Poetry and Revelation

ALSO AVAILABLE FROM BLOOMSBURY

Beckett's Words, David Kleinberg-Levin
Kierkegaard's Religious Discourses, David J. Kangas
The Ethics of Time, John Panteleimon Manoussakis

Poetry and Revelation

For a Phenomenology of Religious Poetry

KEVIN HART

Bloomsbury Academic
An imprint of Bloomsbury Publishing Plc

B L O O M S B U R Y
LONDON · OXFORD · NEW YORK · NEW DELHI · SYDNEY

Bloomsbury Academic

An imprint of Bloomsbury Publishing Plc

50 Bedford Square	1385 Broadway
London	New York
WC1B 3DP	NY 10018
UK	USA

www.bloomsbury.com

BLOOMSBURY and the Diana logo are trademarks of Bloomsbury Publishing Plc

First published 2017

© Kevin Hart, 2017

Kevin Hart has asserted his right under the Copyright, Designs and Patents Act, 1988, to be identified as Author of this work.

British Library Cataloguing-in-Publication Data

A catalogue record for this book is available from the British Library.

ISBN: HB: 978-1-4725-9831-8
       ePDF: 978-1-4725-9832-5
       ePub: 978-1-4725-9833-2

Library of Congress Cataloging-in-Publication Data

A catalog record for this book is available from the Library of Congress.

Typeset by Fakenham Prepress Solutions, Fakenham, Norfolk, NR21 8NN
Printed and bound in Great Britain

For Sarah Hart

Contents

PART FOUR *Religio Poetæ*

PART FIVE Morning knowledge

Acknowledgments

Earlier versions of some of these chapters have appeared in various journals and edited collections. My thanks to the editors for allowing them their first lives elsewhere: a version of Chapter 1 was published in *Pacifica: Australian Theological Studies* 18 (2005): 259–80; Chapter 2 has been revised from its initial appearance in *Material Spirit*, edited by Carl Good (Johns Hopkins University Press, 2012); a version of Chapter 3 appeared in *Christianity and Literature*, 64: 3 (2015); most of Chapter 4 was included in *Sacred Worlds: Religion, Literature, and the Imagination*, edited by Mark Knight and Louise Lee (Continuum, 2009), 23–36; an early version of Chapter 5 was published in *Studia Phaenomenologica* 8 (2008): 219–39; Chapter 6, now recast, first appeared in *Gazing through a Prism Darkly*, edited by Keith Putt (Fordham University Press, 2009), 116–38; almost all of Chapter 7 was included in a discussion of Geoffrey Hill in *Religion and the Arts* 16 (2012): 563–74; a version of Chapter 8 was published in *Southerly* 71 (3) (2012): 76–97; Chapter 9 has been lightly revised from a talk that was included in *Imagining Australia*, edited by Judith Ryan and Chris Wallace-Crabbe (Harvard University Press, 2004), 305–19; an earlier draft of Chapter 10 appeared in *Southerly* 69 (2) (2009): 17–49; Chapter 11 has been expanded from a short piece in *Verse* 24 (1–3) (2007): 240–53; Chapter 12 has been revised from a long review that appeared in *Heat* 14 (2000): 166–82; and Chapter 13 was published, in a shorter version, in *Religion and the Arts* 8 (2) (2004): 174–99, and has been brought up to date with the poet's more recent works. All the other chapters appear here for the first time. Chapter 3 was read in French translation at a conference at the Institut Catholique de Paris in February, 2012, and Chapter 15 was read at a conference held at Wayne State University in October, 2007. My thanks to all my editors and hosts.

Many friends have read these chapters at different stages of their composition, and I am indebted to them for their criticisms and suggestions. In particular, I would like to thank Harold Bloom, Larry Bouchard, Gerald L. Bruns, Stephen Cushman, Jacques Derrida, Alan Gould, Brad S. Gregory, Paul Groner, Geoffrey Hartman, Jean-Yves Lacoste, Claire Lyu, Paul Mariani, Charles Mathewes, Michael L. Morgan, John Nemec, Kate Rigby, Claude Romano, Kurtis Schaeffer, Michael A. Signer, Richard Strier, Alan Toumayan, Henry Weinfield, Siân White, and Robin Darling Young. I would also like to thank the monks of the Abbey of Notre Dame, Tarrawarra, Australia, for their hospitality while I drafted the penultimate chapter of this book.

Permissions

This book includes quotations from the following sources, reproduced with grateful thanks to the following people and places.

From T. S. Eliot, *Four Quartets* (London: Faber and Faber, 1944) in Chapter 3.

From Geoffrey Hill, *Broken Hierarchies* (Oxford: Oxford University Press) in Chapters 4, 5, 6, and 7.

From A. D. Hope, "The Double Looking Glass," *Collected Poems 1930–1970* (Sydney: Angus and Robertson, 1972), Geoffrey Hope and Curtis Brown, in Chapter 8.

From Judith Wright, "The Lost Man," *Collected Poems, 1942–1985* (Manchester: Carcanet, 1994), Meredith McKinney, in Chapter 9.

From Robert Gray, *New Selected Poems* (Sydney: Duffy and Snellgrove, 1998), the author, in Chapter 10.

From Charles Wright, *The World of the Ten Thousand Things: Poems 1980–1990* (New York: Farrar, Straus and Giroux, 1990), *Negative Blue: Selected Later Poems* (New York: Farrar, Straus and Giroux, 2000), *Bye-and-Bye: Selected Late Poems* (New York: Farrar, Straus and Giroux, 2011), *Caribou* (New York: Farrar, Straus and Giroux, 2014), in Chapter 13.

From James McAuley, "Pietà," *Collected Poems, 1936–1970* (Sydney: Angus and Robertson, 1971), Philip McAuley and Curtis Brown, in Chapter 14.

From *The Collected Works of St. John of the Cross*, translated by Kieran Kavanaugh and Otilio Rodriguez © 1964, 1979, 1991 Washington Province of Discalced Carmelites ICS Publications 2131 Lincoln Road, N.E. Washington, DC 20002–1199 U.S.A. (www.icspublications.org), in Chapters 3 and 9.

From Virginia Woolf, *Orlando* (London: Hogarth Press, 1928), in Chapter 9, HMH Trade Publishing.

Disclaimer: *While every effort has been made to trace the copyright holders, if any have been inadvertently overlooked, the author and publishers will be happy to make necessary arrangements at the first opportunity.*

Introduction

Poetry and Revelation: My title seems to speak of two connected things, how revelation of the divine is reflected or refracted in poems. And so it does. Yet it also speaks of a third thing: revelation as the manifestation of phenomena. So while this is a book about what is called, sometimes all too quickly, "religious poetry" it is also a phenomenological study of this poetry; it seeks to approach responses to positive revelation by way of what the poetry makes manifest in all manner of modes of presence and absence: perception, recollection, anticipation, fantasy, and so on. The care that phenomenology requires of a reader serves to challenge the judgments that are sometimes cursorily made with respect to "religious poetry."

The chapters in this book therefore have the conceptual shape of triangles, the apexes of which are poetry, religion, and philosophy. Sometimes the triangle is equilateral, or very close to it; sometimes it is isosceles, or very close to it; and sometimes it is scalene. Always there is a focus on at least one poem, which is read in conjunction with a question or a problem that has been received from the tradition. Apart from some Marian lyrics considered in the penultimate chapter, the poems are all modern ones, and the poets are sometimes very well-known (Gerard Manley Hopkins, T. S. Eliot, Philippe Jaccottet, Eugenio Montale, and Geoffrey Hill), on the way to being well known (Charles Wright), or deserving of having a far wider audience in the United States and Europe (A. D. Hope, Judith Wright, and Robert Gray). Some of the questions, too, are familiar: Why do we think of religious poems as minor? Are we right to think of them in that way? What role or roles does the category of experience play in the writing and reading of poems, especially those written out of experience of God? Others are less so: Are all religious poems in the West answerable to the medieval and modern category of revelation, or are some of them answerable to its conditions, namely revealability? What differences, if any, are there between the two groups? And yet others are perhaps unfamiliar, at least in contemporary literary criticism: Can phenomenology help us to read poetry, especially (as here) religious poetry? If so, what modes of phenomenology are the most helpful?

This last group of questions has imposed itself on me not because I inherited from "the criticism of consciousness" practiced decades ago by

Georges Poulet, but rather largely because of the technical work I have been doing in the overlaps of philosophy and theology over the past decade, work that can be read in other books that have appeared, or that are soon to appear.[1] Here, I have sought to show how phenomenological analyses, conducted in my own way, can be used to read poems and answer judgments made by literary criticism. There are three main questions any thinker can and should ask: What? Why? How? The first two are conducted within the "natural attitude" and belong to metaphysics; the third is the animating question of phenomenology. What philosophers call the "phenomenological reduction" is the passage from either or both of the first two questions to the third one.

Artists of all kinds tend to be very good at performing this reduction, even if (like most philosophers) they leave it incomplete. They do not always lead us back to the same place, in the same way, in the same direction, or to the same depth. There are some who lead us inwards to consciousness, so that the poems they compose show us how phenomena become meaningful for them from that region of subjectivity that Husserl dubbed "transcendental." Others instinctively recoil from the idealism they detect in this approach, and are committed in advance to realism: their aim is to lead themselves and us back to the phenomena that manifest themselves to us in the world about us and to see them freshly, as though for the first time. For my part, I have frequently been interested to see in what ways some poems yield an excess of intuition over intentionality: it is something that Jean-Luc Marion has taught us to watch for in his analyses of saturated phenomena. In addition, however, I have sometimes found that poems composed in the dimension of Christian faith perform what I call the "basilaic reduction": they lead us back from "the world" to "the Kingdom." They are not concerned with signaling that we can respond to phenomena without making any presuppositions but rather with affirming that there is one presupposition we need to make in order to view reality properly: that God is the Creator of all that is.

In the opening essays of this book, I seek to show, through close readings of poems by Hopkins and Eliot, that great Christian poets are not bound by what I call the "supernatural attitude": regarding creedal truths as though they referred to states and situations of the same modal status as states and situations in the natural world. They may credit these propositions as true yet their poems embody a passage from religious theses to phenomenological concreteness. The poems are properly read when we recognize that they suspend theses about the nature and acts of God and invite us to participate in pre-thetic experience of being in relation with God. Whether God exists, or exists as the poet thinks, is beside the point when it comes to reading a poem. Phenomenology not only leads us back to this layer of pre-thetic experience but also it gives us ways in which to read the poem. In my study of the opening section of "Burnt Norton," for example, I try to show how intentional analysis can give us a surer, more nuanced way of reading that elusive section (and hence the *Four Quartets* as a whole) than we have been used to since its publication.

The second section of the book offers four essays on poems by Geoffrey Hill, who I take to be one of the strongest poets, writing in English, of recent times, at least in his books from *For the Unfallen* (1959) to *Canaan* (1996). Here I am drawn to read a poet who is in no clear sense a Christian, let alone a "Christian poet," yet whose lyrics sometimes involve second-order reflections on faith and the possibilities of talking about God in poetry. The issue of transcendence comes up time and again in his book *Tenebræ* (1978): religious transcendence (God's irreducible otherness), epistemological transcendence (our difficulties in making any judgments about the divine), and phenomenological transcendence (all that is above or beyond consciousness). Here I step away for the first time from Christian themes and try to attend to the horror of the Holocaust and Hill's response to it in his lyric "September Song." The Holocaust should be a torment for Christians as well as Jews, for non-religious persons as well as religious ones, though not in the same ways; it is an event that Christians have not yet fully recognized in all its dimensions and implications and the weight of which we have not taken properly on our own account. Hill's poem is a test case of how a poem can speak to this horror. It is not a "religious poem" in any clear sense, yet it is a poem that responds to a state of moral and spiritual desolation, and so has religious significance.

In the third section, I consider poems by three major Australian poets, none of whom is very well-known in the United States or Europe. A. D. Hope's "The Double Looking Glass" is a gorgeous midrash on the story of Susannah and the Elders; Judith Wright's "The Lost Man" must be read, I argue, besides a little known, almost forgotten, book about a plane crash in southeast Queensland; and Robert Gray's "Dharma Vehicle" is one of the major Buddhist long poems of our times. If there is no religious revelation at issue in this poem, there is talk of enlightenment and a profound meditation on the manifestation of the sensuous particulars of nature.

French and Italian poetry, and an American who learned deeply from Italian poetry, constitute the third part of the book; and here my focus is on poets who are more devoted to revealability than to revelation. Not one of them is religious in a confessional sense, though all of them reset and relaunch motifs from Christianity in the service of thinking about the writing of poetry and what is called these days "belief without belief." Finally, I look at phenomenological concretion as it may be found in four Marian lyrics, from the late Middle Ages to the late twentieth century, and conclude with a wide-ranging chapter on the different ways in which silence can be read in modern poetry and its various religious resonances.

PART ONE

Experience

1

Poetry and revelation

Hopkins, counter-experience and *reductio*

We are driven to use the expression "religious poetry," and even "Christian poetry," though usually with reservations and regrets. For they come with a concession, now more or less traditional, that this is a minor poetry at best. Strangely enough, the verse that mostly invites the qualification "religious" is written after the Middle Ages: the adjective bespeaks irruptions of modernity going on around it. We remember Bishop Sprat's address to Abraham Cowley, "You first the Muses to the Christians brought," and are more surprised by the claim than his audience would have been, and not only because we do not read Cowley, let alone relish his prosody.[1] Exceptions in English to the judgment that religious poetry is minor occur only rarely. If Milton's "On the Morning of Christ's Nativity" is a case in point, Spenser's "An Hymne of Heavenly Love" probably is not. Milton's *Paradise Lost* (1667) also excuses itself from the general rule, yet even here people are more at ease in talking of religion in the epic rather than it being religious poetry. In terms of the blank verse tradition, it is in Milton's impress on later poets such as Samuel Catherall and Elizabeth Rowe that we find clearer examples of "religious poetry," and we tend not to be overjoyed when we discover them. Of course, Blake's lyrics are exceptions as are, in quite another way, his prophetic books. Yet to say that Blake is exceptional is only to say that Blake is Blake.

Closer to our own times, Eliot's *Four Quartets* (1943) presents another exception, yet the chances are that the category of religious poetry will not be the only one brought into play when discussing the poem.[2] If it is introduced, it will be treated with care, not least of all because Eliot agreed "up to a point" with those who taught that religious poetry tends to be minor poetry.[3] Whether that stricture applies to "Ash-Wednesday" (1930), or whether that poem's taut energy makes us doubt the conclusions of Eliot's essay would be a question worth considering. Eliot did not relegate "Ash-Wednesday" to the section of his *Collected Poems* called "Minor Poems," but perhaps he was thinking only in the context of his own work. Certainly, the Eliot of "What is Minor Poetry?" is of little help to us, since he only circles around the word "minor."[4] What makes George Herbert for Eliot a minor poet in "Religion and Literature" (1935), and later a major poet in "What is Minor Poetry?" (1944) is never satisfactorily explained; we leave Eliot's criticism unconvinced that the word "minor" can be used descriptively but not evaluatively.[5] Let us, therefore, consider another perspective. There are ways of reversing the general judgment that religious verse is always minor. For example, one can argue, as bards sometimes do, that all poetry is religious—or at least spiritual—in one way or another.[6] Or one can agree with Erich Auerbach that the gospels changed the nature of representation in the West and that all literature composed since patristic times is Christian in an important sense.[7]

Auerbach's conclusion might give one pause, for one does not have to subscribe to everything that Kierkegaard said about Christianity and Christendom in order to feel the force of the distinction between the two.[8] And, in deciding not to be worried by or for the adjective "Christian" because it shelters in the noun "literature," one has to be all the more careful in deploying the adjective "religious." For now, the word takes on a confessional resonance it might not have in other contexts. If all Western poetry is Christian, at least culturally, only some of it—very little, perhaps—will be religious. Poets such as William Cowper and Christopher Smart come to mind, as does the Isaac Watts of *Horæ Lyricæ* (1707), but so, too, does the John Keble of *The Christian Year* (1827). Almost certainly the adjective "religious" will be accused once again of not qualifying "poetry" as much as limiting it. Why a poetry that is written *coram deo* is regarded as necessarily narrower than a poetry written *coram hominibus* is scarcely self-evident, and it is worthwhile to examine the assumptions that have led us to think that it is.

Like many other people, when I find myself using the expression "religious poetry" I hear Samuel Johnson ringing warning bells in my head. He says in his "Life of Waller" (1799), "Contemplative piety, or the intercourse between God and the human soul, cannot be poetical. Man admitted to implore the mercy of his Creator, and plead the merits of his Redeemer, is already in a higher state than poetry can confer."[9] His reasons are solid ones:

> The essence of poetry is invention; such invention as, by producing something unexpected, surprises and delights. The topics of devotion are few, and being few are universally known; but few as they are, they can be made no more; they can receive no grace from novelty of sentiment, and very little from novelty of expression.[10]

Another critic who offers counsel when I talk of "religious poetry" is Harold Bloom who is in some respects Johnson's heir in our times, although, to be sure, his project is very much his own. In his Charles Eliot Norton lectures of 1987–8, he offers us a choice: "If you wish, you can insist that all high literature is secular, or, should you desire it so, then all strong poetry is sacred. What I find incoherent is the judgment that some authentic literary art is more sacred or more secular than some other."[11] His conclusion is an unnerving one: "Poetry and belief, as I understand them, are antithetical modes of knowledge, but they share the peculiarity of taking place *between* truth and meaning, while being somewhat alienated both from truth and meaning."[12]

Before going any further, it is evident that talk of religious poetry is bedeviled by three adjectives that are often used rather loosely. Eliot is not the only critic to slide from "religious poetry" to "Christian poetry," and then to "devotional verse." Johnson writes with more care, yet his strictures on "contemplative piety" are commonly folded into the more general topic of "religious verse."[13] For my part, I will attend solely to Christian poetry, devotional or not, and will offer my reasons for adopting another vocabulary, but not before I return to Johnson. At first, it seems easy enough to launch a counter-attack against him. One can point out that he is chiefly concerned with devotional poetry, lyrics addressing the deity, which is only a part of religious poetry. And one can argue that his insistence on the inappropriateness of poetry as a vehicle of prayer presumes too sharp a dividing line between secular and sacred writing. That the psalms are both prayers and poems was apparent before Robert Lowth satisfactorily explained their meter in his *De Sacra Poesi Hebraeorum* (1753; trans. 1787).[14] Johnson bypasses Lowth's description of Job as dramatic poetry, Jeremiah as elegiac poetry, and the Song of Songs as lyric poetry; and, resisting a powerful movement of his times, he denies that the sublime can subsume the religious: prayer puts one in a "higher state" than poetry ever can.[15] To see Scripture in terms of the categories of secular literature is to devalue it, he would think, while to write sacred poetry is either to overestimate what poetry can do or to underestimate the need for originality in it.

Johnson's emphasis on imploring and pleading suggests that prayer is understood as petition, and not in the more general sense of supplicating God (as St. Gregory of Nyssa taught) or raising the mind to God (as St. John of Damascus maintained).[16] Johnson might be thinking of the many devotional poets of the late sixteenth and seventeenth centuries, including some of the best of them: Crashaw, Herrick, Southwell, Traherne, and Vaughan. Nowadays even the least religious among us would be reluctant to add Fulke Greville, George Herbert, and John Donne to that list. Besides, fine poems such as "Wrapt up, O Lord, in Man's degeneration," "Sin's Round" and "Batter my heart, three person'd God" seem to be conducted at a pitch of fervor that is entirely appropriate to prayer. Turning to the claim that devotion is incompatible with invention, we must concede Johnson's theological point at the outset: "Omnipotence cannot be exalted; Infinity cannot be amplified; Perfection cannot be improved."[17] The argument might lead some to silent adoration and others to ignore God altogether. That said, the best religious verse is seldom concerned with the deity's ineffable qualities. Dante's vision of the Trinity in the last canto of the *Paradiso* is an exception, and is mostly taken up with a relation with God, even if it is, strictly speaking, an infinite relation.[18] Each of us stands before God generally (as human) and specifically (as an individual), and as the relation intensifies or slackens so opportunities for poetry present themselves.

One can mount a case against Bloom by contesting his grounding assumption. It is by no means clear that literature and Scripture are subtended by the notion of "authentic literary art" in the same way, especially when a Romantic sense of "literary" is at issue. A Christian will hold the Bible to be sacred on account of it being the living Word of God, a claim that no believer will make of *Paradise Lost*, even if Milton's characters have become essential reference points in his or her imaginative life. When Johnson asserts that devotional poetry is impeded by its inability to invent, he has already accepted a strict distinction between sacred and secular, as well as a robust doctrine of biblical inspiration. This is not incoherent; it is reasonable. Bloom's view makes perfectly good sense to him as a Jewish Gnostic because no text, however sacred it has been deemed by Church or Temple, bears upon his salvation. He looks to gnosis, not faith. As soon as one speaks of revelation, though, the situation changes utterly: a distinction between the natural and the supernatural intrudes and brings with it the duality of secular and sacred. One can also reply to Bloom that it is doubtful that poetry and belief are antithetical modes of *knowledge*. From St. Augustine to St. Anselm and beyond, we have thought of faith leading to understanding. Only mystical states yield anything like "knowledge" of God, but it is unsayable. Meanwhile, we are used to saying that literature leads us to a deeper understanding of the world. Chaucer, Dante, and Shakespeare expand our sense of being human, partly because of their witness to a wide variety of life and partly because they create fresh exemplars of moral action. Poets who do that are very rare. Most do not give us anything resembling knowledge in the usual sense of the word, and perhaps only Bloom himself identifies a strong reading of strong poetry with gnosis.

It is an index of great critics like Johnson, Eliot, and Bloom that their remarks have force even if they have been refuted to the best of one's ability. Their words return to haunt us when we feel most secure, and they influence how we shape our thoughts and read the poems that matter most to us. So, when I take my bearings from the relatively recent theological word "revelation," I know I am indebted to these critics even if none of them actually uses the word.[19] I choose it over "dogma," "faith," "mysticism," "orthodoxy," "religion," "sacred," and "spiritual," for it enables me to identify those writers for whom poetry is a response to God's call not to the silence of the sacred, to consider something more elusive than doctrine, and to begin with God rather than human beings. Following Johnson's lead, I exclude from consideration didactic poems, concerned as they are with "the motives to piety" and "the works of God," rather than God or a relationship with him.[20] Versified paraphrases of Scripture are also of no interest here. I take as my focus the modern Christian lyric and note at the outset that the lyric is the poetic mode most closely associated, rightly or wrongly, with first-hand experience.[21]

One point on which Johnson, Eliot, and Bloom firmly agree is that religious poetry cannot draw on the experience appropriate for the writing of major poetry. Revelation has been communicated, if at all, only to others long since dead, they say, and no one can write first-class poetry on the basis of allegiance only. The negative evaluation of religious poetry partly turns on the concept "experience," both in figuring poetry and in understanding revelation. I wish to identify the assumption more narrowly and then dislodge it or at least weaken it.

*

The assumption about experience cannot be unearthed without also bringing to light other assumptions that surround it and to some extent cling to it. First of all, it is commonly supposed, especially in the Protestant churches, that religious art must negotiate a profound gulf between revelation and aesthetics and that the effort is of dubious value. A poetic conception of religion, which diminishes its truth claims, is a danger on one side, while a religious conception of poetry, which, for the believer, overvalues its revelatory authority, is a constant threat on the other. Milton strides between the two, justifying the ways of God to man, yet not all believers have been at ease with his attempt to hold together pagan form and Christian content. Hans Urs von Balthasar has examined the consequences of the assumption that revelation and aesthetics are separate spheres, pointing out that even in modern Catholicism being and truth have been prized over beauty, despite the acknowledgment by the schoolmen that the three transcendentals are convertible, and that this bias has impoverished the tradition. His argument is that revelation has an irreducible aesthetic dimension, *Gestalt* or form, and that aesthetics has an equally resistant theological strain.[22] In another context I would develop his case while expressing reserve about his choices of poets and his readings of them, but today I wish to put pressure elsewhere and my allusions to von Balthasar will be muted.

Closely related to the first, the second assumption is that revelation imposes a severe limitation of the poet's imaginative freedom, that there is insufficient room to move if one must at all times respond to *locutio Dei ad homines*. It is at this point that we need to recognize that "revelation" means several things and that this assumption answers to a particular historical under-standing of the word. I call on Avery Dulles whose theology of revelation can help us move quickly through difficult terrain. He distinguishes five models of revelation: as doctrine, history, inner experience, dialectical presence, and new awareness.[23] It is only the first model that is at issue here. It gains traction among conservative Evangelicals in the mid-nineteenth century and among Catholic neo-scholastics a little later, two groups that set themselves firmly against Romanticism and that remain intensely suspicious of its overarching doctrine of the imagination. Without endorsing a high Romantic theory of the creative imagination, it is nonetheless possible to speak of revelation and imagination in terms of the other models of revelation. Neither Dante's *Commedia* nor Herbert's "The Collar" makes one think that the author is writing under unduly tight external constraints, and the very idea would be ridiculous when reading *The Four Zoas* (1807). On the contrary, the awareness made possible by revelation seems to open a wider world to the various poets than they would have otherwise. The third assumption is that there is something called "religious experience," of which "religious poetry" would be a manifestation. Both expressions come to us from the eighteenth and nineteenth centuries: the age of experience, if ever there were one.[24] From adherence to the Inner Light to the rise of Evangelicalism, Christianity oriented itself to individual experience, often enough with little or no theological depth. The appeal to experience did not always pass through revelation; it frequently sidestepped the historicity of the faith in the search for a more fundamental dimension that supposedly unified the world religions and that was regarded, from one viewpoint, as a natural revelation and, from another, as a *philosophia perennis*. When reflection on this search occurred, it did so in the context of a theological anthropology in which conditions for revelation are granted methodological priority over revelation. Religion becomes a matter of "feeling" (Schleiermacher), "prayer" (Sabatier), "the sacred" (Durkheim), "existential decision" (Bultmann), "ultimate concern" (Tillich), "the holy" (Otto), "faith" (Ebeling), or "transcendental experience" (Rahner). The attempt to ground religion in experience goes by way of locating grounding experiences. Because they are found only in extraordinary attunements, these primal intuitions of the divine are easily reset as regional, as "peak experiences," rather than held to be generally available; and, in consequence, religion becomes restricted to a particular range of activity: charismatic, liturgical, or intensely private.

When these experiences fail to offer access to primal intuitions of the divine, religion is deemed not to work or the work is regarded as best done outside church, at home or in nature. Neo-orthodoxy sought to counter the misplaced emphasis on experience in religion, as did post-liberal theology, while others have pointed to the irreducible diversity of revelations.[25] None of these reactions has had any effect on how religious poetry is conceived. It remains a matter of "experience." For those who sought encounters with the divine outside church, there is a wealth of nature poetry to call on for help, a good deal of it written by Wordsworth or indebted to him. I think of the bard in his older years, almost echoing Johnson, when he confesses to the Rev. R. P. Graves that the truths of Christianity are "a subject too high for him," and that his task has been "to elevate the mind to sacred things."[26]

The poetry which Wordsworth made possible is also Wordsworthian, to the extent that it has any interest in religion, in being cautiously aligned with revealability rather than revelation. Hölderlin had no such caution, and it is to him rather than to Wordsworth that we look when contemplating Heidegger's claim that poets open a space in which a new revelation of the holy might take place.[27] Karl Rahner was less bold but broadly of the same view when he commended us to read poetry in order to be responsive to revelation.[28] Eliot would be in general agreement.[29] It has become common for many of our best poets to confine themselves to elevating the mind to sacred things without actually affirming them. At the end of his oratorio "For the Time Being" (1941–2), W. H. Auden has his narrator outline the modern attitude to revealability. For him, it has happened, as it has time and again, that "the actual Vision" has been seen and people have been able to do no more than ponder it as "an agreeable / Possibility."[30] By and large, the generation of poets after World War II concurred with Auden's narrator. Of memorable poets, perhaps only Francis Webb followed the young Robert Lowell in his passionate early religious verse. A. R. Ammons is more characteristic of contemporary poets when, in his beautiful "Hymn," he begins by saying, "I know if I find you I will have to leave the earth."[31] The conditional "if I find you," repeated twice, indicates that the poem is more concerned with the possibility of finding God than with a response to a God who has revealed himself in the world. In their own ways, Geoffrey Hill and Charles Wright are also oriented to revealability rather than revelation, Hill being more anguished about it than Wright.[32]

There is another way of looking at this situation. The notion of religious poetry we have inherited in the twenty-first century partly derives from a broad sense of religious experience, while doubts over "experience" in the twentieth century call the notion of religious poetry into question. It could be argued that since World War I we have been faced with a world that limits experience, that prepackages it or consigns it to the non-experience of images, and to which its major thinkers respond by talking of *Entleben* (Heidegger) or the impossibility of *Erfahrung* (Adorno). And it could also be argued that poetry itself has rejected "experience" as bequeathed by the nineteenth century, and from the association of *Erlebnis* and *Dichtung* in particular, in order to value experiment, especially the attempt to see how automatic writing, mechanical devices or voices disconnected from persons can generate experience that no one has actually lived through. Flaubert's *style indirect libre* is one starting point, Eliot's *The Waste Land* (1922) is an important station along the way, while OULIPO and L=A=N=G=U=A=G=E poetry are recent examples of the adventure.

At any rate, before we can talk sensibly of religious poetry we will need to rethink both "religion" and "poetry" with respect to experience. I suspect that the rethinking would end with us putting aside "religious experience" and turning to an expression that is not less fraught but fraught in ways that are worth taking on board. I mean the phrase "experience of God." Part of the sharpness that is gained in this formulation repulses it from us, for we must ask, "Does God offer himself to experience?" It would seem not: *Finitum non capax infiniti*. Yet if that is strictly true, at the penumbra as well as in the center of consciousness, many biblical narratives—those of Samuel and Isaiah, for instance—as well as testimonies of the mystics, lose their apparent truth value, and we have to put aside the theology of deification running from St. Athanasius to Origen to St. Maximus the Confessor and beyond.[33] The old theological tag concerns comprehending God, not encountering divine love, and it may well be that a life spent *coram deo* does not have a single moment of "religious experience." I do not propose to delve more deeply into the issue, since that would call for technical discussions in philosophy and theology best served in other places, but I will indicate how the question must be reset for it to make sense and I will offer some guidelines for thinking about it with respect to poetry.[34]

To do so I will have to lapse into my native tongue, the language of phenomenology. Let me start then by identifying the fourth assumption. Even when revelation is understood with some sophistication, as a reveiling as well as a revealing of God, critics have tended to emphasize the fact of the supernatural order its status as positive fact and to figure revelation as *veritates e coelo delapsoe*.[35] I am not thinking of those seventeenth-century poets whose devotions are informed by a *theologia supernaturalis*, which must be taken into account when reading them. My concern is with modern critics who appeal to revelation in order to frame "religious poetry." Revelation is still widely regarded by critics as supernatural in a naïve sense of the word, as though the supernatural order were a distinct, static region of being that functions for believers who appeal to it as an abstract explanation of reality. In literary criticism, this leads some readers, like Johnson, to regard a religious poem as merely representing received truths.[36] It entices others to sheer away revelation altogether and focus exclusively on the poetry, trusting that it will carry the belief.[37] Still others attend solely to the poem's language, with the result that paradoxes inherent in the faith itself are interpreted as working solely in the economy of the poem.[38] And it brings others to appeal to metaphor or symbol as a means of bridging the gulf between two worlds.[39] To rethink revelation so that it is immanent, able to be derived from consciousness, as some theological modernists sought to do last century, does not fundamentally change this assumption, render it less one-sided, make it more answerable to the divine mystery, or place us on firmer ground as readers of religious verse. Revelation still functions as an abstract mode of explanation, although one that is now more likely to fall victim to psychologism than superstition. Needless to say, all this is a long way from a strict theological understanding of the supernatural order as that which exceeds *ens creatum*. What is needed is a sense of God as the mystery of the world, a phrase I deliberately take from two distant realms in the modern Christian world: Erich Pryzywara's *Gottgeheimnis der Welt* (given as lectures in 1924), and Eberhard Jüngel's *Gott als Geheimnis der Welt* (1977).

If we shift our perspective so that we pass from the supposed fact of revelation to its phenomenological concreteness, we can begin to rethink religious poetry. Of course, no conversion of the gaze can turn weak religious poems into strong ones. The verse of Giles Fletcher, Christopher Lever, and William Strode will remain just as dull as it has always been. However, the change of perspective can discharge or modify an assumption that renders memorable religious poems—lyrics by George Herbert and Gerard Manley Hopkins, say—minor by definition. Another preliminary point needs to be made. To bracket revelation as fact is not to deny the absolute reality of the supernatural order. Not at all: it is to switch off uncritical understandings of it as an explanation of the world, whether it be revelation as doctrine, history, inner experience, dialectical presence, or new awareness, and to pass from fact to meaning. Phenomenology has taught us to suspend the "natural attitude," our habitual reliance on common sense to determine the being and mode of phenomena. It should also teach us to abstain from what I call the "supernatural attitude," the believer's uncritical use of revelation as a thesis about an alternative world similar in its mode of being to the one we experience now. Pious or impious, the poet writes "without authority" in Kierkegaard's sense of the expression.[40]

I will organize my thoughts around a poem that is very well-known indeed, "God's Grandeur," written by Gerard Manley Hopkins in 1877. I choose it because it appears to be a poem of awe, one of the standard "topics of devotion" that Johnson suggests cannot be poetical, because it seems to be a test case for judging whether poetry and belief are indeed antithetical, as Bloom would have it, and because it has the air of being somewhat programmatic. We are to talk about a poem that declares that it is a "religious poem," that insists on its verticality even while it looks about the world. Before going any further, though, here is the poem:

> The world is charged with the grandeur of God.
> It will flame out, like shining from shook foil;
> It gathers to a greatness, like the ooze of oil
> Crushed. Why do men then now not reck his rod?
> Generations have trod, have trod, have trod;
> And all is seared with trade; bleared, smeared with toil;
> And wears man's smudge and shares man's smell: the soil
> Is bare now, nor can foot feel, being shod.
>
> And for all this, nature is never spent;
> There lives the dearest freshness deep down things;
> And though the last lights off the black West went
> Oh, morning, at the brown brink eastward, springs —
> Because the Holy Ghost over the bent
> World broods with warm breast and with ah! bright wings.[41]

*

The first thing to be said about this sonnet is that it does not attempt to write or rewrite any revealed truths. Doctrine, as Hopkins the Jesuit understands it, is a series of "sufficient propositions" (Suárez) about the world that are binding upon the believer. He is hardly less strict in his sermons.[42] Yet this poem does not adopt a thetic approach to God: it is not concerned with His greatness, *magnitudo*, about which one can frame theological theses, and it sidesteps even talk of glory, *kabod*, in order to evoke God's grandeur, a word deriving from the French that introduces a strangeness into the poem from the very beginning, that points us to the sublime, and that bespeaks a relationship of lordship between the divine and the human. At the risk of stating the obvious, the poem is not concerned with what Johnson calls "the grandeur of Nature" but with the grandeur of God.[43] It takes its cue from Psalm 71:19, "And blessed be the name of his majesty for ever: and the whole earth shall be filled with his majesty" (Douay-Rheims), which it emphasizes in an Ignatian manner. Nor does it seek to place God in an abstract relation with the world, as happens when one calls the deity *causa sui*, ground of being, or being of being, in order to explain why there is something and not nothing. Only in the lyric's closing two lines is an explanation of anything seemingly offered, but it explains little in the manner of scholastic logic, as we shall see.

That God exists, is triune, created the heavens and the earth, expects the obedience of all men and women, and cares for them and for all creation: all these creedal propositions are suspended, put out of play *as theses*, while offered to us *as acts* (of perception and judgment) that can still disturb the security of our lives. It needs to be stressed at the outset that these acts are made in and through language. Hitherto unnoticed horizons of consciousness are rendered apparent in metaphors and similes, which embody the meaning of those items to which consciousness is intentionally related and, as we know, add further meanings, perhaps not "lived through" by author or reader, that nonetheless orchestrate the very movement of the poem from its first words. The poem does not tell us "The presence of God fills the heart with awe," nor does it illustrate any revealed truths. It synthesizes and singu-larizes diverse regions of experience in sense, not quality (as would happen in a thesis about an object), when responding to what is given as "divine grandeur." Nor does the poem simply represent an experience. Because it is a poem, working with concentrated and concatenated language, it keeps open the possibility of further unfolding the meanings of what has been offered to consciousness and already rendered significant by it.

The poem begins by declaring something about "the world." It is "charged with the grandeur of God," and, since the third and fourth feet of the opening line are reversed iambs, the phrase must read, "chárged / wíth the / grándeur / of Gód."[44] Only with the second line and its references to "flame," "shining" and "foil" do we take the verb to link the divine and electricity. Here the natural and the supernatural are perceived as one, not in order to downplay the transcendence of God but to emphasize his invisible power and the danger to which one is exposed when standing before him (or, for that matter, when avoiding him). Notice that it is not "the earth" that is charged with divine grandeur, and it is too early in the poem for it to be "nature." It is "the world," the planet on which we live, and also the cosmos; the ordered totality of things, as Plato and Aristotle thought, and the sum of created being, as the New Testament teaches: the world as the theatre in which God's mission is perormed with no spectators, only participants. The world is "charged," full of divine majesty, and also, more darkly, accused on account of our not heeding that power.

It is remarkable that a poem that begins in a sublime context, at once biblical and natural, concludes its introductory image by inviting us to fuse the ancient and the modern: "shook foil" refers to gold foil, perhaps in an electroscope (invented in 1824), or held in someone's hands.[45] The majesty of God "*will* flame out" [my emphasis] not only in the Last Judgment but also by dint of the divine nature, which cannot be limited.[46] To evoke the "grandeur of God" by way of sheet and fork lightning is traditional, and to do so by way of electricity would have been sufficiently modern to satisfy and disturb many a Victorian reader. Yet the image is not one of grandeur in any usual sense. We are directed not to a city paved with gold but to gold foil that consists of thousands of tiny creases, and the greatness of God is

registered in the small as well as the immense. No one image, not even one
that holds together the sublime and the beautiful, could possibly evoke divine
transcendence, and Hopkins quickly switches to an entirely different register:
"It gathers to a greatness, like the ooze of oil / Crushed." The enjambment is
violent, not only in its abuse of the line but also in the exclusion of all mention
of olives: it is as though the very oil, made by crushing, is itself crushed again
to be refined further. From lightning we pass to an olive press, and from the
Father to the Son, indeed, to the Son at Gethsemani (Heb. *Gat* = press +
semen = oil), at the base of the Mount of Olives, who is soon to be crushed.
It would be fitting to remember Song of Songs 1:3 and especially St. Bernard
of Clairvaux's fifteenth homily on the Song of Songs in which he meditates
on the name of Jesus as oil that is poured out.[47] Yet Hopkins is closer to St.
Bonaventure who, in his sixth of the *sermones domincales*, imagines Christ
on the cross as a bunch of grapes in the winepress. The teaching and deeds
of Jesus finally "gather to a greatness" in his passion and, indeed, in his
Ascension, and the oil indicates not only the Son's kingship but also the sacra-
mental value of his suffering and death. Later, we hear of the Spirit brooding
over the planet Earth, and so find another kind of grandeur, one that Simone
Weil was to identify, "*Mais, il n'y a, à mes yeux, de grandeur que dans la
douceur.*"[48]

I pause to underline that to speak of the deity for Hopkins in this poem
is not to appeal to an abstract explanation of reality; it is to evoke the dread
of being placed in the hands of the living God (Heb. 10:31).[49] It is because
revelation is not merely abstract doctrine or simply exterior to life but is
registered as meaningful in experience that Hopkins can ask, with urgent
concern, "Why do men then *now* not reck his rod?" [my emphasis]. The
question asks why people do not acknowledge divine authority (and the
possibility of retribution) now, and we can hear there the isolation of a
Catholic convert in the Victorian era. Yet, since it is posed immediately after
the allusion to Gethsemani, it is not unreasonable to let "rod" make us think
of "rood," which is just the kind of etymological association that Hopkins
likes to make. Also, it is hardly stretching the sense of the poem to suggest
that the cross is the lightning rod that conducts the terrible anger of the
Father. In Hopkins's day, the crosses on church steeples were still the most
common conductors of lightning.[50] The Christological controversies of the
fourth century, as well as Tridentine notions of atonement, are, as I have
said, suspended as creedal formulations and doctrines. Yet Hopkins's rapport
with the Father is embedded in a horizon established by the relations of the
Father and the Son, and which can be summarized in the dark phrase "penal
substitution."

*

That Hopkins is awestruck when confronted by the divine is plain, and that he responds in Trinitarian terms is also evident to believers before we reach the sonnet's closing lines: the Holy Spirit is present through the gift of speaking in faith and with wisdom. We might say that we are given "an experience"—the observation of a tremendous storm, say—yet that remark remains banal. The poem is a site where many intuitions, not all of them sensible, are gathered, each of them being an *intus legere*, a reading inside things, a discernment of original form and pattern not apparent before our gaze is converted from a concern with the positive and superficial.[51] The "in" of "inscape" does not indicate an immanence that has abolished all transcendence; it suggests that immanence is the way given to discern the meaning of transcendence. "God's Grandeur" reads revelation from deep inside the things of the world. It regards revelation not as a comet that has flicked the world but more as a king wave that has finally broken and soaked deeply into things.

When we examine it with care, we see that the sonnet is not so much about "an experience" as "experience itself." It is an exposure to a peril from which Hopkins has emerged, doubtless shaken or wounded, so that he can bear witness to it.[52] "God's Grandeur" is not a poem of *Erlebnis*, lived experience, along the lines that Dilthey drew in *Das Erlebnis und die Dichtung* (1905), in which an event is encompassed, internalized and processed as knowledge. The fecundity and variety of the metaphors suggest that not everything presented in the poem can be lived through and rendered meaningful in the one movement or even in several movements. It is a work of *Erfahrung*, a passage that never quite reaches an end, partly because the experiencing "I" impinges on a "me" that in turn changes the "I," and partly because there is always more meaning to be found in the consideration of multiple interactions: trope and trope, idiom and trope, form and idiom, structure and theme, and so on.

We read a little better, I think, if we say that "God's Grandeur" bespeaks what Eberhard Jüngel calls *"eine Erfahrung mit der Erfahrung,"* an experience with experience, an event that is used to judge other events, and that calls for a re-evaluation of one's past and future.[53] Experience, here, is not a cipher for revealability; it is a sign of revelation as interruption. What has been "experience" in the past can no longer be counted as such, and from now on we will measure future events against what has been revealed to us. Jüngel's formula points us in the right direction in interpreting Hopkins's poem and also in thinking about religious poetry. A religious poem is not one that is restricted in advance to a narrow range of experience, and secondhand experience at that. It is an exposure to the otherness of God, which characterizes experience at its most radical, which might be marked in a structural fashion but will involve making that mark legible as a theme. One aspect of that otherness is that God impinges on us in contrary ways at the same time: His grandeur is given in Trinitarian terms as lightning, oil and wings. And an aspect of the radical nature of the encounter is that we may well find ourselves talking of an experience of nonexperience. How can this be?

The opening stanza of "God's Grandeur" is as good an instance as any of what Jean-Luc Marion, in a remarkable rethinking of Husserl's "principle of principles," calls a saturated phenomenon, that is, a phenomenon in which the concept is exceeded by intuitions, whether sensible or not.[54] Here, the phenomenon that gives itself, the holiness and lordship of God, cannot be adequately matched by a concept. The image of a storm is joined by another metaphor, the slow gathering of oil from an olive press, and together they suggest a wide range of intuitions: a sudden, infrequent discharge of energy that has been building invisibly, and a gradual collection of a nourishing and healing oil. At no time does God appear as an object, not even when the Spirit is figured as "bright wings." And here I have an opportunity to modify what I have been saying about experience. God cannot be experienced in anything like the strict sense of the word because He does not offer himself as an object or submit to an objectifying gaze. Yet since his grandeur appears in the poem, without being foreseen or aimed at by a subject, we can talk of what Marion calls "counter-experience," that which contradicts the conditions of possibility for experiencing an object.[55] The subject's intentional gaze is rebuked by the intuitions to which it is exposed, not necessarily because he or she is bedazzled but perhaps because of being disappointed by unfulfilled or displaced expectations, and in any case by the sheer resistance of the phenomenon to objectification.[56]

To live *coram deo* might be to have counter-experience of God, to find oneself unexpectedly turned around, to have the desires of the will changed, even in a life already consecrated to religion. The cross shatters every image of God that comes from within, and there is no life of faith that does not pass beneath the cross. To recognize that God imposes himself suddenly, violently and at large, and also that he allows himself to be recognized as coming gradually, in oozes that have the capacity to heal and anoint, and in wings that enfold, is to admit that he discloses his grandeur as phenomenon but does not appear as object or fall under a well-defined concept. Hopkins does not encounter God as such, but even so we cannot speak of him having an "experience of non-experience" without a significant qualification. He suffers a sense of awe, recoil and insignificance before God, as well as responding to the hope for a care and a healing that will come without any perceptible agent. He is cast as witness rather than subject, not rendered passive but required to respond, doubtless inadequately, without comprehension, and without the ability to persuade others that an event has taken place. Such is "God's Grandeur." Approaching the same issue from the side, as it were, we can say that Hopkins is exposed to a peril that cannot be seen, let alone lived with or contained, as well as to that which establishes and succors.

How the two quatrains of the octave hang together is not at all clear on a first reading or perhaps even on a second or a third. The evocation of generations treading, treading, treading provides justification for Hopkins asking why his contemporaries ignore God's authority. After all, the production of oil has been traditional: "thou shalt tread the olives" we hear in Micah 6:15. Yet Christ's sacrificial offering, suggested in the crushing of olives, has sacramental efficacy only if his authority is acknowledged. The earth has been subdued but has not been replenished; dominion has been exercised without stewardship, and man has become alienated from the earth (Ruskin) and from his labor (Marx). Nothing in the second stanza speaks explicitly of divine greatness, however. The poem is about God's grandeur insofar as it rethinks "grandeur" in a threefold manner—power, sacrifice, care—but, equally important, it is about the lack of recognition of his sovereignty and the consequences that follow from it. The earth has been "seared" not by a bolt of lightning from the heavens but by the human labor that is a direct consequence of original sin ("man's smudge") and, more particularly, by the actual sin of greed. The plowed earth looks as though it has been scorched; it is "bare" in that trees have been felled and the soil has been over cultivated. Our feet are "shod": we recognize no holiness at all in nature. Performed without grace, and solely with finite ends in mind, human labor does not lead to order and clarity but to their opposites. It is for this reason that God's grandeur "*will* flame out" [my emphasis], and that there will be an eschatological sign of Judgment.

With the sestet we pass from "the world" to "nature," and we do so not in the spirit of contrast but in a surprising continuity with the octave. Hopkins says, and stresses it, "Ánd for all this, nature is never spent," not "*But* for all this, nature is never spent" [my emphasis]. To know why this is so, we need to know the "all this" that is at issue. Is it the sinfulness of man, his poor stewardship of the earth? Yes, indeed. Yet the broken relation between God and man is also relevant. Although God is all-powerful and all just, and although we have been thoroughly disobedient, He does not destroy the planet or let us do so. We are not allowed to "spend" nature as though it were realized as so much money, even though that is precisely what the poem suggests we try to do. Its "dearness" does not give itself as commodity but as intimacy with creation. Revelation is given on the inside, as it were, and it is the poet's task to read things from within—*intus legere*—and so to encounter the divine by way of inscape.

Always, it seems, there is more to encounter; and that is because the divine grandeur does not reveal itself simply as anger and power but also discloses itself as self-sacrifice and healing. It is here that the poem against which "God's Grandeur" defines itself, Wordsworth's "The world is too much with us" (1807), comes into focus. In the earlier sonnet the poet laments being out of tune with nature. He exclaims, "Great God! I'd rather be / A pagan suckled in a creed outworn" and conditionally wishes to see Proteus or Triton. Such a sight would be preferable to living with revealed truth in a world in which we are alienated from nature. Hopkins's response in his sonnet is precisely that intimacy with nature need not make one revert to paganism in order to regain religious vitality; on the contrary, it will disclose the grandeur of God not in experience but in counter-experience.

In general, this reading finds support in the final line of the lyric, the Miltonic image of the Holy Spirit "brooding" over the earth.[57] It will be seen that we have passed from "nature" back to "world" in order to find a cosmic perspective on the scene and accordingly to stress that God's holiness is given in maternal solicitude as well as in dynamic power and self-sacrifice. The West is "black"—we think of night and the dire effects on the environment of the industrial revolution—and the world is "bent" not only because its curve is seen in a cosmic perspective but also because of the crushing weight of sin and its consequence, work. Or is it because the world itself, if not its human population, is bent in adoration of the Holy Spirit, offering us a model of how to respond properly to God? Certainly Hopkins does not identify the Holy Spirit with the dawn. The metaphor is of the moment before the rising of the sun, before it becomes visible, when distinct rays of light can be made out against the dark. It is the time that Hölderlin valued in "Wie wenn am Feiertage …," the moment when nature, which precedes the gods, reveals herself. Hölderlin says, "das Heilige sei mein Wort," the holy be my word, meaning not that he will represent what is holy but rather that his words will *be* sacred speech and thus open to a new revelation.[58] Orthodox in his Trinitarian faith, Hopkins would never affirm nature in quite that way. Rather, he tells us that morning does not come merely as part of a mechanical diurnal round but that it springs into being because of the many opportunities for a life nurtured by the Spirit. The "because" does not have a strong thetic role in the poem; it indicates a leap from the natural to the divine rather than a logical relation of *consequentia or inferentia*. That morning "springs" to life recalls that specific acts are the fruit of the Spirit, and it stands in sharp contrast to the earlier talk of being crushed. The sestet has more active verbs ("spent," "lives," "went," "springs," "broods") than the octave ("is charged," "is seared," "bleared," "smeared"); it is as though nature asserts its epiphanic power in response to the Holy Spirit. That the poet grasps the *Gestalt* of divine grandeur is itself a gift of the Spirit. Yet in saying these things it is the critic who is doing theology, not the poet.

Those who demur about the possibility of religious poetry will point to the final line, in which the Spirit is seen as a dove, as a biblical symbol (Matt.

3:16) that betrays, right at the end of the lyric, the impossibility of escaping from umpteenth-hand experience when talking of God. That the dove is a dead metaphor for the Spirit is entirely true, and we need to remember it was just as dead for Milton when he wrote *Paradise Lost*. Yet Milton did what strong poets always do with a dead metaphor: he revived it. Which is what Hopkins has done, partly by having rays of light before dawn becoming wings and partly by the signature exclamation "ah!" that interrupts the poem with an immediate affective response to the Spirit, a final moment of adoration and relief. The experience of language in "God's Grandeur" is strongly felt here, for, as Robert Bridges recognized, one peril to which Hopkins exposes himself is that the dead metaphor cannot be revived without undue force.[59] That would mean there would be no poetic invention, no change to the field of literary possibility by something unforeseen, something that "comes in" from nowhere and is a revelation of originality. Without this doubling of religious and poetic revelation there would be no religious poetry worth reading.

*

The main argument against religious poetry turns partly on the narrow range of experience available to the poet and to its derivative quality. Yet it seems that a poetry written *coram deo* can engage with experience in a far more radical manner than most poetry can ever do. This claim can be clarified a little more, and so I will conclude this chapter by reflecting on one or two aspects of the style of criticism I have been practicing. All poetry involves a bracketing of the natural attitude; it marks the possibility of the multiple logics, the repeated foldings, refoldings and unfoldings of metaphors and motifs, which are the very life of poetry.[60] Similarly, religious poetry requires a suspension of the supernatural attitude. All poets, religious or not, perform, to some extent, the phenomenological reduction: they are led back to a consciousness whose intentional rapport with the world renders meaningful those events that might otherwise be dismissed or overlooked. Yet, at the same time, poetry frustrates the phenomenological reduction. The act of writing introduces differences and deferrals that prevent consciousness from closing on itself.[61] A partial or frustrated reduction admits traces of transcendence: we pass from sign to meaning. In the case of religious poetry, where we are concerned with the transcendence of God, there will be effects of counter-experience but little or no appeal to the supernatural attitude construed as a thesis.

The failure of the phenomenological reduction in religious poetry brings to mind other species of reduction. I recall the *reductio* that St. Bonaventure details in his *De Reductione Artium ad Theologiam* and that he drew from Hugh of St. Victor.[62] This is a theological, not a philosophical, reduction; it does not lead us to the absence of presuppositions, as Husserl wanted, but to the non-ground, given only by Grace, that *ens creatum* is exceeded by *creatio activa*. It can be debated whether St. Bonaventure properly suspends the supernatural attitude, and perhaps this is one of the things that Pryzwara was contemplating when he coined the expression *reductio in mysterium*, meaning by that the movement of being led back to a living relationship with the divine mystery.[63] Pryzwara thinks that, properly considered, theology is this *reductio*, and I do not think he would object if I included the finest religious poems in that category, especially in the case of a poem such as "God's Grandeur" that affirms the triune God. Perhaps also Jüngel would not oppose me when I say that, for Hopkins too, "God is ... grasped as the mystery of the world as he *comes* to the world" while exceeding the world's possibilities.[64] To live in that mystery, to be *coram deo*, is not to "have" positive experience of the invisible and unknowable God but to be marked at every level of one's being by counter-experience. There *intus legere* becomes a species of *lectio divina*. It is the place where Hopkins takes us time and again.

2

"For the life was manifested"

On "material spirit" in Hopkins

What is it to hear with Christian ears, to see with Christian eyes, and to touch with Christian hands? It would be, first of all, to live in a full, rich interpretation of the first epistle of John, to live in response to "the life" that "was manifested" (1 Jn 1:2), that "was from the beginning, which we have heard, which we have seen with our eyes, which we have looked upon, and our hands have handled" (1 Jn 1:1).[1] It would be a matter of "bear[ing] witness" to that life, of showing others "that eternal life, which was with the Father, and was manifested unto us" (1 Jn 1:2). It would be to live in the truth of what is preached in this epistle: "Hereby know ye the Spirit of God: Every spirit that confesseth that Jesus Christ is come in the flesh is of God: And every spirit that confesseth not that Jesus Christ is come in the flesh is not of God" (1 Jn 4:2-3). To hear with Christian ears would be to hear differently now that one has heard and accepted the κήρυγμα, namely that Christ, the Son of God, has come "in the flesh." To live in an interpretation of 1 John would be to devise, haltingly or more fully (and both only through gifts of the Holy Spirit), a theology of the senses and a theology of manifestation, and—for those who work in systematic theology—to be able to hold the two together.

One approach to living deep inside the words of 1 John 1:1-2 would be by way of the spiritual senses. For Origen, St. Gregory of Nyssa, St. Augustine, all the way up to St. Bonaventure, and continuing in the contemplative religious orders, the spiritual senses have provided a way in which we, material creatures often at odds with spirit, can be in partial contact with the spiritual world: the outer man signifies the reality of the inner man, and the inner man signifies the reality of the divine.[2] The author of 1 John speaks of Christ in his mortal life and perhaps also after his resurrection. He was seen "by the fleshly eyes that see the sun," as St. Augustine says.[3] But those of us who have come after the manifestation of the Christ can at best feel his spirit by way of the spiritual senses.[4] That there are competing interpretations of what these great theologians thought goes without saying, though each proposed that the spiritual senses are distinct from the corporeal senses. And that there are arguments as to the rightness of what they thought is also plain. Whether the spiritual senses act best when the corporeal senses have been put to sleep, or whether, once purified, they act in concert with them is a fault line of modern debate.[5]

There is also disagreement among the advocates of the spiritual senses. Origen, for one, speaks of the prophets who "tasted and smelt, so to speak, with a sense which was not possible," and St. Gregory of Nyssa says that "the soul will see God in a divine watchfulness," while St. John of the Cross holds that the spiritual senses do not give access to the divine but must be rendered inactive before God can be encountered.[6] (A different but contributive emphasis can be detected in the thirteenth and fourteenth centuries: we must pass from the light of *intellectus* to the darkness of *affectus*.[7]) For Origen and his school "being human" means, as St. Paul said, being "spirit and soul and body" (1 Thess. 5:23), with the spiritual senses mediating the outer and the inner person.[8] By the time the Alexandrian school was flourishing in the third century, Christian theology had overcome the idea of the soul as "material spirit."[9] That was the description Tatian gave it in his *Oratio ad Graecos*, written in the late second century, his point being that we should pass from a material soul to an immaterial, divine soul. In the patristic age, a doctrine of the spiritual senses is attained only when the human being, considered as a whole, can be seen as material spirit.[10] The spiritual senses help us ascend from the material to the spiritual world; they are to be cultivated as ways of taking us on a journey into the darkness of unknowing.

That vision of "being human" has mostly faded under the intense glare of successive philosophical criticisms, mainly circling around the rejection of a self-sufficient inner life, although the words "material," "soul" and "spirit" have survived with different denotations and connotations.[11] "Material spirit" would be a self-contradiction within programs of naturalist reductionism, while in phenomenology it need not be, in part because here "spirit" [*Geist*] is not a substance but the intentional activity of consciousness: not just a matter of cognition but, as Eugen Fink makes clear, the very movement of life.[12] "Soul" and "spirit" name different things for Husserl: the soul is the bearer of my experiences, and the spirit is the life of my consciousness. There is no Cartesian "inner life" for Husserl; our statements about the world are about the world, not about mental representations of the world. The "inner man" is transcendental life.[13] And yet it still makes sense to speak of imagination, memory and understanding: the staples of the doctrine of the "spiritual senses" as usually considered.[14] "Experience teaches us," Husserl writes in *Ideas* II, "that real spirituality [*Geistigkeit*] is connected up with material Bodies only," and he later observes, "The unity of Body and spirit is a two-fold one, and, correlatively, a two-fold apprehension (the personalistic and the naturalistic) is included in the unitary apperception of the human."[15] Husserl's concern in this study is with the phenomenology of the body. *Leib*, the lived body, *is* material spirit for him: its stratum of ὕλη grounds the flow of noesis. ("*The intentional functions*," he writes in *Ideas* II, "*are bound to this stratum*; the matter receives a spiritual forming, just as ... the primary sensations [ὕλη] undergo apprehension, are taken up in perceptions" [160].) More generally, he opposes the naturalist reduction of spirit to nature: the spiritual cannot be fully explained by cause and substance, he maintains. Although Husserl largely puts God out of play in *Ideas* I, he nonetheless seeks to find a phenomenological path to God that does not rely on what the positive religions have said about him.[16] Also, without intending to do so, he gives us clues how we might rethink the teaching of the spiritual senses today so that we might keep faith as firmly as one can with 1 John 1:1-2.[17]

As is well known, Husserl maintains that by performing the ἐποχή and transcendental reduction we may pass from the natural to the transcendental attitude, and we can there examine a phenomenon as it is concretely embedded in our intentional horizons.[18] When I perceive something my intentional ray exceeds itself, involving other intentional relations that are implicit in the act; there is always a "meaning more," he says, and when I examine the phenomenon in its implicit as well as its explicit horizons I may gain a fuller, deeper understanding of my relationship with it.[19] I grasp *how* I am intending, and *how* the phenomenon is giving itself.[20] The phenomenon flashes and fires in ways it would not were it perceived solely in the natural attitude (or indeed the naturalistic attitude or theoretical attitude) and allowed to remain abstract. "Phenomenological explication makes clear what is included and only non-intuitively co-intended in the sense of the cogitatum," Husserl writes in the *Cartesian Meditations*, and adds that it does so "by making present in phantasy the potential perceptions that would *make the invisible visible*" (48; my emphasis). I shall return to "make present in phantasy" a little later. For now it need only be stressed that the question whether the phenomenon exists inside or outside consciousness has been turned off: for the time being it illuminates nothing at all. We are left to consider how something has given itself, not its pre-given state or the causal structure of its givenness.

We may add to phenomenology another protocol that does not change it but that clarifies its range. For we may observe that for the Christian there is also a supernatural attitude.[21] Within this attitude, as when devoutly reciting the Nicene-Constantinopolitian Creed, one has a thetic relation with all manner of presumed realities and real events concerning the nature of God and the activities of Christ. One may say, "I believe *in*," not "I believe *that*," but when used liturgically the Creed is either declarative or interrogative in mode. So when saying or singing the Creed one is attesting to revelation as interpreted by the Church, and declaring that this picture of reality is solid and reliable, although not open to verification. When a person of faith performs the ἐποχή and reduction, he or she passes from the natural and supernatural attitudes to the transcendental attitude. The truths professed in the Creed are not denied but allowed to fade as theses, and we gain the opportunity of pre-theoretical experience of what they point to. One understands better that when one attests *Credo in unum Deum* one is confessing that one believes oneself into God. In perceiving something, a Christian can make explicit other intentional horizons that until then had been implicit, and one of these will be faith. The faith I have in mind is not the belief that is implied in all the positings of anticipations, perceptions and memories, or the rational faith that Karl Jaspers urges, but religious faith, *fides qua*.[22] Dogmatic elaborations of faith—*fides qua iustificat, fides salvifica*, and so on—cannot become issues for the person explicating intentional experience. Similarly, exactly what Christians name by "divine spirit" (the nature of *ipsum esse subsistens*, for example) loses its urgency as a question.

Yet a Christian does not cease being a believer after performing the ἐποχή and reduction. The self has been stilled, not changed; the world remains, though no longer as one's goal. Faith too remains; it has been sedimented in the psyche as a number of acts of which one is unconscious although they can be recovered, sometimes by accident and sometimes by discipline ("spiritual exercises," for example). In part, faith is passive, a number of associations and habituations, but it is also in part active, for a new association can jog the mind so that sedimented acts return to consciousness with vivacity and power and / or so that one will make one sort of intentional act rather than another. Reflection can move backwards to passive synthesis or forwards to the world, or backwards in order to go forwards. Faith remains, passively and actively (as faith *in* or *into*, not faith *that*), since the person of faith continues to be passionately invested in the divine.[23] Now, though, that person's intentional life is open to his or her inspection. So one might see, when looking at a landscape—sunlight on clouds in the sky, blue hills in the distance—that it is charged with unforeseen significance because it is being intended in a manner that, until then, had not been noticed, let alone explored. One sees that it is beautiful but that is not all that touches one. Now both the meaning and the construction of it can be considered. Doubtless one has always been oriented to the world as such but intentionality has put one concretely in relation with the clouds and the landscape in such a way that neither the subject nor the object has priority over the other. Only after the fact has one's thought been founded, and by what it has constituted as meaningful by implicit as well as explicit intentional acts.

Accordingly, a Christian might see not just clouds and mountains but also, on reflection, see them through the eye of faith, perhaps with other common intentional horizons in place: anticipation and hope, desire and imagination, love and memory, for example. One might experience pre-theoretically what the thesis "I believe in one Lord Jesus Christ, the only begotten Son of God" asserts in a creedal mode. One could say, in a manner recalling St. Gregory of Nyssa (though not St. John of the Cross), "I can 'see' Christ in the clouds, and the landscape as supported by Christ." It would take a very long time to unfold this judgment with full phenomenological rigor. For tacit support, I turn to Husserl, much as one touches a banister when climbing a steep set of stairs. Reflecting on the exclusion of transcendence, Husserl notes that even so "there must be, therefore, modes in which transcendencies are made known other than the constituting of physical realities as unities of harmonious appearances; and ultimately there would also have to be intuitional manifestations to which a theoretical thinking might conform, so that, by following them rationally, it might make intelligible the unitary rule of the supposed theological principle."[24] Our lived experience leads us to affirm a divine, transcendent reality but we do not presuppose that reality in order to explain our lived experience. Husserl inches forward from here in one of his research manuscripts: "God can be no object of experience (as in the sense of a thing or a human)," he writes. "But God would be 'experienced' in each belief that believes originally-teleologically in the perceptual value of that which lies in the direction of each absolute ought and which engages itself for this perpetual meaning."[25] This is the closest that Husserl comes to touching the tradition of the spiritual senses: God would be "experienced" only in the understanding. It is this "would be 'experienced'" that interests me. The scare quotes indicate that God is experienced in a doxic positing of an absolute ought: not directly but only indirectly and vaguely, without profiles.[26]

Some distinctions are in order. St. Augustine tells us that there are three ways of seeing: the "bodily," the "spiritual" (imagination and memory) and the "intellectual."[27] Husserl shows how the first involves the second and third. When reflecting on acts of perception, one can make other implicit intentional acts—faith, to be sure, but also hope and love—explicit, and in so doing "see" God in the world. Intentional acts may be considered as "spiritual" [geistige] senses, a modern counterpart to the older spiritual senses. Notice that not all senses are spiritual, even in this particular sense: non-intentional sensibility is left aside here. And notice, too, that no epistemological claim is being made about an objective "religious experience": that Christ has appeared in the clouds or has revealed himself in a visionary way in the landscape. The intentional experience is noetic and what it sees (the clouds, the hill) is the noema with "Christ" inscribed on one or more strata of the noematic structure. Strictly speaking, with intentional acts the existence of God is irrelevant to the experience of God. (This is another reason to read "experience" here as "'experience.'") The second point is the bolder, though, and is drawn from Husserl himself: when reflecting on lived experience one may apprehend a deep pattern that leads one to posit God as real. The transcendent deity is always and already an irreducible trace in consciousness.[28] Here one may "experience" God in the sense of his transcendence being implied by enough lived experience and then posited as real by the subject. Going further, one may contend without leaving phenomenology that there is a region of being in which God may offer himself to be intuited in one way or another, and that this region supplies its own evidence (in the sense of *Evidenz*: making evident), which is unlikely to be indubitable.[29] There are mystics and visionaries, after all, and they brood over what counts as evidence in their experiences.

Let us take a step back from these three points. On my understanding, the person who greets what has been made manifest to us in Christ is not only converted from death to life but also has converted his or her gaze.[30] To respond to the κήρυγμα is to return to listen closely to what Jesus tells us; it is to have these two conversions taking place, the one superimposed upon the other. For Jesus's preaching, especially his telling of parables of the kingdom—for which, after the cleansing of the Temple, he was ruthlessly punished by crucifixion, and the truth of which was vindicated by his resurrection—prompts a reduction that allows people to shift their gaze from "world" to "kingdom."[31] In parable the kingdom is briefly phenomenalized in and through ordinary words. A parable changes how we see things, regardless of whether we have heard it from Jesus in the flesh or heard it millennia later in scripture and preaching. Jesus is a phenomenon that was made manifest, both in his life and after his resurrection, and the kingdom is a phenomenon that was disclosed not only to his disciples and the others who heard him preach but also to those who stand in the light of God. To be sure, we mostly have empty intuitions of the kingdom, but on occasion they are filled, partly or wholly, in such a way as we can glimpse what its full reality might be. So, too, we may pass from αἰών and κόσμος, *orbis terrarum* and *imperium mundi*, to the possibilities of the βασιλεία. The Christian is no longer one of those people who, as Maurice Blondel said, "see too clearly to see properly."[32] Reborn, he or she has a gaze that can see the kingdom breaking into the world (and can see Christ as αὐτοβασιλεία), and who has a calling to develop that adjusted sight through prayer, reception of the sacraments, and by living a life through which goodness shines.[33] He or she does not always find a new range of experiences ("mystical experiences," let us say), and often enough blurs his or her gaze by living bluntly. But a Christian always has the chance to experience "experience" anew.[34] As material spirit, Christians can look at the material world and also "experience" the kingdom.

What becomes manifest in the world is the possibility of something other than "world."

I do not propose to reject the spiritual senses as attested over the centuries from Origen to their fading in the writings of St. John of the Cross but only to rethink them on the basis of spirit rather than soul. The spiritual senses are quite real, but they do not constitute an inner life that is independent of the external world. In phenomenology, as we have seen, there are three ways in which we can talk about seeing God: (1) by way of various implicit horizons being made explicit; (2) by discerning a pattern that has a teleological unity, that cannot be regarded as purely immanent in consciousness, and that cannot be reduced; and (3) by intuiting a particular region of being in which God reveals himself with the *Evidenz* appropriate to that region. Now it may be that (2), and even (3), may cue ἐποχή and reduction, but what is cued is primarily of interest here. The spiritual senses of intentional analysis do not point us out of this world to another one above or beyond it, whether through inner sight or through a blinding of that sight; rather, they help us pass from "world" to "kingdom." On making the ἐποχή and reduction, we see, first, that things are *with* us, not outside us or within us: they are not there to be mastered, and we are not already masters of them. We abide in a relation of mutual constitution—the phenomenon as meaningful, and I as the subject pole of the relation—that exceeds any asymmetric subject-object relation. Perhaps we can even show "from beneath how God constitutes the world."[35] That much Husserl can teach us, and it is a great deal.

However, a Christian who has reflected on what he or she sees and who has made explicit what was only implicit, stands in a world that is no longer just a world. If Husserlian phenomenology seeks to do without transcendent entities as presuppositions, Christian phenomenology, taking its lead from St. Bonaventure's *reductio* as much as Husserl's reduction, acknowledges the absolute presupposition, God: the light of God, the power of God to manifest himself, the fleshly manifestation of God in Christ.[36] The transcendental turn, the "inquiring back into the ultimate source of all the formations of knowledge," is to the unconditioned: not the "I" but the Creator of the "I" and all that it engages.[37] One sees oneself not just constituting events as meaningful but, as created, able to constitute creation as meaningful in my lived relation with it. We begin to glimpse what Jesus meant by "the kingdom," its presence in the world and above all its many and terrible absences. Here at least ἐποχή and reduction do not disengage one from the world so that one is free to contemplate the kingdom without commitment to it; they place one in a situation so that one may be claimed by the kingdom, emptied of "the natural man" by that claim and pulled ever more deeply into the mystery of Christ. This is not mysticism; it is everyday Christianity: *lived* Christianity, Christianity as *life*. Unless we are mystics, the phenomenality that presses on us is the manner in which phenomena are given to us in faith as well as perception, anticipation, memory, imagination, and other intentional horizons. Yet the language of fulfilled and unfulfilled intentions breaks down when entering the kingdom; instead, one needs to speak now of being overwhelmed and now of desolation. To enter the kingdom is to risk humiliation and death before being raised again.

Of course, what St. Ignatius Loyola in the *Spiritual Exercises* calls an "application of the senses" is relevant here, for in any religious education, however basic, the imagination and memory are trained.[38] Yet I am not thinking first of all of the need to impress scriptural scenes on the mind and heart but rather of indicating a way in which lived experience can be implicitly oriented by faith and then made explicit, a way of passing from world to kingdom. The kingdom is not given to us as a system of explanation of what happens in this world ("revelation," "miracles," "visions," and so on), or so many items of knowledge, but rather, as George Herbert so beautifully said, as "The land of spices; something understood."[39]

*

"I can 'see' Christ in the clouds, and the landscape as supported by Christ."

In order to continue exploring what is involved in this judgment, and to do so more concretely, I want to stay close to a poem, a Petrarchan sonnet, by Gerard Manley Hopkins, "Hurrahing in Harvest," written in the September of 1877. It was, as he said to his friend Robert Bridges, "the outcome of half an hour of extreme enthusiasm as I walked home alone one day from fishing in the Elwy."[40] In its singular way it offers clues how to develop a theology of the senses and a theology of manifestation. Here is the poem:

> Summer énds now; now, bárbarous in béauty, the stóoks rise
>   Around; up above, what wind-walks! what lovely behaviour
>   Of silk-sack clóuds! has wilder, wilful-wávier
> Méal-drift moulded ever and melted acróss skies?
>
> I wálk, I líft up, Í lift úp heart, éyes,
>   Down all that glory in the heavens to glean our Saviour;
>   And, éyes, heárt, what looks, what lips yet gáve you á
> Rápturous love's greeting of realer, of rounder replies?
>
> And the azurous hung hills are his wórld-wíelding shoulder
>   Majestic—as a stallion stalwart, very-violet-sweet!—
> These things, these things were here and but the beholder
>   Wánting; whích two whén they ónce méet,

The héart réars wings bóld and bolder
And hurls for him, O half hurls earth for him off under his feet.[41]

Two straightforward observations should be made in order to situate
the poem and the reading that I propose, a reading less concerned with
literary appreciation or evaluation than with continuing the phenomenological
theology already introduced. For this poem, like many others, proceeds
phenomenologically; it works within ἐποχή and reduction. Yet, unlike many
poems, it also extends our notion of reduction: it leads us from world to
kingdom. First, I note that Hopkins tells Bridges that he "walked home
alone" (my emphasis): there is no question of intuiting the presence of
Christ on his return from fishing in the Elwy, a claim that Bridges would
have found incredible, though one that Hopkins would not have been afraid
to put to him had he reason to do so. The poem has bracketed that sort of
miraculous event and makes explicit the meaning of Hopkins's relation in
faith with Christ. The entire poem is set in the mode of *how*, not *that* or
what; it is concerned, as we shall see, with how the kingdom manifests
itself to the speaker, Hopkins, and how he lives with respect to it. Second,
this *how*, this relation in faith, has been educated, specifically by Hopkins's
intense formation as a Jesuit, which means being immersed in the *Spiritual
Exercises* of St. Ignatius Loyola.

Viewed from far enough away, we can see that "Hurrahing in Harvest"
was composed between two "long retreats" of thirty days: the first, under-
taken in 1868, when Hopkins was a novice, and the second in 1881, when
he was a tertian. Over the course of his life as a Jesuit, he took a further
twenty retreats, each of eight days. He commented, quite selectively, on the
Spiritual Exercises in 1881, and, less fully, in 1883. Of particular importance
to Hopkins's poems is the second week of the long retreat. When meditating
on the Incarnation of Jesus Christ, St. Ignatius directs the exercitant to follow
a particular sort of mental prayer, one that has grown out of the monastic
practice of *meditatio*, "the unraveling of something complicated," as Hugh
of St. Victor says, which for St. Ignatius involves responding in a highly
disciplined manner to specific images.[42] The imagination is to be used in
meditatio, as Richard of St. Victor reminds us.[43] St. Ignatius agrees, and asks
those taking the retreat to produce *compositio loci*; for example, "to see in
particular the house and rooms of Our Lady, in the city of Nazareth in the
province of Galilee," "to listen to what the angel and Our Lady are saying,"
and then "to see in imagination the road from Nazareth to Bethlehem." The
directions are specific: "Consider its length and breadth, whether it is level
or winds through valleys and hills. Similarly, look at the place or cave of the
nativity: How big is it, or small? How low or high? And how is it furnished?"[44]
This "mental prayer," then, is not strictly mental: it involves all the senses. Nor

is it neutral phantasy, as Husserl conceives it, for the exercitant posits the reality of the scene he or she imagines.

Hopkins translates St. Ignatius's instructions, originally written in Spanish and then twice translated into Latin in 1548, on how to conduct the fifth contemplation of the nativity of Jesus. They are clearly of more than usual significance to him:

> The first point is to see the persons with the eye of the imagination, *meditating and contemplating in particular their circumstances* [meditando et contemplando in particulari circumstantias eorum], and from the seeing of them to get some fruit.
>
> Secondly, to hear with my hearing what they say, or might say, and by reflecting on myself to get some fruit.
>
> Thirdly, *to savour and to taste*, by smell and by taste, the infinite delicacy and sweetness of the divinity, of the soul and of the virtues and of the rest of the things that belong to the person whom I am contemplating, and by reflecting on myself to draw hence some fruit.
>
> Fourthly, *to touch* by touching, that is to say to kiss and to embrace the ground where such persons leave their footprints and the places where they recline, always with a view to the fruit that I may draw from thence.[45]

To which Hopkins adds the following glosses on the Latin version:

> "Meditando … circumstantias earum" / inferring what they must have been, "contemplando" / observing what they are. . .
>
> "Odorari" etc—Here he speaks of metaphorical taste and smell. You may suppose each virtue to have its own sweetness—one rich, another fresh, a third cordial, like incense, violets, or sweet herbs, or, for taste, like honey, fruit, or wine.
>
> "Tangere" etc—I suppose that St. Ignatius means us to do what we might have done if present and not to do what we should not have ventured to have done, and this also shows how strongly he means us to realize the scene. (175–6)

Hopkins is impressed by how strongly St. Ignatius wants those on retreat "to realize the scene": it is a matter of imagining oneself in the particular material circumstances of the Holy Family. Yet Hopkins distinguishes, perhaps more firmly than St. Ignatius intended, and other than how the medieval tradition usually specifies, between meditation and contemplation.[46] When meditating, he takes himself to be instructed to impress the scriptural scene upon his heart and mind, and when contemplating he believes himself to be called to observe what the same people are in themselves. They are to be detached to some degree from the particular scene, which means that they can be reconceived and attached elsewhere: in the clouds, in the hills, anywhere.

Contemplation, as Hopkins conceives it here, is not quite what the monastic tradition has deemed it to be, a loving gaze on the changeless God (who first gazes lovingly at us) rather than on the world, in part because St. Ignatius has reset the distinction between *meditatio* and *contemplatio* and hence redirected the meaning of "contemplation."[47] No distinction is drawn between active and passive contemplation, for example, as has been standard practice since Denys the Carthusian in the fifteenth century. Contemplation is entirely active, consisting of observation of *what* things are, their quiddity, not of passing beyond the spiritual senses. It is done, as St. Augustine observes, in faith for the most part, not through a vision.[48] Also, knowingly or unknowingly, Hopkins remains close to Richard of St. Victor's understanding of the third species of contemplation in *The Mystical Ark*: the grasping of the "quality of invisible things by means of the similitude of visible things" and the knowing of "the invisible things of God by means of visible things of the world."[49] A contemplative may rise above this level, although a contemplative *as poet* must always write at this level. Even "Una noche oscura" is pitched, as poem, at the lower level, although it speaks of a higher level of spiritual attainment, passive contemplation.

Some years before writing his commentary on the *Spiritual Exercises*, while still at Oxford, Hopkins addressed the theme of contemplation. There are "two kinds of energy" in the mind, he wrote, one concerning the transitional and the other the abiding. Contemplation absorbs the mind, "for contemplation in its absoluteness is impossible unless in a trance and it is enough for the mind to repeat the same energy on the same matter."[50] He then notes that the prayerful gaze in its highest moments is close to the aesthetic gaze, though the latter adds something to it: "Art exacts this energy of contemplation but also the other one, and in fact they are not incompatible" (307). He goes on to talk about the complex relation between form and matter in art, and then steps back and distances himself from transitional energy: "The saner moreover is the act of contemplation as contemplating that wh. really is expressed in the object" (308).

St. Ignatius seeks to immerse the exercitant in the materiality of a scriptural scene, and Hopkins seems temperamentally inclined to follow him. It is not a question of perceiving, through the spiritual senses (as conceived by Origen and all), the odor of sweetness in divine things, although one may "*suppose* each virtue to have its own sweetness" [my emphasis]; it is an activity of the imagination (rather than, say, the stirring of associations). At the same time Hopkins also contemplates what is expressed by what he observes. To contemplate is to see properly: the *what* is preceded and carried by the *how*. The best vehicle for this *how*, the young Hopkins says (and it is hard to imagine the older Hopkins entirely disagreeing with him), is art. "Hurrahing in Harvest" certainly keeps an eye on the transitional, while also revolving the essence of what grips his attention. It is contemplative in that Hopkins detaches a biblical person, Christ, from particular scriptural scenes in order to see what "really is expressed" by him.

*

The poem begins with a strong opening statement, much like some of Horace's odes, yet immediately distances itself from canons of classical elegance: the stooks, bound sheaves of barley, are "barbarous in beauty."[51] They are not Greek, Roman, or Christian but savage in their appearance, as though they have unkempt beards. We are in the midst of an event, or rather two events that come at the same time: "Summer ends now," we are told, and "now, barbarous in beauty, the stooks rise / Around" as Hopkins walks past them. He sharply registers the phenomenality of each: the end of summer in the presence of the stooks, and (in a violent enjambment) how the stooks are giving themselves to him, rising together as one, pointing to the sky, even though they are purely natural and their arrangement suggests a pagan ritual. The sheer beauty of the stooks in the fields around him also encourages the mind to ponder higher things. So Hopkins looks "up above," detaches himself from the world before him. Unlike pagans, he cannot view the harvest without also experiencing how the Bible has used the metaphor, as a figure of impenitence (Jer. 8:20) and the end of the world (Matt. 13:39). The eschaton is taken wholly positively here with no fear of judgment or damnation, as there is in "The Wreck of the Deutschland" and some of the terrible sonnets.[52] He sees, first, large clouds with the roughness and bulk of sacks and the smoothness of silk. Like him, they are walking: as below, so above. The clouds pass in a dignified manner along "wind-walks," moving not stiffly but gracefully, calling forth our admiration and even affection ("lovely behaviour," he writes). At least that is what we are likely to think at first. On reflection, it may be that the clouds are wearing sackcloth, and that because of their perfect penitence they are now as smooth as silk. Or, again, it may be that the clouds are wearing sacks (from the French *saques*), silk gowns that hang loosely from the shoulders of ladies and flare out a little as they promenade.

The clouds are like the blessèd walking through the heavens in the fullness of the kingdom. Looking higher, Hopkins sees cirrus clouds, wild and wavy, also barbarous in beauty; and we remember that in "Pied Beauty" he praises "All things counter, original, spáre, strange." If he sees like Ruskin, it is not entirely so, and decidedly not to Ruskin's ends.[53] For he sees with the eye of faith, even when it is not made immediately apparent. Already, in a single glance, the stooks have imaginatively been transformed into "Meal-drift," for the high small clouds resemble coarsely ground grain. Hopkins anticipates the separation of the wheat and the chaff in the great judgment (Matt. 3:12) and sees it concretely prefigured now in actual cirrus clouds. Has there been anything more beautiful in this way? Perhaps not, but there surely will be—so the implied answer runs—when we come to speak of the end of time, which will be not in terms of wind but of what the wind stands for: the Holy Spirit. The more we interpret the poem the more we nudge it closer to the supernatural attitude. In order to avoid passing wholly over into the supernatural attitude, we must perform the reduction ourselves. "Poetry is in fact speech only employed to carry the inscape of speech for the inscape's sake," Hopkins says, and we need to be able to pass from speech as thetic to speech as inscape, "that is species of individually-distinctive beauty of style."[54] To interpret a poem is always to risk losing the poem as poem.

It is with high anticipation, as well as with memory and faith, that Hopkins begins the second quatrain. Already implicit horizons are beginning to become explicit. "I wálk, I líft up, Í lift úp heart, éyes, / Down all that glory in the heavens to glean our Saviour," he writes. The buoyant first line is saturated with his experience of literature and the Bible, especially the Authorized Version of his Protestant days. As Hopkins walks along the road back to St. Beuno's College, he follows the hint of the stooks ("rise"), though in his own way. We are likely to think first of Milton's Adam raising his head to the heavens on waking:

> Straight toward heaven my wondering eyes I turned,
> And gazed a while the ample sky, till raised
> By quick instinctive motion up I sprung,
> As thitherward endeavouring, and upright
> Stood on my feet.[55]

Also, though, it is likely that we shall recall the situation of Joseph in prison ("Yet within three days shall Pharaoh *lift up thine head*, and restore three unto thy place" [Gen. 40:13; my emphasis]). Hopkins looks to the heavens in hope of the fullness of the kingdom; it is a release, though, that will come only with the παρουσία. In the meantime he knows full well the injunction, "*Lift up your eyes*, and look on the fields; for they are white already to harvest" (Jn 4:35; my emphasis). He does not mechanically repeat scripture but, as the marking of the rhythm makes plain, fully appropriates in his lived body what is said there: "I *líft* up, Í lift úp" (my emphasis).[56]

Notice that Hopkins raises his heart first, and then his eyes: his perception is informed by his heart, which is prior to cognition and which is suffused by his attachment to Christ. *Affectus* precedes *intellectus*. The poem's focus is

Christological; more particularly, it is soteriological and eschatological. The "skies" are now "heavens," and their glory is more than sunlight shining through the clouds; it has become divine majesty. It is there that one can "glean our Saviour," the allusion being to Ruth 2:3, though doubtless mediated by Keats's "To Autumn," now bespeaking the marriage of the soul to Christ, and pointed to indicate that in natural beauty one can find vestiges of Christ. The allusion is not accidental. Matthew tells us that "Boaz begat Obed of Ruth" (Matt. 1:5) in the royal line that extends all the way to Joseph, the husband of Mary. Because perception when properly informed can find Christ manifest in the world, Hopkins now addresses his eyes first and then his heart: "And, éyes, héart, what looks, what lips yet gave you a / Rapturous love's greeting of realer, of rounder replies?" Things have changed since "Nondum" (1866) when he wrote, "God, though to Thee our psalm we raise / No answering voice comes from the skies." Now he has an answer. And we also see things differently from "The Wreck of the Deutschland" (1875): there we heard in stanza V, "For I greet him the days I meet him, and bless when I understand," and now it is Christ who greets Hopkins. Yet in "Hurrahing in Harvest" Hopkins figures this greeting by way of an address to himself—himself as material spirit (physical eyes and spiritual heart)— because he has become the object of a vivid counter-intentionality, Christ's. "What you look hard at seems to look hard at you," Hopkins sharply observes in his journal in 1871.[57] More specifically, what at first was the gathering of the *vestigia dei* has suddenly become something more whole and more real than could ever be anticipated. The gleaning has resulting in a rich harvest: Christ greets Hopkins in a manner that could not be "realer" or "rounder." In the *Spiritual Exercises* the contemplation ends with a colloquy that realizes the encounter with Christ; here a colloquy takes place in the middle of the poem, and adumbrates the possibility of other colloquies for other people ("whích two whén they ónce méet").

No English poet, unless it was Blake, would say that Jesus Christ has actually appeared in the clouds. To talk of supernatural vision here would be to go badly wrong in reading this poem (but not when reading "Jerusalem" by Blake). There is no special revelation, only a conversion of the gaze that inten- sifies the meaning of general, public revelation for the poet. When Hopkins looks at the clouds he passes from speaking simply of himself ("*I* wálk, *I* líft up ..." [my emphasis]) to recognizing "*our* Saviour" [my emphasis]. We glide from the self and its world to the possibility of the kingdom, and Hopkins, for whom, like all the living, the kingdom is not yet fully present, can only *glean* Christ in natural beauty, cannot see him whole and certainly not in his glory. Looking at the clouds, and making implicit intentional horizons explicit, allows Hopkins to say that he "sees" Christ in natural beauty, understands him to be there, finds "that wh. *really* is expressed" by the clouds [my emphasis]. He grasps the μορφή of Christ, not the ὕλη of a resurrected body or tiny droplets of water; there is no intuition of another "phenomenological I," no question of empathy, only an inscape that attracts him, that is part of the "constitutive duet," and that is perhaps aroused by the sort of teleology that Husserl evokes when thinking of the "experience" of God.[58] It is not even a phantasm that he beholds. Husserl tells us that "In lively intuition we 'behold' centaurs, water nymphs, etc.; they stand before us, depart, present themselves from this side and that, sing and dance, and so on. All, however, in the mode of the 'as if'."[59] There is no "as if" in Hopkins's perception, though: he directly sees an inscape in the clouds that bespeaks a transcendent ordering of the matter of the clouds that he identifies with Christ. "All the world is full of inscape," he writes, "and chance left free to act falls into an order as well as purpose."[60] But perception tires; one must continually refresh one's mind to perceive inscape.[61] Husserl would add that one must repeatedly perform the reduction. It too is a "spiritual exercise."

Instead of speaking of Christ as a phantasy, we should speak, rather, of an intentional correlative that has been long since formed in the tradition and is inscribed on the noematic strata of the poet's experience. Christ is made "present in phantasy," to use Husserl's expression, not in the sense of being merely imagined but of being posited as real from within presentification rather than presentation, *Vergegenwärtigung* rather than *Gegenwärtigung*.[62] Not that this is merely a subjective projection, for any Catholic with a decent awareness of the iconographic tradition and with sufficient piety and imagination would be inclined to "see" the same thing. Not every Catholic sees inscape, however. Hopkins grasps things in his own way and only, it seems, if there is a peculiar and rich beauty that calls to be registered. Consider a passage from his journal of 1871. "What is this running instress, so independent of at least the immediate scape of the thing, which unmistakably distinguishes and individualizes things?" he asks himself (215). It is not something purely subjective. "Not imposed outwards from the mind as for instance by melancholy or strong feeling: I easily distinguish that instress" (215). He had known how to do so since he was an undergraduate at Oxford when he was struck by Parmenides's insight that being is and non-being is not. "I have often felt when I have been in this mood and felt the depth of an instress or how fast the inscape holds a thing that nothing is so pregnant and straightforward to the truth as simple *yes* and *is*."[63]

At risk for him now, though, is something that exceeds mood as an opening onto being, though in speaking of mood in this way he anticipates Heidegger on mood, *Stimmung*, or attunement, *Befindlichkeit*, and indeed attunements as triggers to reduction.[64] The instress in question is the power of the divine to hold nature and arrange it in unique and usually hidden patterns, which are nonetheless manifestations of divine transcendence for those who have eyes to see. One might say that when these patterns are experienced through ἐποχή and reduction they may be called "inscape." To find inscape in nature is to find spirit in matter; it is the manifestation of God in and through nature, not by way of mystical experience but by way of the spiritual senses as conceived by way of spirit rather than soul. Often inscape is descried in clouds, as Hopkins' journal testifies time and again, although a particularly suggestive passage has him studying it not in the clouds but in trees in early Spring, "for the swelling buds carry them to a pitch which the eye could not else *gather*—for out of much much more, out of little not much, out of nothing nothing: in these sprays at all events there is a new world of inscape" (205; my emphasis). There is a sense that at sundry times nature reaches a pitch, there is a ripening of something so that its individuality is distinctly felt; then there is permitted the gleaning of a unique material pattern that has intense religious significance.

I return to the poem. Having raised his eyes in the context of his heart, Hopkins now addresses his eyes first and then his heart: his perception has already been oriented to see not material nature but rather material spirit, Christ in the natural beauty of the clouds. A limit to experience, having to *glean* the Savior in the clouds, is now overcome by Hopkins passing from being the subject of perception to being the object. The focus is less on a being than on a relationship, one that is concretely experienced in faith. No one has ever given him "rounder" replies because the relationship is of sinner and Savior, and no one has ever given him "realer" replies because Christ is himself that which is most real. Needless to say, these replies are not audible sounds. With the exception of mystical auditions, such as the one that Margery Kempe claims to have heard, only human beings, who characteristically reply to greetings with far less honesty and less weight in their words, talk to one another in words.[65] God speaks "in the voice of an inward essence through the mind," as St. Gregory the Great says.[66] Or, in the terms I have been developing, Christ replies fully to Hopkins's greeting by way of his intentional horizons: scripture that he remembers, the kingdom that he anticipates, and the beauty that he perceives. The "replies" exceed any temporal organization of question and response. Notice that even this experience of fullness is linked to a non-experience: the promise of fulfilled life with Christ in the kingdom. All the same, one material spirit, Hopkins, finds Christ by way of quite another sort of material spirit: inscape.[67]

Lowering his gaze a little, Hopkins sees the mountains, now blue in the distance, and sees them with eyes educated by Ruskin ("azure" being one of the sage's favorite adjectives). Yet he looks with a doubled gaze, at once theological and aesthetic. The hills are described as "azurous," Hopkins's version of "azureous," coming presumably from the Late Latin masculine adjective *azureus*. These hills are "hung," supported from above. Earlier the stooks seemed to "rise," and so directed his gaze to the heavens, and now that Hopkins's heart has informed his perception he realizes that when seen properly the hills are suspended from the heavens by the will and power of God who has also decorated them with the blue haze of a late summer afternoon. Held from above, these hills are also a sign of the earth being supported from beneath; they are Christ's "world-wielding shoulder." The one majestic shoulder looks like two hills, one at the top of the arm and the other sloping up toward the neck. This is Christ as the true Atlas, supporting the whole world, and we recall the description of him in stanza XXXIII of "The Wreck of the Deutschland" as "Our passion-plungèd giant risen." Notice that Christ is not phenomenalized here: we do not see him with our physical eyes or with one of the spiritual senses in the older understanding of the expression. Hopkins "sees" Christ on the noematic structure of the phenomenon "Christ as value." How is Christ given to him? In a contradictory manner, it seems, in two profiles at once: "as a stallion stalwart, very-violet sweet!" What Hopkins sees with his bodily eyes is the saddle of the hills, which suggests the stallion, and he sees it at the coming of evening when the color of the hills changes from azure to violet. This avowal of sweetness is the closest that Hopkins gets in "Hurrahing in Harvest" to the spiritual senses as classically conceived. Christ is "very-violet-sweet," yet we remember the poet's gloss on St. Ignatius's *Spiritual Exercises*: "You may *suppose*," he tells himself, "each virtue to have its own sweetness—one rich, another fresh, a third cordial, like incense, *violets*, or sweet herbs" [my emphasis].

We have passed from a glimpse of the kingdom to Christ as himself the kingdom, and now the lyric ends with the possibility of anyone, not just Hopkins, recognizing the singular relation that one may have with Christ, of passing from "world" to "kingdom." The next lines show us how this happens. "These things, these things were here and but the beholder / Wánting." The repetition suggests the excitement of what Hopkins calls "pitch" and what, in a quite different register, Husserl calls the conversion of the gaze.[68] But what are "these things"? They are the stooks, the clouds and the hills: reduction does not change what is there to see only how it is seen. ("The question is not what you look at—but how you look & whether you see," as Thoreau said so well.[69]) They were *here*, had been created, and the manifestation of Christ was indicated by the stooks and given through the clouds and hill; only the dative moment of the manifestation, a particular person, was needed for the manifestation to be received. It was always possible not to see these things as "world," as so many representations, but as "kingdom," as a life lived in the emptiness and fullness of a relation with divine love itself. The surprise is that the *kingdom* was here too, not just the natural world, and only someone properly attuned to it was lacking to see it. Once attuned, Hopkins responds to the phenomenality of the kingdom as it breaks into the world.

Something in the stooks, their beauty and the Greek–Christian association of beauty and elevation, urges Hopkins to make a reduction and so "see" the kingdom, and turn him from being merely a viewer, someone who lifts up his eyes, to becoming a "beholder," someone who sees the true significance in what is shown, who contemplates, and is beholden, tied to what he or she sees. Earthly beauty leads to heavenly Beauty: "I do not think I have ever seen anything more beautiful than the bluebell I have been looking at," Hopkins writes in his journal, "I know the beauty of our Lord by it."[70] To return to the less elegant language of Husserl, at least in English translation, the movement here is from "presentation" [Gegenwärtigung] to "presentification" [Vergegenwärtigung]. Hopkins has clear, vivid intuition of the landscape's beauty that also gives rise, by way of a highly trained memory for scripture and images, to an anticipation of a higher Beauty that is posited as real. In this poem, however, the movement from beauty to Beauty does not have the structure of a Platonic ascent but rather of a basilaic temporal paradox: the kingdom is already here but not yet fully here. We can glean Beauty by way of the beauty of the stooks and the clouds, yet once gleaned that Beauty will also be found embodied in the beauty of the hills. The "spiritual senses" as rethought by phenomenology are in constant movement between Gegenwärtigung and Vergegenwärtigung, between positing the beauty of nature (gleaning what is here) to positing the reality of Christ in Beauty (not yet here). We contemplate that movement, and in doing so we contemplate the kingdom. It happens not in the neutral mode of phantasy but in the shuttling back and forth of presentiation and presentification and, within the latter, from memory to anticipation.

Now contemplation is not without outcome, as Blondel reminds us: "even in the most 'contemplative' form of activity, θεωρεῖν (contemplating), there is a material fashioned: and this material we sculpt in thinking and willing, is our members and, through them, the milieu where they make their impression."[71] Contemplation changes us, and we can change the world. Here the beholder enters the kingdom, to the extent that he can, in joy, and celebrates the moment in making a sonnet, following the tradition of Herbert who in The Temple (1633) effected the change in sonnets from being secular love poems to religious love poems. In that very moment of entering the kingdom, though, Hopkins realizes that the kingdom has not yet fully come, that there are beholders "Wanting." The Welsh, in fact so many of the British, are not yet in the kingdom or even close to it, though perhaps they are wanting to enter it in an inchoate way. It is not irrelevant that Hopkins, now walking back to the seminary, has been fishing. His background thought is of being a fisher of men. ("Come ye after me, and I will make you to become fishers of men" [Mk 1:17].)

In the final three lines we slide from the first to the third person. When someone, anyone, "meets" Christ it is through the realization that he is already there, invisible, behind the play of representations that make up "the world." The meeting presumes eyes, but the focus is solely upon the heart: it "réars wings bóld and bolder." The heart does not *grow* wings; it *rears* them, like a loving parent, and it can do so because it is has been affected and is now affecting. Also, there is a suggestion of a stallion rearing on its back legs, shaking off a burden, or simply expressing joy. Hopkins fully appropriates *Phaedrus* 249d, of course, but also Psalm 55:6 ("Oh that I had wings like a dove! *for then* I would fly away, and be at rest") and perhaps also Isaiah 40:31 ("But they that wait upon the LORD shall renew *their* strength; they shall mount up with wings as eagles"). It is what Richard of St. Victor calls *sublevatio*, the raising of the mind, except that it is also a raising of the body.[72] The new wings "hurl for him," we are told at first; they throw the earth down with impetuous force, finely captured in the sprung rhythm. Then we hear a modified claim, "O *half* hurl earth for him" [my emphasis]. First we experience the feeling of hurling without limit, of pushing down and rising, and only then the realization that even an ecstatic leap can be at best a half measure: we leap to some degree, but not wholly into the clouds to enjoy the fullness of the kingdom. Richard of St. Victor would say that contemplation through the imagination is insufficient to stay in heaven, that only the highest contemplative "begins to dance and to make gestures in a certain way because of its excess of joy, to make some unique spiritual leaps, to suspend itself above the earth and all earthly things."[73] For Hopkins, though, things are different. It is enough, more than enough, to half hurl oneself, for Christ is also *here*, in the landscape, and is supporting it from beneath. Hopkins hurrahs not only in the time of harvest but also in the act of harvesting Christ and finding him not only above but also below. The kingdom has given itself in anticipation, as much as in other ways. For the kingdom into which he has surely come, indicated by the Society of Jesus and indeed the seminary to which he is walking home after fishing, is not yet fully the kingdom of heaven. Material spirit, a human being, Hopkins must wait until he can become a spirit, though of an infinitely different sort from Christ who can support the world with instress and appear as inscape: material spirit of quite another kind.

*

"Hurrahing in Harvest" begins with an ending, and meditates on another ending that has not yet come. It marks the presence of nature and even the glory that is beyond nature, while responding with joy to a presence that has not yet come. It is a lyric of the divine phenomenality being received in different ways: the beauty of nature, the surprise of the kingdom breaking into the world, and the "not yet" of the kingdom and of Christ as kingdom.[74] Hopkins does not subscribe to Tatian's notion of the soul as "material spirit" yet if we talk of "material spirit" to evoke human beings in their intentional life the expression tells us something about this poem. The different ways in which Hopkins can respond to Christ, the limitations of that response, and that our existence on earth, in the world and in the kingdom, is a middle stage of "already-not yet": our spirit, or rather our soul, is still weighed down. Yet it is still in contact with inscape that gives us glimpses of the kingdom. Divine spirit does not disdain the material: the Incarnation bespeaks that its beauty is good and, if looked for properly, the spiritual may be found in what has been created. Indeed, it offers itself here and now to be seen, heard and touched in anticipation of a closer vision of the divine phenomenality. The theology of manifestation and the theology of the senses, Hopkins teaches us in fourteen lines, are to be found in a theology of the kingdom.

3

Eliot's rose-garden

Some phenomenology and theology in "Burnt Norton"

I wish to read the opening passage of T. S. Eliot's "Burnt Norton," the first of *Four Quartets* (1944), because I find it the most difficult part of the poem, as well as one of the richest sections of it. The difficulty and its richness of the passage are co-ordinated in ways that need to be specified, and while *Four Quartets* as a whole continually interprets the opening passage while further enriching it, it is also true that this passage establishes the lines along which we interpret the whole of the *Quartets*, including what we understand to be the character of its wholeness. "Burnt Norton" was written in the autumn of 1935, and published before the idea of the further three poems came to Eliot.[1] That *Four Quartets* forms a whole can scarcely be denied—its unity is thematically and formally insisted upon in "East Coker," "The Dry Salvages," and especially "Little Gidding"—and yet "Burnt Norton" also exists as a poem in its own right. More exactly, one might say that it once existed simply by itself but now does not: it was progressively taken up into a greater unity, and now the later three sections permeate the first, ramifying and deepening some if not all of its lines. This first poem, section, or movement of *Four Quartets* has two epigraphs taken from Heraclitus, which frame the whole. Let us begin with them.

The first epigraph is the second of Heraclitus's fragments: τοῦ λόγου δὲ ἐόντος ξυνοῦ ζώουσιν οἱ πολλοὶ ὡς ἰδίαν ἔχοντες φρόνησιν. In English: "Though wisdom [λόγος] is common, yet the many live as if they had a wisdom of their own." And the second epigraph is the sixtieth of the fragments: ὁδὸς ἄνω κάτω μία καὶ ὡυτή. In English: "The way up and the way down are one and the same." Puzzled as one might be by the title, "Burnt Norton," one is not likely to be entirely bewildered by the epigraphs, for we are told that they are from Heraclitus's fragments, indeed from Hermann Diels's edition, *Die Fragmente der Vorsokratiker* (1903).[2] One might not frequent the redoubtable Greek scholarship of the Germans or even be able to read pre-Socratic Greek, yet one knows that these remarks are *philosophy*, taken from the very fount of Western thought. Eliot's audience is expected to construe Greek, it would seem, or at the very least be able and willing to read poetry with philosophical resonance. Doubtless, too, Eliot's intended audience, in 1935, is educated and Christian, for the most part, and would be quite capable of performing the hermeneutical task of adjusting pagan Greek insights to Christian teachings, of giving λόγος a Johannine spin ('Εν ἀρχῇ ἦν ὁ λόγος, καὶ ὁ λόγος ἦν πρὸς τὸν θεόν, καὶ θεὸς ἦν ὁ λόγος ["In the beginning was the Word, and the Word was with God, and the Word was God"]), perhaps by way of early *Logos*-theology. Diels encourages his readers in this enterprise by translating λόγος as *Wort*.[3] Certainly the poem is often taken to bring philosophical fragments into the field of theological remarks.[4] When read in the context of "Burnt Norton," the first epigraph would thereby come to mean something like, "The Christian revelation is given to all, though many persist in following their own minds," and the second, "One transcends one's sinful state only through humility, by becoming *alter Christus*." So readers of "Ash-Wednesday" (1930) or people who had seen *Murder in the Cathedral* (1935) might think as they come across "Burnt Norton," knowing very well that Eliot converted to Anglo-Catholicism in 1927. Yet, by the time they complete the poem, they may wonder if the translation is simply and fully from pagan philosophy to Christian doctrine or a Christian theology. That wonder may well persist if they read the whole of *Four Quartets*, though that is an issue I cannot consider in any detail here.

Even before one has construed, let alone interpreted, the epigraphs, the reader will have pondered the title, "Burnt Norton," which names the remains of a seventeenth-century manor house not far from Chipping Camden in Gloucestershire. Over Norton House was set alight by its owner, Sir William Keyte, one night in 1741 while in a drunken rage, and he burned alive. Eliot and his friend, Emily Hale, visited the deserted gardens of the house in the summer of 1934. Of course, those who read the poem at the start of *Four Quartets* meet it after encountering a metaphor drawn from music: the overall title suborns the title of the first poem. Eliot had listened to Beethoven's "String Quartet in A Minor" (Op. 132) in 1931, and, in a letter, had written to Stephen Spender saying, "There is a sort of heavenly, or at least more than human, gaiety about some of his later things ... which one imagines might come to oneself as the fruits of reconciliation and relief after immense suffering; I should like to get something of that into verse before I die."[5]

For the reader of *Four Quartets*, music and philosophy are guiding figures for engaging the poem, each of which lends itself to be translated or trans-posed into Christian motifs—or perhaps it would be more judicious to say religious or spiritual motifs—without quite erasing themselves.[6] Naturally, the reader who begins "Burnt Norton" as the first of *Four Quartets* will ask himself or herself what makes it a "quartet," and the best answer likely to come is that it involves four themes—the garden, the tube, the still point, and the limits of language when faced with the ineffable—that interplay to form a complex whole. Successive embodiments of the four elements (air, earth, water, fire) and the four seasons also mark *Four Quartets*, though as a structural feature of each quartet, rather than as a way of justifying the choice of "quartet" in the first place.

Already we have been doing a little phenomenology, for "Burnt Norton" offers itself as a choice instance of the distinction between independent piece and non-independent moment, as discussed by Husserl in his *Logical Investigations* (1900-1), and *Four Quartets* is an example of a group or combination, something with both objective and subjective aspects, a phenomenon that interested Husserl as early as his *Philosophy of Arithmetic* (1891).[7] Of "Burnt Norton" we might ask if it is detachable from the whole or inseparable from it, a delicate question that has no clear-cut answer so far as I can see.[8] We have also touched upon secondary passivity in reflecting on the epigraphs from Heraclitus: Eliot writes not only as an individual, but also as a member of a literary and philosophical community, and his words silently appropriate history and tradition as he writes. These associations are not necessarily restricted to his evocation of Heraclitus, even to a Christian absorption of the fragments, for the poem does not state the one philosophical position or even develop in to the one philosophical mode. Part of the poem is phenomenological in procedure, as we shall see, while another part reads more like moments in a lecture in the philosophy of internal time consciousness. To be sure, the motifs of time and ecstasy are developed in the later three quartets, though they are fully, if elusively, introduced in the first section of "Burnt Norton," and I shall limit myself to it with occasional references to the complications and embellishments of the larger poem. Needless to say, the phenomenology of composition presents us with all manner of questions about the poem, as does the phenomenology of reception, but I shall set these aside and focus instead on what is given to us in the first part of the poem itself.

*

"Burnt Norton" begins with a passage that, as we know, is revised from a speech culled from *Murder in the Cathedral* (1935). Originally to be spoken by the Second Priest, the lines were dropped before the first performance of the play when the Director, E. Martin Brown, decided that improving suggestions he had made to Eliot, which prompted the composition of the lines just mentioned, were in fact unnecessary.[9] Whatever the theatrical virtues of Eliot's third play (counting the fragmentary *Sweeney Agonistes* as his first), these lines contribute little or no drama to the poem. They serve to announce the main theme of a meditative poem. Let us take them slowly since they have been read all too cursorily. It is an attitude that is understandable when faced with a highly abstract introduction to an exquisite lyrical passage about a rose-garden. But in reading poetry all haste is regrettable, even when over unwelcoming ground:

> Time present and time past
> Are both perhaps present in time future,
> And time future contained in time past.
> If all time is eternally present
> All time is unredeemable.
> What might have been is an abstraction
> Remaining a perpetual possibility
> Only in a world of speculation.
> What might have been and what has been
> Point to one end, which is always present. (*ll.* 1–10)

It is, as critics say, a "philosophical meditation on time," though we should be careful not to take this description too narrowly.[10] Nor should we allow Eliot's distinction between "philosophical *belief*" and "poetic *assent*" to turn the task of reading a demanding poem into an opportunity merely to appreciate its poetry.[11] One of Eliot's less well-known distinctions, drawn in a paper given in French in 1952, is more apt. There are two senses to the expression "la philosophie d'un poète," he says: "Une 'philosophie' qu'il a empruntée ou qu'il a cherchée à construire lui-même *dans le langage de la philosophie*" and "Une 'philosophie' qui ne peut s'exprimer que *dans le langage de la poésie*."[12] Clearly, with the lines quoted we are in the orbit of the second sense.

I would like to draw attention to several things in these opening lines. First, the speaker's prudence: the present and past are *perhaps* present in the future, a doxic modification of a philosophical belief in a τέλος of time—a final cause, perhaps—or merely a protention of the past into the future; the same sort of modesty applies to the claim about the future being retained by the past. For all the philosophical framing of the poem, we are not given definite philosophical theses but two plausible, provisional statements that could readily be revised. Second, while the lines have a flat donnish tone, they are not philosophical in the sense of the academic discipline of western philosophy, not even the philosophy current when Eliot studied it when a young man (Henri Bergson and F. H. Bradley, above all). It seems likely that Eliot has in mind an Indian philosophical tradition, one coming from Nāgārjuna's verse on the "middle way," the *Mūlamadhyamakakārikā*.[13] In academic European philosophy to set "present" and "contained" in parallel, as seems to be done here, would lead to confusion. Besides, it is not evident at the moment whether the speaker is ruminating on time in its subjective or its objective aspect, whether (as McTaggart has it) the A-series (past, present, and future) or the B-series (before, now, and after) is at issue.[14] To say these lines have an "austere exactness" is to credit them with an ambition that they do not have.[15] Eliot himself is on track when he places "philosophie" in scare quotes in his gloss on "la philosophie d'un poète." He is concerned with how one thinks in verse, not how one translates philosophy into poetry.

Third, we should note the speaker's modulation of temporal claims, since we slide from what is "*eternally* present" to "a *perpetual* possibility" to that which "is *always* present." The word "present" occurs four times in ten lines, and calls for vigilant reading. It would have been different in 1935, though no one now would pass easily over the word "present" in these lines. Husserl has made us conscious of different shadings of "presence" and "absence": we think of an original presentation to consciousness (*Gegenwärtigung*) that is intuitively present, and of representation of currently absent sides of an object (*Vergegenwärtigung*). And we think too of empty, full, and fulfilling intentions. An empty intention gives us an object, without any intuition of it, purely in language: all we have are signs, not perceptions. A full intention carries the object in its sensuous presence, while an intention is fulfilling when it refers to an earlier empty intention. All these distinctions will help us to read the opening of "Burnt Norton"; more, phenomenology will help us to understand their difficulty and appreciate their richness. Whatever further innocence we may have had with respect to presence Heidegger and Derrida, among others, have taken from us.[16] Today we are likely to question the *presence* of the present moment, what Heidegger calls its *Anwesenheit*. Also, we are likely to be more vigilant with respect to "possibility" than Eliot's first readers, for we read the poem after Husserl and not just after Aristotle, and are aware of eidetic possibilities and not just metaphysical ones, that is, of possibilities that contrast with actualities rather than realities. A poem with philosophical motifs may well resonate with the philosophical concerns of another age and *vice versa*.

On a first reading, one conducted with western eyes and ears, we might say that the opening lines pass from a philosophical to a biblical vocabulary and then back again. Certainly when we hear the conditional, "If all time is eternally present / All time is unredeemable" (*ll.* 4–5) we seem to be in the realm of biblical thinking, indeed a biblical thinking that is already modified by philosophical reflection. Unlike the first two statements, this third one is categorical. We think of St. Paul: ἐξαγοραζόμενοι τὸν καιρόν, ὅτι αἱ ἡμέραι πονηραί εἰσιν ("Redeeming the time, because the days are evil") (Eph. 5:16), and readers of Eliot will also recall, "Redeem / The time. Redeem / The unread vision in the higher dream" from the fourth section of "Ash-Wednesday." Yet the poem gives us no right to think simply and exclusively of Christianity here: Buddhism and Hinduism are both concerned with redemption. A problem for all religions concerned with redemption, whether they are theistic or not, is how to overcome the consequences of past faults. If the presence of the past is freighted into the present and the future, all time is strictly unredeemable. Christianity resolves the problem with the doctrine of Christ's atonement; Buddhism teaches that redemption is achieved through the cessation of desire; and Hinduism proposes that many lives of selfless devotion to one's *dharma* can overcome bad *karma*, brought about by wrong doing, and finally attain *moksha* or the state of endless bliss.

"What might have been" is not only an abstraction, as Eliot says, but also almost always an empty intention: it has no intuitive content. Bypassed potential cannot be redeemed, cannot be brought into the present, because it has never entered the stream of time, the speaker tells us. So it remains "a perpetual possibility / Only in a world of speculation" (*ll.* 7–8), a possibility only in the sense of never being able to be realized, made real, and not in the sense of being able to be realized at any given moment. Because "what might have been" was never realized, it has not influenced the course of lived experience. And yet we know very well that such things can impinge on our lives; they inform our decisions by way of felt disappointments, regrets, remorse, and lingering hopes, usually by way of the imagination. They may not have been actualities but they still have a certain reality for us. Even if they influence how we act, they, nonetheless, indicate the same *terminus ad quem* at any moment of our lives, the here and now, where we find ourselves because of what we have done and not done. In the end, the most powerful adverb or adjective in these lines is not "eternally," which is tacitly rejected, or "perpetual," since it is sequestered to a world that can never be actual, but "always": it is the present, the passing now, that is paradoxically always with us though never with us for more than a moment. No matter what we have done or not done, even if we have brooded endlessly on choices we did not make, we are invariably led to the present moment of time.

With the next few lines the voice changes, becoming more surely embodied and personal. This is now someone who is part of a scene, however minimal it may be—a corridor with a door in it—and, more, one of a "we" who is also in contact with a "you" and so not speaking into a void. We are told about a memory of a choice not made, and so the poem slots itself into the terms of McTaggart's A-series:

Footfalls echo in the memory
Down the passage which we did not take

Towards the door we never opened
Into the rose-garden. My words echo
Thus, in your mind. (*ll.* 11–15)

The recalled corridor echoes with remembered footsteps, though not those of the speaker and not by anyone else who is named or alluded to: profiles of the past enter the present, though only in the mode of presentiation (*Vergegenwärtigung*) and, for the reader who does not have the speaker's memories, by way of an empty intention (with respect to those memories) and presentiation (with respect to his or her own). Others have gone that way, it seems, actualizing possibilities that the speaker has not, even though he always knew that the door in the passage opened onto a rose-garden. The possibilities perhaps relate to two people, the "we" (which perhaps includes Emily Hale), and the speaker is either addressing this person or us, inviting the reader to contemplate missed opportunities in his or her life. Immediately, though, the speaker steps back from any consequential knowledge of the reversal of time's passage through the agency of memory: "But to what purpose / Disturbing the dust on a bowl of rose-leaves / I do not know" (*ll.* 15–17). The memory of the garden in the other person's mind is no more than a bowl of potpourri now covered with dust, and since "what might have been" cannot be realized now and abides "Only in a world of speculation," it will scarcely respond to the speaker's words. Yet we have passed from certainty as to an end to a disclaimer of any grasp of a possible end or purpose: the speaker may know his thoughts well but not the intentions of the person he addresses.

*

Suddenly the speaker passes from passivity to action, from philosophical musing to participating in a unique experience, whether internal or external. It is the consequence of an indefinite intention, one that never actually becomes definite and perhaps never turns on an actual object.[17] The sound of apparently real, not metaphorical, echoes in the present form the first prompt to action, though as we shall see there are three prompts in all, growing in intensity as we pass from the one to the next:

Other echoes
Inhabit the garden. Shall we follow?
Quick, said the bird, find them, find them,
Round the corner. Through the first gate,
Into our first world, shall we follow
The deception of the thrush? Into our first world. (*ll.* 17–21)[18]

These echoes, neither footfalls nor words, permanently occupy the rose-garden, at least in imagination, and presumably were the original attraction to go down the passage and perhaps the reason why the door was never opened in the first place. The second prompt comes from the speaker himself, as he responds to the recently heard echoes. "Shall we follow?," he invites (rather than asks) his companion and ourselves—meaning shall we pursue these echoes, even take them as our guides? Third, there is a bird that urgently insists, "Quick ... find them, find them." That we cannot return to "our first world," our childhood or early adulthood, and that we cannot relive elapsed time, decide differently and remake our present selves, is known all too well by everyone concerned. We cannot even represent an object that was never present to consciousness, and must content ourselves with presentiation, and so Eliot asks if we really should entrust ourselves to "The deception of the thrush."[19] The thrush's song is widely regarded as one of the most beautiful among birds, and here it entices the speaker to cross a line that is perhaps forbidden to him, and to give him and us mistaken hope of changing the past and hence the present and the future.

This section of the poem has long been associated with a range of literary allusions, all of which can be discerned by the experienced reader of English literature. Eliot himself recalls Lewis Carroll's *Alice's Adventures in Wonderland* (1865), and (after the fact) Rudyard Kipling's story "They" (1904), while there is also reason to think of Elizabeth Barrett Browning's "The Lost Bower" (1844).[20] To these, I add J. M. Barrie's *Dear Brutus* (1917). One line from the play explains why: "A might-have-been? They are ghosts, Margaret. I dare say I 'might have been' a great swell of a painter, instead of just this uncommonly happy nobody."[21] Above all, I think, one feels the slight pressure of the thirteenth-century poem *Le Roman de la Rose*, with its birds in the garden that sing like angels, and also like the Sirens that deceive sailors, its garden with many roses and its sense of order.[22] Yet it is worthwhile considering that the three prompts lead to ἐποχή and reduction. These are weighty philosophical words used nowhere by Eliot but nevertheless germane to the poetry. Phenomenology was developed and articulated in early twentieth-century philosophy, and once established lit up what many artists had always known in a pre-reflective manner. It is not inherently philosophical in the sense of working only within an academic discipline called "Philosophy," though it is inherently thoughtful. The language of phenomenology can sometimes help us to identify and clarify cognitive moves in poetry that does not make use of any philosophy.

In the lines under consideration we have already suspended any belief or non-belief in the philosophy of time being offered to us, and now we bracket the explanatory power of naturalism and the ingrained logic of the priority of cause over effect.[23] Now this is not a thoroughgoing leading back to transcendental consciousness, as Husserl commended, or the adoption of an attitude so that one can discern being instead of beings, as Heidegger proposed; but it is surely a bracketing of the natural attitude, and involves a passage beyond it.[24] On the hither side of reduction, above or beside his natural being, the speaker experiences a shift of perspective; no longer captivated by the world, he or she can be open to everything that is in the world.[25] The reduction does not lead Eliot into another world, certainly not a spiritual world behind our own. Rather, he undergoes a change of awareness, not a change of place; he passes from experiencing the echoes in the garden to focusing on the experience in which the echoes are given.

Yet the experience Eliot is to undergo with these presences is not recollected, but is rather lived as present, something more like a hallucination than a memory. The presences are merely intentional objects, having a meaning but no independent existence, but since Eliot is writing a poem, not an essay, he figures them in terms that are appropriate to a poem. He phenomenalizes them:

There they were, dignified, invisible,
Moving without pressure, over the dead leaves,
In the autumn heat, through the vibrant air,
And the bird called, in response to
The unheard music hidden in the shrubbery,
And the unseen eyebeam crossed, for the roses
Had the look of flowers that are looked at. (*ll.* 23–9)

Note that the speaker is not neutrally conscious of these presences: they appear to him in a certain way, as respected. He recognizes them as dignified before he concedes them to be invisible. Are we to figure their invisibility in terms of intuitive presence (they are spirits) or by way of a lack of intuitive presence (they are memories or literary figures)? The lines give us no sure way of telling.[26] Yet the opening phrase ("There they were") lightly suggests a fulfilling intention, and Husserl allows fantasies to have intuitive content.[27] "What might have been" has intuitive content, then, as *meaning* but not as *object*. The presences exist not in time but in a quasi-time that cannot be redeemed. As poetry, the lines credit the "they" with phenomenality, while leaving us philosophically undecided as to what Eliot is asking us to believe. Note too that this eerie situation takes place in a time that is itself peculiar: there are dead leaves, suggesting that autumn is well along, and yet it is hot, with "vibrant air." It is a day in which death and life coexist, each exhibiting its power. Thrushes would not usually sing in autumn unless, as here, it is a warm day.

The bird calls again, this time in response to "unheard music." Is this because the speaker has missed hearing some music, because human ears cannot usually hear it, or because we can never hear it? We cannot say, although I tend to think that Eliot inclines us to believe that this is heavenly music which our sinful state prevents us from hearing. If we are attentive, we recall that the bird is deceptive, and so it may well be that no music is heard: the bird's song might actually respond to nothing at all. Of course, we recall Keats ("Heard melodies are sweet, but those unheard / Are sweeter"), yet we think equally, and in a more spiritual register, of "la música callada" [silent music] that St. John of the Cross evokes in his "Cantico Espiritual."[28] And, in doing so, we know we are dealing with signs, not intuitions. More intriguing is the line about the "unseen eyebeam," an odd expression since we do not usually think of beams of vision as being observable in the first place. "Eyebeam" is an unfamiliar word in the twentieth century. It is found in Marlowe and Nashe's play *The Tragedie of Dido Queene of Carthage* (1594), when Dido says to Anna of Aeneas, "But tell them none shall gaze on him but I, / Lest their gross eye-beames taint my lovers cheeks," as well as in Donne's lyric "The Ecstasie" (1634). Given that the lines that follow speak of an ecstasy, though one without any romantic element, it is possible that the reference to Donne is the one to keep close.[29] Of course, it could be that the eyebeam is no more than an ordinary "shaft of sunlight" that fills the pool and is styled that way toward the end of the poem.[30] At any rate, this unseen counter-gaze crosses the scene, and the speaker is partly reshaped in response to it.

To feel the gaze of someone who cannot be seen is common in experiences of shame. Here, though, the speaker does not feel the gaze directly: it is inferred from the roses that have "the look of flowers that are looked at." In one sense, the image is straightforward: Eliot is in a garden, and flowers in a garden are planted so that they may be viewed. (We might think of Proust: "les grandes roses vivantes 'posant' encore dans les vases plein d'eau."[31]) Yet there is a sense of the garden being an enchanted world, as though the flowers are posing by way of a response to a gaze.[32] It cannot be the gaze of one of the echoes or presences, since there is more than one of them and they are not individuated in any way. It may be going too far to invoke Bishop Berkeley's *esse est percepi*, but we may at least suppose that the gaze comes from the "eye of providence" or the "all-seeing eye" of God—an eye with rays of light radiating from it that is usually set in a triangle—an image that was common in Victorian parlors and cemeteries, as well as on the American dollar bill, and one that would have been very familiar to Eliot. Not that this image therefore restricts the poem to confessing the Christian triune God, for it may also be found in Buddhism.

The strong sense of the supernatural impinging on the scene—invisible presences, unheard music, and unseen eyebeam—is unsettled by an alternative explanation that is entirely naturalistic, as we have been seeing.

Another of these details that caution us against a religious reading in general and a Christian one in particular is the image of the "vibrant air." It could be that the speaker is experiencing a minor distortion of perception due to the shimmering heat. By the same token, it could be that this unseasonable heat is the trigger to make the speaker aware of things that otherwise he would not see. A similar hedging with regard to perception or misperception occurs at the start of "East Coker," where, before the speaker encounters the spirits of the dead villagers dancing around a bonfire, he walks down a lane "in the electric heat / Hypnotised," specifying "a warm haze" and "sultry light" (*ll.* 19–20). Yet we are not supposed to believe in the presence of the dead villagers in the way we are invited to consider the lotos rising. Even less are we asked to believe that Eliot actually encounters a "ghost" (*l.* 95) in the second section of "Little Gidding": the imitation of Dante makes it clear that if there is testimony here it is folded within literature. As with the presences in the garden, it is uncertain whether the lines about the lotos result from an empty intention, a full intention, or a fulfilling intention. The imagination may be variously in play in all three: in literary allusions, in unanticipated acts of the imagination, and in using the imagination in order to fill an intention. As important as the distance taken from the natural attitude is the reserve taken with respect to what we may call the supernatural attitude. No attempt is made to code the invisible, the unheard and the unseen with creedal statements, despite the speaker's allusion to redemption in the opening lines and the later image of the eye of providence.

Yet it needs to be underlined that there is not just one reduction in the opening passage of "Burnt Norton," that which leads us *into* the garden, but also, as already noted in passing, a reduction that takes place *in* the garden itself. This does not turn on the speaker realizing that he constitutes phenomena but instead that *he* is constituted by the "unseen eyebeam" as it crosses the garden. It is only in the divine gaze that the meaning of his life may be found, and the first inkling of this occurs in his encounter with the echoes or presences.

*

The next section begins by repeating the existential claim, "There they were," the speaker being entirely unflustered by invisible presences. In the lines that follow it feels far less likely that either the speaker or the reader will seek naturalistic justification for what happens:

There they were as our guests, accepted and accepting,
So we moved, and they, in a formal pattern,
Along the empty alley, into the box circle,

To look down into the drained pool.
Dry the pool, dry concrete, brown-edged,
And the pool was filled with water out of sunlight,
And the lotos rose, quietly, quietly,
The surface glittered out of heart of light,
And they were behind us, reflected in the pool.
Then a cloud passed, and the pool was empty. (*ll.* 30–9)

This is a curious situation: we have entered "*our* first world" [my emphasis] at the particular prompt of the thrush, who has perhaps encouraged us to trespass in a world *not* our own, and now we are told that the dignified echoes who "*Inhabit* the garden" (*l.* 18) [my emphasis] are "as *our* guests" [my emphasis]. The echoes can be guests if they are hosted in the speaker's memory or imagination, or if the dead require the living as hosts so that they may be present to someone. And so, once again, it is not entirely clear whether we are dealing with empty, full or fulfilling intentions, though the meaning (not the object) given in imagination inclines us to think, in one direction at least, of the last option. Also, the passage moves from an "empty alley" to an "empty" pool and in between there is a sense—perhaps deceptive—of remarkable intuitive fullness; we seem to pass from memory or imagination (that is, from image as broadly conceived) to lived event. It is as though the echoes and the speaker walk ceremoniously toward the "box circle," the circle of box shrubs, where they will have a privileged view of the pool. They see the drained pool, and doubtless passively take in some details of its historical strata. (A concrete pool would have been an improvement on the original pool, if there was one, modern concrete having been invented by John Smeaton in 1756, some fifteen years after Over Norton House was burned to the ground.[33]) More important is the expression "box circle," which has a secondary sense of a place to view something staged. The presences are "*as* our guests" [my emphasis again], which underlines their condition or their capacity, and yet it can also be taken lightly to suggest that they are playing a role.

Utterly unexpected, the pool is "filled with water out of sunlight," which means at the most basic level that a sudden stream of light crosses the empty pool and makes it seem as though it has miraculously filled with water. Yet more than this appears to be intended; it is as though the speaker sees the pool as it was when the house was lived in. Even this is insufficient when read with the following lines in mind: "And the lotos rose, quietly, quietly, / The surface glittered out of heart of light." We recall Tennyson's "The Lotos Eaters," which evokes the land that "seemed always afternoon," although we primarily think of the lotos in Buddhism and Hinduism.[34] There are various possibilities: in Buddhism the white lotos symbolizes Bodhi, the state of mental purity; the red lotos, love and compassion; the blue lotos, triumph over the senses; the pink lotos, divinity; and the purple lotos, the mystical. In Hinduism, Krishna is known as the "Lotos-eyed One."[35] The lotos *rises*, manifests itself, and by convention indicates a change of state in the speaker. If the speaker is having a spiritual experience, it is plainly not coded as Christian unless, of course, one identifies the "shaft of sunlight" with the "unseen eyebeam," and even here there is room for doubt because of the Buddhist use of the motif of the all-seeing eye. If we stall when reading the poem, the expression "lotos rose" may seem to synthesize eastern and western symbols, though it is impossible to keep both as nouns in the syntax of Eliot's sentence. We might say that as the lotos rises, so it displaces the rose, associated with England and Christianity; or, maybe, the Christian rose attains its true spiritual significance only in a verbal form.[36] Certainly the softness of the lotos contrasts with the hardness of the water's surface that "glittered out of heart of light." Again, we think of *Le Roman de la Rose* where the water's surface, in the midst of the garden, is a "miroërs perilleus" because of is capacity to seduce one to narcissism.[37] (And we recall also that "heart of light" appears in *The Waste Land* [1922] in the romantic scene of the Hyacinth garden.) For Eliot, though, there is more loss of self at issue than self-love. What the speaker sees, it seems, is not his image but that of the echoes who are reflected in the water: individuality disappears in the face of tradition. If we think first that invisible presences cannot have reflections, we are being overly literal; the distorting play of light in the pool gives the sense of broken images.

At the same time that we are oriented by *Le Roman de la Rose*, we are pointed to the end of Dante's *Paradiso*, where St. Bernard of Clairvaux identifies the blessed in the heavenly white rose. Before he prays to the Virgin Mary, Bernard indicates to Dante the children in the mystic rose, and Eliot alludes to "*le voci puerili*" in the lines of dismissal from the scene: "Go, said the bird, for the leaves were full of children, / Hidden excitedly, containing laughter."[38] The "hidden music" of several lines earlier is now heard. What at first seems a peculiar reason to leave the garden, the laughter of hidden children, is a strong reason when we associate it with the children in the mystic rose, for "human kind / Cannot bear very much reality," and we would willingly believe while reading the poem that heavenly children are more real than children in this life. (And yet we have a lingering reservation, for the bird was introduced to us as deceptive.) There is also another strong reason: Eliot, who had no children, might have become a father had he chosen differently in life, by marrying Emily Hale, say.[39] (It is not wholly irrelevant that the bird, the tutelary spirit of the passage, is a thrush, since wood thrushes mate for life.) In any case, these are not children *hiding* in the shrubbery; they are *hidden* there: concealed with the suggestion of being kept safe by another in heaven or in another possible world. The shrubbery contains their laughter in the sense that only giggles that can be heard; the children themselves cannot be seen.

The passage seeks closure by returning to the terms of the opening lines, though now greatly condensed:

Time past and time future
What might have been and what has been
Point to one end, which is always present.

What might have been and what has been still bring one to the present moment in time, as we heard at the start of the section, and the past flows toward the present while the future seems to pour toward the same point. Or, as St. Augustine showed in the *Confessions*, the past that abides in the soul is the present of the past (memory) and the future that abides in the soul is the present of the future (anticipation).[40] The present is the mode of access to the past and the future, though only in highly limited ways; and it has no presence in and of itself: such presence is to be found only out of time, the poem proposes, and is marked by divine love rather than *Anwesenheit*.

*

What is given to us in the opening passage of "Burnt Norton"? The question is not easy to answer, for in much of the description of the rose-garden it is unclear whether the speaker records an ecstasy of some sort or an entirely natural experience brought about through distorting heat. To be sure, the bird's injunction to leave the garden inclines us to think that the experience has been supernatural; the speaker has encountered more reality than he can bear. Yet we have been warned from the outset not to trust the bird, and we have warrant to acknowledge a distinction between object and meaning. Certainly the passage gives us no reason to look for the Christian confession alone as able to explain the event: the sudden filling of the pool does not provide adequate *Evidenz* for a Christian "mystical experience," most references allude to eastern religions as well as Christianity, while the most compelling Christian reference, to the heavenly children, is literary, a matter of signs and not intuition. Nonetheless, the event in the rose-garden may still be a "religious" experience in the sense that the speaker has been converted to see things from a new perspective. Is it that he now has the world, given not pre-given, before him as a correlate of his subjectivity, and that this world is richer and stranger than he ever imagined? Or is it that his subjectivity has been challenged by a counter-experience that has made him shift his way of seeing things? Even if we were to grant that the speaker has had a full or fulfilling intuition of the "heart of light" in the garden, it would not of course protect that intuition from doxic modification. What was once felt to be certain can thereafter be regarded as partly or wholly illusory.[41] Needless to say, there must have been a perception at first for modification to occur later in the writing of the poem by way of phrasing and allusion. By the same token, the perception may have been only of "a shaft of sunlight" that was itself subject to doxic modifications of its substance and meaning so that an ordinary event became charged with religious significance.

Let us look at the final passage of "Burnt Norton" where the "shaft of sunlight" is evoked. It reflects on the very lines we have been considering:

> The detail of the pattern is movement,
> As in the figure of the ten stairs.
> Desire itself is movement
> Not in itself desirable;
> Love is itself unmoving,
> Only the cause and end of movement,
> Timeless, and undesiring
> Except in the aspect of time
> Caught in the form of limitation
> Between un-being and being.
> Sudden in a shaft of sunlight
> Even while the dust moves
> There rises the hidden laughter
> Of children in the foliage
> Quick now, here, now, always—
> Ridiculous the waste sad time
> Stretching before and after.

To return to Eliot's distinction between philosophy in the language of philosophy and in the language of poetry, one might almost wonder if he is imitating here the awkward prose of some modern philosophy (but not his beloved F. H. Bradley). A philosopher might use the word "movement" three times in a short space because of the demands of verbal precision in developing an argument; a poet, concerned with precisions of other sorts, would usually seek alternatives. (The same might be said of the repetition of "presence" in the poem's opening lines.) The final lines that see endless temporality as "ridiculous" may well be a rejection of Bergson's understanding of immortality, which Eliot had earlier dismissed as an "exciting promise" that has a "somewhat meretricious captivation."[42] Yet to my ear they are a devaluation of time with respect to eternity as experienced in the rose-garden, lines whose complete confidence in isolated moments of ecstasy Eliot will weaken over the course of the *Quartets*.

The pattern is first mentioned when the speaker moves "in a formal pattern" with the presences toward the box circle, and it is found again in the pursuit of the boar by the boarhound in the second section of the poem, and in the evocation of the pattern of words in the fifth section of the poem where it is asserted that the pattern is the formal cause whereby "words or music" can "reach / The stillness." Pattern presumes movement, at least in this poem, though Eliot refers us to another poem, St. John of the Cross's "Una noche oscura," and specifically to this stanza:

A oscuras, y segura	In darkness, and secure,
Por la secreta escala disfrazada	By the secret ladder, disguised,
— ¡ Oh dichosa ventura!—	— Ah, the sheer grace!—
A oscuras y en celada,	In darkness and concealment,
Estando ya mi casa sosegada.	My house being now all stilled.[43]

In his commentary of this stanza in *The Dark Night*, St. John of the Cross says that the secret ladder is a figure for "dark contemplation," which has ten stairs. We begin with the first step of love, which is sickness "for the glory of God," and end with the tenth step, which marks the soul's assimilation into God.[44]

To ascend this dark staircase calls for self-purgation with the aid of divine grace; it is "movement / Not in itself desirable" that is prompted by God, conceived here in the terms of perfect being theology as the Unmoved Mover, outside of time and without desire. However, this God can be "caught" in the sensuous world, grasped in and through time, in the mode of becoming, which is between non-being and being. The privileged moment is given while the dust moves on the bowl of rose-leaves, in "a shaft of sunlight," and allows one to hear "the hidden laughter / Of children in the foliage." Once again, nothing in these images points ineluctably to a "mystical experience"; the children could well be imagined, could well be no more than imaginative contact with one's past that has the effect of a sudden release from the power of time, as in the "spots of time" passages in Wordsworth's *The Prelude* (1805; 1850) or the moments of temporal recovery in Proust's *À la recherche du temps perdu* (1913–27). Only the theological introduction to the concluding image leads one to read the sunlight as a figure for ecstasy and to do so in Christian terms. "Burnt Norton" begins with a quasi-philosophical framing and concludes with a robust theological framing; indeed, by the time we get to the end of the poem, the speaker is thinking in terms of cause and effect. At the start of the poem, it was the tight linking of cause and effect that seemed to stymie the possibility of redemption. Something was required to break that linkage, and at the end of the second section it turns out to occur through time itself:

only in time can the moment in the rose-garden,
The moment in the arbour where the rain beat,
The moment in the draughty church at smokefall
Be remembered; involved with past and future.
Only through time time is conquered. (*ll.* 85–9)

Conquered, not redeemed: the language has become much more forceful in the second section, and the lines remain within Christian orthodoxy only if it is God who conquers time through the gift of his grace. A moment in and out of time suffices to overcome the power of time, the supposed presence of the past in the present and the future, to render us unredeemable. Once again, these lines obey the inexorable logic of cause and effect: if there is a privileged moment, then one can escape the domination of time. But this is not the case throughout the poem; the first section shows us something quite different.

After the speaker's initial meditation on time, we pass to another way of thinking of our relations with the world. We hear of "Other echoes" that "Inhabit the garden"; we hear a response to "unheard music" without a call, and long before we gather what this music really is; and we see roses that "Had the look of flowers that are looked at": effects precede causes in the garden, and the culminating event is a series of effects without an identified or named cause. We pass from the echoes to the presences, and from the look of the flowers to the divine eye that sees everything, to a sunlit pool that is filled for no apparent reason. In the garden Eliot lives phenomenologically; only outside it does he think in terms of a metaphysical philosophy or a perfect being theology. This is not to say that in the garden he enjoys full or fulfilling intuitions; it is perfectly possible that the entire experience is given in memory or even hallucination, and that he receives meanings and not objects or being or any mode of phenomenality. Thereafter in *Four Quartets* one finds many doxic modifications of the event in the rose-garden, none of them as affirmative as at the closing lines of "Burnt Norton." It happens even before the poem has ended. In the fifth section, we are invited to entertain the possibility,

        that the end precedes the beginning,
And the end and the beginning were always there
Before the beginning and after the end,
And all is always now. (*ll.* 146–9)

Here the experience in the rose-garden is not deflated by a return to that "which is always present" but instead is recoded in Augustinian terms as touching on the eternity of God before Creation.[45] We approach eternity through time, and this eternity, this "still point" or Love, is a joy rather than a burden; the "present" is not burdened with a hardened presence so as to be irredeemable.

In "East Coker" there are elders who are deceitful, and we are warned that, "knowledge imposes a pattern, and falsifies" (*l.* 84), which suggests that we should not trust reflections on first-hand experience, perhaps even the very passage about the rose-garden. Also we are told that, "You must go by a way wherein there is no ecstasy"(*l.* 137).[46] The roses are now associated with the flames of purgatory both in "East Coker" and "Little Gidding." The "intense moment" is placed in a wider context, and we are warned that "experience" and "meaning" do not coincide. In "East Coker" we are told that "echoed ecstasy" is "Not lost" but requires as a supplement "the agony / Of death and birth" (*ll.* 131–3). In "The Dry Salvages" the event in the rose-garden is depreciated somewhat by being called "The distraction fit, lost in a shaft of sunlight" (*l.* 208), and, more, is regarded as one of a number of "hints and guesses," the rest being "prayer, observance, discipline, thought and action" (*ll.* 212–14). What principally counts is not ecstasy but "Incarnation." *Four Quartets* develops by unfolding and progressively interpreting the episode in the rose-garden, among other motifs, and this interpretation tends to downplay the event rather than magnify its significance. "To apprehend / The point of intersection of the timeless /With time, is an occupation for the saint" (*ll.* 201–2) we are told in "The Dry Salvages," the implication being that the author is no saint.[47]

*

"East Coker" tells us that what is most important is not "the intense moment / Isolated, with no before or after, / But a lifetime burning in every moment" (*ll.* 192–4). Our aim should be to live a pattern of burning moments in life, moments of "sudden illumination" ("The Dry Salvages," *l.* 92). What most matters is not even localized in the life of one person: "And not the lifetime of one man only / But of old stones that cannot be deciphered" (*ll.* 195–6), namely, the tombstones in the graveyard of East Coker. Even in the frame of "Burnt Norton" the event in the rose-garden is not promoted simply as a "mystical experience": we are warned of deceit and the possibility of misperception. We recall the first epigraph from Heraclitus: τοῦ λόγου δὲ ἐόντος ξυνοῦ ζώουσιν οἱ πολλοὶ ὡς ἰδίαν ἔχοντες φρόνησιν ("Though wisdom [λόγος] is common, yet the many live as if they had a wisdom of their own"). If our reading of "Burnt Norton" inclines us to think of this fragment as prizing the Christian revelation over common human wisdom, a reading of *Four Quartets* may well edge us toward another interpretation: we should follow the path of mere Christianity and not seek special revelation or private spiritual consolation. For all of the involvement of Buddhism and Hinduism in the poem, it becomes more and more solidly Christian when we hear of "the one Annunciation" and "Incarnation" ("The Dry Salvages," *ll.* 84, 215) and as it seeks closure in "Little Gidding." At the same time, one of the developing themes of *Four Quartets* is a discrediting of *experience* as such. Quite early on in "East Coker" we hear the weary disclosure, "There is, it seems to us, / At best, only a limited value / In the knowledge derived from experience" (*ll.* 81–2). Individual experience is to be subordinated to tradition.

The second epigraph, we recall, is ὁδὸς ἄνω κάτω μία καὶ ὡυτή ("The way up and the way down are one and the same"). In "Burnt Norton" this fragment indicates the deep identity between what is above and what is beneath, between the immense and the tiny; the cosmic dance is beyond us and yet we participate in it here. By the time we have finished *Four Quartets*, however, we are likely to reflect also that the way to God is the path of endless humility. When we are told in "The Dry Salvages" that "the way up is the way down, the way forward is the way back" (*l.* 129), we are being asked, by way of Krishna rather than Christ, to "consider the future / And the past with an equal mind" (*l.* 153–4), as though "all is always now" ("Burnt Norton," *l.* 149). We do not ascend to God through industry—by chairing many committees, for instance—but are redeemed, as we are told in "Little Gidding" (with a bow to Julian of Norwich), through "the purification of the motive / In the ground of our beseeching" (*ll.* 198–9). In the fourteenth of the "shewings" (long text) we overhear Jesus say to Julian, "I am grounde of thy beseking," namely, the foundation of her prayer.[48] These lines touch lightly on the opening passage of "Burnt Norton," on the questionable motive of following the "deception of the thrush" that led us into the rose-garden. It is not the fullness of intuition granted there (if it *is* granted) that counts in a life devoted to God but rather the purification of one's motives rising from an awareness of what is likely to come to all of us, "the shame / Of motives late revealed, and the awareness / Of things ill done and done to others' harm / Which once you took for exercise of virtue" (*ll.* 139–41).

The final lesson of *Four Quartets* is perhaps the religious significance of a certain mode of reduction. In the phenomenological reduction the gaze is converted, and we recognize that phenomena are lodged on our intentional horizons. This kind of reduction takes place not just the once but—if we are attentive in life—continually. Yet *Four Quartets* also asks us to consider that "the ground of our beseeching" performs a reduction on *us*, one that may occur just the once or many times. It cannot be brought into focus, cannot be rendered meaningful in the usual ways, and hence mastered by us; rather, the phenomenon of divine revelation, centered in Incarnation, saturates our intentional horizon, leads us more to frustration (and thereafter humility) than to exaltation or ecstasy.[49] We are led back to find ourselves not centered in our intellects, our wills or our consciousnesses but to what is revealed, divine Love, "the unfamiliar name" ("Little Gidding," *l.* 208). In the end, Eliot undergoes and describes a transformation prompted by divine love: God overcomes distinctions between the real and the ideal, the real and the imagined, the real and the possible as a counterpart of Eliot purifying his motives in ordinary earthly actions. All these distinctions are displaced and set in another pattern when we practice humility before Love.

All this is said in poetry. Yet "The poetry does not matter" ("East Coker," *l.* 71) on its own account, as embellishment or "heightened language," or anything of the sort, but only insofar as it points to God who is capable of leading us back to our true selves in him. (Eliot may well be thinking of the poetry of the *Commedia*.) Were it to matter deeply, it would pose a serious problem for Eliot, since the imaginative use of language opens up a quasi-time that competes for our attention with God's ability to overcome time. Besides, poetry might itself be kin to the song of the thrush. So Eliot diminishes the power of poetry in the hope of being led back to a state of "being human" in God. And yet there is no doubt that his words "echo" in our minds ("Burnt Norton," *l.* 14) because they are poetry of a high order. The poem lives between the claim that poetry does not matter and the hope that it echoes in our minds. Certainly the poetry is not desired to obscure the thinking of the poem. The movement of what I have been calling counter-reduction is the most difficult of all reductions to perform in the entire repertoire of phenomenology, whether one is a poet or not, for as "Little Gidding" teaches—and the pedagogical aspect of the *Quartets* needs to be acknowledged—it brings us to "A condition of complete simplicity / (Costing not less than everything)" (*ll.* 253–4). *Everything*: our sense of self-development, our hopes for the future, our regret for the past, all these things must be set aside if we are to live attentively in the now and participate in the divine simplicity. Julian came to see that, for God, the Fall of Adam and the Atonement of Christ are the one act; and she teaches "the fulhed of joy is to beholde God in alle."[50] In his turn, much influenced by Julian, Eliot comes to see that "the end and the beginning were always there / Before the beginning and after the end. And all is always now" ("Burnt Norton," *ll.* 147–8). That "which is always present" (*l.* 10) is not just time's cursor, the now, but is the all. In reaching this insight, we are released from the chain of time, able to be redeemed, though not absolved from "prayer, observance, discipline, thought and action" ("The Dry Salvages," *l.* 214). For we have not yet reached the end of time "When the tongues of flame are in-folded / Into the crowned knot of fire / And the fire and the rose are one" ("Little Gidding," *l.* 257–9).

PART TWO

On Geoffrey Hill

4

God's little mountains

Young Geoffrey Hill and the problem of religious poetry

In 1917, a year before World War I would finally end, Mary Webb published her second novel, *Gone to Earth*. It is the story of Hazel Woodus, an unlettered girl, daughter of a gypsy and a harp player, who lives in the Callow, "a spinney of silver birches and larches that topped a round hill," apparently one of the Stiperstones bordering on Wales, in the sparsely populated southwest of Shropshire.[1] She lives flush with the hard, beautiful country of those parts, freeing trapped wild animals and looking after her fox cub, "Foxy." Without having any great desire to do so, she marries Edward Marston, a Non-Conforming minister. He lives "on a hill five miles from the Callow, called God's Little Mountain" (15), where one finds a chapel and minister's house, "all in one—a long, low building of grey stone surrounded by the graveyard, where stones, flat, erect, and askew, took the place of a flower garden" (63). On the day he sees her for the first time, Marston hears Hazel singing to the accompaniment of her father, a song about singing to Christ accompanied by a "splintered harp without a string" (68). "Poor child!," Marston thinks to himself, "Is it mystical longing or a sense of sin that cries out in her voice?" (69).

It is neither of those things, the narrator tells us. "It was the grief of rainy forests and the moan of stormy water; the muffled complaint of driven leaves; the keening—wild and universal—of life for the perishing matter that it inhabits" (69). Certainly God's Little Mountain does not at first attract the earthy, pagan Hazel. Yet she listens to what the hills tell her. "They were of a cold and terrific color, neither purple nor black nor grey, but partaking of all. Kingly, mournful, threatening, they dominated the life below as the race dominates the individual. Hazel gazed up at them. She stood in the attitude of one listening, for in her ears was a voice that she had never heard before, a deep inflexible voice that urged her to do—she knew not what. She looked up at the round wooded hill that hid God's Little Mountain—so high, so cold for a poor child to climb. She felt that the life there would be too righteous, too well-mannered" (130). Her intuitions are partly right: the marriage is not consummated. Beautiful and vital, Hazel soon finds herself the object of Jack Reddin's passion, who she dislikes at first because he hunts foxes, and who is as sensual and narrow in his worldliness as Edward Marston is spiritual and gentle in his otherworldliness. "Love that was abnegation was to his idea impossible" (254), the narrator says of Reddin, yet that is the love affirmed and practiced on God's Little Mountain.

Her sexual desires awakening, Hazel hastily interprets a blue petal on her path to be a sign to go to Reddin. And so she does. He rapes her, yet she is nonetheless drawn to him, even after that act. Indeed, the violence is figured as protection. "He caught her and flung her into the bracken, and suddenly it seemed to her that the whole world, the woods, herself, were all Reddin. He was her sky, her cloak" (215–16). Thereafter, Hazel lives with Reddin at Undern Hall, while also yearning for the love she has known on God's Little Mountain. Pulled in different directions by her sensual desire and spiritual longing, she is torn apart, while rural Shropshire broods in the background, sometimes flexing itself and becoming the foreground: pre-Christian, lyrical, almost suffocating its inhabitants with the intensity of its timeless presence. During a storm Hazel looks toward her former home: "Yet the Mountain shone in paradisal colors—her little garden; her knitting; the quiet Sundays; the nightly prayers; above all, Edward's presence, in the aura of which no harm could come—for all these things she passionately longed" (287). She goes back to Marston, who has now lost his faith precisely because he realizes that in introducing Hazel to Christianity he has given her a "mortal wound" (313). "He only knew he must care for Hazel as Christ cared for the lambs of His fold. And darkly on his dark mind loomed his new and bitter creed, 'There is no Christ'" (296). There is to be no happiness for the injured couple, however, in this new Godless world: Hazel and Foxy are torn in pieces by the hounds on one of Reddin's foxhunts. She has gone to earth, although her hiding place will be the grave, as it already is for so many British soldiers in the Great War. Nature and humankind respond alike: "There was silence on God's Little Mountain for a space" (320).

*

In 1952, the expression "God's Little Mountain" was doubled: the original remained in *Gone to Earth* while its copy became the title of a poem in Geoffrey Hill's first booklet of poems, the eleventh in Oscar Mellor's Fantasy

Press series, and so took on a new life. At the time Hill was an under-graduate reading English at Keble College, twenty years of age, having come up to Oxford in 1950 from Bromsgrove, Worcestershire, south-east of the Shropshire countryside so densely and piercingly evoked by Mary Webb. The booklet contained only five poems, the second one being "God's Little Mountain":

> Below, the river scrambled like a goat
> Dislodging stones. The mountain stamped its foot,
> Shaking, as from a trance. And I was shut
> With wads of sound into a sudden quiet.
>
> I thought the thunder had unsettled heaven;
> All was so still. And yet the sky was cloven
> By flame that left the air cold and engraven.
> I waited for the word that was not given,
>
> Pent up into a region of pure force,
> Made subject to the pressure of the stars;
> I saw the angels lifted like pale straws;
> I could not stand before those winnowing eyes
>
> And fell, until I found the world again.
> Now I lack grace to tell what I have seen;
> For though the head frames words the tongue has none.
> And who will prove the surgeon to this stone?[2]

Anyone opening up the Fantasy Press's *Geoffrey Hill* would have recognized the author to be a highly literary young poet. The first poem is entitled "To William Dunbar," the fifth, "For Isaac Rosenberg," while others pay homage to eighteenth-century poets: "Genesis: A Ballad of Christopher Smart" and "Holy Thursday of William Blake."[3] Only the second poem, "God's Little Mountain," is not immediately recognizable as offering tribute to another writer unless, of course, one has read Mary Webb's novel, and even if one knows *Gone to Earth* the relations of the lyric to the novel are less than clear, if there are any in the first place. We know with hindsight that Hill has long meditated on the moral weight of World War I, as registered in English poetry, and so the allegory of *Gone to Earth* would have lodged as firmly with him as the evocation of the countryside.[4] Neither landscape nor war is marked in the poem, though; and we are more likely to read "God's Little Mountain" as establishing a distance from the visionary Blake of *Songs of Innocence and Experience* (1794), perhaps by way of Housman's *A Shropshire Lad* (1896), than as creating a space for itself inside the narrow world of *Gone to Earth*. Why then does Hill draw the title of his poem from Mary Webb's novel?

Also on opening the booklet, the reader will sense that the poet admires from a studied distance different things in the semantics and rhetoric of several contemporary American poets: Allen Tate (a poem such as "The Traveller"), Richard Eberhart ("The Groundhog," in particular), and Robert Lowell ("The Quaker Graveyard in Nantucket," among others). The young Hill is a formal poet, and as he says in "The Poetry of Allen Tate" (1958), "The ideal of 'form' dismisses the legend of the 'mad' disruptive poet, and affirms the social value of the Respectable Artisan."[5] He is not a formal poet in search of smoothness, however; he is drawn to a "wanton roughness of form," apparent in his preference for slant rhymes.[6] He may not play a splintered harp, but his harp has splinters nonetheless. Yet what distinguishes Hill, even at this early stage of his writing, is less an interest in the formal possibilities of the modern lyric (an interest shared, after all, by a good many other English-speaking poets at the time) than a stress on the value of the letter of the poem. In the essay from which I have just quoted, Hill quotes with approval from Tate's essay "The Man of Letters in the Modern World" (1952). The task of the man of letters, Tate says, "is to preserve the integrity, the purity and the reality of language wherever and for whatever purpose it may be used. He must approach his task through the letter—the letter of the poem, the letter of the politician's speech, the letter of the law; for the use of the letter is in the long run our one indispensable test of the actuality of our experience" (8).[7] "How splendid and how true this is!" Hill exclaims after quoting it. And how well its lesson is taken to heart by the young poet, as we shall see.

Lastly, anyone opening up the thin booklet would have identified Hill as a religious poet, and would have asked, as though with Edward Marston, whether he speaks here out of mystical longing, or a sense of sin, or both. If he is a religious poet, he is one of a peculiar kind, someone for whom Christianity has been received as a blunt ache and a quiver of sharp questions, and a poet for whom "religious poetry" has become a problem more than a means of expressing immortal longings.[8] "Genesis," a highly condensed, postlapsarian hexameron, as powerful in its lyric way as the more orthodox homilies on the six days of Creation by St. Basil of Caesarea, St. Ambrose of Milan, and St. Bonaventure,[9] concludes with stanzas that will disconcert believer and non-believer alike:

On the sixth day, as I rode
In haste about the works of God,
With spurs I plucked the horse's blood.

By blood we live, the hot, the cold,
To ravage and redeem the world:
There is no bloodless myth will hold.

And by Christ's blood are men made free
Though in close shrouds their bodies lie
Under the rough pelt of the sea;

Though Earth has rolled beneath her weight
The bones that cannot bear the light. (4)

The speaker (call him Hill) reflects not on the creation of human beings on the sixth day but, rather, on a postlapsarian human act: he digs his spurs into the horse's sides in order to make it go faster.[10] Is Hill actually doing God's work or is he merely running around observing it? Either way, his attention to God leads him to cruelty. In turn, the horse's blood prompts him to ponder the Fall and the Atonement. And in a sense he has repeated the sin of Adam in the wake of Adam's sin, for he plucks the horse's blood as the first man plucked the fruit of the Tree of the Knowledge of Good and Evil, an act that quickly led to the spilling of blood in the murder of Abel.

His meditation is far from orthodox. We are likely to read the second stanza as saying that only blood-myths—those of infanticide, matricide, patricide, self-sacrifice, and war—have sustaining power, and that while they ravage us they also redeem us from insignificance. The thought rubs up against Pascal's *pensée* that "Man's greatness lies in his knowing himself to be wretched."[11] Other myths, such as the story of the Pleiades or that of Atlanta, do not have holding power; they explain something or entertain us but do not enter deeply into the mystery of being human. Things change with the third stanza. We are told in no uncertain terms that "And by Christ's blood are men made free," which catches on the earlier verb "redeem" as well as on 1 Peter 1:18-19 ("ye were … redeemed … with the precious blood of Christ"). What are we to make of this? We seem to have two choices. First, we may fold the allusion to the Atonement back into the general claim about blood-myths, which makes the Atonement into a myth. The claim is certainly possible to make in a poem written in 1952: Rudolf Bultmann's controversial essay, "Neues Testament und Mythologie" (1941), with its sharp insistence that we must strip away myth from the New Testament in order to reveal its κήρυγμα, was already well-known and widely discussed.[12] The speaker of this poem *needs* the myth of the Atonement, it seems, although one may well wonder whether one can need a myth when it is known to be a *myth*. Second, we may see the allusion to the Atonement as contrasting with what we have been told of blood-myths. The Christ-event bespeaks the truth and has genuine power to redeem us, unlike all blood-myths. For no myth, whether bloody or unbloody, can support belief because, being a myth, it is ultimately bloodless. Only the suffering and death of Christ can "ravage and redeem the world."

If we accept this second interpretation the poem does not remain for long in the comfort of orthodox hope. For what is a Christian to make of the final statement, "Though Earth has rolled beneath her weight / The bones that cannot bear the light"? Is it merely a conventional remark that the bodies of the drowned sailors are dead (with the hope of the general resurrection being understood)? Or is it a more final statement, at odds with Christian doctrine about the last things, that some of the dead will not rise again? The ambiguity turns first on the verb "bear." It could be that the bones of the drowned cannot endure the light because they are in inky darkness on the ocean floor, or it could be because they cannot affirm the revelation of God in Christ. And the ambiguity turns, second, on how we read "Though." We might take it to be an adjective in which case the final couplet maintains that, in spite of the terrible pressure at the bottom of the ocean that crushes their bones, the drowned will be resurrected in the flesh. Or we might take it to be a conjunctive adverb that modifies what has been asserted so that the line says the drowned who have lost faith in Christ have been ground to nothing by the Earth and Ocean to which they have foolishly entrusted themselves.

As an undergraduate reading English at Oxford, Hill's education was regulated at a distance by, among others, J. R. R. Tolkien, then Merton Professor of English Language and Literature. Tolkien had worked on the Oxford English Dictionary after World War I, and on his return to teach at Oxford in 1926 was concerned to revise the curriculum of the School of English Language and Literature. He did so in 1932, and the new curriculum remained solidly in effect while Hill was at Keble. That revision was essentially to overcome the old (and sometimes bitter) divide between philology and literature at Oxford, requiring students to balance, if not always to interlace, philology and literature.[13] Hill grew up hearing lectures and participating in tutorials that presented the need for sound philology almost as a moral imperative, to which he added—in his poetic practice if not in his tutorial papers—elements of the formalism of the New Criticism with its emphasis on the letter, which leads readers to maintain a focus on ambiguity and paradox. Both were in the air, and had been since William Empson's *Seven Types of Ambiguity* (1930). Many critics of the day, Christian or not, read English poetry, confessional or not, in terms of the paradoxes inherent in the faith (Jesus as God-Man, Mary as Mother of God, suffering as redemptive, weakness as strength, and so on), sometimes in a manner than can only seem reductive for poetry and faith alike. They did not do so for long with impunity.

After completing *The Structure of Complex Words* (1951), Empson turned from doubleness in literature to more ethical concerns, setting himself with fierce determination against the Christian faith, which he thought promoted a wicked view of God and life in general, and sideswiped those critics— "Neo-Christians" he called them—who reduced the complexities of moral experience to the paradoxes of the faith in the service of "Eng. Lit."[14] Helen Gardner, Hugh Kenner, Rosemond Tuve and W. K. Wimsatt were readily caught within his sights. What seems particularly to have upset Empson is the ease with which critics would appeal to the interpretation of the Atonement known as "penal substitution" in order to explicate poets as different as Donne, Marvell and Coleridge. It is, as he put it in later life, "The belief that the Father could be bought off from torturing mankind eternally (or rather, a tiny remnant of mankind) in exchange for the specially intense pleasure of having his Son tortured to death."[15] It is hard to know who to credit with this blood theology when it is caricatured so freely. Empson associates Tertullian with the teaching on the basis of the theologian's idea of hell, but in fact Tertullian had very little to say about the Atonement.[16] Anselm's *Cur deus homo* is a case in point, as is Luther's 1535 commentary on Galatians, and in the *Institutes* Calvin speaks of the Atonement in terms of criminality.[17] No one, though, conceives the Father taking pleasure in the suffering of the Son. In their different ways, each speaks of the unity of love and justice. Empson's is a crude misunderstanding of the Atonement and of sacrifice in general, one that shows no awareness of κένωσις or of personal love as self-sacrifice.[18] Clearly, he liked his Christianity vulgar.

What one finds in "Genesis," however, is not something that would have given the Neo-Christians much satisfaction, or given Empson cause to savage Hill.[19] We find there an abiding interest in the letter of the word, one that is fastened to what Tate calls the "actuality of our experience," which for Hill means that the double nature of some words in his poem bespeaks an ambivalence to what they denote: in particular, an ambivalence to the claims of visionary experience and the Christian teachings that underwrite it.[20] If Hill would come highly to value certain martyrs and saints—St. Edmund Campion and St. Robert Southwell, in particular—he would also deepen his interest in the pathology of martyrdom and sainthood.[21] This ambivalence would be practiced at a high level in *Tenebræ* (1978), especially in "The Pentecost Castle" and "Lachrimæ," although the particular worry of those poems is already in evidence in Hill's first poems, in "Genesis," to some degree, though more clearly in "God's Little Mountain."

*

To which I turn, beginning with the title, which, taken from *Gone to Earth*, is left with the sixteen lines beneath it and an open set of references produced by the conjunction of "God" and "mountain" (not to mention the teasing qualification "little") to help make sense of it. Plainly, the speaker of the poem has climbed the mountain and failed to be worthy of a revelation at its summit, or even to be able to articulate what has been heard there. The questions remain, "Which mountain is it?" and "Why is it little?"

The poem begins with Hill high on the mountain. "Below," we are told, "the river scrambled like a goat / Dislodging stones." This small disturbance pales to nothing when compared with what comes next. "The mountain stamped its foot, / Shaking, as from a trance." The title constrains us to think of God, but the lines themselves suggest that a fairy tale giant, like the one that bothers Hop o' My Thumb, has been woken from a deep sleep. It is a far cry from the self-denying love one finds at the top of God's Little Mountain in *Gone to Earth*. We may well wonder if this great being is angry for good cause or is merely petulant. In an odd way Hill is protected by the sudden noise; it is the means by which he experiences "a sudden quiet" that blots out every other sound. The quiet, I take it, is wholly interior or entirely beyond the senses. The huge thunder may well have "unsettled heaven" if the stillness is any index.[22] What could have caused this catastrophe? Only, it seems, Hill's presumption in attempting as an impure man to climb the holy mountain. And how could this show of anger or petulance have rendered heaven no longer at ease?

That last question is engaged, if not fully answered, by a metaphor in the sixth line, "And yet the sky was cloven," that picks up the allusion to the goat in the first line and extends it, since the Devil is often represented as a goat.[23] The sky is not simply divided; it is demonically torn in two by flame. If we thought the good, great God rules heaven while the Devil is consigned to Hell we must revise our judgment. For now, we have no coercive reason to draw a strong clear line between God and the Devil, either because there is no such distinction in fact or because we cannot tell the difference between them in the first place. Hill protests that he waited "for the word that was not given," and yet something seems to be have been given to him: the flame leaves the air "cold and engraven." Commenting on Deuteronomy 33:2, Rashi observes in the Jerusalem Talmud that Torah existed before Creation. "It was written with letters of black fire upon a background of white fire" (*Shekalim*, 13b). Rabbi Isaac the Blind, the father of Kabbalah, suggests that the mystical, written Torah is engraved in the white fire while the oral Torah is persevered in the black fire.[24] Mystical Torah is illegible, and will remain so until the Messiah comes. Could it be that Hill expects the legible Torah and consequently misses the offer of the mystical Torah? If so, he is neither Moses, who receives biblical Torah and fully understands the mystical Torah, nor the Messiah who will actually receive the mystical Torah.

Hill is "Pent up into a region of pure force," and we may wonder whether this purity bespeaks raw, elemental power or a more elevated moral or spiritual strength. Either way, he is constrained by the divine will to remain on the mountain, and is subject to great cosmic powers. Also, he is strained by what is overfull within him. Is this his desire to receive the word? It would seem so. Equally, it could be that he is overfull with what he wants to say and is unable to express it, whether because it is forbidden or because he fears competing with the great poets of the past ("the stars"). The "pure force" may be outside him, confining him, or it may be what is deep within him, wanting to get out but blocked by what Harold Bloom calls "the anxiety of influence."[25] Certainly Hill sees poetry in visionary terms. As he writes in "A Letter from Oxford" (1954), "the young student, the poet, maybe, hunched in his mackintosh on the top of the bus in the Banbury Road, sits apart from the crowd. Or he follows in the wake of a vision of life that goes before him and which he cannot grasp, a cloud by day and a pillar of fire by night."[26] And certainly Hill is not denied a vision in the poem: "I saw the angels lifted like pale straws." The point is that the vision is too intense for him: "I could not stand before those winnowing eyes." It is a biblical image of divine judgment. We think of Isaiah, "You shall winnow them, the wind shall carry them away, and the whirlwind shall scatter them" (Isa. 41:16) and Jeremiah, "And I will winnow them with a winnowing fan in the gates of the land" (Jer. 15:7). In Hill's poem, though, the impure prophet or poet is winnowed, not the wayward children of Israel. He is not allowed to descend the mountain with dignity but falls and finds "the world" again.

Back in "the world," an expression slightly stained with a Pauline sense of distaste, Hill finds that he lacks "grace" to tell what he has seen. Reading this line with Christian mystical visions in mind, we recall St. Paul saying how someone he knew (himself, in all likelihood) "was caught up into paradise, and heard unspeakable words, which it is not lawful for a man to utter" (2 Cor. 12:4). There is no grace given to Paul to repeat the holy words of paradise. Yet Hill has already told us what he has seen: "I saw the angels lifted like pale straws" and "those winnowing eyes." There must be more that he has seen but cannot report or express. At the same time, we may take "grace" to be elegance and charm, in which case the complaint is that he cannot write the visionary poem he has in mind for want of inspiration or refinement of poetic skill. "God's Little Mountain" would therefore be the workmanlike, fallback poem that can be written but that is composed without grace. And so the poem provides its own defense against criticism for some stiffness in its lines. The slightly arch question that remains, "And who will prove the surgeon to this stone?," asks both who will enable Hill to speak properly of his religious vision and who will help him to write the visionary poetry that is pent up within him or, if not that poetry, then another kind.

*

Hill has climbed part of the way up God's Little Mountain. Stripped of all particulars, it does not seem at all like the mountain in *Gone to Earth*. Except for the river at its base and the allusion to the Devil, it appears to be like a smaller version of Mt. Sinai. We have only to open the Bible to make the identification. "And mount Sinai was altogether on a smoke, because the LORD descended upon it in fire: and the smoke thereof ascended as the smoke of a furnace, and the whole mount quaked greatly" (Exod. 19:18). Yet Hill is no favored prophet like Moses. "And the LORD came down upon mount Sinai, on the top of the mount: and the LORD called Moses *up* to the top of the mount; and Moses went up" (Exod. 19:20). While Moses is on Mt. Sinai, the children of Israel urge Aaron to build an object of worship. Angered by his people's turn to idolatry, God sends Moses down to the people; the prophet smashes the tables of the Law that God has given him. After praying for the people, Moses returns to Mt. Sinai, God allows him to see his "back parts" (Exod. 33:23), and new tablets of the Law are made.

Must we take God's Little Mountain to be another peak, not the great mountain of the Lawgiver? Not necessarily, for God did not choose Mt. Sinai because it was the tallest mountain in the area but because it was the most desolate and the most pure. The Talmud points us in the right direction. "R. Joseph said: Man should always learn from the mind of his Creator, for behold, the Holy One, blessed be He, ignored all the mountains and heights and caused His *Shechinah* to abide upon Mount Sinai" (*Sotah* 5a).[27] God overlooked mountains higher than Sinai, such as Mt. Tabor and Mt. Carmel, even though those peaks each thought it deserved the honor of hosting the Lord God. And He did so because idols had been placed upon them and had rendered them impure. Only Sinai was untainted, and so it became God's little mountain, its relative smallness being a sign of God's modesty and a challenge for us to be modest as well. Indeed, so unassuming is Mt. Sinai that we are told in *Midrash Tanhuma* that it had to be miraculously expanded in order to be able to receive the glory of God and the "thousands and thousands and a myriad of myriads" of angels and chariots that accompanied Him when He descended in order to give the Law to Moses.[28] "The Holy One said to it: Widen and lengthen yourself to receive the children of your Lord" (224).

Perhaps, though, there are other mountains that are qualitatively little in comparison to Mt. Sinai. One contender, with a plausible basis in the poem, is Mt. Parnassus in central Greece, the home of the muses and therefore the mountain sacred to poetry, music and learning, three things that are very important to Hill. There are several possibilities here. One is that Hill tries to climb Mt. Parnassus and fails: the muses disregard him, or at least the one he especially wants to court shuns him (maybe Polyhymnia, the muse of sacred song). Yet the allusion to angels in the lyric cannot be decently accommodated by this interpretation. Another possibility is that Hill climbs Mt. Sinai but as a poet rather than as a prophet, thinking—with Eugenio Montale, among others—of poetry as a *scala a Dio*, which would mean that he wishes to use poetry as a means of ascending to God or that he proposes to make poetry out of "religious experience."[29] For climbing the sacred mountain in the wrong spirit or with impure motives he is inevitably judged by God and thrown back to "the world." The third possibility is the most complex. Here Hill climbs the sacred mountain, doubtless believing that he is called to do so, yet is judged unworthy of high prophetic calling. Falling back into the world, he turns his experience into poetry: not, to be sure, a religious poem but a poem that analyzes failed religious experience. He is no Moses, no Joannes Climacus, no Guigo II, no Dante, neither a prophet nor a mystic.[30] Nor is he a visionary poet, let alone a mystical one. He is, rather, an artisan who examines the desire for vision and its consequences.

It is instructive to look sideways for a moment, and to consider another twentieth-century poem, a far greater one, that is concerned with descending from on high. In "Tea at the Palaz of Hoon" (1921) Wallace Stevens introduces us to the spirit he will later call "that mountain-minded Hoon."[31] It is a memorable meeting. In his dignified descent, hearing hymns of his own composition, Hoon maintains his visionary intensity. He wears the purple and has been anointed with ointment: so he holds Episcopal office, or, better, is a priest-king. Despite his elevation he has not lost himself in ecstasy, as the implied questioner has presumably suggested before the poem begins, but rather has found his self in that high state. Where "God's Little Mountain" figures Hill as waking an angry or petulant deity, and being summarily dismissed by Him, Stevens's Hoon has consecrated himself as priest, prophet or king (or all three), and speaks to us in tones of supreme self-confidence. "Out of my mind the golden ointment rained," he declares. Where Hill asks for a surgeon to loosen his tongue, Hoon is sublimely indifferent to anyone other than himself, his ears making "the blowing hymns they heard." And where Hoon finds himself Hill merely finds "the world again." In his fall from the mountain, Hill is unable to express himself properly. Yet in his stately descent Hoon finds himself "more truly." He does not find himself "more strangely," as we would expect from the grammar, since the poem ends more strongly if it places an emphasis not on *how* he finds himself but on *what* he finds: his irreducible strangeness.

That Hill ends his poem with a question rather than with the assurance of Hoon's self-discovery indicates a sharp division between the visionary Stevens and the Hill who must content himself with examining failure of religious vision.[32] At first, we might say that the question does not seem to be a stumper. The surgeon who can treat his wound—we think of the "mortal wound" that Hazel receives—and make him able to speak of what he has seen is God. T. S. Eliot, whose later poetry is not greatly admired by Hill, is nonetheless surely in the background here when Eliot writes in "East Coker" (1940), "The wounded surgeon plies the steel / That questions the distempered part," the surgeon being Christ.[33] And the surgeon who can help Hill speak with more elegance and charm is the muse, or perhaps none other than his true self. The reader of Hill's later books, especially *King Log* (1968), *Tenebræ* (1978), and *The Mystery of the Charity of Charles Péguy* (1983), recognizes that the surgeon has finally performed his operation, enabling Hill to say everything while using just a few words. A second look at the question, though, shows it to be more difficult. *Who* will prove to be the surgeon who can make me speak? That is the question on which the poem ends, and it is a genuine, urgent question: Is it God or is it the Muse? Is Hill's silence, his inability to write the poem that "God's Little Mountain" should be, due to a religious failure or an artistic one?

*

What is "the problem of religious poetry" for the young Geoffrey Hill? First of all, as "God's Little Mountain" makes plain, it is that he cannot write religious poetry (as Blake, Hopkins, Claudel, and Eliot can, despite their many differences of confession and style) but only a poetry that considers failed or flawed religious vision. Part of the reason that a more elevated poetry is out of reach for him is because, as he says in "The Bidden Guest" (1953), "The heart's tough shell is still to crack."[34] But hardheartedness is not all. In falling back into the world he has been unsettled far more than heaven has in his bid to be considered worthy. The problem is with him, at least in this early lyric: he is not a mountain (like Milton, like Blake) but a hill. Still an under-graduate poet, he is God's *little* mountain, Geoffrey *Hill*, using a pun that was waiting dormant for him in *Gone to Earth* ("a hill five miles from the Callow, called God's Little Mountain"). God's true little Mountain is actually south of Shropshire in Worcestershire: such is the hidden joke of the poem. Second, the problem is that Hill cannot decide whether he needs surgery from God or the Muse. Is his problem in writing visionary poetry to do with the state of his heart or with the state of his poetic skill?

In "God's Little Mountain" the problem is posed simply at the level of indecision, which tends to make the final question seem a little coy. It is a beginning, and only a beginning. With "Lachrimæ" the problem will be raised to a higher power, and Hill, no longer so little, will worry more deeply whether art is constitutively a distraction from authentic spirituality. Art, "this trade," will become identified with "Self-love," and the religious poet—Southwell or Hill—will come into focus as a "Self-seeking hunter of forms."[35] Are these poetic forms, which turn the poet into a martyr for his art, or are they the forms of martyrdom, which turn the martyr into an artist, perhaps distracting him from his or her religious vocation? That is the cruel ambiguity around which "Lachrimæ" is constructed. But for the Hill of "Genesis" and "God's Little Mountain" that was unimaginable. He must first address himself to "the unfallen," those who, unlike him, have not fallen from the mountain or fallen in the more recent Second World War, and he must also pass through the difficult years of *King Log* (1968) and *Mercian Hymns* (1971).

5

"it / is true"

Phenomenology, as properly practiced, is an attentive response to what is given rather than a single procedure that can be perfected. Responses can take various forms—essays, treatises, paintings, conversations, narratives, plays, and poems—each of which has constraints that, whether respected or transgressed, inflect phenomenological observation in different ways. Literature certainly gives us a range of examples for understanding phenomenology. When reading Italo Calvino's *Invisible Cities* (1972), we see exactly what "free phantasy" is, and when watching *Othello*, we grasp the εἶδος of sexual jealousy far better than in reading a paper about that obsessive state in a psychology journal.[1] Yet literature also does phenomenology itself, though usually more implicitly than explicitly. Has any philosopher performed the ἐποχή and phenomenological reduction more effectively than Franz Kafka, supreme artist of the opening sentence? When observing the world through K., we recognize that consciousness is implicitly founded by what it constitutes. Similarly, William Faulkner performs a startling phenomenology of time consciousness in *The Sound and the Fury* (1929) without knowing anything about Edmund Husserl's reflections on the topic in the ninth volume of the *Jahrbuch für Philosophie und phänomenologische Forschung* (1928).[2] And Francis Ponge, perhaps the closest we get to a major poet explicitly interested in phenomenology, attends to the things themselves in *Le parti pris des choses* (1942).

The list could be continued, the names of the authors varied. We have competing analyses of the work of art, from diverse phenomenological perspectives, those of Roman Ingarden and Martin Heidegger, Maurice Merleau-Ponty and Mikel Dufrenne. Yet there is still much to be learned from Husserl who, in 1907, just before giving the lectures that would comprise *The Idea of Phenomenology*, wrote of the kinship of the phenomenological and aesthetic gazes.[3] I would like to center my reflections on this proximity. At the same time, I would like to touch lightly on the "theological turn" that phenomenology is said to have taken in recent years, and to do so not with the question of divine transcendence in mind, but rather with the central event for western religion of the last century—the unique horror of the Shoah—an event that unleashes many questions for Christian theology as well as Jewish thought, questions that I will not directly engage with here. Throughout, I want to remain close to one poem: its title, "September Song"; its author, Geoffrey Hill. It first appeared in *Stand* in 1967, and was reprinted, with slight changes, in Hill's second full volume of verse, *King Log*, a year later.[4]

Why this poem? Not because it was written out of an overt engagement with phenomenology nor has it been situated in its wake. To my knowledge, Hill has neither quoted nor alluded to Husserl nor any of those continuing or redirecting the philosopher's thought. Literary criticism, as he practices it, is a modification of British empiricism. I choose the poem, instead, because it is a "poem of our climate," if I may borrow an expression from Wallace Stevens. We know that Stevens often composed with the Oxford English Dictionary close at hand, sifting through etymologies and unusual senses of words, and perhaps when he wrote "The Poems of Our Climate," he had in mind the Greek root of "climate," κλίνειν or "to decline."[5] Geoffrey Hill's "September Song" is a poem about the slope of our times, a precarious decline that falls in several directions at once. It is a poem of, and about, the "moral weather" of our culture—his part in it, as well as ours. It is one of the first testaments to the Shoah in English, coming just a year after the publication of Richard L. Rubenstein's *After Auschwitz* (1966), and in the very year of the Six-Day War.[6]

SEPTEMBER SONG
born 19.6.32—deported 24.9.42
Undesirable you may have been, untouchable
you were not. Not forgotten
or passed over at the proper time.

As estimated, you died. Things marched,
sufficient, to that end.
Just so much Zyklon and leather, patented
terror, so many routine cries.

(I have made
an elegy for myself it
is true)

September fattens on vines. Roses
flake from the wall. The smoke
of harmless fires drifts to my eyes.

This is plenty. This is more than enough.[7]

*

"Literature has never been as 'philosophical' as it has in the twentieth century," says Maurice Merleau-Ponty, "never has it reflected as much upon language, truth, and the significance of the act of writing."[8]

Why does Merleau-Ponty place "philosophical" in scare quotes? Presumably to respect the distance between literature and philosophy, and to allow a philosophical mode of activity that is not philosophy as such. Jacques Derrida would agree. He tells us that modernists share a common situation: "they are inscribed in a *critical* experience of literature," he says. "They bear within themselves, or we could also say in their literary act they put to work, the same one, but each time singular and put to work otherwise: 'What is literature?' or 'Where does literature come from?' 'What should we do with literature?'"[9] Modernist writing may not create concepts or adduce arguments but it folds questions of a philosophical type into the literary models that it receives and revises. As Derrida implies, the border between "literature" and "criticism" becomes blurred and divided in modernist writing; and if that is the case for Eliot and Joyce, it is all the more so for a belated modernist such as Hill, and especially so in a poem such as "September Song." Critical objections to writing poetry after Auschwitz, to the morality of representing the Shoah, if it is even possible to do so, must be engaged by the poem itself.

Derrida goes further, and talks about literature's rapport with philosophy in general and with phenomenology in particular. When he does so he makes liberal use of quotation marks, sometimes to hold the word at a distance and sometimes to show that is a quotation:

> Poetry and literature provide or facilitate "phenomenological" access to what makes of a thesis a *thesis as such*. Before having a philosophical content, before being or bearing such and such a "thesis," literary experience, writing or reading, is a "philosophical" experience which is neutralized or neutralizing insofar as it allows one to think the thesis; it is a nonthetic experience of the thesis, of belief, of position, of naivety, of what Husserl called the "natural attitude." The phenomenological conversion of the gaze, the "transcendental reduction" he recommended is perhaps the very condition (I do not say natural condition) of literature. (46)

Note that Derrida begins by saying "Poetry *and* literature" [my emphasis]. They are not one and the same, however. Literature becomes a way of framing poetry, prose fiction, and drama only in the late eighteenth century, at least in Britain. It is a modern formation, and while it impinges on how we think of poetry, it is at heart alien to poetry, which is always a making although not always a fiction. Since I will be answerable to a poem, I will talk only of poetry, while remaining mindful that modern poetry, including modernist works, strives with and against its framing as literature.

We might wonder why Derrida places the word "phenomenological" in scare quotes. He does so because a poem performs the ἐποχή and transcendental reduction without, in most cases, the author having any deep familiarity with either. A poet is already doing phenomenology as soon as he or she starts to write, for composition—at least the sort of composition we call poetry—suspends the natural attitude, and shows the writer's intentional consciousness to be concretely embedded in the horizons that "common sense" occludes. With the first line, the passage from mundane experience to phenomenological truth is already taking place. The poet is able to think in and with a given situation rather than to use thought to manipulate it to one or more ends. We might add that a poet can undertake a phenomenology of the invisible. It can be done by attending to what gives itself but does not show itself, as happens in faith, or by responding to one's auto-affection. We look to Jean-Luc Marion for the former and to Michel Henry's non-intentional phenomenology for the latter.[10] Derrida says nothing of either commitment, confining himself to the experience of writing, of which literary inscription would be exemplary, and which is precisely what dislodges the phenomenology of Husserl, "self-presence of absolute transcendental consciousness or the indubitable *cogito*, etc."[11]

Let us grant that writing, in Derrida's sense of the word, does all these things. We might still wonder if a poem could dislodge classical phenomenology and yet open onto another formation of the discipline, one that is not entirely based on Franz Brentano's teaching that acts of consciousness depend on either presence or representation.[12] It might tell us something new about phenomenology, or might respond to the sorts of insights that the new phenomenology has developed. Henry's analysis of auto-affection is a case in point, Marion's attention to saturated phenomena is another, and, as I have already stressed, we need not sharply separate these two from those who have bequeathed them questions and problems. Can we be sure that literary criticism has learned all it can from Levinas? I do not think so. We also need to recall that a poem will never be merely illustrative of a method completely foreign to it, if phenomenology is a method in the first place, since there can be no poem without ἐποχή and a partial reduction. It would be better to think of reading a poem as an engagement between two styles, two practices, two itineraries, or two intensities, of phenomenology.

*

"September Song": the title both situates the poem in time and characterizes it as a poem. It is a *song*, we are told, a lyric, heir to a tradition that in the West goes back to Alcman's "Maiden-Song" of the seventh century BCE, and, east of Europe, reaches back to the Song of Songs, which, in turn, has roots in the ecstatic poetry of Sumer in the third millennium BCE. Among the many songs in English poetry, we think first when reading Hill's poem of Blake's *Songs of Experience* (1794) and perhaps of one of the *Poetical Sketches* (1783), "To Autumn," with its evocation of the season "stained / With the blood of the grape."[13] No more than Blake does Hill naively celebrate the time of harvest. Indeed, any positive suggestion of "harvest," as well as celebratory song, is quickly put into question by the lapidary inscription beneath the title, which immediately adjusts our expectations of the genre of the work. Set in italics the line reads, "*born 19.6.32—deported 24.9.42.*" And so the poem is partly framed again, this time as an elegy, and another September is evoked, one twenty-five years before when the child in question was deported. We do not need to labor the point that to be deported was a prelude to death by malnutrition, exhaustion or execution, nor do we need to surmise why the child was deported. So this lyric will not inherit from songs addressed to a god or a great man, nor from drinking songs or folk songs, but from the memorial lyric addressed to the dead, such as Aristotle's paean for Hermias. As we shall see, the lapidary inscription is as important for what it does not tell us as for what it does. No name of the child is given, nor the reason why, out of all the children deported in 1942, this one is addressed.

Already, the lyric has folded poetic traditions tightly into itself, not by virtue of its form but by allusion to genres. It begins by addressing the dead child, using prosopopoeia, the figure for crafting a face. The figure is barely used, however, for the profile of the child that begins to appear does so entirely in terms of negatives. The child was "undesirable" but not "untouchable," certainly not "forgotten" or "passed over." If we needed more evidence than is given by the word "deported" that the child is Jewish, it is supplied in the allusion to the Passover (Exod. 12:12). This time, in 1942, the Lord did not pass over the child. He or she is "undesirable," a word for deportees that was in use long before the Second World War, but which here indicates a group deemed by the Nazis to be the *Untermenschen*, or subhuman, namely Jews, Slavs, and Gypsies, homosexuals, dwarfs, and those suffering from mental illness. Others, mainly communists and democrats, were also deemed undesirable, but only Jewish deportees marked for "resettlement" were classed *Rückkehr unerwünscht*, "return undesirable," and consigned to death camps such as Auschwitz-Birkenau, Gusen, Mauthausen, and Treblinka. The child was not "untouchable," however, the allusion being to the lowest Hindu caste, the *Dalits* or Scheduled Caste, or, as Ghandi called them, *Harijans* or children of God. If the child was deemed to be an outcaste by the Nazis, it was not because he or she could not be touched. On the contrary, the pollution the child represents for those who, like Hitler, believe in the purity of the Aryan race, renders him or her all the more vulnerable.[14] He or she is well within the reach of informers, *Einsatzgruppen*, and the Gestapo. Not positively "remembered," which could happen only to an individual, the child is merely "not forgotten," one of many who fall within the scope of a government program, and we even hear the bureaucratic language of the time, and of all times, when told that there is a "proper time" for deportation to a camp.[15]

We continue to overhear a bureaucratic voice behind the poet's voice, "As estimated, you died." Not only does deportation imply death in the near future but also, and more chilling, the child is included in an approximate calculation as one of so many Jews judged to be living in Berlin or Paris, this part of Poland, or that region of Romania. Yet the death of the child has already been announced, more quietly, in the changes of tense in the first stanza. We pass from "you may have been" to "you were" and then to the simple past tense, "Not forgotten / or passed over at the proper time." We see the child solely in terms of one horizon, the race laws. "Things marched," events and dehumanized soldiers alike, to the "end." This is not "the end of life," as the expression is commonly used, but an end as an outcome, the realization of a purpose; it is the direct consequence of a plan of social purification, *die Aktion*. As we know, in executing that plan responsibility was deflected from the self to others, whether superiors in the chain of command or abstract entities such as policy or government. If we read "September Song" in the frame of *King Log*, we will recall the opening poem of the collection, "Ovid in the Third Reich," in which Ovid says in the voice of one all too experienced in the ways of the world, "Things happen."[16]

Again, the discourse of official calculation is remarked by the word "sufficient," that which is adequate, competent, or—in a word we will hear later—enough. The stanza ends with a sentence without a verb, without the "you": "Just so much Zyklon and leather, patented / terror, so many routine cries." A precise amount of Hydrogen cyanide, a few blue tablets, is all that is required to poison the child and those with him or her. The guards performing the "fumigation" are "so much … leather," and with this image the word "untouchable" presses on the poem from another direction. Among Hindus, cows are sacred, and leather is generally worn only if it has come from an animal that has died of natural causes. Here, though, it is the German soldiers who are morally impure, not the child. The sudden reversal occurs in a slight shift from "so much" to "so many" which opens a cruel ambiguity. From the perspective of the guards, the "fumigation" generates only the usual number of cries within the twenty minutes it takes for death to ensue after the release of the gas. It is "patented / terror." The adjective, which recalls "patent leather," qualifies "terror." A metonymy distributes the qualification associated with the firm of Tesch and Stabenow, which manufactured the poison, to those who die inhaling it. Protected by the law, the cries are Nazi property; they are made "proper" to the régime. The reader knows at once that "so many" also means an unbounded number of cries, and that it would be inhuman even to think of counting them.

And so the child is murdered. A whole world of experience, as tenderly evoked in the "September Song" of Maxwell Anderson and Kurt Weill's *Knickerbocker Holiday* (1938), is denied the child. And so he or she passes out of the poem. There is no more prosopopoeia, no more making of a face for the dead one, no more addresses to a "you." Indeed, the poem shifts from the "you" to the "I," and does so in a stanza that attracts notice, one that shows, as Merleau-Ponty would have it, reflection "upon language, truth, and the significance of the act of writing." Let us read it very closely:

(I have made
an elegy for myself it
is true)

*

Set in parentheses, the third stanza seems to be in retreat from the rest of the poem; it is as though it turns away from the poet's public utterance in order to reflect on what has been said and how it has been said. In a poem in which lines are run on more often than not, this stanza has a particularly violent enjambment—"it / is true"—in which more than one philosophical issue is at stake. Yet the third stanza does not hide from the poem in all respects. The lapidary inscription announces that the lyric will be an elegy of a peculiarly modern sort, one in which "deportation" has become official jargon for "death"; but now we are quietly told that the elegy is for the poet who presumably has never been face to face with horror.

Is this a moment of self-reflection, as in Wordsworth's lines about the "Boy of Winander" in *The Prelude*? Not quite: Wordsworth is more oblique, less self-conscious, than Hill, and the child's experience in "September Song" differs sharply from that of the boy who was "taken from his mates" and died "ere he was full ten years old."[17] Nor does "A Slumber did my Spirit Seal" seem an appropriate lyric for comparison; the "touch of earthly years" that the child Lucy does not seem to feel is a long way from her not being untouchable. Is Hill's a moment of judgment akin to Hopkins's gesture in "Spring and Fall"? There "a young child," Margaret, is seen to be grieving over "Goldengrove unleaving," and is told at the end of the lyric, "It is Margaret you mourn for."[18] Hopkins and Hill meet here only for a moment, if at all: Hopkins's child mourns nature and herself as a part of it. The mourning at work in "September Song," though, is the consequence of an atrocity, and

Hill is led back from the mourning of the child by virtue of reconsidering the imaginative identification with him or her and the rectitude of talking about it. Yet there is a reason why *this* child is mourned, and why Hill turns from him or her to himself. No one fully performs the reduction, Merleau-Ponty teaches, and certainly it is never completely achieved in a poem.[19] This poem can be seen to turn on a transcendent event that remains outside the world of the lyric. It is this: Geoffrey Hill was born on June 18, 1932, one day before the child who was deported in September, 1942. That single day stands for the slight change of circumstances that, in bad outbreaks of history, can mean life or death, everyday existence or sheer horror, and it also helps to explain the emotional link he feels with this one child. That said, this empirical fact is of limited help in reading the poem. More significant, I think, is that the "you" of the poem, the Jewish child, remains somewhat abstract until the "I" appears to disown him or her; and, disconcertingly, the sheltered appearance of the "I" draws attention to something uneasy in the elegy and perhaps in all elegies.

Addressing the child in the first two stanzas, Hill is utterly powerless as a speaker. Because the child is not present, all he can do, strictly speaking, is report an empty intention. Yet he addresses the child nonetheless, and thereby turns the dead child into a phenomenon that is both invisible and irregardable. There is little for Hill to aim at, surely not a memory, perhaps only the memories of others. Only as a poet does he have power, a way of enchanting himself and us with words, and a rhetorical power over life and death. Only by way of prosopopoeia can the child be made to enter what seems to be the field of experience, even if it is not. Thus poetry becomes the means by which non-experience is violently changed to counter-experience, and counter-experience is passed off as experience.[20] The prosopopoeia feigns a bringing back of the child to life, feigns to a relation between the poet and the child, an act that can be terminated by a shift of attention as required by the shape of the poem, in other words, by aesthetic ends. All the face can say, Levinas and Marion agree, is "Thou shalt not kill," a command to which Hill must respond as a poet as well as a man, a distinction that he would rightly distrust. In talking of the child, the poet is envisaged, as well as envisaging; his act of representation is "ruined," as Levinas puts it, by an ethical *Sinngebung* or bestowal of meaning that does not depend on a perceptual context.[21] Hill the poet has created a counter-gaze that accuses Hill the man in the very moment of calling it into being since its recreation is only momentary and, to a greater or lesser extent, intended for aesthetic ends. It is as though the child's face says, "Do not kill me again," as though the child knows with Stevens (but otherwise than Stevens) that poetry can kill.[22]

I recall another poem from *King Log*, "History as Poetry," with its talk of "The tongue's atrocities" and its wariness of poetry that "Unearths from among the speechless dead."[23] The first two stanzas of "September Song" do indeed exhume the child. Also, they allow us to "to think the thesis," as Derrida says, to suspend a thetic relation to reference, and in doing so they let us contemplate the suffering of an innocent as a theme, without being required to take any responsibility for the act. The contemplation of what happened, perhaps with even a degree of imaginative variation, is not in itself immoral. It can mark a disturbance of the making of a theme; the poem can be *itself* a relation with the dead child, a relation of unsaying, not simply of the said. Yet the contemplation can become immoral if it remains at the level of phenomenological description without a *reductio* such as the one we witness in the third stanza. Eugen Fink alludes to the reduction as a passage from the natural attitude to a far more disinterested gaze, as though one has become like one of the gods, "the player of the world [*Weltspieler*]."[24] Long before then, Husserl had noted the proximity of the phenomenological and aesthetic gazes, as we have seen, but did not remark the moral danger of that closeness. In "September Song" Hill is finely alert to the threat.

The turn from the second to the third stanza is marked by parentheses. They indicate less a neutralizing of positivity than an awareness of the impropriety in continuing the poem by way a purified gaze.[25] It is, if you like, a reduction of reduction. I doubt that I am alone in hearing an oblique acknowledgment of Dylan Thomas's well-known poem, "A Refusal to Mourn, the Death by Fire, of a Child in London" (1945).[26] Thomas's child is also a victim of war, a German air raid on London late in the Second World War. Here, too, are Jewish references, though ones that have been thoroughly naturalized and neutralized—"Zion of the water bead," "synogogue of the ear of corn," and "valley of sackcloth"—as has the Christian reference to the Stations of the Cross. The lyric is a sustained instance of *occupatio*: in saying he will not mourn the child until his death, he does precisely what he says he will not do.[27] Yeats is a vanishing point in Thomas's poetic world, and even more than Yeats's poems, including his elegies, "A Refusal to Mourn" is a high-toned and supremely self-confident rhetorical performance, one that luxuriates in language and in the freedom of the poet to refuse to mourn, and yet to mourn, to involve both nature and himself in the event, to use biblical and ecclesial language while denying a central Christian teaching in the final line.

Nothing could be further from "September Song." Formally, the poem eschews the satisfactions of ripe stanzas of varying line length and intriguing rhymes. If we look at *King Log* we find that "September Song" is the fifth poem in the collection, and the first both to break with form and not to begin each line with a capital letter. Not only is the amplitude of a bardic voice declined but so too are conventional signs of its own status as a poem in conversation with a rich tradition. Notice too the rhetorical movement of the lyric: we pass from talking *to* the child to talking *of* the child, and before the poet could begin to talk *for* the child, as is done in many elegies ("Who would not sing for *Lycidas*?") or poems with an elegiac strain (James Dickey's "The Sheep Child," for example), he recoils from the very possibility, and not in the freedom of acceptance or refusal. Thomas may assure us that "I shall not murder / The mankind of her going with a grave truth" but he does so anyway ("After the first death, there is no other"). When Hill speaks of truth, it is in quite different ways, as we shall see. Yet before we can be in a position to judge what "true" means for Hill in this poem, we must recognize that the lyrical "I" here is less one that abides in the freedom of a *cogito* than in the responsibility imposed upon him by the other person, here the child.

What does the third stanza say? And what does it do? I will begin with the first question. The first line and a bit are the least difficult: "I have made / an elegy." Notice that the "I" figures himself as a poet, while stressing the element of craft, that he is a *makar*. It is as though he is well aware of the claim of art to remove the artist from the world, to engage in what Jean Wahl calls "transascendance," a rising to the ineffable heights without term, and he insists on drawing attention to the element of craft in the work.[28] For the Levinas of "Reality and its Shadow" (1948), this gesture is a first sign of ethics irrupting in the artwork, requiring it to make contact with the world. An older Levinas would see here a refusal to make the child a phenomenon, to allow him or her to remain an enigma, and also a reduction of the Said to the Saying. Yet we must respect the tense of the statement; it reads, "I have made," not "I am making." A division is marked between the first two stanzas and the third: the address to the child is an elegy for himself, and for the first time in the poem we have an explicit registration of a fulfilled intention. Does this change come about because Hill has been imaginatively identifying with the child but really writing about himself? Or has it come about because he has no right to speak as he has been doing of another's suffering? Both, I would say.

Only the first reason for recoiling from his own poetic stance brings Hill into relation with the poems by Wordsworth and Hopkins. The second reason is the more original and the more sobering, and it prompts us to reflect further on the expression "an elegy *for myself*" [my emphasis]. For it also means that Hill has made an elegy, a poem, for his own aesthetic delight, for the enlargement of his poetic repertoire, and at the cost of erasing the child. Adorno's well-known remark, dating from 1949 and appearing definitively in *Prisms* (1967), comes to mind, "To write poetry after Auschwitz is barbaric" [*nach Auschwitz ein Gedicht zu schreiben, ist barbarisch*].[29] Of course, Adorno later resiled from the judgment, and observed, even before the essay was collected, in *Negative Dialectics* (1966), "Perennial suffering has as much right to expression as a tortured man has to scream; hence it may have been wrong to say that after Auschwitz you could no longer write poems. But it is not wrong to raise the less cultural question whether after Auschwitz you can go on living—especially whether one who escaped by accident, one who by rights should have been killed, may go on living."[30] There are many ways of escaping horror by accident, many sorts of contingency, and in "September Song" the difference of a single day is secretly felt by the author to be one of them. More pertinent for Hill than Adorno's reflections, I think, is Levinas's argument in "Reality and its Shadow." In presenting itself, we are told, a thing produces both a phenomenon and an image, and attending to the latter leads us away from the world and the inexorable demands of justice for other people. Levinas's judgment on aesthetic delight is among the harshest in western philosophy. "There is something nasty, selfish, and cowardly in artistic pleasure," he writes. "There are times when one could be ashamed of it, as if carousing in a town struck by the plague."[31] Most writers will recoil from the judgment, crying "Unfair!" But the Hill of "Annunciations," "Poetry as History," and "September Song" would be in firm agreement.

It is easy to imagine a "new phenomenologist" seeking to interpret the brackets of the third stanza. One might say, following Michel Henry, that here we have the invisible revelation of the poet's subjectivity.[32] The poet's intentionality is unable to determine a relationship with the dead child, and so his mourning must be explained in another way. What Hill's concern for the child manifests is precisely itself—"I have made / an elegy for myself"—and the manifestation is invisible. Or, following Levinas, we might see the brackets as performing a reduction of the Said to the Saying, a leading of the speaker back from the world in which poetic declaration is one with a rhetorical freedom to create and observe, to a site where his speech is vulnerable and well aware of the wounds it can make. Yet the passage from ontology to ethics is not one that can ever be reassuring in a poem. The sacrifice of poetic power can always be a subtle way of gaining pathos, of laying claim to another, more legitimate sort of power, one that is infused with moral concern. There can be no assurances of moral purity in the world of poetry, a judgment that should not let us draw too sharp a distinction between the aesthetic and the ethical, and should not blind us to the testimonial power of high art. Celan's "Todesfuge" and Hill's "September Song" bear witness to the Shoah in ways that are more piercing than many films, many stories, many analytic studies, and their drive to satisfy aesthetic hungers are neither simply fulfilled nor simply refused. No one has a secure place to stand on this slope.

"Todesfuge" is not the only poem Celan wrote about the Shoah, and perhaps not the closest one to Hill's poetic sensibilities. A later lyric such as "Die Fleissigen" might be a more exact parallel in terms of a shared poetics.[33] Yet "Todesfuge" provides the sort of contrast that is needed here.[34] Celan had to bear Adorno's judgment about poetry after Auschwitz, and his pain in doing so must be acknowledged, while Hill responds elliptically to that same judgment in the writing of his lyric. In its insistent, almost hypnotic rhythm, its surprising figures, its powerful juxtapositions and its imaginative reach, "Todesfuge" is a lyric in the high modernist manner. If it does not withhold its speech or reflect on its intensity, it is because of the "right to expression" of which Adorno spoke. Hill does not exercise such a right because it is not his to exercise. To speak in empathy for a dead child is one thing, to speak in the third person plural in the context of the Shoah is quite another. Hill could not be part of that "we," as Celan was, and his "I" is less hesitant about speaking of the Shoah (as impossible or immoral to represent) than about speaking of it in poetry.[35] On the one hand, Hill's poem evokes "what otherwise mocks every description," while on the other hand it restrains itself from saying too much.[36] "September Song," as Gentile speech, can be responsible only if it heeds Adorno's warning about "poetry," only if it expresses a reserve about speaking for the Jewish dead. "We grasp, roughly, the song," as he says in "Two Formal Elegies: *For the Jews in Europe*" (30), poems that should be read in close conjunction with "September Song." Roughness, here, would seem to be offered as an ethical gesture.

Which brings us to the enjambment, the "it" hanging at the end of the line without even a dash to keep up appearances. Hill says "it / is true," and we must ask if the truth claim refers to the *making* of an elegy for himself or if the elegy itself *speaks* the truth. In the latter case, are we being told that, if the elegy is for him, then it is true, and that the first two stanzas are presumably untrue. We might think of them as untrue, according to the logic of the poem, because the poet knows only the general circumstances of the child and nothing particular about him or her. We have heard much in a phenomenological key in recent years about the mourning of friends but little about the mourning of people one does not know.[37] Death cancels the relation one has with the deceased, but what if the relation is entirely general and abstract, as with someone never met and never known?[38] Proust evokes the danger of "posthumous infidelity" toward the end of *À la recherche du temps perdu*, and Hill courts a version of that specter, an infidelity to the memories of others about the child.[39] Perhaps Hill's affectivity is consequent on an intentional rapport with a photograph of the child, a story about him or her, or a sense of compassion for the suffering of another human being. Does this suffice to write an elegy in a responsible fashion? How does the death of another person impinge on me? In his 1975–6 lectures on death and time, Levinas reflects on an issue that is prior to these questions:

> The death of the other who dies affects me in my very identity as a respon-
> sible "me" [*moi*]; it affects me in my nonsubstantial identity, which is not
> the simple coherence of various acts of identification, but is made up of

an ineffable responsibility. My being affected by the death of the other is precisely that, my relation with his death. It is, in my relation, my deference to someone who no longer responds, already a culpability—the culpability of the survivor.[40]

Hill may have no particular responsibility for the child's fate, but the child nonetheless burdens him with a responsibility to bear witness to his or her plight. The emotions that spur the poem are difficult to disentangle. Grief, to be sure, and guilt for surviving, but at least some of the affectivity is without intentionality, as Henry would say, because it is a relation with Hill's own death to come, which offers no response to him, no more than the child does, and which cannot appear as a presence or a representation.[41]

Not that "September Song" is a lyric of undiluted auto-affection, or that the third stanza offers such a moment. We might compare it with W. S. Merwin's well-known lyric, "For the Anniversary of My Death," a poem that is almost pure affectivity with limited intentionality, an "elegy for myself" that plays elegantly with knowing that death is certain but that, unlike birth, does not yield knowledge of its date.[42] If "September Song" concerns a seasonal repetition after the fact (the recurrence of September), Merwin's lyric responds to an illegible repetition before the fact. The self is seen as other, enabling the poet to find a minimal intentionality ("in life as in a strange garment"), though one that multiplies pathos. To be sure, the lyrical "I" looks around and takes stock of "the shamelessness of men," but this is the notation of an observer who takes refuge in his inner life, and any inclusion of himself in that category is tacit. Like "September Song," the poem has a moment of self-reflection. Merwin indicates that he is writing now, presumably the very poem we are reading, and this introduces a complication into the lyric that becomes apparent only when another mode of non-knowing is declared in the final line. The poet bows in reverence but does not know to whom or what. Could it be God? Or Love? Or Life? Or Death? Or the poem we are reading? Or the poet's creativity that enables him to write the poem? Doubtless the lyric allows all these possibilities. Yet its mode of ambiguity is not self-lacerating in the manner of "September Song."

Let us return to Hill's poem. It addresses truth, not knowledge, though not in the straightforward manner of a thesis. We are not told of something that "it is true" but of each of more than one thing that "it / is true," which is hardly the same. For the third stanza puts at risk whether a truth claim is actually being made in the first place. The enjambment "it / is true," can mean, "I concede that the elegy, which seemed to be for the child, is in fact for myself." And it can also mean, "the elegy is true to life, it shows that we seek to speak for the Other even when we do not know what we are saying or even have the right to speak" or "the elegy is in good tune, a proper poem, despite appearances" or "the elegy shows loyalty, faithfulness, it is true to myself, to my feelings for the child, if not the child himself or herself and the child's inner experiences which are hidden from me." Inevitably, anyone interested in phenomenology will recall that "truth" here could mean correctness or disclosure. So "I have made / an elegy for myself" would be correct if it confirms the way things are, and true if it indicates a disclosure of a state of affairs, such as the poet recognizing that only he is present, not the child. Is this a poem that admits correctness or displays the truth? There is, I think, a prior question: Is the poem true in the sense of offering testimony? The lyrical "I" of the poem is unusual in that it assumes responsibility for the child it addresses, not just freedom to determine an aesthetic response to a situation, and, with this in mind, we might pose the question that Levinas has taught us to ask. What is primary, truth or justice?[43]

If this question takes us more deeply into the poem, it does so by more than one route. To be making an elegy for myself when apparently talking about another person might be true, although it might not be just, which for Levinas would mean that it revolves entirely in a world of aesthetic pleasures. Or to make an elegy for myself might be both true and just, which for Levinas would mean that it interrupts or retards its movement of self-transcendence.[44] The latter alternative fits with a high modernist insistence on the breaking of form, yet it has become such a familiar gesture in contemporary literature that it is difficult to credit it as having any ethical force, assuming in the first place that we believe that the aesthetic and the ethical are as distinct as Levinas takes them to be in "Reality and its Shadow." Even if the third stanza enacts a movement from the Said to the Saying, it does not step far outside the order of meaning. Hill figures the ethical situation by way of difficulty, one of his favored words, and here "difficulty" is to be understood, as William Empson would have us do, in terms of ambiguities.[45] If asked what the third stanza does, the answer must surely be that it "unwrites" the poem as read so far, that it is an attempt to make the poet as well as the reader "lift his eyes from the page."[46] Also, though, the third stanza does other things. First, it enacts a passage from the Jewish child to the Gentile poet. Hill shares mortality with the child, yet he does not share the horror to which the child was exposed. The lyric that might have marked a place for Jewish-Gentile dialogue about the Shoah erases that place in its very performance. Second, the third stanza is an economical means of keeping the poem open to all intuitions. This is of course a desire of phenomenology, one remarked and revived by Marion. It has also been a desire of literature. In its multiplication of languages, and its passivity with respect to their interaction, *Finnegans Wake* (1939) allows all intuitions to be received by the novel above and beyond the intentionality of James Joyce or any narrators he might employ. It is one way in which modern literature has performed its desire to say everything, *tout dire*.[47] Hill may not wish to encompass everything in the manner of Joyce, or to say everything (including what is forbidden) in the style of the Marquis de Sade, but he does want to say everything, as Celan does, by staying within the confines of a lyric.[48]

*

How can a poem continue once it has turned aside from itself, once it has disowned itself as poetry? Certainly Hill no longer speaks of the child, and presumably the remainder of the poem would aim to be responsible speech. There is no talk of the Shoah, certainly no appeal to theodicy. The poem seeks closure in five simple declarative sentences:

> September fattens on vines. Roses
> flake from the wall. The smoke
> of harmless fires drifts to my eyes.
>
> This is plenty. This is more than enough.

Unlike Christopher Ricks, I do not hear any hint of a fattening for sacrifice in the first of these lines.[49] The "fattening" is one of fullness, marked by the surprising conjunction in an English setting of "vines" and "roses" before we reach the deflation of "flake." The lines hint at complacency in nature (and the cultivation of nature) far beyond the ripeness that Rilke evokes in "Herbsttag" with its bid for the last fruit to grow ripe on the vine.[50] The point of "September fattens on vines," rather, is the sharp contrast of Hill's September with the child's. A complex experience of time is marked in these lines. There is a repetition of September, underlining the fact that the poet has survived, not the child. Also let it be noted that the child's experience of time differs from the poet's: September is the month, in Gentile time, of two high Holy Days, Rosh Hashana and Yom Kippur. And, as already seen, "September Song" may also retain an echo of Blake's "To Autumn" with its image of the season "stained / With the blood of the grape," and Hill's September is stained with the death of the child, as the "harmless fires" (in contrast to the fires of Auschwitz) and the suggestion of tears caused by the two sorts of smoke imply.

September is the month of fullness and decay, grapes ripening, and roses fading, of leaves that are burned in bonfires. Such is Hill's world, the one from which he has never been deported, and which he has survived to take part in. It is his judgment on what he has just stated that makes the final lines responsible speech. The ordinary world he has inherited is "plenty," "more than enough." The final word might recall "sufficient" earlier; it might also make us think, with a bitter irony, of the "Da-Yaynu" in the Passover Haggadah with its refrain that the Lord has done enough, more than enough, many times over, in bringing the Jews out of Egypt, in giving the Sabbath, and in giving Torah.[51] Certainly Hill has nothing about which he can decently complain. Yet the final line is also a judgment on the poem, on the presumption of talking to and of the child, of the failure of offering testimony for another's suffering. "I have said plenty," it says, "I have said more than enough about the child and about myself—I have risked an excess of poetry, I have both staged and queried 'the tongue's atrocities.'"[52] If the question "What should we do with literature?" is folded into the poem, as Derrida suggests, so too is an answer: we should be vigilant with respect to the proximity of aesthetics and phenomenology, lest the ethical be occluded. Adorno may have retracted his judgment about poetry after Auschwitz, but it has left its mark on Hill's poem.

6

Transcendence in tears

There is good reason to think of Geoffrey Hill as a religious poet, though only if the adjective is taken to mark a field of inquiry, one in which doubt and analysis rival faith and even the desire for faith. A key poem in any consideration of Hill in this regard is his sequence "Lachrimæ," from the collection *Tenebræ* (1978).[1] To consider "Lachrimæ" in the context of Hill's poetry would call forth a vast commentary, as would placing it within theology without any boundaries marked: martyrology and Christology would press incessantly on the poem, as would theologies of prayer and sacrifice. Hill himself cautions us that if we are to develop "a theological view of literature" we should be careful not merely to re-state "neo-Symbolist mystique celebrating verbal mastery."[2] I agree, although I also think we can go in directions other than the one Hill takes, namely the equation of style and faith in Milton, Donne, and Herbert. As Hill readily concedes, "In most instances style and faith remain obdurately apart."[3]

Hill insists on the strangeness of his poem even before we start to read it. His title, "Lachrimæ or Seven Tears Figured in Seven Passionate Pavans," repeats the title of a haunting and austere piece of Tudor consort music by John Dowland. This composition for five viols, or violins, and lute, was first heard in 1595, published in 1604, and soon won deep admiration.[4] In a sonnet to "his friend Maister R. L.," Richard Barnfield wrote, "*Dowland* to thee is deare; whose heavenly tuch / Upon the Lute doth ravish humaine sense."[5] Another sixteenth-century horizon is set in place by the epigraph. It, too, is formed by a Catholic, the British martyr St. Robert Southwell whose St. *Mary Magdalens Funerall Teares* (1591) reads, "Passions I allow, and Loves I approve, only I would wish that men would alter their object, and better their intent." With sixteenth-century Catholicism, we enter a world in which theology has long since classified tears as signifying penitence, love, or compassion for the crucified Jesus.[6] Southwell focuses on the Mary Magdalene whose penitential tears were shed years before, and who now weeps out of compassion and love for the dead Jesus. In his turn, Hill uses the figure of tears of compassion and love, while a resistance to penitence, hardness of heart, exerts a pressure throughout the sequence.

"Lachrimæ" refers to, and participates in, a world where "tears poetry" has already been inaugurated. We can take Luigi Tansillo's madrigals "La Lagrime di San Pietro" (1568) as a model, one that was brought from Italy to Britain by Southwell (partly translated as "Peeter Playnt") and adapted in his own "Saint Peters Complaint" (1595).[7] We think also of *Marie Magdalenes Lamentations, For the Love of Her Master Jesus* (1601), perhaps by Gervase Markham, and Nicholas Breton's *The Ravisht Soul and the Blessed Weeper* (1601), both influenced by Southwell. In prose there come to mind Thomas Nashe's *Christ's Tears over Jerusalem* (1593) and Thomas Lodge's *Prosopopeia Containing the Teares of the Holy, Blessed, and Sanctified Marie, the Mother of God* (1596).[8] Hill has testified to his admiration for Richard Crashaw's verse, especially the use of technique to shape and sharpen emotional and ethical response as well as to respond to purely formal issues.[9] Doubtless this admiration is at the root of his interest in the hard-won welding of style and faith in Donne's sermons and elsewhere. Yet "Lachrimæ" avoids the rather maudlin and sometimes bizarre "tear poetry" of a poem such as "The Weeper." There Crashaw says of Christ and Mary Magdalene, "He's follow'd by two faithfull fountains / Two walking baths; two weeping motions, / Portable, & compendious oceans."[10] Nor does "Lachrimæ" bypass positive religion for a primal religiosity, as happens when René Char meditates on the cave paintings at Lascaux. "La bête innomable" becomes for him "La Sagesse aux yeux pleins de larmes."[11] Completely unsentimental, "Lachrimæ" is highly, almost painfully, self-conscious both as poetry and in its stance with respect to religious belief. Yet it is in a positive relation with the Christian faith.

If we think that Hill's sonnets are a literary counterpart to or a translation of Dowland's music, we will be mistaken. Only four sections refer directly to Dowland's sequence—"Lachrimæ veræ," "Lachrimæ coactæ," "Lachrimæ antiquæ novæ" and "Lachrimæ amantis"—and these are not in the same order as the original pavans.[12] The other three sections—"The Masque of Blackness," "Martyrium," and "Pavana dolorosa"—develop from other works or Hill's imagination.[13] And if, once we begin to read them, we think that the sonnets are lyrics "by" Geoffrey Hill in any simple or straightforward sense we will be in error. Several of them are translations or adaptations from Counter-Reformation Spanish lyrics. Whose tears are these? If they are Hill's, they are refracted through Dowland and Southwell, Lope de Vega Carpio, Francisco de Quevedo, and anonymous poets of the same age. One of the things that some readers find strange about Hill's poem is that it refuses to remain as either first-order religious discourse, prayers to God, or as second-order theological discourse. The poetry is at once ardent and dialectical. It also transcends its sixteenth-century sources, becoming a poem on its own account, while allowing them to live on in new ways. More importantly, the poetry transcends the "I" of apparently unmediated experience. The poem may examine, and even offer, testimony but it confesses little or nothing.

For ease of exposition, I begin in the middle of Hill's sequence, and will gather the other sonnets, insofar as it is possible, into my discussion as I proceed.[14] Here then is "Lachrimæ coactæ":

Crucified Lord, however much I burn
to be enamoured of your paradise,
knowing what ceases and what will not cease,
frightened of hell, not knowing where to turn,

I fall between harsh grace and hurtful scorn.
You are the crucified who crucifies,
self-withdrawn even from your own device,
your trim-plugged body, wreath of rakish thorn.

What grips me then, or what does my soul grasp?
If I grasp nothing what is there to break?
You are beyond me, innermost true light,

uttermost exile for no exile's sake,
king of our earth not caring to unclasp
its void embrace, the semblance of your quiet.

Is this a lyric *of* forced tears or *about* forced tears? Both and neither. Its twofold manner is characteristic of the entire sequence, as is the motif of doubling, especially a doubling of prayer and poem, and yet two streams of meaning cannot be separated and analyzed by themselves. "Crucified Lord": the salutation immediately marks the utterance as prayer, the tears as those inspired by the Passion, and nothing that follows completely erases that mark, although "Lachrimæ coactæ" like the sonnets before and after it also allows prayer to be regarded as a literary genre, by reader and writer alike. Is Christ "Lord" because he is confessed as such, or because the title is conventional? Who is addressed, Christ or a representation of Christ? Or, if you wish, is Christ regarded as transcendent with respect to Hill or is he immanent in Hill's imagination, one figure among others? The problems and the pathos of the sequence arise from the speaker being unable to answer these questions as clearly as he wants to and needs to. Attracted to the faith, he is also repulsed by it.[15] Drawn to what transcends him, he is unable to follow Southwell's advice and change his object and better his intent. He writes poems as prayers, while fearing that Coleridge might be right when he says, "Poetry—excites us to artificial feelings—makes us callous to real ones."[16]

The speaker (call him Hill) does not burn for paradise, but only "to be enamoured" of it. To want to be inspired to desire heaven suggests a working up of emotion, such as those crocodile tears evoked in the title. Certainly, as the first stanza makes plain, only *attritio*, imperfect contrition, motivated by fear of divine justice, is achieved, not the *contritio* that is free love for God in himself alone, and that indicates true repentance. So Hill "falls," suddenly switching the valence of "burn" in the first line. It is not a direct plummet into hell but into a situation that paralyzes him. He finds himself caught between "harsh grace" and "hurtful scorn." If the adjective in the second expression seems a little lazy, the one in the first expression rubs up the noun in the wrong way and in doing so recalls the Tridentine doctrine of justifying grace as the pardoning of the ungodly. Or maybe "harsh" does not qualify "grace" so much as underline the difficulty of a life lived after accepting it, or even a repugnance to that life, a life without life in the eyes of the world which are partly Hill's. Not to accept grace is to express contempt for God. Yet to accept grace is to expose oneself to the contempt of the worldly; and, either way, it could leave one prey to self-contempt in any number of overt or covert ways.

Even if we assume that Hill sincerely addresses Christ as "Lord," he is nevertheless not fully converted, as he attests. Why not? Because, as Jesus says to his disciples, "he that taketh not his cross, and followeth after me, is not worthy of me" (Matt. 10:38) and "If any man will come after me, let him deny himself, and take up his cross, and follow me" (Matt. 16:24). Recusant Catholics under Elizabeth could hardly avoid images of Christians carrying crosses if they used contemporary manuals of prayer.[17] Robert Southwell goes further than others of his time and painfully combines the figures of bridal mysticism and martyrdom: "Thy soul is espoused to the Crucified One," he tells himself, "and therefore thou must be crucified both in soul and body."[18] And Christ's injunction finds its way into Hill's consciousness by other means as well. "All or Nothing," says Ibsen's Brand, and Brand is never far from Hill's religious imagination.[19] Nor, for that, is the Kierkegaard who stands behind and to the side of Brand.[20] Christ is indeed "the crucified who crucifies": he places Hill in an excruciating position, "between harsh grace and hurtful scorn," while demanding that if he accepts grace he will be crucified to himself, if not actually martyred for his belief. Yet the situation in which Hill finds himself is even worse than this. For Jesus, as Hill directly tells him, is "self-withdrawn even from your own device." I do not find any hint here of Christ as the supreme artist withdrawn behind his work.[21] Rather, I see the Savior having distanced himself from the emblematic figure of himself on the cross, not because of the resurrection (for the death, resurrection and ascension of Christ form a deep unity) but because the crucifix is a token of what happened centuries ago on Golgotha. The crucifixion has long been a frozen image, even in churches, calling forth devotion at the risk of containing it or misdirecting it. Such images can become caricatures, as Hill realizes when he speaks to Jesus, with a flicker of humor, of his "trim-plugged body, wreath of rakish thorn."

"Lachrimæ coactæ," like the entire sequence to which it belongs, leads us to ask about the relations of religious devotion and art, and in order to get clear about these relations I turn to Emmanuel Levinas's essay "Reality and its Shadow" (1948) where art receives criticism at least as fierce as that urged by Plato in book ten of *The Republic*. Levinas begins that essay by silently borrowing a distinction drawn by Jean Wahl between "transascendance" and "transdescendance."[22] Art is disengaged, not because it transcends the world, pointing us up toward the ineffable, but because it passes beneath the world, pulling us toward an impenetrable darkness. The concept is *"grasped"* [saisi], known; it is "the intelligible object."[23] The image, on the other hand, neutralizes any relation between reality and the viewer. Now if art substitutes the image for the object, as Levinas maintains, it is not properly spoken of in terms of creation and revelation. Instead of the highest spiritual categories, magic and enchantment are the proper terms in which it should be discussed. "The image is musical," Levinas says (79), intending this as anything but a compliment. Images enmesh us in rhythm, he thinks, distracting us from our responsibilities in the world. Never an icon, art is always only an idol; it requires sharp criticism, not passive appreciation.

Levinas begins his case insouciantly enough: "Let us say that the thing is itself and its image" (82). That is, when a phenomenon gives itself to consciousness it gives not only itself but also its image. It is as though there is "a split in being," a gap between "being and its essence" (85), so that essence can be detached from being and used to divert it from its proper path (the real, the true) into a deviant course (the non-real, the non-true). A sharp distinction, originally Sartrean, between two irreducible modes of intentionality is drawn, and distributed in a way foreign to Sartre.[24] For Husserl, imagination is a modification of perception. Sartre insists they are distinct but does not use them to distinguish different sorts of person or generic activity.[25] Not so for Levinas. When a philosopher looks at something, he suggests, he or she performs a reduction, and thereby grasps the phenomenon. Yet when an artist looks at something, he or she tries to hold onto the image, the unreal and not the real. As Levinas puts it in a fine sentence, "So art drops the prey for the shadow" [*L'art lâche donce la proie pour l'ombre*] (89). In missing the phenomenon, art does not produce a symbol but an "allegory of being" (82); it arrests time, not as a flash that captures a moment and holds it aloft above time, as it were, but as a passage beneath time to a "life without life" (86) in which the future is suspended for ever. The image is a tableau, a "caricature of being" (85): classical art seeks to correct the element of distortion, while modern art, which incorporates philosophical critique of the image, draws attention to it. The only ethically responsible art, for Levinas, is iconoclastic.[26] Da Vinci's "Mona Lisa," which stands as a prime example of art that erases the signs of its non-being and non-truth, is for Levinas a constant temptation to "nasty, selfish, and cowardly" pleasure (90). Art takes us away from the world and our responsibilities there. What then of Philippe Halsman's "Dali as Mona Lisa" (in which Lisa del Giocondo is given Dali's eyes and moustache)? Presumably it would be ethically sanctioned by virtue of emphasizing the element of caricature in Da Vinci's masterwork.

Of course, it would be utterly implausible to argue that Halsman's painting is superior as a work of art to Da Vinci's, that the Renaissance man is "just an artist" (91) while the modern man is somehow more than one, and hence his work is to be valued the more highly. Yet Levinas seems unable to explain why this is so, if indeed he is not already committed on ethical grounds to prizing the later work over the earlier. The criticism of art that he develops rests on the "literary absolute" of Friedrich Schlegel and his friends, and uncritically affirms avant garde assumptions about art that, endlessly repeated, have tended to become gestures and nostalgias.[27] To figure ethics in art solely as criticism of the image is to fix ethics too narrowly in that sphere, while to correlate ethics and modernity in art is unhistorical and fantastical. When Levinas allows "modern literature" to begin as long ago as Shakespeare (91), he is not finding a moment when literature becomes ethical by acts of self-criticism but extending the assumptions of Jena Romanticism back to Elizabethan England. Expanding "criticism" to include technique is a valuable concession, although it does not go sufficiently far. "Technique" is not something learned only by Shakespeare and those who come after him, nor is it always used in the service of the concept. Pound's comment is closer to what poets do at their best: "The poet's job is to define and yet again define, till the detail of surface is in accord with the root in justice."[28] Yet not all poets are the same. So I would not only add justice but also wisdom, and not only the wisdom of the Greeks, Romans and English but also that of the Bible.[29]

My first, general criticism of Levinas opens the way to other worries about "Reality and its Shadow." One might argue that it is the task of philosophy to investigate the deepest level of reality, which for Levinas would seem to be prior to the distinction between being and essence, namely the "split in being" that he identifies. If the artist attends to this ontological fissure, then it would be the artist, not the philosopher, who responds to what is most profound. Such is the position developed by Levinas's friend, Maurice Blanchot.[30] Besides, can we be so sure that the artist *as artist* differs so fundamentally from the philosopher? Could it not be that when Leonardo paints Lisa del Giocondo's portrait he puts out of play the natural attitude and leads us back to something deeply mysterious in the human being? Gazing at that face for five minutes might make one understand the vulnerability of the other person, her infinite preciousness, more concretely than any argument proposed in a philosophy seminar. And could it not be that, in terms of ethics, the philosopher at his desk, reading *Totalité et infini*, is like the person in the next room who is admiring a painting? Could not they be equally deaf to the call of the widow, the stranger and the orphan precisely because the work in hand is so absorbing?

That "Lachrimæ" incorporates a critique of "mere art" is not to be doubted; it harbors an iconoclastic impulse, as does all his poetry, though one that is animated by another concern than the one that motivated either Constantine V or Levinas. And that poetry has a "menace" is something we know from Hill's inaugural lecture at the University of Leeds, even if he is insufficiently clear about what he means by the word.[31] The doubling that sends a tremor through Hill's poetry in general, and that to some degree stimulates it, is not simply one of image and concept but, as Christopher Ricks sees, one of prurience and imagination.[32] Poetry allows one to speak of anything, even the most terrible suffering, while distancing itself from it in the name of art. "Lachrimæ" may well be partly about the distraction of images in a life of religious faith but the self-criticism that Hill folds into his poetry is a sharp objection to the complacency and self-regard that accompany art and the appreciation of art. That it is embodied by way of technique is evident to any reader of the poetry sensitive to paradox, line endings, ambiguity, scansion, and punctuation. Hill's self-criticism is not motivated by a perceived fissure in being but by an all-too familiar and deeply felt failure to realize an intention with sufficient purity. It is the self-criticism of a moral rigorist, not that of someone drawn to attack Orthodoxy or to propound ethics as first philosophy.

After noting that Christ has withdrawn from all images of himself, Hill asks, "What grips me then, or what does my soul grasp?" The two questions need to be separated. Notice that he does not ask, "*Who* grips me?" No personal experience of the risen Christ is explicitly entertained, but he registers the horror of Christ's suffering even in the caricature of the Passion that is the crucifix before him. Or, as he admits in the second question, there is no objective reality that grips him; there is only him grasping for something, longing for a reality that might not be there. The slight asymmetry between "grip" and "grasp" needs to be registered: Christ, or something trans-cendent (in either the phenomenological or religious sense of the word), grips Hill, holds him firmly, or he grasps at Christ, clutches at him greedily. A hesitance in the subject requires notice, for we pass from "What grips *me* then" to "what does *my soul* grasp?" to "If *I* grasp nothing" [my emphasis throughout]. The self in the accusative is perhaps gripped whereas only the soul grasps—understands spiritually—which is quickly modulated into the self in the nominative perhaps grasping nothing. It may be that the soul can grasp something intellectually yet the whole self, emotional as well as spiritual, cannot grasp anything. At any rate, no sooner is the second question uttered than the possibility of delusion is raised and an answer is touched in imagination: "If I grasp nothing what is there to break?" The problem here is to work out exactly what is being asked. There are many possibilities, and I give only their general matrix, (1) If I grasp nothing, if God does not exist, then nothing will break, neither my relation with God, nor my heart in true contrition because these things are unreal. (And yet the heart may break because there is no God.); (2) If there is no God, no light will ever shine on me; (3) If I understand nothing because I have no faith—*Crede ut intelligas*, as St. Augustine said—there will be no illumination for me;[33] (4) If I grasp nothing because Christ has removed himself from me and is detached from my plight then what follows? I must hope for him to come closer to me.

Every believer of any sophistication or honesty prays at times in the midst of anxieties and doubts, although seldom as many or as virulent as these. They are not overcome but tightly folded into the final sentence of the sonnet, which needs to be read in the awareness that Hill's first question "What grips me then?" has neither been answered nor dismissed. "You are beyond me," Hill says to Christ, partly in exasperation, partly in affection, partly in praise: I do not understand you or your ways, nor can I because you are beyond being. Christ's absolute transcendence does not contradict his immanence in the depths of the soul. He is "innermost true light," *lumen gratiæ*; he is *deus interior intimo meo*, the God who is closer to me than I am to myself. The paradox of Christ being outer and inner is Christianity's, and only the delicately managed tone of "You are beyond me" makes it Hill's as well. That, and the poet's own relish for paradox, for without a pause he figures Christ as "uttermost exile" because of his radical κένωσις (Phil. 2:7-8). Why does Christ leave heaven? For sinners like Hill, of course, whose faults must be atoned for "on the hill" as we hear in "Lachrimæ veræ," even though Hill in 1978 is not an exile from his homeland, and not one of those who while on earth pray *nobis post hoc exsilium*. Looking still at the crucifix, and presumably at the inscription *INRI* (*Iesus Nazarenus Rex Iudæorum*), Hill addresses Christ as "king of our earth," perhaps also half-recalling the title in use in the late sixteenth century, "King of the Glorious Martyrs." With arms outstretched on the cross, Jesus seems as though he stands with the earth embracing him. At first one thinks of lines from Boris Pasternack's second poem entitled "Mary Magdalene": "Thy arms, O Lord, upon the Cross / Embrace too many in the world."[34] Yet the embrace that concerns Hill holds nothing, not too much. It is a "void embrace" for two reasons, because Jesus holds only empty air, and because natural life on earth promises only the void after death.

By the time we get this far into any of the parts of "Lachrimæ" we can see that the poem gambles everything it has and is not once but twice. Every sonnet implicitly proposes a scansion of the history of the form. Little in these sonnets recalls sixteenth-century religious verse, certainly not Henry Lok's *Sundry Christian Passions, Contained in Two Hundred Sonnets* (1593) or Barnabe Barnes's *A Divine Centurie of Spirituall Sonnets* (1595). Donne's "Holy Sonnets," from the early seventeenth century (1607–19), are the most secure point of contact with Hill's poem one can find in English religious verse. It cannot be a surprise, for Hill inherits many streams of "metaphysical poetry" from Donne, as well as from critics such as Eliot and Empson who affirm Donne's poetry as a model for modernist poetry. The flair for paradox is common to Donne and Hill, of course, and so too are certain themes, such as the fear of pandering to God ("Oh, to vex me, contraries meet in one") and the experience of "harsh grace" ("Batter my heart, three-personed God").[35] Yet the baroque era in the history of the sonnet is brought to the fore, mostly by allusion to Spanish poets, perhaps ones that Donne had read, and the risk is run of appearing overly literary, even of the English verse reading as though it has been translated (albeit with great skill). The poet's mask could seem contrived, self-conscious and fussy. Second, the poem highlights baroque Catholic spirituality, and takes its chances as being read as trading in theological commonplaces. For all its risks, however, the poem has a directness that almost completely overcomes its weaker moments (as in the sestet of "Lachrimæ coactæ"). Hill tells us that, "ambiguities and scruples seem to reside in the object that is meditated upon."[36] This is true, but only if one acknowledges that the "in" ventured here does not exclude a structure of subjectivity in the writer. Those ambiguities and scruples, along with the literary devices and theological commonplaces, are "in" the noemata as *irreal*, Husserl would say; they are linked to the noetic pole of the writer's gaze.[37] They are not objective in a naïve realist sense, and responsible action with respect to them involves an acknowledgement of the self's involvement with them. The problem at issue is not that of self-criticism of prurience but the styling of one's relation to the world so often in terms of "difficulty." That the events that stimulate poetry are given to us in an excess of intuition is not to be doubted, but to consider that excess so often by way of difficulty— rather than mystery or richness, say—is to yield to intellectualism.[38] To say repeatedly that something is difficult, whether or not it is overcome, is a subtle form of self-aggrandizement. In this sense, difficulty and mystery are very far from one another. Mystery is compatible with an affirmation of the simple, though never the simplistic, and in its world to speak of difficulty is already reductive.

The final image is of doubling once again, and once again it is ambiguous. Here, as elsewhere in Hill, we do not find the "fruitful ambiguity" that the New Critics talked about so much as what we might call a "thornful ambiguity." We might say that just as Christ's embrace of Hill is quiet ("If I grasp nothing ...") because it is empty, so the earth promises Jesus only the void. The dying Jesus does not care to unclasp the earth's embrace in a triumphant gesture, or he does not bother to do so: it is far too late for that or anything. On the first reading, Jesus maintains the embrace to the very end because he must bear the full weight of sin for the redemption of the world to be efficacious. His quiet is not a deathly silence but a submission to the will of the Father that we are enjoined to imitate. On the second reading, however, Jesus cannot shake off the embrace of the void. He cries out, "My God, my God, why hast thou forsaken me?" (Matt. 27:46). The poem has brooded on the crucifix as an image of Jesus on the cross, yet in its final line it is the earth that becomes an image of Jesus. Is it that the silent earth is a poor copy of Jesus's quiet, and instead of calmness and peace it reveals emptiness and blankness? Or could it be it that both Jesus and the earth are finally still, a dead body and a place of execution facing the void? The questions are not answered, no more so than the one that haunts the sestet, "What grips me then?"

*

Can one pray in a poem? Should one pray in a poem? An important critical tradition, running from Samuel Johnson to Donald Davie, answers both questions firmly in the negative. With non-scriptural verse, at least, either the poem will be compromised as art, or the speaker will delude himself or herself.[39] Yet there are many strong poems that are also prayers, from the psalms to anonymous lyrics of the thirteenth and fourteenth centuries, seventeenth-century devotional verse, T. S. Eliot's "Ash-Wednesday" and beyond. Other poems—George Herbert's "Jordan" I and II, for instance—explicitly query religious lyrics, prayers or not, that prefer metaphor to plain speech. The metaphor required to express the transcendence of God can distract writer and reader from the truth of the faith. Detaching the rhetoric of prayer from belief in God is a familiar practice: Jules Supervielle and Yves Bonnefoy have composed poems that address a God who does not exist.[40] And that prayers not intended to be poems can have literary qualities is well-known: *The Book of Common Prayer* (1559) provides many examples. Similarly, prayers that might have no literary value whatsoever may be informed by deliberate exertions of the imagination, as St. Ignatius Loyola commended in his *Spiritual Exercises* (1548). Prayer can be regarded as an art itself, an exemplary discipline.[41] Even acts of devotion, up to and including martyrdom, can be regarded as works of art. Ibsen's Brand exhorts us, "Don't forget / life's the real work of art!," and Pierre Janelle tells us that St. Robert

Southwell's "trial and execution are in themselves a work of art of supreme beauty."[42]

In his essay "The Absolute Reasonableness of Robert Southwell" (1979), Hill glosses Janelle's comment by way of "transfiguration," a word that for Hill, at least here, is associated with art and not faith.[43] In *Tenebræ* (1978), though, he is more doubtful that a religious vocabulary can be transferred to art. "Lachrimæ coactæ" has already shown a concern with the image, and a vigilant awareness of the ambiguities of the imagination can be found throughout the sequence. In the first sonnet of "Lachrimæ" the crucified Christ is told, "This is your body twisted by our skill," meaning not only Roman techniques of torture and execution but also the craft of making images, both crucifixes and poems. Christ's words "Take, eat; this is my body" (Matt. 26:26) are themselves twisted in the poem, as though in acknowledgment of how the spiritual can be distorted to fill aesthetic hungers. And when Hill tells Christ, "I cannot turn aside from what I do" it is important that the "I" be recognized as both sinner and poet, the two being impossible to separate in his case. The sinner cannot achieve *conversio*, conversion, partly because he is a poet, committed in advance to tropes or turns, with a hardened tendency to drop the prey for the shadow. In the sixth sonnet he will talk of our devotion that is "bowed beneath the gold," indicating both an attitude of prayer and a distortion. The current of criticism of the Church's self-distraction with icons and art is also a self-criticism: the casting of religious devotion as art, as "Lachrimæ," introduces self-regard in moments of what could have been sincere prayer. Religious transcendence in prayer is contaminated by literary transcendence in composing a work of art. In Hill's terms, the desire for atonement runs aground in the quest for at-one-ment.[44] Whether it must do so or whether it usually does so is left undetermined.

The first and sixth sonnets, "Lachrimæ veræ" and "Lachrimæ antiquæ novæ," have titles drawn from Dowland. More attention to the possibilities of corruption in art (or, more darkly, art as corruption) is given in the three sonnets that depart from the titular musical work. Consider the second of the series, "The Masque of Blackness":

Splendour of life so splendidly contained,
brilliance made bearable. It is the east
light's embodiment, fit to be caressed,
the god Amor with his eyes of diamond,

celestial worldliness on which has dawned
intelligence of angels, Midas' feast,
the stony hunger of the dispossessed
locked into Eden by their own demand.

> Self-love, the slavish master of this trade,
> conquistador of fashion and remark,
> models new heavens in his masquerade,
>
> its images intense with starry work,
> until he tires and all that he has made
> vanishes in the chaos of the dark.[45]

The sonnet is about art, as well as striving itself to be highly polished art. It cites the title of Ben Jonson's *The Masque of Blackness* (1605), which was performed before James I of England and in which the king's wife, Anne of Denmark, acted with blackened face and arms. (Dowland dedicated his "Lachrimae" to Anne.) Also it adapts Francisco de Quevedo's sonnet "Retrato de Lisi que traia en una sortija."[46] Some preliminary comments on these two works are needed in order to clarify the lyric.

Brought to a high pitch of spectacle by the architect Inigo Jones, Jonson's masque was a great success as art, if not for consolidating Anne of Denmark's reputation at court since people talked about the flimsiness of her costume.[47] The masque traced the passage of Ethiopian daughters, who desire perfect beauty, from Africa to England. It is a piece about tears of vanity, for the River Niger ("in form and color of an Ethiop") speaks of his daughters crying: "They wept such ceaseless tears into my stream, / That it hath thus far overflowed his shore / To seek them patience."[48] The cause of this vanity is traced by the River Niger to the poets, "Poor brain-sick men" who have "sung / The painted beauties other empires sprung" and let "their loose and winged fictions fly / To infect all climates, yea, our purity" (*ll.* 130–5). Eventually the daughters reach Britannia, and bathe in the rays of James I, the sun, who can turn black into white:

> For were the world with all his wealth a ring,
> Britannia, whose new name makes all tongues sing,
> Might be a diamond worthy to enchase it,
> Ruled by a sun that to this height doth grace it,
> Whose beams shine day and night and are of force
> To blanch an Æthiop, and revive a cor's.
> His light sciental is, and, past mere nature,
> Can salve the rude defects of every creature. (*ll.* 221–8)

A ring also forms the conceit of Quevedo's sonnet in which he speaks of a portrait of Lisi, which is imprisoned ("aprisionado") in a ring. Here the empire is not that of James but of Love ("y grande imperio del Amor cerrado"). Like many others of its day, the sonnet reworks sacred motifs in a secular register.

Lisi's teeth are pearls set in diamond ("en un diamante"). Hard like diamond, she speaks with scorn, like tinkling ice ("con desdén sonoro yelo"), and tyrannical fire ("fuego tirano").

The masque gorgeously contains in its narrow limits all the magnificence of life at court: dance, costume, music and poetry, combined with coruscating visual effects. The Queen played Euphoria, an Ethiopian, while various ladies of the court played lesser roles. Blackened and heavily jeweled, Anne came on stage in a mother-of-pearl shell drawn by seahorses, accompanied by tributaries of the River Niger and several sea monsters.[49] Watching her is James I, absolute monarch of Britain (the "new name" that Jonson speaks of) who also holds the nominal title King of France. As a Stuart, James believes that his authority derives from God and takes himself to be Christ's sovereign representative. Masque and court are the "east / light's embodiment," the metaphor applying to James I in particular. He is able to revive the dead, as the *Masque* proclaims. Yet he is less Christ than he is "the god Amor" with his empire of conquest spread before him in the court, and his "eyes of diamond" suggest rarity, artificiality, hardness or even tears. He is fit to be caressed—by male or female. (*Rex fuit Elizabeth: nunc est regina Jacobus*, people in the know said wryly after the coronation in 1603.) In its brightness and pomp, not to mention its decadence, the court exhibits "celestial worldliness." Yet the court also knows *angelica mens*, "the intelligence of angels," in the sense that Pico della Mirandola gives to the expression in his "Oration on the Dignity of Man" (1486). "It is a commonplace of the schools that man is a little world, in which we may discern a body mingled of earthy elements, and ethereal breath, and the vegetable life of plants, and the senses of the lower animals, and reason, and the intelligence of angels, and a likeness to God." [*Tritum est in scholis*, he says, *esse hominen minorem mundum, in quo mixtum ex elementis corpus et spiritus coelestis et plantarum anima vegetalis et brutorum sensus et ratio et angelica mens et Dei similitudo conspicitur.*[50]]

Hill's poem explores the "little world" of James I's court, and the way in which the King and the artist both seek to be free creators of their own worlds, and, in mistaking "self-love" for "love," become prisoners of desire rather than free creators of new worlds. Pico has God tell man at his creation, "We have set thee at the world's center that thou mayest from thence more easily observe whatever is in the world. We have made thee neither of heaven nor of earth, neither mortal nor immortal, so that with freedom of choice and with honor, as though the maker and molder of thyself, thou mayest fashion thyself in whatever shape thou shalt prefer. Thou shalt have the power to degenerate into the lower forms of life, which are brutish. Thou shalt have the power, out of thy soul's judgment, to be reborn into the higher forms, which are divine."[51] Hill's "Lachrimæ," and "The Masque of Blackness," in particular, explores this Renaissance Platonic theology, not merely dramatizing its options, but underlining the difficulty of choosing between them in the world of art, in the making of beautiful things, and in the world of religion, in the making of a life that God sees as beautiful. The very diagnosis of corruption in "The Masque of Blackness" is itself contaminated by "self-love," as Hill indicates when he refers to poetry (and the writing of the poem in question) as "this trade," a matter of craft.

The court itself is "Midas' feast," a familiar scene from Ovid. Or rather two scenes: the ten-day party to welcome Silenus, and the dinner in celebration of the gift from Bacchus—the ability to turn anything into gold. It is the second feast that presses the harder in the poem, the image of the king as "both a wretch and rich," as Arthur Golding has it in his translation of the *Metamorphoses*.[52] Hill may well have a contemporary version of the myth in mind. We think of what Apollo says in John Lyly's *Midas* (1589), performed before Elizabeth I: "To be a King is next being to a God" (IV: i, 65–6).[53] Hearing that, though, we remember that Mellacrites has already told Sophronia about the feast: "Your highnes sees, and without griefe you cannot see, that his meat turneth to massie gold in his mouth, and his wine slideth downe his throte like liquide golde" (II: i, 46–8). The luxury of court life is anything but nourishing for the soul. "Stony hunger" is overcome only by listening to "every word of God" (Lk. 4:3). Dispossessed, like Narcissus—*inopem me copia fecit*, Ovid writes in *Metamorphoses* III. 466, he has been made poor by his possessions—James and Anne are locked into the brilliant yet superficial life at court "by their own demand," that is, by their legal claim, their imperious requests of Parliament for more money, and their almost unlimited desires. They live in a false Eden, not even the forest of Arden where one feels "not the penalty of Adam," but a twisted version of the society that B. L. Joseph calls "Shakespeare's Eden."[54]

Thus far the sonnet has shifted from the concerns of "Lachrimæ veræ" to courtly entertainment at the very time when Dowland was composing his "Lachrimæ" and the baroque poets of Spain were writing sensuous religious sonnets. It comes as a jolt in the sequence in its definitive arrangement: although, as king, James I is the representative of Christ, "The Masque of Blackness" is not a Christological poem so much as an exploration of what happens when "the god Amor" is substituted for Christ, and there is sufficient power to make the substitution take hold for a while.[55] The structure of doubling is clear and, here as elsewhere in the poem, Southwell's desire for men to "alter their object and better their intent" is pertinent. The sestet is more direct in its criticisms. The "trade," whether in gold, colonial slaves or sex, is directed by "Self-love," the fuller name of "Amor" who cannot separate himself from what he does, and who sets *le bon ton* in all the registers of cleverness and cruelty. Yet "this trade" is surely also the writing of poetry, as we have seen, including at the edge of all condemnation the very sequence "Lachrimæ" that we are reading. There is a shift from *The Masque of Blackness* to the masks worn by the poet of *Tenebræ*.[56] A similar move will be made in "Pavana dolorosa" where Southwell is addressed as "Self-seeking hunter of forms," and told "there is no end / to such pursuits," a comment that flicks back on Geoffrey Hill, who can be seen equally to be addressing himself. His project of self-criticism, his hunt for "good form," can never end, for his version of the literary absolute can always be admired by himself and others precisely for its moral integrity. The "verbal mastery" of the Symbolists can always be criticized and the poet's words become a higher form of mastery, one that rises above ethical concerns by dint of having addressed them and turned them into tropes. And of course there is a sense in which the writing of prayerful sonnets is pointless if the aim is the salvation of one's soul. Like Southwell, at least to the extent that both are artists, he is "self-seeking," in quest of his true self and promoting that self. To exhibit free beauty, Kant says in the third *Critique*, an artwork must have "finality without end" [*Zweckmässigkeit ohne Zweck*]; it must be cut off from religious purposes as well as all others.[57] For Kant, a poem that is also a prayer would not exhibit free beauty, and most certainly would not have a proper understanding of prayer.[58]

To return to "The Masque of Blackness," the new heavens are not those of Revelation 21:1 but others devised by Inigo Jones. They are modeled like the latest fashions in clothes, the passing moment being deemed a success only because of the enormous amount of misdirected work behind it. Yet self-love cannot sustain any interest beyond itself, and the *Masque*, along with everything like it, "vanishes in the chaos of the dark." The final metaphor is biblical, referring us to the *tohu wa-bohu* of Genesis 1:2: "And the earth was without form, and void; and darkness was upon the face of the deep." A certain sort of art, such as that exemplified by Jonson and Jones, passes from creation to un-creation.

*

"Lachrimæ" represents a poem as a funeral monument, a martyrium, and casts doubt on the image of the martyr as someone testifying purely and simply for his or her faith. Martyrs, both secular and sacred, if the distinction can be trusted here, appear throughout Hill's poetry, for he is deeply interested in the equation of witness and suffering, and of the possible atonement that comes from suffering. Consider the third sonnet, "Martyrium":

The Jesus-faced man walking crowned with flies
who swats the roadside grass or glances up

at the streaked gibbet with its birds that swoop,
who scans his breviary while the sweat dries,

fades, now, among the fading tapestries,
brooches of crimson tears where no eyes weep,
a mouth unstitched into a rimless cup,
torn clouds the cauldrons of the martyr's cries.

Clamorous love, its faint and baffled shout,
its grief that would betray him to our fear,
he suffers for our sake, or does not hear

above the hiss of shadows on the wheat.
Viaticum transfigures earth's desire
in rising vernicles of summer air.

I take the "Jesus-faced" man to be Southwell, and "Jesus-faced" to summon
"Janus-faced": for Catholics the saint-to-be is indeed looking to Christ,
though the Protestants of Elizabeth I's time believe him, and all Jesuits, to
be in league with Beelzebub, Lord of the Flies. While studying at the English
College in Rome in 1585, Southwell received a letter describing the exami-
nation and martyrdom of George Haydock. "The Catholic faith, the devel's
faith," standers-by cried out at Tyburn when Haydock asked for prayers from
"Catholicks" and defined the word to mean members of "the Catholick
Roman Church."[59] The writer of the letter had been standing "under the
gibbet" (61), like the priest imagined in the first stanza. Now, though, the age
of Christians dying in *odium fidei* has faded; what remains are reliquaries and
images, which call forth devotions, real and florid, appropriate and skewed.
Considering them, Hill parallels what Southwell says in St. *Mary Magdalens
Funerall Teares*. "Passions I allow," the saint concedes, which Hill adapts in
the third person, "Clamorous love … he suffers for our sake." The martyr
allows tearful, importunate devotion, stemming from grief, which can easily
become a displaced figure of our own fear of death. Yet "suffers" also takes
on the usual, darker sense; the martyr experiences pain for us, just as Christ
did upon the cross, and to the same end. Or is the "Clamorous love" entirely
earthly, the tears of Eros that have not been directed to a divine object or
bettered in intent? And can we trace the border between the holy and the
profane with any confidence in the devotion of the time, the poetry of the
time, or in "Lachrimæ"?

At any rate, as the lyric makes plain, it could be that the martyr does not
hear our cries, by dint of the intensity of his focus, as a recipient of special
grace, or in a more dubious state of abstraction. The lines in the sestet are

more elusive than one usually finds in Hill, perhaps most obliquely so in "the hiss of shadows on the wheat." Is this an allusion to John Wilkinson, the silk mercer who stood beneath the scaffold where Henry Garnet was executed in 1606 in order that the linens he had brought with him might be spotted with the martyr's blood? Garnet's blood fell on a wheat stalk caught in Wilkinson's clothes and some thought that one of the grains miraculously assumed the features of Garnet's face.[60] Or are we directed to the parable of the wheat and the tares (Matt. 13:30)? More likely, I think, Hill's line alludes to the Eucharistic metaphor of the martyr as bread to be consecrated by his or her witness to Christ. The metaphor is patristic, although of course patristic sources were much used by recusant Catholics, including Southwell, and those who suffered in the early Church were liturgically commemorated in the *Roman Martyrology* (1584). They were hardly distant figures for sixteenth-century Catholics.[61]

So we think of St. Ignatius of Antioch writing in his letter to friends at Rome before he suffered: "I am the wheat of God, and am ground by the teeth of the wild beasts, that I may be found the pure bread of God."[62] And we think of *The Martyrdom of St. Polycarp*: "The fire produced the likeness of a vaulted chamber, like a ship's sail bellying to the breeze, and surrounded the martyr's body as with a wall; and he was in the center of it, not as burning flesh, but as bread that is baking or as gold and silver refined in a furnace!"[63] Those who would harm a recusant martyr are no more than shadows when considered eschatologically, even though they rail against him or make flames hiss around the cauldron in which his heart will be thrown. A figure of the Eucharist, the martyr becomes viaticum for those who witness his or her testimony, and this has the power to transfigure worldly desire, including all longings for self-preservation. Whenever the martyr's blood is shed, Southwell says, it "engendereth a wonderful alteration in men's manners, making them embrace the truth."[64] Just as the Veronica was revered after Jesus's death, so too was the handkerchief with which Southwell wiped his face before he threw it into the crowd assembled to watch his execution. He is "Jesus-faced," and never more so than at his martyrdom.

To be sure, reliquaries, a martyrium, or even the desire for martyrdom, can be a distraction for the believer. The form of a religious devotion, and a formal adherence to it, can reverse its value: a fast can become a feast of asceticism, and one can seek martyrdom for the wrong reason. If love can be misdirected, endangering self-transformation, so too can passion. "Pavana dolorosa" begins by tilting Southwell's concession "Loves I approve and passions I allow" so that it flips into "Loves I allow and passions I approve." With a slight push, Hill edges Southwell's deeply incarnational theology further in the direction of sensuality than the saint would wish to go.[65] Where Southwell affirms a proper ordering of love and passion under grace, Hill reflects that the order can never be absolved from possible distortion. Art is a passion that flirts with and mimes love; it can create the truths of religion, and encourage the artist to pass from creation to un-creation, or indeed to pass to a Creator who does not exist. "Decreation," the movement from creature to Creator, is Simone Weil's coinage. She says in her *Notebooks*:

> The universe is so made that a creature is able to love God in a pure manner.
>   In other words, creation contains within itself the condition for de-creation.[66]

The Hill who wrote, "Our God scatters corruption," meaning both that God eliminates corruption and that He spreads it, is unlikely to agree without qualification.[67] Doubtless the terrible ambiguity stems from the thought of the deity being "*Our* God"; but can the possessive with its hints of church and party, ever be completely removed? There are times when Hill seems to rail against our embodied state, seeking a purity we can never find. So when Hill talks (in a tone reminiscent of *Four Quartets*) of "the decreation to which all must move" it could be an undoing of the self in a slide toward death, what I have been calling un-creation, as much as an act of self-transcendence. The poet may become a martyr to his art: the sacrifice of the "I" in the quest for a self-transcendence that never comes. It is a theme familiar to readers of Hölderlin and Blanchot.

I have been attending to the relation of devotion and art in "Lachrimæ," yet it needs to be underlined that this relation, like any other, is framed by a broader political context, one that has variously compelled Hill's attention for many years. When the "Bloody Question" was put to Catholic priests and others, it was to force them to make an hypothetical choice between the Monarch and the Pope, and if they answered in favor of the Pope, or were taken to equivocate, they were executed for treason, not for their faith as such. A rather different imbrication of religion and politics can be seen in the concluding lines of "Lachrimæ antiquæ novæ." Christ is told, "We find you wounded by the token spear. / Dominion is swallowed with your blood." What wounds Christ is that our faith is perfunctory. Were we to take Southwell's advice and better our intent, we might fully accept Christ's sovereignty when taking Communion. Yet this possibility is always contaminated. Dominion, the right to govern in Church or State, is "swallowed" when the Eucharist is taken: Christianity and Christendom are inextricably entwined, a fact we must accept, and Christendom (as Kierkegaard recognized so well) can be a perpetual distraction from the practice of Christianity. When we take Communion we "swallow" Christ's Lordship, we repress it in the very gesture of apparently accepting it. According to the first sonnet,

"Lachrimæ veræ," we merely "pander" to Christ's name. Or, in the words of the final sonnet, "Lachrimæ amantis," we keep ourselves "religiously secure," grounded in creed and ritual, rather than opening our hearts to accept Christ.

"Lachrimæ amantis," and the entire sequence, ends with the lines,

> So many nights the angel of my house
> has fed such urgent comfort through a dream,
> whispered "your lord is coming, he is close"
>
> that I have drowsed half-faithful for a time
> bathed in pure tones of promise and remorse:
> "tomorrow I shall wake to welcome him."

The sonnet freely translates Lope de Vega Carpio's "¿Qué tengo yo que mi amistad procuras?," and it is instructive to compare the original Spanish with Hill's version:

> Cuántas veces el ángel me de decía:
> "¡Alma, asómate agora a la ventana,
> verás con cuanto amor llamar porfía!"
>
> Y cuántas hermosura soberana:
> "¡Mañana te abriremos"—repondía,
> para lo mismo responder mañana![68]

Notice that in the Spanish the speaker has postponed conversion time after time, although finally he has welcomed Christ. The closing lines represent the procrastination in a plangent manner of intense regret. For Hill, however, the situation is more ambiguous. It is not at all clear that his speaker has welcomed Christ, and indeed the weight of possibility is that he will continue to defer the moment of intimacy. Nonetheless, one can read the translation as suggesting that he might open the door on the morrow. For the colon can be taken to indicate not only a statement often said and often bringing remorse but also a resolution that contrasts with past behavior. We do not know if the speaker will act on his resolve, but we at least experience more fully that act than we do in de Vega's original.

"Lachrimæ" ends without it being clear whether the poet personally affirms the transcendence of Christ. Does Hill counter-sign the theology in Lope de Vega's poem, or just his poem? Even if we take the preponderance of evidence to be that Hill wishes to believe in the transcendence of God, the poem concludes without any sign of the poet's self-transcendence, except, to be sure, in the writing of the poem itself. The poem, as poem, achieves transcendence in tears; the poet remains in tears, though whether real or forced we cannot say. He is "bathed in pure tones of promise and remorse," the frightening word being "pure." If we search for an explanation of this failure of religious self-transcendence, we will find it, at least partly, in the poet's allegiance to "difficulty," especially in his defense that it comes from an objective situation in which his subjectivity plays no part.

7

Uncommon equivocation in Geoffrey Hill

Toward the end of "Dividing Legacies" (1996), a long review of Eliot's Clark Lectures of 1926, *The Varieties of Metaphysical Poetry* (1993), Geoffrey Hill turns to consider *Four Quartets* (1944). He laments that Eliot's poetry deteriorated from "The Love Song of J. Alfred Prufrock" to "Little Gidding." Whereas the earlier poem exhibited what Hill calls "pitch," the later poem is guided merely by "tone." The word "pitch" is taken less from music than from Gerard Manley Hopkins, for whom it means "distinctiveness and selving, this selfbeing of my own."[1] Elucidated only by Hopkins for his own purposes, the word remains too vague for general literary analysis, and Hill offers no gloss to render it more precise, either in itself or in contradistinction with "tone." In "Prufrock," Hill says, "the distinction between I, me, my, we, us, our, you, your, his, her, they, them, one, it, its, is a proper distinction in pitch."[2] It is difficult to see how "pitch," as evoked here, differs from the usual grammatical terms— subject, object, possessive, and so on—and can pick out "this selfbeing of my own." One might get further over the same terrain, and do so more quickly, by way of Jacques Derrida's notion of "idiom," which denotes the trace of the absolutely singular in literature.[3] Be that as it may, Hill finds no pitch in Eliot's late poetry: the speaker of *Four Quartets* is "a commentator on the general tone or tonelessness of things" (378). I think that this criticism does not do justice to the range of meditative and lyrical voices in the *Quartets* as well as Eliot's unmistakable idiom. The widely admired passage of imitation *terza rima* in "Little Gidding" does much of what Hill values in "Prufrock," and the four poems continue to press on the mind and linger there. We remember the "rose-garden" passage, the lines about sailing off the coast of New England, the "blitz" stanzas, and several others, even if we also regret some pages of unsatisfactory verse, including those that Eliot staged as such in "East Coker."

Not content to disparage the *Quartets*, Hill also takes a swipe at Christopher Ricks as a critic of the poems. In *T. S. Eliot and Prejudice* (1988),

Ricks comments on some lines from "Little Gidding" and reflects on the same passage from Eliot's earlier poetry to his later poetry that attracts Hill's ire. Ricks, though, notes at least one aspect of Eliot's trajectory that he approves. "Antagonism to clichés—like the expression of antagonism through clichés—has been succeeded by confidence in their good sense, in their generous common humanity."[4] Hill does not reject the general claim about clichés; he even points to the value of cliché in Whitman's "Drum-Taps." Instead, he recalls a letter written by Eliot to the editor of the *Athenaeum* in 1920 where he writes of "apathy ... more flagitious than abuse" (378) and associates the verse of the *Quartets* with this villainy. This is strong stuff; and, having unleashed the younger Eliot upon the older Eliot, Hill turns to Ricks and observes in a manner reminiscent of a very cross Headmaster of ages past speaking to a schoolboy, "I would ask him to place 'his generous common humanity' within the field of Hooker's common equivocation and to determine how much weight and pressure that generous humanity can sustain" (379). Not much at all, is the very clear implication; and thus emboldened Hill goes on to make two more hits at those who have inherited from the *Quartets*. The first is Anglican "literary 'spirituality'" (the last word is suspended by quotation marks in order to hold it at arm's length); and the second is the poetry of Philip Larkin. The justification for yoking together two such different things is "a common species of torpor" (379). Once again, Ricks is called into the Headmaster's study, and this time the boy who is usually top of the class has been very bad indeed: "he is pleased to be numbered among Larkin's advocates," Hill sighs. This remarkable tirade ends with Hill searching for a possible reason for this horrid aberration: How could a critic as sensitive as Ricks (someone who greatly appreciates Hill's poetry) admire the poetry of Larkin? "I anticipate," Hill writes, "that he might answer, 'Because he [Larkin] speaks to the human condition'" (379).

In *True Friendship* (2010), Ricks responds to Hill's essay of fourteen years before. "Yes, I am pleased to be numbered among Larkin's advocates, but no, I would not answer with something about the human condition for I don't find myself uttering those words."[5] His reason is a little lame, and he says nothing about how his expression "generous common humanity" would fare "within the field of Hooker's common equivocation," and it is worthwhile to ponder the expression for a moment or two. It is clear why Hill appeals to Richard Hooker: he falls within the historical period that Eliot discusses in his Clark lectures (though Eliot does not mention Hooker in his lectures, which Hill takes to be a fault, since he thinks that Hooker supplies Donne's center of gravity [372]). Yet one does not think first of Hooker when the topic is equivocation. If one is looking for formal or informal fallacies, one would tend to go to logicians who diagnose the fault of giving a word different meanings in separate lines of a syllogism; and if one is looking for a discussion of moral equivocation, one might go to Navarrus or Robert Southwell (to name just two) who offer more detailed considerations of the fault than Hooker does. For Hooker, moral equivocation is an effect of the Fall of Adam and Eve, compounded by actual sin. Our will is "hardly inclinable" to search for true knowledge. "The root thereof, divine malediction; whereby the instruments being weakned wherewithall the soule (especially in reasoning) doth worke, it preferreth rest in ignorance before wearisome labour to knowe."[6]

In "Divided Legacies," Hill dilates on the different pitches that "common" has in Hooker's *Of the Laws of Ecclesiastical Polity* (1594–7, with posthumous additions), and he also points to Hooker's own equivocation regarding them. On the one hand, Hooker thinks of the different pitches of the word "common" being correlated to Romans 13, the chapter of the epistle in which St. Paul reflects on the Christian's civic responsibilities. On the other hand, there is Hooker's "tacit invitation to his readers to accept that hierarchical distinction and brute natural obduracies are alike resolved into equity by fiat of the commonweal and the administrations of the 1559 *Book of Common Prayer*" (375–6). Nowhere, though, does Hill explain the expression "common equivo-cation," and he does not point us to Hooker or quote a passage in which the expression occurs. Indeed, there seems to be a disconnection in his essay between "common" and "equivocation," certainly no basis for speaking later of "common equivocation."

What, then, does "common equivocation" mean in Hill's essay? Is he thinking of an equivocation that is common in the sense of being widely spread? Certainly Hooker talks about the prevalence of the fallacy of equivo-cation in one of those sonorous sentences that mark his style. Here is Hooker pondering the claim that reason is an enemy of divine wisdom:

> The cause why such declamations prevaile so greatly, is, for that men suffer themselves in two respects to be deluded, one is that the wisdome of man being debaced either in comparison with that of God, or in regard of some speciall thing exceeding the reach and compasse thereof, it seemeth to them (not marking so much) as if simplie it were condemned: another that learning, knowledge, or wisdome falsely so tearmed, usurping a name whereof they are not worthie, and being under that name controlled, their reproofe is by so much the more easily misapplied, and through *equivo-cation* wrested against those things whereunto so pretious names do properly and of right belong. (*Laws*, III. viii. 5; my emphasis)

We are deluded when we think that human knowledge is simply condemned by God, and deluded too when we confuse human knowledge with wisdom. That confusion occurs through the logical fallacy of equivocation, although, to be sure, we may be led to commit that fallacy through the effects of the Fall of Adam and Eve. Our will is no longer sufficiently strong to do the hard work of reasoning, and so we settle for ignorance, which is a moral fault as well as a cognitive one. Hill may well be drawn to this aspect of Hooker, for the poet tells us that he come to believe in the doctrine of original sin.[7]

One might almost be forgiven for entertaining the idea that Hill is thinking of the word "common" as equivocal in Hooker's prose, that Hooker is finely aware of this equivocation, and makes good use of it, while Ricks is quite unaware of it and falls victim to it? This would mean no more than that Hooker draws on the full semantic range of "common" in the English of the late sixteenth century, and Ricks presumably is not fully aware of this range in the twentieth century. When Ricks writes of "generous common humanity" is he suggesting, Hill prompts us to ask, that all people *share* a sense of generous humanity? Or is he proposing that this "generous humanity" is *familiar*? Or that it is *habitual*? Or that it is *undistinguished*? Or that it is *mean* and *cheap*? The list could continue, right through the extensive entry on "common" in the Oxford English Dictionary. I take it that Hill is suggesting, mostly through tone, that the sort of "generous humanity" one finds in *Four Quartets* and in Larkin's poems cannot exclude the senses of being undistinguished, mean, and cheap.

Finally, is Hill perhaps thinking that Ricks is equivocating in just the way that Hooker does in *Of the Laws of Ecclesiastical Polity*? As an "unrivalled" critic of literature (379), Ricks is certainly aware of hierarchical distinctions, of the nice differences involved in ranking poems and poets, and yet with the cases of Eliot and Larkin he resolves those distinctions, which should be rigorously established by critical analysis and judgment, in the commonweal and Anglican "literary 'spirituality.'" The commonweal, however, is the degraded "little Britain" of the 1990s, and Anglican "literary 'spirituality'" (of which he nowhere gives an example) is, I suppose, thought to be merely insipid. It is Hill's contention that the Eliot of *Four Quartets* and the poetry of Larkin, uplifted by Ricks by way of an appeal to "generous humanity," cannot sustain much weight and pressure at all, and that is because this "generous humanity" is "common" in the sense of being undistinguished, mean and cheap. I think that this *is* what Hill is driving at, and clearly it takes quite a bit of work to discover his point. It is not a pleasant point at which to arrive, and we may well ask why he goes to such lengths to be so ungenerous to two poets who, as Ricks shows very clearly in *True Friendship*, are hardly alien to Hill's own practice as a poet.

The answer may be found in Hill's poetry, especially his earlier poetry, the sequence of books that runs from *For the Unfallen* (1959) to *Canaan* (1996), where one finds almost all of his strongest verse. There is much to be said of this body of work, and I have said a few things about it in the preceding chapters, and certainly one of the first observations would be that it is deeply invested in equivocation. I am not thinking of the logical fallacy but of the ethical and rhetorical senses of the word. It is not common equivocation, since it is neither widespread nor undistinguished; it is, rather, uncommon equivocation, ambiguity of a sort that is quite different from that embraced by the New Critics, less binocular than Janus-faced. Of course, this style of equivocation has long been Hill's signature, has been admired, leagued with Freud's short essay on antithetical words, and many of his earlier poems have been decoded in terms of it.[8] I am not sure, however, that its moral and theological dimensions have been clarified. In an effort to go a little way in that direction, I would like to comment on an exemplary early lyric, "Annunciations":

1.
The Word has been abroad, is back, with a tanned look
From its subsistence in the stiffening-mire.
Cleansing has become killing, the reward
Touchable, overt, clean to the touch.
Now at a distance from the steam of beasts,
The loathly neckings and fat shook spawn
(Each specimen-jar fed with delicate spawn)
The searchers with the curers sit at meat
And are satisfied. Such precious things put down
And the flesh eased through turbulence the soul
Purples itself; each eye squats full and mild
While all who attend to fiddle or to harp
For betterment, flavour their decent mouths
With gobbets of the sweetest sacrifice.

2.
O Love, subject of the mere diurnal grind,
Forever being pledged to be redeemed,
Expose yourself for charity; be assured
The body is but husk and excrement.
Enter these deaths according to the law,
O visited women, possessed sons! Foreign lusts
Infringe our restraints; the changeable
Soldiery have their goings-out and comings-in
Dying in abundance. Choicest beasts
Suffuse the gutters with their colourful blood.
Our God scatters corruption. Priests, martyrs,
Parade to this imperious theme: "O Love,
You know what pains succeed; be vigilant; strive
To recognize the damned among your friends."[9]

A full reading of this demanding poem—almost, in some respects, a meta-poem: a poem about poetry—would take far too long in a short chapter. Harold Bloom has suggested that it offers a key to Hill's poetry, and perhaps post-Romantic poetry as such, and it is noteworthy that it is the only one of his poems that Hill has sought to paraphrase.[10] Bloom's reading of the poem follows the guidelines that Hill supplies.[11] So Hill has cut a key that opens his tightly locked poems; it has been copied and is taken to be a Yale key, and has been freely used ever since when seeking to gain entry to the highly wrought intellectual treasures of his poetry. In those notes to the lyric, Hill ranges his poem against the *Four Quartets*: for both, he says, "The Word is an Explorer" (392). Nothing is said there about Eliot's tone, yet Hill's "Annunciations" can be read as an essay on what he will later call the various "pitches" of words such as "sacrifice" and "Love." Interestingly enough, Hill's own key to the poem makes no comment on the evident theological dimension of the poem.

The first part of "Annunciations" puts in play both the Christian mystery of the Annunciation and the smaller annunciations that poets make when writing poems. It considers Christ as the Eternal Logos, and poems as words that strive for literary immortality by way of agreed aesthetic value. Let us focus on the Christian reading first. Hill records the economy of Trinitarian action after the fact: the Logos has been born through the Spirit, has suffered, died, been resurrected by the Father, and is now ascended into heaven. The "steam of beasts" in the stable outside Bethlehem is now a distant memory; he enters heaven "with a tanned look," with the mud of the grave still on him from his short time there, with the signs of having been whipped, and having been turned already into a leather bound book, the New Testament. (The perspective of eternity allows for a dramatic foreshortening of worldly history, it would seem.) His crucifixion has been a "cleansing," as far as sinful humanity in Pilate's Jerusalem sees things. Doubtless the thirty pieces of silver given to Judas were indeed "Touchable, overt, clean to the touch." More, the "reward" is Christianity as an established religion, which has churches, benefices, properties, artworks, and so on, that are also "Touchable, overt, clean to the touch." To be sure, the tanning of Christ—his flagellation—and his crucifixion have been no more than toil and trouble to the Roman soldiers assigned the tasks; the hard work has "killed them" for the day, as we say colloquially. Now we see Christ as pure in holy images, as though his turbulent time on Earth was no more than a holiday from heaven. His Middle Eastern flesh even looks as though he has a suntan: the dirt of the grave has been conveniently edited out of the picture, and even biblical scrolls and printed Bibles have become beautiful and valuable objects.

Once the Church is established, celibate clerics set themselves apart from the vulgar faithful with their odious bestial acts, and analyze their sins in penitential handbooks and moral theologies. The "searchers" (priests, martyrs and all) and "curers" (theologians and confessors) present themselves before the altar to receive the flesh of Christ. The sacrifice of Christ has achieved "satisfaction" or atonement, though the Mass is seen as a banquet of exquisite artistic riches that also satisfies all who attend it in quite other ways. The bread and the wine are "put down," consumed, yet also demeaned because taken without due reverence, and the soul "Purples itself," supposedly becomes one with Christ the King. Yet Christ's sacrifice has had the effect of generating a form of life that is no more than feasting, materially and aesthetically, of easing "the flesh," a metaphor for concupiscence, and getting purple in the face through overindulging at table. Each "eye squats full and mild": it rests on the fat flesh of the cheeks. At the same time, we hear that each "I" squats on a toilet and expels what has been consumed as so much waste. Christian culture, whether low or high ("fiddle" or "harp") is used for "betterment": moral improvement by aesthetic means or, just as likely, pulling the strings and complaining endlessly until one gets what one wants in life. Christians have "decent mouths"—they take themselves to be moral beings—while they consume the Word that is at once the innocent Jesus who was tortured to death and the Christ who has been aestheticized in icons and cleaned up in saccharine popular religious art so as to become "the sweetest sacrifice."

Much more could be said of this account of Christianity doubled with a severe criticism of the faith, but I wish to note that the same poem also speaks of poetry and literary criticism, and more generally of the entire literary world. For Hill, this *is* the meaning of "Annunciations," though I think it would be hard to rule out the reading I have ventured first. On my understanding, the poetic word is a phased counterpart of the Christian Logos: poets and their critics all benefit from the sacrifice of the poet. Mallarmé and Eliot both sought a poetics of purity. The one wanted, as he said by way of Edgar Allan Poe, "Donner un sens plus pur aux mots de la tribu" while the other translated the same sentiment in "Little Gidding," taking it as his own, as "To purify the dialect of the tribe."[12] Yet this act of cleansing through artistic sacrifice has become literary parricide, and a rather hard job at that, for the tribe apparently keeps on multiplying its filth, and thereby making more business for art. Poets and critics are ultimately complicit; together they feast on their benefits of the literary world (fame, prizes, professorships, grants, residencies), and the sacrifice that art calls for from the artist is itself rendered in aesthetic-religious terms ("inspiration") and becomes an aesthetic object that supposedly provides an avenue for moral improvement or, more likely, a way to climb the greasy pole of social status.

Clichés about the economy of salvation and the life of the Church, or literary production and evaluation, can be seen to be ordered to a range of meanings, high and low, in the key words of the first of "Annunciations." The second of the two poems would also yield a long reading marked by double inscription, one that would delineate the various "pitches" of "Love." The Love that is addressed is at once God and the speaker's beloved, and the address takes the form of a prayer. God is the "subject" (as Barth insists), never the object, and always has the daily motion of the Earth before him, which includes many prayers that resemble pawning one's sins.[13] From another perspective, romantic love becomes subject to habit and everydayness, including routine sex ("the daily grind"). Marriage is seen as a contract: love is pledged and redeemed in sex. So the beloved is asked to reveal herself for the sake of love, and also, *sotto voce*, to make herself sexually available because mortality is forever pressing on us. (We think inevitably of Marvell's "To His Coy Mistress.") Women visited by angels or by demons, good men and bad, are enjoined to "Enter these deaths according to the law," that is, to honor the contract that life ends in death and also to submit to the law of marriage and yield to the husband's desire for sex and for *les petites morts*.

At the same time, men are addressed; they are "possessed sons," dominated by evil spirits or subject to Government or another power. The lines that follow give a strong sense of an invading army raping women; there is sexual death (orgasm) and physical death after the sex is over (women dying in the gutter), the latter regarded by way of aesthetic value ("colourful blood"). The poem rises to its central line, "Our God scatters corruption," which means at once that the God of European Christians is Almighty, able to eliminate evil and bring on the Kingdom of the pure, and that this same God makes the Earth more corrupt by evils caused by the complacency, violence, and immoral practices of the Church, whether through crusades, missionary activity overseas or collusion with the established political order at home. Love, whether it be God, the Church, or the poet's beloved, is enjoined to "recognize the damned among your friends," namely to purify the "faithful" and to keep a watchful eye on those who may frustrate your ends. They may be evil, and your ends may be evil as well. When God or the speaker's beloved is instructed to recognize the damned, the addressee may well be being told to watch out for the one speaking the poem or even for himself or herself.

What are we to make of a poem such as "Annunciations" that is systemically given to equivocation? Hill's answer in his notes to the poem and in later interviews, and one that has been very widely accepted by his readers, is that the poetry is a diagnosis of the difficulty of life, especially moral decision. "Difficulty," of course, is Hill's preferred word, and we should first hear in it the meaning "the opposite of *ease* or *facility*" (*OED*), the very things that Hill associates with late Eliot and Larkin. Hill's poetry would therefore perform the critical task of helping we fallen creatures to see that moral, religious and political situations are not guided blandly by clichés, but properly require a differentiated sense of shaded meanings, which run from the vulgar to the elevated, from the everyday to the sublime, and that conceal one another at our cognitive and moral risk. On this understanding of Hill, we value him for repeatedly drawing our attention to the danger of simplifying situations, of failing to recognize ambivalence, and of aestheticizing that which is properly moral, political or religious, and, in doing so, apparently neutralizing such situations only to add more disreputable moral, political and religious consequences to our account. His poems draw unflinching attention to their own status as poetry, and once again we are reminded of how Emmanuel Levinas calls for art to abandon its will to perfection on ethical grounds in his fierce essay "Reality and its Shadow."[14] Not only "September Song" but also each and every early poem seems to whisper, "This is more than enough," because it fears its own will to art at the risk of moral misadventure.[15] We are checked by the very poem we read, although of course we may well pick up on the very equivocation of the poem we are reading, and admire Hill's poetry all the more for exceeding all aesthetic economies and overflowing with ethical significance. What appears to be self-criticism can be received as self-protection against criticism.

There is another sense of difficulty in play, however, that is also in line with the uncommon equivocation practiced by Hill. I am thinking of "difficulty" as meaning "hindrance to action" (*OED*). Many things can hinder someone from action, beginning with moral scruples, continuing to weakness of will, and ending with a rooted resistance to charity. To recognize that virtue has a dark side, to understand that everything that can be used can also be abused, is to be wisely, if sadly, informed about human nature. Thus informed, one can make a choice, wear it, and put off the temptation of being what Hegel calls a "beautiful soul," yearning for something but being unable to act in order to get it.[16] Yet Hill's uncommon equivocation differs from this reasonable preparation for any decision. To regard everything human as systemically equivocal, to abide in a state that Husserl calls "inhibited decision," is to leave oneself and the reader in moral paralysis.[17] Modalization of one's views, even one's certainties, happens, as we know, but it tends to prepare one to make a decision rather than block the possibility forever. If one cannot affirm God because the fear of corruption comes to the fore alongside the desire for purity, then one stands outside religion. Of course, one does not thereby stand securely on a secular ground, for precisely the same situation obtains with any political or social program: it too is caught in an aporia of purity and corruption. And yet we should note that Hill equivocates himself in the central line of the second part of "Annunciations." There, as we know, we are told, "Our God scatters corruption." We need to distinguish between belief in divine power and the acts of the self-proclaimed agents of that power, both ecclesial and earthly. Belief in the almighty God does not, in itself, imply corruption, and to suggest that it does is equivocation as a logical fallacy with moral import. The person who reads the line "Our God scatters corruption" and finds himself or herself caught between the will to believe and repulsion at hypocrisy is the unwitting victim of equivocation. For it is always possible to fight to improve the state of things, including the moral character of Christianity.

Hill's preferred vocabulary is drawn from Christianity, in his understanding of poetry as well as more generally: he speaks of the poet's sense of "atonement" and "grace."[18] And while he is adept at recovering economic metaphors at the heart of doctrine, it is not those metaphors that he works the hardest. His most persistent religious belief seems to be in original sin; he has a theological anthropology even when writing on political, social and moral themes. It is this primal sin, Hooker thought, which prevents us from engaging in hard reasoning and making difficult decisions. In a sense, Hill's poetry exemplifies less the sheer difficulty of moral, political and religious situations than the fallen nature of the one who delineates the difficulty in such a way that it hinders making any decision about it. The poetry is more about the effects of original sin, as Hill conceives it (and, doubtless, as influenced by Hooker), than has been credited; it is a poetry that stands at a remove from the Grace that overcomes the effects of original sin even while it sees no alternative. Except of course in one sphere, that of poetry, where Hill finds the possibility of atonement and grace because he ventures into the arena and composes poems. Hill may regard the Word with suspicion, but he nonetheless deals with words, and does so with attention and respect: the second sense of "difficulty" always recurs to the first sense, without, however, ever being quite dispelled.

PART THREE

Three Australian poets

8

Susannah without the cherub

In Fragment A of "Jubilate Agno" (1758–63) Christopher Smart intones, "Let Susanna bless with the Butterfly—beauty hath wings, but chastity is the Cherub."[1] The allusion is to the history of Susannah and the elders, one of the Additions to the Book of Daniel—along with the Prayer of Azariah, and the story of Bel and the dragon—that enters the Christian Bible by way of the Septuagint and, more surely, Theodotion's translation of the Hebrew Bible into Greek. In placing the story at the end of the book of Daniel, St. Jerome allowed it into the Vulgate, the new Latin translation of the Bible. During the Reformation, however, Protestants relegated the story to the Apocrypha, although the Fathers of the Council of Trent in their fourth session (April 18, 1546) confirmed Jerome's judgment, declaring the whole of the Vulgate to be binding for the faithful.[2] Only later, in 1566, did Sixtus of Sienna coin the word "deuterocanonical," designating those texts accepted by Trent but omitted in some earlier canons, mostly eastern. One of these texts is the history of Susannah. Neither a Catholic nor a Protestant would find much to dispute in Smart's line about the story, however. In just one sentence he condenses its drama and a good deal of the tension that has marked its reception in literature, the visual arts, and opera, as well as biblical studies.

Largely because of its extensive treatment in the arts, especially in cinquecento painting, the story of Susannah, or at least an imaginative construction of it, is well-known. Let us content ourselves for the moment with what the Bible says. Susannah was living in exile in Babylon with her prosperous husband, Joacim, with whom she has had children. One day as usual she goes out into the garden for a walk, and two elders—judges, no less, and friends of Joacim—see her and, we are told, "their lust was inflamed toward her" (Dan. 13:8), and, thereafter, they watch her day by day. Walking another day in the garden and, finding it a hot afternoon, Susannah sends her two maids back to the house for oil and washing balls so that she may bathe; and when she is apparently alone, she is accosted by the two elders who have been laying in wait for her and have locked the garden gates. They propose that she sleep with them or they will bear false witness against her, declaring that they will say that they discovered her having sexual intercourse in the garden with a young man. Susannah cries out, as Torah requires her to do when threatened (Deut. 22:24), is shamed at her trial by the removal of her veil, and is about to be stoned to death for adultery, when the young Daniel intervenes and, with some clever cross-examination of the elders, saves her, and has the two elders executed instead.

Right at the start of the story, the narrator stresses two things about Susannah, that she is "a very fair woman, and one that feared the Lord" (Dan. 13:2). In Smart's words, she is both butterfly and cherub, beautiful and chaste. It is the first of the two qualities that has excited or worried painters, poets and exegetes, some of whom have quietly transformed beauty into seductiveness, thereby making Susannah into a highly ambiguous figure.[3] She can be associated with the temptress Eve in the Garden of Eden, or with the virtues of the Virgin Mary, the *hortus conclusus* or enclosed garden.[4] More generally, the narrative can be pushed toward the profane or the sacred, becoming the story of an attempted rape, supposedly provoked by female beauty, or the story of a good woman's moral fortitude. Some details in the thirteenth chapter of Daniel lend themselves to either interpretation. The garden is one example, as the figures of Eve and Mary show. Another is the water and oil that Susannah's maids are to bring. They allow us to imagine a nude woman about to bathe (as one finds in paintings of the scene by Tintoretto and Ludovico Carracci, for example).[5] Equally, though, they can prompt us to meditate upon the water as signifying baptism and the oil as a symbol of the Holy Spirit (as one finds in Hippolytus of Rome's commentary on the story).[6] And, of course, it is possible to hold the fleshly and the spiritual together, as some early Christians did, and take the story to be a defense of marriage and, hence, of human sexuality.[7] After all, at the end of her trial, Susannah's parents "praised God for their daughter Susanna, with Joacim her husband, and all the kindred, because there was no dishonesty found in her" (Dan. 13:63).

The history of Susanna is a short narrative, only sixty-four verses in the King James Bible. Over the centuries, the plot has been stretched so that it begins before the beginning depicted in Daniel. Sometimes this stretching is in order to make more of the characters of the two elders, allowing them to be treated as comic or tragic figures, or both.[8] Sometimes it is to give a bigger role to the young Daniel, so that he may rival Susannah as the central figure of the drama.[9] Also, the narrative has been contracted to a single point, the bathing scene, which, interestingly, is not a part of the biblical story. There never is a moment in Daniel 13 when Susannah begins to take off her clothes. Now the story does not need its narrative frame made larger in order to be cast as a *Bildungsroman*, moral exemplum, legal debate, or reversal tale.[10] Yet the more that it is expanded, the more the story tends to become a moral or divine narrative. And the more it is contracted to the imaginary point of the bathing scene, the more the morality fades before the allure of a naked young woman. The contrast is most acute in the sixteenth century. On the one hand, in Italian painting we find rather a lot of exposed, illuminated female flesh. And on the other hand, in British drama and narrative poetry, we hear much about the triumph of virtue.[11]

A. D. Hope's poem "The Double Looking Glass" (1960) is decidedly at one with the Italian painters and not with the English poets.[12] This is partly because of the poem's intense sensuality and partly because, like the paintings, it attends to a stretched moment that is imagined to occur between verses seventeen and eighteen in Daniel 13, the undressing and bathing of Susannah. One might well say that Hope, although he is an admirer of Smart, nonetheless relates the story of Susannah without the cherub.[13] She is surely the most highly sexualized of all literary representations of Susannah, more so than Wallace Stevens's Susannah in his "Peter Quince at the Clavier" (1915), a strong poem, though one more concerned with the effects of female beauty on men than with Susannah's self-eroticism.[14] Stevens's Susannah may sigh "For so much melody," but the center of the poem's concern is "the strain / Waked in the elders," and the old men's reaction to seeing her bathing. Stevens focuses on Susannah but not to the exclusion of the elders; he presents at least the bare outlines of the action before he meditates on it. Hope concentrates more intently on just the one imagined moment in the biblical narrative, and drains the elders of almost all character. They have no comic or tragic dimension; they are, in effect, the male gaze presented at maximum intensity and spiced with as much wickedness as possible.

To speak of Susannah without the cherub is not to say that Hope slights the biblical heritage of the story. On the contrary, his poem relates and extends the story in a familiar biblical way, midrash, albeit in an unfamiliar direction. The poem also remains consistent with a traditional understanding of Daniel 13 as a reading of the Song of Songs. Nor does the recognition of Hope's Susannah as a sexually mature woman, fantasizing about a lover on a warm afternoon, carry an implication that she is a temptress. The storyteller of Daniel 13, presumably a man of the Second Temple period, must think that Susannah is at least likely to entice men in order to tell the story the way he does.[15] Not so Hope: she is a perfectly normal young woman as far as he is concerned; and the very painting which gave Hope the idea for the poem, Paolo Veronese's "Susanna al Bagno" (distinct from his "Susanna e i Vecchioni"), presents a more demure, more covered, woman than one finds in other Italian paintings of the imagined bath scene.[16] The poem is a complex one, formally and thematically, drawing on modern poetics as well as biblical narrative and lyric, and, to my mind, its central concerns have never been properly explicated, beginning with the title.[17] What is a double looking glass? Is it something depicted in the poem? Or is it the poem itself? What are we to make of the image of a looking glass, and of the motif of doubling? What do all these things tell us about Hope's view of human sexuality, both male and female? These are the questions that will guide my reading of the poem.

I will begin by letting the title hover over the poem, whether like a butterfly (for it is a beautiful title) or like a cherub (for it seems to know a great deal), and move directly to the poem itself.[18] The first line takes us deeply into the poem and into Hope's poetics: "See how she strips her lily for the sun." The image of the flower is hardly accidental. Susannah, in Hebrew, is Shoshana, which signifies "lily" and which is taken by the early Church Fathers to mean chastity.[19] More directly, we recall the well-known lines from the Song of Songs: "I *am* the rose of Sharon, *and* the lily of the valleys. As the lily among thorns, so *is* my love among the daughters" (Song 2:1-2). And, like Philo of Carpasius, we take them to be spoken by the Bride, not the Bridegroom.[20] Accordingly, the history of Susannah in Daniel can be read as a long, parabolic gloss on these lines in the Song of Songs, in which the elders are the thorns, and needless to say other lines can be brought in to support such a reading, especially "A garden inclosed *is* my sister, *my* spouse; a spring shut up, a fountain sealed" (Song 4:12).[21] About a third of the way through the poem Susannah looks around her and murmurs, "Safe in their sunny banks the lilies grow, / Secure from rough hands for another day." She thinks or half-thinks of herself as a flower among other flowers, not realizing that she is scarcely secure from rough hands this very day. And later she imagines a young man making love to her: "[H]e lies / And feeds among the lilies." Again, she is a flower, and she daydreams on what her mother most likely has told her about flowers and bees.

Throughout the poem Hope eschews allegorical interpretation of the history of Susannah, for which we can be thankful, and draws on the eroticism of the Song of Songs in a perfectly frank way. It should be said at the outset that "The Double Looking Glass" is not a Christian poem in any sense, not even hermeneutically (the phoenix, for example, is not a figure of Christ), nor is it a Jewish poem in any significant way, except for a naturalized use of midrash.[22] Yet it is, as we shall see, a religious poem, one whose religiosity is one with human sexuality. So when we hear the word "lily" in the first line, we think rightly when we think immediately of the whiteness of Susannah's flesh. From the very beginning we are directed to look at her: "*See* how she strips her lily for the sun" [my emphasis]. She is not performing a striptease, yet we are invited to see her undress not with us in mind, as though we are looking at her through a peephole. The reader is invited to become a voyeur.

That voyeurism courts violence is acknowledged quickly and lightly, for the adverb "how" is fulfilled not only by a visual image of the girl lifting

off her silk garment but also by the sound of it being removed, "The silk
shrieks upward from her wading feet" [my emphasis]. The first lines of the
poem anticipate the last lines when the hidden elders run up to her, and
Susannah cries out in a rush of plosives, "I am undone! / What beards, what
bald heads burst now from the bush!" The meeting of beginning and end is
elegantly managed, although it hardly distracts us from the introduction of
other dualities: the upward gesture of undressing, and the movement of the
water down in the pool; the slow wading of Susannah in the pool and the
echoes that quickly run, as though the consequences of her action hasten
to bring about a dénouement; and the encounter of "shade and substance."
The brightness of the water meets with the whiteness of Susannah's flesh;
each is candid—frank and fortunate. Yet the meeting of shade and substance
sends other ripples through the poem: the coolness of the shade welcomes
the warm flesh, sure, but also the unreal meets the real (the young man
Susannah imagines as a lover will be a "melancholy shade"), and a real
darkness touches the body (anticipating the attack of the elders now lurking
in the dark bushes). Susannah's candor in her desire for refreshment, as
well as in her sexual fantasy, is more than matched by the elders' candor in
their predatory gazes. It should be clear that the symmetry of "Candour with
candour" is followed by what will be developed as an asymmetry: Susannah's
idle fantasy of having a young, strong lover, and the elders' plot to force her
into having sex with them.

The narrative glides from viewpoint to viewpoint, first from the narrator to
Susannah to the elders, and thereafter as the drama of the poem requires.
Susannah imagines eyes that "Lurk in the laurels," although for now she
allows them perhaps to belong to birds, just as at first the whisper she hears
is that of the "crisp air" in the "dimple of her belly." Yet with the mention
of the birds' eyes we cut to the elders who note Susannah's armpit as she
raises her arm ("Yawn of the oxter") and so moves her "liquid breast." Their
emotion underlines more heavily the theme of doubling that has already been
sounded: "this rage of double double hearts," by which we are to picture two
old men, outwardly pious yet inwardly sinful, hiding in the bushes. No sooner
than this theme of doubling is marked than it is lightened by Susannah's
rationalization of her vague sense of being watched:

Here all things have imagined counterparts:
A dragon-fly dim-darting in the stream

Follows and watches with enormous eyes
His blue narcissus glitter in the air.
The flesh reverberates its own surprise
And startles at the act which makes it bare.

It is hard to decide whether "imagined" or "counterparts" is the more disturbing word in these lines. "Imagined" carries us along lightly at the start, for we think of reflections and shadows, and we enjoy the delicate modulation by way of Narcissus into a brilliant image of auto-affection, which assures Susannah of her animal nature and her rights in "the great web of being," and will in turn give rise to the sexual fantasy to which much of the poem is devoted. Yet the idea of Susannah being "Laced with quick air" should give us pause; it may prettify her nakedness but, at the same time, it fortifies the elders' lust. We know that there are humans in the bushes who are real, not imaginary. Later, Susannah will imaginatively suppose the glints in the bushes to be "the gleam / Of eyes; the eyes of a young man in love," and the sharp irony will be that all along they have been the eyes of the men who want to force her into having sexual relations with them. The elders are her "counterpart" only in the most bitter sense, as predators to her prey, an image of them that is inevitable given the elders' dreadful questions, "Who shall be first upon her? Who shall stand / To watch the dragon sink its fangs in blood?" Yet we are prompted to think of Daniel slaying the dragon in Daniel 14:23-30. It is the only time in the poem when there is an allusion to justice, and it is a very faint one at best.

Although we are only a few stanzas into "The Double Looking Glass" it should already be clear that Hope was not misleading us when he said that "I had the idea of writing a poem in a style suggested by certain poems of Mallarmé and Valéry."[23] One vanishing point of Hope's poem is Stéphane Mallarmé's "L'Après-midi d'un Faune" (1876), itself inspired by a painting, François Boucher's "Pan et Syrinx" (1759). Reading Mallarmé's poem with Hope's beside it, and as though with his eyes, we quickly recognize a shared love of a heavy, warm afternoon, and a sharply registered sensuousness in the presentation of it. Think of Mallarmé's "*l'immobile et lasse pâmoison / Suffoquant de chaleurs le matin frais s'il lutte*" ["the still and weary fainting / Suffocating the fresh morning with heat"].[24] In several of Hope's stanzas we can imagine him being spurred to match the lyric splendors of the lines toward the end of Mallarmé's poem:

Tu sais, ma passion que, pourpre et déjà mûre,
Chaque grenade éclate et d'abeilles murmure;
Et notre sang, épris de qui le va saisir,
Coule pour tout l'essaim éternal du désir. (165)

[You know, my passion, purple and already ripe,
Each pomegranate bursts and murmurs with bees,
And our blood, in love with anyone who wants it,
Flows in all the eternal swarm of desire.]

More generally, in placing Mallarmé's eclogue beside Hope's poem, we find an emphasis on our life as grounded in our animal nature (*"blancheur animale"* ["animal whiteness"]); observe desire being transmuted into art; and find dualisms aplenty, including that of illusion and reality. We also find a stress on imagination and sexuality as each being able to perpetuate the objects of desire. And we even find lilies. The faun's question—*"Aimai-je un rêve?"* [Did I love a dream?]—almost could be Susannah's. She tells herself, "And I could dream myself in love as well / As dream my lover in the summer trees," and reveals herself as somewhat more self-knowing and self-confident than the faun. Just one more parallel: *"le splendide bain de cheveux"* ["Splendid cascade of tresses"] seems to be repeated, with gorgeous inflections of its own, in Hope's lines about Susannah's "full / Cascade of tresses whispering down her flanks." Perhaps what inspired Hope the most in Mallarmé's poem, though, is less its local images and euphony than its tone and general ambience. "L'Après-midi d'un Faune" is a narrative that is almost overwhelmed by its lyricism; "The Double Looking Glass" sometimes approaches the same condition.

Like "L'Après-midi d'un Faune," "The Double Looking Glass" seems to embody what Paul Valéry called "harmonious exchange between expression and impression," and it does so in order that "between the form and the content, between the sound and the sense, between the poem and the state of poetry, a symmetry is revealed, an equality between importance, value, and power, which does not exist in prose."[25] As with many others, Valéry was taken with Mallarmé's essay "Crise de Vers" (1886–96), especially with the view of poetry as a supplement that smoothes over the mimetic failures of languages. Here is a well-known passage:

> Put beside *ombre* [shade], which is opaque, *ténèbres* [shadows] is not so dark; what disillusion, before the perversity that has *jour* [day] sound dark and *nuit* [night] sound light. The hope for a word of brilliant splendor, or being extinguished, inversely; when the alternatives of light and dark are at issue.—*Only*, we must understand that poetry would not exist: philosophically, it makes up for what language lacks: it is a superior supplement.[26]

Following Mallarmé, Valéry espoused what Gérard Genette calls a "secondary Cratylism," namely the idea that each word is doubled, being both raw and essential, and that although language itself cannot reduce the arbitrary nature of the sign, which would be "primary Cratylism," poetry can compensate for this loss.[27] Certainly the initial shriek of the silk is heard in the whispers, real or imagined, of the elders in the bushes: "Susannah! ... what hiss, what rustle in the sedge; // What fierce susurrus shifts from bush to bush." Yet more generally the world that Hope evokes in the poem is a motivated one, in which "earth and water, branch and beast and stone / Speak to the naked in their nakedness." Motivation is a formal and decorative feature of the poem but more importantly it is its thematic ground. It supports the central image of the mirror in which there is delusive commerce between inside and outside, essence and accident, and which leads to Susannah's fantasy.

The image of the mirror is introduced and then almost immediately doubled. As the sun warms her, Susannah relaxes and muses. That she has no good reason to feel so calm is delicately suggested first by the allusion to the "hairy bee" that is a "bold ravisher" of flowers. (When the elders burst upon the scene the first thing Susannah exclaims about them is "What beards …!") Second, her precarious position is hinted by the image of the fig tree that touches her "with warm broad hands of harmless shade." (Presumably, since it is noon, she stands directly under the fig tree, which must grow over the pool.) We know from the Talmud (*Berachos* 40a, *Sanhedrin* 70a) that the fig tree is a strong candidate for the Tree of Knowledge of Good and Evil: Adam and Eve cover themselves with fig leaves, suggesting that they are close to the fig tree. And the image of the fig as the tree's genitalia is a familiar one. Thinking of the shade as "harmless" (while we also think of how "shade and substance" have met innocently and will soon meet violently), Susannah reflects:

> My garden holds me like its private dream,
> A secret pleasure, guarded and apart.
> Now as I lean above the pool I seem
> The image of my image in its heart.
>
> In that inverted world a scarlet fish
> Drifts through the trees and swims into the sky,
> So in the contemplative mind a wish
> Drifts through its mirror of eternity,
>
> A mirror for man's images of love
> The nakedness of woman is a pool
> In which her own desires mount and move,
> Alien, solitary, purposeful.

Susannah is a female Narcissus, as we have seen, the allusion being to book three of Ovid's *Metamorphoses*, the story of how Narcissus cannot possess his beloved image, and perhaps also to Valéry's various poems on Narcissus— "Narcisse parle," "Fragments du Narcisse" and his *La Cantate Narcisse* (1941)—with their meditations on the deep self and the purity of gazing at oneself rather than on others.[28] Ovid has the young man say "*inopem me copia fecit*," that his own possessions, his good looks, have dispossessed him; and this turns out also to be true of Susannah, although in a different way. (Arthur Golding renders the line "my plentie makes me poore."[29]) Later, though, Susannah sees herself as an image when she says to herself of her imagined lover that he is "Possessed by what he never can possess."

In Ovid's version of the myth, the sixteen-year old boy who had refused the advances of Echo, lay down beside a pool. Arthur Golding translates as follows:

> The stripling wearie with the heate and hunting in the chace,
> And much delighted with the spring and coolnesse of the place,
> Did lay him downe upon the brim: and as he stooped lowe
> To staunche his thurst, another thurst of worse effect did growe.
> For as he dranke, he chaunst to spie the Image of his face,
> The which he did immediately with fervent love embrace.
> He feedes a hope without cause why. For like a foolishe noddie
> He thinkes the shadow that he sees, to be a lively boddie. (75)

For Ovid, Narcissus falls in love with his own image and pines away. Yet for Hope, Susannah becomes fascinated by an image of her nakedness, and far from wasting away enjoys desiring herself, which she takes to be a natural right. She has entered a dream world in which she is an image of an image, here a metaphor of liberation rather than diminishment. It is noon, and it is as though time has stopped. The mind has become a "mirror of eternity": in his phrasing Hope follows Thomas Traherne rather than St. Paul in thinking that in love we can perceive the eternal clearly rather than obscurely (1 Cor. 13:12). In the fourth lyric of "Thoughts" Traherne prays, "O give me Grace to see thy face, and be / A constant Mirror of Eternity."[30] Not that Hope uses the allusion to Traherne to establish a religious context: the relation between the two poems is too delicate and too distant for that. Besides, the wish that drifts through Susannah's mind as though in eternity is presumably a wish for erotic love, and is the beginning of her sexual fantasy. The logic of the poem in these central stanzas means that eternity, rather than real, is itself an image of an image. Nor does the poem's logic stop here, for the pool is transferred from a natural object to a metaphor. Thus the image of inversion is doubled, and at once inverted and doubled *as image*, for now the mirror has become female flesh rather than the mind, a flesh that was not so long ago an image of an image.

The significance of the poem's title now begins to come into focus. It does not denote a two-way mirror and simply invite voyeurism. That is impossible because Susannah sees herself in the pool, and we see her in the poem. The pool is a mirror that reflects Susannah's desires that are slowly stimulated by auto-affection, while Susannah's nakedness is itself a mirror for male desire, which is produced by imaginative hetero-affection. (Again we may well think of Traherne, this time of the line "At once the Mirror and the Object be."[31]) The poem is about a double looking glass, a clear pool that invites female nakedness, which in turn is figured as a mirror of male desire. Part of the point of the poem, however, is that desire is not symmetrical along the male-female axis. A man's desire is for a naked woman; a woman's desires are generated by the act of looking at her image, and only then are developed as a response to male desire. Because the poem figures both pool and female nakedness as mirrors it is itself a double looking glass, a mirror that directly reflects the two irreducible sources of human desire, male and female. And yet the implied reader of the poem is not doubled. The reader is anticipated as male (hence the coding of female desire as "alien"). For his desire becomes visible in Susannah's nakedness, and the only chance of the poem facilitating auto-affection is the unlikely one of a female reader seeing herself, not anyone else, in Susannah.

"The Double Looking Glass" is a poem that is characterized by distinct modes of saturation, as Jean-Luc Marion would say, different ways in which intuitions exceed any intentional rapport that its characters have with other characters or that its male readers have with the object of their desire. For the elders, and for male readers, Susannah is saturated with respect to quality: she exceeds any concept, including the ones offered in Daniel and in patristic commentaries, of her person and character ("a very fair woman and one that feared the Lord"). Her beauty is almost unbearable in its extreme visibility: as a character Susannah is like a work of art (she seems, as she says, to be the "image of my image") and needless to say she *is* a work of art. Susannah dazzles us with her "glowing thighs," her "liquid breast," "the braided treasure of her hair," the "silver rising of her arms," her "ripeness," and all this even before we get to "the white embraces of [her] thighs." No mention is made of her husband or her children: she is never seen as wife or mother but only offered to the gaze as a nubile young thing. In Marion's terms, she is an idol, an "invisible mirror" that fits exquisitely into the male gaze and returns it, giving us not the satisfaction of erotic experience so much as counter-experience, in which the conditions of possibility for experience are contested.[32] Strictly speaking, even if we talk of Susannah as a "sexual object" she is not really an object; we see more of a glow than a woman, we encounter more of a rush of eroticism than the bringing into focus of a face and a body, let alone a person. Men do not experience her so much as realize sadly that she cannot be experienced.

For Susannah herself, however, it is the category of relation that is saturated, and the phenomenon of her flesh is given to her in the identity of what is felt and the one who feels. In a poem that is intensely visual in its registration of the garden and the pool, we find momentarily a high poetry of the invisible: "The flesh reverberates its own surprise / And startles at the act which makes it bare." It is this auto-affection that introduces Susannah's desire in the poem, a "voluptuous heat" that the narrator declares "alien," doubtless in part because it is "solitary," not needing a man, at least not at first. This auto-affection individualizes Susannah even as she comes to know her place "In the great web of being," feel its rightness, and claim her rights. Solitary as her desire is, it nonetheless prepares her for an imaginary relation in the fantasy of the young man who is in the garden and secretly watching her. "My garden holds me like its private dream," she tells herself, and later concedes that the young man, her imagined counterpart, "lives but in my dream," which makes her lover a dream within a dream.[33] "The Double Looking Glass" is not only one of the great poems of afternoon (like "L'Après-midi d'un Faune," which it rivals in formal perfection), but also, like Mallarmé's eclogue, a great poem of languorous daydreaming, although with a more overt element of sexual fantasizing. It is hard to think of other works with which to compare it in this regard.

Finally, the event evoked in the poem is presented as saturated with respect to quantity. The event is given in three horizons—Susannah's, the elders' and the narrator's—which cannot be made to converge. It is strictly unforeseeable. For although we anticipate what will happen in the poem merely from knowing the biblical narrative we have no clear idea how the event will be played out or indeed what will be the main event of the poem. One might argue that the main "event" of the poem, which surely takes us by surprise, is the sexual fantasy in which Susannah luxuriates. Because it is an internal event, overheard rather than heard, no one other than Susannah can master it, and she of course takes pleasure in that mastery, saying to herself, "for I may end it when I please." Even more persuasive would be an argument that the crucial event of the poem is the vision that is the culmination of the fantasy. If the elders see Susannah "in the flush / Of her desires" as she daydreams about the young man, they are denied seeing the vision. In good biblical fashion, they dream dreams—albeit nasty ones—while the young see visions (Joel 2:28). In point of fact the vision is not properly seen by anyone, not even by Susannah; it is barely apprehended, and only then in highly symbolic terms. The truth of the event is essentially withheld from us, perhaps because it cannot be spoken.

Susannah imagines a young man who "watches from the grove" and crouches "Beside the pool to see me at my bath." She speculates that he has "seen me only by the way," and that he ventures all he has "Only to see me in my nakedness." Having admired her own beauty, Susannah's fantasy now is of being the object of a male gaze, and she figures her sexuality in terms of it, picturing herself kindling "my fire at his imagined fire." The sexual act,

as she conceives it, passes from the dreamlike to the visionary. Her young
man is on a quest romance, though one that has a surprising dénouement:

> In ancient woods that murmur with the sea,
> He finds once more the garden and the pool.
> And there a man who is and is not he
> Basks on the sunny margin in the full
>
> Noon of another and a timeless sky,
> And dreams but never hopes to have his love;
> And there the woman who is also I
> Watches him from the hollow of the grove;
>
> Till naked from the leaves she steals and bends
> Above his sleep and wakes him with her breast
> And now the vision begins, the voyage ends,
> And the great phoenix blazes in his nest.

The visionary narrative is also a reversal tale, though not as in Daniel where
the elders rather than Susannah are punished. In terms of Hope's own
poetry, the vision turns the tables on the image of alienated man in "The
Wandering Islands" (1943) where we see "the shipwrecked sailor" who
"sits on the shore and sullenly masturbates."[34] It revises the image of female
sexuality suggested in "Imperial Adam" (1952) in which Eve is a "tender
parody" of Adam and is "Sly as the snake."[35] And in terms of the Susannah
in the book of Daniel, the narrative is reversed in two quite different ways.

First of all, "The Double Looking Glass" turns around the biblical narrative
in which the elders make up the young man in order to blackmail Susannah
and then to bear false witness against her. Now this reversal has been
attempted before, however. Hippolytus of Rome proposes that, in a sense,
the elders were right, even when intending to tell a lie: "there was in reality
a young man with her ... one from heaven, not to have intercourse with
her, but to bear witness to her truth."[36] Daniel was spiritually present in the
garden with Susannah all along. Hope's reversal is entirely his own, though,
and is also a turnabout of Hippolytus's reading of the situation. The fiction of
the young man, purveyed with bad intent by the elders in the Bible, turns
out in the poem to be Susannah's fiction; and indeed she is imaginatively
committing adultery. When she cries out "I am undone!" she recognizes
that she is in danger from the elders but also perhaps acknowledges that
she has been discovered doing something amiss. Certainly the elders think
themselves less guilty because they propose to abuse a woman caught in the
act of adultery rather than a virtuous wife. In a peculiar but all too common

twist of reasoning they justify their intended act by positing Susannah as its cause. They tell themselves they are chastising Susannah through forced sex precisely because she is so alluring.

In the second place, in the heat of lovemaking the young man finds that the lovers' roles have been reversed, and that it is Susannah who gazes at the man who dreams of her and who takes the sexual initiative. It is with her rousing her lover that "the vision begins." A new cycle of life has started and, with it, another doubling. No doubt Hope construes the coitus as procreation—we remember his lines in "Chorale" about "the womb / Sighing for the wasted seed"—but there is more at issue than reproduction.[37] The young man has become a new Adam, and Susannah a new Eve; and we remember rabbinic legends—given in *Sanhedrin* (108b) and the *Jalkut* on Job—that the phoenix was the only creature in Eden that did not eat the fruit of the Tree of Knowledge and therefore was not banished from the Garden.[38] In any case, the phoenix is associated with a paradise. Lactantius tells us in his poem on the bird that it lives in a "grove of the sun" [*nemus Solis*].[39] Only in paradise does the woman make a sexual advance, Hope's poem tells us; or does it tell us that in the paradise of climax the man realizes that it was indeed the woman who made the sexual advance, although she effectively disguised it at the time? Either way, the final truth of love for Hope is that the man secretly desires the woman to make or to have made the initial sexual approach. Her sexuality is the more complex of the two, for it has phases of self-eroticisation, mimicking of the gaze, and a disclosure of the initial sexual approach after the fact. This final truth of love can be abused, needless to say, as happens when the elders justify their attack on her by pointing to her overt sexuality. But it is primarily the truth of a renewing vision.

"The Double Looking Glass" fills—or, better, overfills—a passing moment between verses eighteen and nineteen of Daniel 13; it is, if you like, a midrash on that imaginary moment in the biblical narrative, though one that has the effect of naturalizing the history of Susannah, removing it entirely from the realm of the sacred narrative.[40] Many signs are given in the poem that Susannah is "a very fair woman," though nowhere is it in evidence that she is "one that feared the Lord." The biblical narrative is largely uninteresting for Hope in its historiographic aspects but intensely interesting in its aesthetic possibilities, in revealing what has not been seen before in poetry deriving from the story: the presentation of Susannah as idol and as flesh, not least of all.[41] There is one exception, however, since it needs to be noted that, unlike the author of Daniel 13, Hope gives Susannah a voice: she speaks at length in the poem, to herself, granted, but nonetheless we overhear the voice of a mature woman speaking of her desires and her pleasures. So the poem is not exclusively oriented toward aesthetics. Which is not to say that it is primarily ethical, despite the mention of natural rights: as we have seen, the question of justice is barely posed. Instead, it is a poem that is concerned with and committed to a vision of sexual fulfillment, a paradise regained.

We may call "The Double Looking Glass" a religious poem if we do so with care and respect the fact that it has no confessional dimension and makes no mention of the deity. For we must recognize that it affirms transcendence of the human condition; we overcome our mortality and our separateness in the act of love, Hope thinks, and not merely by reproducing ourselves. Again, the image of the phoenix is nicely placed in the economy of the poem. Traditionally, the bird nests over a clear pool, and in this poem perhaps its home is in the fig tree. Also, in the Middle Ages it was believed to be the only animal that contains both sexes in its body.[42] The phoenix suggests the sort of transcendence that is possible for men and women when we "die" in lovemaking: we can overcome the particularity of our gender. In making love we glimpse "another and a timeless sky," that of paradise, before we are brought back to earth. All we are granted in the poem is the instant between dream and vision, between our own unconscious musings and what is given to us. The poem has an iconic moment, in which something outside our phenomenal world tries to reveal itself, but what is rendered manifest is not an object or even being but rather the possibility of a transfigured self. And so the poem has two imaginary points, only one of which, the bathing scene, is cast as a narrative; the other point, the vision itself, remains a vanishing point.

The title "The Double Looking Glass" hovers over the poem like a butterfly, to be sure, telling us that it is beautiful. And so it is. Yet the title also hangs magisterially over it, like a cherub, who, as we know, guards entrances and exits. This cherub flies over a poem that is itself a garden, a paradise, one that almost overwhelms its readers with its dazzle of sensuality and its blinding vision of human sexual fulfillment as transcendence of our mortal state. What we see of Susannah in the poem has not all been seen before; it was never so visible. The poem is not a "translation" of Veronese's "Susanna al Bagno," for instance; the painter's Susannah does not see a vision, nor does any other Italian Susannah. Like another garden, though, "The Double Looking Glass" also harbors a corrosive sense of evil, one on which it scarcely comments and certainly not directly. What urges us toward transcendence can degrade us when misdirected: such is one lesson that the butterfly and the cherub combine to teach us. It is an old, dark truth about religion, and in the final rush of the elders upon Susannah it is allowed to interrupt and truncate the vision. In a cruel irony, Susannah's sense of mastery over her daydream—"for I may end it when I please"—is already undone by dint of the elders watching her and intending to take her by surprise. The worst is to be played offstage, and we are left with a dream that became a vision and that will be smashed, at least temporarily, by a brutal reality. Of course, reality is precisely what many readers have steadily denied to the history of Susannah in consigning it to the Apocrypha or regarding it as merely a piece of pious fiction. Yet, in Hope's imaginative treatment of it, the story becomes a visionary narrative, a poem in which sensuality and transcendence cooperate rather than compete.

9

Darkness and lostness

How to read a poem by Judith Wright

One vanishing point of literary criticism, as established in the academy last century, is indicated by the title of I. A. Richards's *How to Read a Page* (1942). This remarkable little book can stand not only for the new criticism, which was already sharpening its knives, but also for the tendency, shared by various critical schools, to find the whole in the part. One might think that Richards was responding, somewhat belatedly, to Ezra Pound's tract *How to Read* (1931), or Virginia Woolf's essay "How Should One Read a Book?" (1932). Not so: he was reacting to Mortimer Adler's immensely popular *How to Read a Book* (1940), and we can take this as the balancing vanishing point of literary criticism as practiced in the twentieth century. Adler's concern was, as his subtitle puts it, "the art of a getting a liberal education," which for him was reading the canon of Western writing or, if not quite all of it, then a judicious selection. The value of tertiary education was not in question for Richards, even though he was not entirely at ease with American college and university curricula, especially the increasing emphasis being placed on higher degrees. His concern was more philosophical: did a "great books" program provide sound intellectual training? And his answer was in the negative. As he had found teaching at the University of Cambridge, even undergraduates from the best public schools might know the cultural valences of canonical authors without having anything like a decent grasp of what they were reading.[1]

Adler and Richards disagreed about speed, not value; and Richards, in particular, must have relished the title he chose for his new book. Surely it gave just the right tweak to the popular culture of "self-help" that Adler was aiding and abetting. No undergraduate at Cambridge would be seen dead with *How to Speak French Quickly and Well* (1918), for instance. One already knew how to speak French well, and one smiled faintly at the conjunction of "quickly" and "well." As we know, the popular culture of self-help expanded rapidly in all directions; and today any bookshop will offer titles that promise to teach you how to be—well, almost anything you like, from your own stock-broker to your own therapist. We find Adler's and Richards' titles listed in thick directories of "how-to" books. Of course, one still finds ironic wrinkles in this popular culture of "do it yourself": think of Harold Bloom's *How to Read and Why* (2000). Far from being a belated intervention in a culture war of sixty years before, Bloom's little book underlines that, with regard to reading at least, the culture of self-help converges with Emersonian self-reliance.[2]

Needless to say, the culture of speed has been a long time in the making. To give just two philosophical indices: Descartes regarded his greatest achievement, an infallible method, as a quick and easy way of leading "those who have not studied" to the truth, while Leibniz valued his logic because "the mind may be dispensed from the labor of having to think out clearly."[3] It would be a mistake to believe that poetry abides outside the culture of speed because it has no particular investment in method or logic. William Carlos Williams wanted to accelerate the line of modern verse, and others have followed him; besides, lyric poetry is speed itself: it does not dutifully follow the steps of method or logic. Yet readers have a lingering suspicion that poetry stands somewhere to the side of that culture. It is a haven, vaguely timeless and best approached, as Edward Hirsch puts it in his *How to Read a Poem* (1999), "in the middle of the night."[4] Publishers have long recognized that poetry readers will pay rather a lot for a nicely produced book of only a few pages. Marianne Moore's *Nevertheless* (1944) has just six poems.[5] More surely outside the culture of speed, and—we like to think—quite untouched by "speed pollution," is the spiritual life.[6] Poets may have to wait for the Muse, yet all of us must wait for God, even if we believe in prevenient Grace. As Thomas à Kempis instructs his reader, "never act in a hurry, and always be ready to alter your preconceived ideas."[7] Of course, none of this prevents people writing "how-to" books about the spiritual life: Adler himself penned one entitled *How to Think About God* (1980), and twenty-odd years later it would be no great surprise to find in Barnes and Noble a paperback on how to get instant, positive answers to your prayers or how to achieve unity with the Godhead while waiting for your fries.

In coming up with a title for this talk, I wanted to allude to Richards's book *How to Read a Page* because, after all, it was written while he was teaching at Harvard and I would be speaking here, and I thought I would take the opportunity to give a slow reading of Judith Wright's lyric "The Lost Man" from her collection *The Gateway* (1953), a lyric that is frequently taught in Australia and much loved there. Judith Wright's poems are not always conceptually exact (in the way that A. D. Hope's are, for instance), but they are never confused; and even admiring readings of "The Lost Man" tend to make it appear confused. Now the culture of speed in academia requires us to abstract from what we have not written. So I was surprised when I started to read "The Lost Man" slowly—"looking cautiously before and aft, with reservations, with doors left open, with delicate eyes and fingers," as Nietzsche says—that it is a "how-to" poem, a lyric that apparently tells us how to conduct the spiritual life.[8] I knew of course that Wright was directly or indirectly referring us to St. John of the Cross who reads his piercing poem "Una noche oscura" more slowly than any literary critic would dare to read another's lyric. Yet when I started to reread *The Ascent of Mount Carmel* I was taken aback to find that the *incipit* begins "This treatise explains how to reach divine union quickly." And when I immersed myself in "The Lost Man" I found that it was not quite the self-contained poem taking up just one page that I had believed it to be, though neither is it a poem that makes sense by referring it solely to the great books.

*

Before continuing, however, let us attend to "The Lost Man":

To reach the pool you must go through the rain forest—
through the bewildering midsummer of darkness
lit with ancient fern,
laced with poison and thorn.
You must go by the way he went—the way of the bleeding
hands and feet, the blood on the stones like flowers,
under the hooded flowers
that fall on the stones like blood.

To reach the pool you must go by the black valley
among the crowding columns made of silence,
under the hanging clouds
of leaves and voiceless birds.
To go by the way he went to the voice of the water,
where the priest stinging-tree waits with his whips and fevers
under the hooded flowers
that fall from the trees like blood,

you must forget the song of the gold bird dancing
over tossed light: you must remember nothing
except the drag of darkness
that draws your weakness under.
To go by the way he went you must find beneath you
that last and faceless pool, and fall. And falling

find between breath and death
the sun by which you live.[9]

"The Lost Man": how are we to understand the title? The usual response
is that we are invited to see a man lost in the Bush, and the assumption
is supported by the opening lines of the poem but then perplexed by what
seem to be allusions to Jesus. Critics respond not by questioning their initial
assumption and starting over but by casting doubt on the appropriateness
of Wright's use of Christian imagery or, more mildly, by distancing the poem
from any explicit commitments that this imagery suggests.[10] Yet why, apart
from the title, should we regard the speaker as talking to someone lost in the
Bush? The instructions needed to be given in that circumstance would point
him out of the rainforest, not to a pool deep inside. No matter how danger-
ously hot it is in the Bush—and we are told it is "midsummer"—it would be
foolish for anyone lost to go further into dense rainforest in search of water.
Rather, one should follow a creek or a track in the hope of finding a way out.
When they come, the allusions to Jesus walking the Via Dolorosa, if that
is what they are, offer little comfort to the interpreter who begins with the
assumption that the speaker is addressing someone lost in the Bush. We do
not think of Jesus as lost, even on his way to Mt. Calvary: on the contrary,
the lost are precisely those who have not followed the Messiah, those who
have been morally or spiritually ruined.

If we reject the assumption that the person addressed is already lost in the
Bush, we are left with two alternatives. We can regard the man as spiritually
lost but able to be saved by entering the rainforest and undergoing the depri-
vations and sufferings it embodies. (It is easy to imagine the young Arthur
Boyd painting such an image.) Or we can regard the speaker of the poem
as not addressing a man who is lost, either geographically or spiritually, but
rather giving directions to an experienced Bush walker who is on a mission
of mercy. On this reading, the directions are communicated to a rescuer who
by his very deed, is acting out the *imitatio Christi*. Once grasped, the first
alternative offers a viable reading of the lyric—the rainforest is an Australian
equivalent for Mt. Carmel, the pool being coordinate with the summit—and
the poem itself does not invite us to consider the second alternative. Yet it is
the second alternative I wish to explore, partly because I think there are good
reasons for doing so and partly because doing so will help us to reflect on the
horizon of literary criticism that I invoked at the start.

The reading I am proposing becomes more plausible if we place "The
Lost Man" in the broad context of the rescue of the survivors of the Stinson
plane crash. On February 19, 1937, a Stinson tri-motor, *The City of Brisbane*,
was flying over South-East Queensland on a routine trip from Brisbane to
Sydney via Lismore when the weather rapidly deteriorated and conditions

became cyclonic. Unable to gain sufficient altitude to cross the McPherson ranges, the plane crashed just below the summit of Point Lookout on the Lamington Plateau. Four men were killed instantly, the two pilots and two of the passengers, leaving three survivors—Joe Bimtead, John Proud, and Jim Westray—whose fate, after a few days, must have seemed even worse than that of their fellow passengers. The isolated and inhospitable jungle in which they found themselves, injured and without supplies, threatened a cruel death by exposure and starvation. Once they escaped from the wreckage, only Westray could walk. An Englishman visiting Australia on business for Lloyds of London, Westray was used to climbing alone in the Highlands of Scotland, but he was unprepared for making his way through virgin Bush in a Queensland summer.[11] Nonetheless, he set out through the misty jungle for help. While on his quest—"a valiant but hopeless attempt," as the *Sydney Mirror* put it—he fell over a waterfall near Christmas Creek and died from the injuries he sustained.[12]

A week after the plane had been reported missing, a local Bushman, Bernard O'Reilly, surmised that *The City of Brisbane* had gone down near the McPherson ranges, contrary to reports that it had been seen south of the Hawkesbury. After making his way from his homestead at Goblin Wood to Mt. Bethongabel and from there to the top of Mt Throakban, O'Reilly saw a burnt tree about eight kilometers away, and after heading in that direction for three hours, heard the cries of Binstead and Proud and discovered the smoldering wreckage of the Stinson. O'Reilly tended the two men, who had survived for ten days, and then set off for help. He followed in Westray's tracks. I quote from the narrative he wrote about the rescue, *Green Mountains* (1941): "As it had been a day of miracles, I had hopes of finding him alive also."[13] He describes walking in Westray's tracks:

> I followed the Englishman's tracks into difficult and dangerous country, down cliffs of loose rock covered with great Bird's Nest ferns which gave a false sense of security, down almost perpendicular slopes of loose earth, studded with tree ferns; down until suddenly, through a screen of palm trees I saw the torrent, boiled white around great moss-covered boulders. (38)

O'Reilly has already told us that Westray's hands were "badly burned" in the process of escaping from the Stinson (32), and later he reports the discovery of "A shoe which had come off when there was no strength left to put it back on." (37). Westray's path through the rainforest was indeed "The way of the bleeding / hands and feet." Before correlating narrative and lyric, though, let us listen to a little more of the former. Here is the moment when O'Reilly encounters Westray:

I expected to find him lying on the broken blue rocks at the foot of that drop, but found instead that he had gone on, crawling this time, miles down that torrent bed with its green, slimy boulders, around four more waterfalls ... Around him in the green twilight of the lofty jungle was the unearthly beauty of palm, fern, orchid and vine; beside him tumbled the wild creek and from around a bend the deep musical note of a waterfall dropping into a deep black pool. (40)

So the body was found near a "black pool" in Christmas Creek Gorge, and when O'Reilly returned with help from Lamington, Westray was, he said, "Gently carried from the creek to the mystic circle of trees where he now lies" (47).

O'Reilly's *Green Mountains* was widely read during and after the Second World War; it sustained many people in a bad time, and has been sadly overlooked in recent years. There is little doubt that Judith Wright knew the book, and my sense is that the figure of the dead Jim Westray near the pool is one of the sources of "The Lost Man."[14] The very title is likely to have been drawn from the narrative: O'Reilly refers to the survivors as "lost men" (32). That the waterfall is near Christmas Creek coheres with the image of Jesus in the lyric, as do the other religious references to be found in O'Reilly's narrative. It is worth noting that O'Reilly declares his openness to the possibility that his part in the rescue is due to "Divine Intervention" (15). There is even mention of "the Hermit of Lamington," Charles Burgess. "The Hermit," O'Reilly tells us, "dwells in a cave down on Christmas Creek, and lives almost entirely on corn which he grows, grinds into meal with a little hand mill and bakes on the coals in unleavened cakes. The great precept of his simple religion is 'Thou shalt not kill,' and this he carries out so thoroughly and sincerely that he refuses to wear leather boots because they involve the killing of animals" (49).

Green Mountains is only one source for "The Lost Man," and by no means the most significant one for reading it as a poem. I wonder, though, if it is possible to make decent sense of the title and the man pictured in the rainforest without any awareness of O'Reilly's story. Certainly a reading of the poem would be impoverished were it to proceed without any sense of Wright's allusions to St. John of the Cross. "You must go by the way he went," the speaker tells us; and, later, "you must forget the song of the gold bird dancing / over tossed light," then, further, "you must remember nothing / except the drag of darkness / that draws your weakness under." Anyone familiar with Carmelite spirituality will immediately recall St. John of the Cross's sketch of Mt. Carmel, and especially the verses that are inscribed at the bottom of the mountain:

To reach satisfaction in all
desire satisfaction in nothing.
To come to the knowledge of all
desire the knowledge of nothing.
To come to possess all
desire the possession of nothing.
To arrive at being all
desire to be nothing.
'To come to enjoy what you have not
you must go by a way in which you enjoy not.
To come to the knowledge you have not
you must go by a way in which you know not.
To come to the possession you have not
you must go by a way in which you possess not.
To come to be what you are not
you must go by a way in which you are not.[15]

Are these central motifs of sanjuanist mysticism folded into "The Lost Man"?
They are; but not, I think, in an unmediated manner. In a letter to Shirley
Walker partly about "Song," another lyric from *The Gateway*, Wright refers to
her reading of T. S. Eliot's *Four Quartets* (1943), and notes that her husband,
Jack McKinney, thought it to be "the greatest poem of modern times."[16]
McKinney was not alone in his evaluation, and the influence of late Eliot had
already been felt in Australian poetry: Kenneth Slessor's "Five Bells" (1939)
answers in its own way to "Burnt Norton" (1936). And equally in its own way,
"The Lost Man" receives St. John of the Cross by way of Eliot's pastiche of
them in the third section of "East Coker" (1940).[17] Eliot both borrows St. John
of the Cross's lines and subtly redirects them so that they point to Brahmic as
well as Carmelite spirituality.[18] Yet while Wright had read a little in the oriental
religions, she remains closer to *The Ascent of Mt. Carmel* than to any of the
Upanishads.[19]

Wright's emphasis, like St. John of the Cross's, is a quest: "To reach
the pool ...," she says, while he directs, "To reach satisfaction in all ...."
Uninterested in the sanjuanist thematic of desire, Wright maintains a steady
emphasis on images of unknowing ("darkness," "black valley," "silence") and
the dangers that attend them. The reading I am proposing distinguishes the
apophatic emphasis on unknowing from the condition of being lost: the "lost
man" is being sought by someone who, in order to imitate Christ, must pass
along the negative way. Not to accept this distinction would be to confuse the
register of the ascent through spiritual darkness with the condition of being
spiritually lost. To be sure, St. John recognizes that souls ascending through
the dark night can sometimes feel that God has abandoned them: "On

account of the apprehension and feelings of their miseries, they suspect that they are lost and their blessings are gone forever."[20] The anguish is familiar to readers of Gerard Manley Hopkins. The "terrible sonnet" that begins "I wake and feel the fell of dark, not day" ends with "I see / The lost are like this, and their scourge to be / As I am mine, their sweating selves; but worse."[21] Notice that the poem concludes with a figure that, understood theologically, is a contrast—the damned and the saved will be utterly separate—but that, as felt by the speaker, is a comparison; and the lyric gains some of its considerable pathos in this difference between the comparison and the contrast.

When Wright folds St. John of the Cross's guide to Mt. Carmel into her lyric it is first inserted into another, shorter sequence. For St. John, the important thing is to supply the reader with a map by means of which he or she can ascend the mountain. Wright also gives directions, but they are oriented by way of sensuous experiences that are linked to the landscape rather than instructions on how to evacuate desire. At first one might think that this is merely a lyrical concretizing of a theology. More than this is happening, however. To begin with, St. John's map of the spiritual life has no sensory dimension whatsoever; unlike the Church Fathers, not to mention other contemplatives, he allows none of the "spiritual senses" a role in his account of the ascent.[22] If we ask in what way the ascent registers as experience, we will have to content ourselves with an answer that is likely to seem curious: in its highest reaches the spiritual life is conducted without experience. On those heights, the *imitatio Christi* has resulted in a κένωσις so rigorous that there is no longer any self that could be the site of experience. Or, if you like, the only experiences one suffers are generated by the sheer absence of experience.[23]

The commonly held view that mysticism's defining trait is ecstatic experience emerges only in the nineteenth and twentieth centuries when, to put it a little too simply, the *Erfahrung* of the contemplative life is casts as *Erlebnis*. At any rate, it is this post-enlightenment understanding of the mystical into which Wright folds St. John of the Cross. The poem begins with one kind of directive ("in order to") but in effect changes to another kind ("how to"): a map becomes a series of lived experiences. Little surprise then that the lyric focuses on the externals of asceticism. O'Reilly is always alert to the rainforest around him—he mentions the lawyer and raspberry vines, for instance (20)—but he makes no mention of stinging trees. To be sure, these may be found on the Lamington Plateau, and because they seek sunlight (and therefore grow in clearings) there is reason to mention them in the poem. They have thick hairs that inject poison into the skin, and the wound can irritate for months. The association of this dangerous plant with priests is Wright's invention, and is doubtless an allusion to the use of the "discipline," a cattail whip with knotted cords, by priests and religious mostly in the years before Vatican II. Yet the metaphor marks the religious imagery a little too heavily—we already have an adequate image of monks with "hooded flowers" and the poem is slowed down by a moment of self-explanation.

If this reading is substantially correct, the "he" who walks the "way of the bleeding / hands and feet" is not Christ. Rather, the Christ figure is the person who is following in the path of the lost man. So I do not find any coercive reason to call on Carl Jung in order to associate the pool with Christ, even though Wright seems to have read quite deeply in the psychologist's work.[24] As we draw toward the ending of the poem, two notes about the narrator's directives are called for, each of which has considerable implications for reading the lyric. First, an obvious point: the poem does not simply recapitulate in lyrical form the story of *Green Mountains*. The primary directive is "To reach the pool," yet on leaving the wreck of the Stinson, O'Reilly had no idea that Westray would be found near a pool. On realizing this, one must suspend the assumption that O'Reilly, or a savior figure based on him, is primarily addressed in the poem. Does this mean that the savior figure is resituated as the "he" in the first stanza? Certainly one can make a case that the "he" is Jesus, though it is not without difficulties, as we shall see. The second point about the directives is not quite so evident: the person being directed is ultimately not guided to the pool but to the reflection of the sun in the water. I do not read this as nature mysticism.[25] Rather, Wright's image is a traditional one, used by Hopkins among others, that the sun is Christ; and if the pool is "faceless," it is because the final stage of the ascent to the deity involves a complete evacuation of self.

*

How are we to read "The Lost Man" then? We can develop an intrinsic reading of the lyric, although the standard interpretation, in which a man physically lost in the rainforest is addressed, moves far too quickly and ends up beleaguered by confusions. A better interpretation of the lyric is available if we take the person addressed to be spiritually lost yet able to be saved by entering the rainforest and enduring its hardships. Here "Green Mountain" becomes an Australian version of Mt. Carmel. I am not convinced, though, that this reading does not make the poem appear confused: after all, in terms of the thematic, why should someone outside a jungle be considered lost? If we take the "he" to be Jesus, it is not easy to see him walking with "bleeding hands and feet" (the wounding occurred only during his execution) or being whipped by priests (the flailing was done by Roman soldiers). One must take "way" metaphorically if the image is to work effectively. Nor is St. John of the Cross a candidate for the pronoun: there is no record of him receiving the stigmata. Of course one might cite his poem "Cantico Espiritual" which has the bride imploring the bridegroom, "let us go forth … to where the pure water flows," but one must acknowledge that she seeks to go further, "deep into the thicket."[26]

Accordingly, I have developed another reading, one that uses the narrative of the Stinson crash in order to render the lyric consistent but that turns its source into a trace. The "he" is Jim Westray, who performs the *imitatio Christi* in trying to save the other survivors and dies in the process. (And so Jesus becomes the "he" behind the "he.") Seen in this way, "The Lost Man" does not mark "the figuration of a new venturing religious mysticism" or "the mystical union of the psyche with the eternal cycles of nature," but refers to a modern, specifically Australian, understanding of Carmelite spirituality in which second-order directions are taken as first-order experiences and in which Jim Westray is remembered in his "mystic circle of trees."[27] The New Criticism would have told us that if "The Lost Man" relies on *Green Moutains* it is less than a fully achieved lyric, while a training in a "great books" seminar would have taught students to expect an allusion to *The Ascent of Mt. Carmel* or "East Coker" but not to *Green Mountains*. Neither helps us to read "The Lost Man." It is a lyric that makes sense only if we find its source in the story of the Stinson crash, and it can be accounted a successful lyric only to the extent that it turns its literary source into a trace. It does so very quickly, no later than the fourth word of the first line, long before we know there is a source to be lost; however, we realize that only on a second reading. Besides, once glimpsed, is a source ever truly lost? Two larger questions remain. What would have happened if the link between the Stinson crash and "The Lost Man" was lost? Such a thing is perfectly possible in a literary culture like Australia's, sustained by a very small population. But would it have been possible without that link to read the poem convincingly?

10

"Only this"

Some phenomenology and religion in Robert Gray

When Husserl enjoined us to go "back to the 'things themselves'," he was proposing that we look for the phenomenon, what actually appears, and not rely on inherited ways of thinking about problems.[1] The remark is as valuable to a poet as to a philosopher: one must learn how to attend to phenomena, and not merely inherit a sense of the "poetic." Philosophers and poets alike are also interested in how a phenomenon gives itself, that is, its phenomenality. In a lapidary remark, Husserl says that it is divided between appearing and what appears, and that it is the mark of the mental.[2] So the essence of a phenomenon requires the phenomenon to manifest itself and it also requires consciousness to aim at it and to receive it in a particular way. In recent decades, we have seen philosophers fall on one side or another of this division. Michel Henry, for one, holds that the auto-affectivity of life is the most basic mode of phenomenality, while Jean-Luc Marion insists that the phenomenon has the right to manifest itself: it contains, as it were, its phenomenality. We might see something similar in the world of poetry. At one extreme, there is John Ashbery, who, in long poems such as "A Wave" (1985) and *Flowchart* (1991), speaks from a profound immanence that fluctuates freely from pathos to joy; and, at another extreme, there is a poet such as Robert Gray for whom phenomena simply give themselves without there being consciousness in the sense of a distinct substance: there is no deep self.[3]

In thinking about poetry and phenomenology, it would be a mistake of the first order to restrict phenomena to the realm of objects, for we have lived experience of many other things—dreams, fatigue, fears, ideas, numbers, memories, musical compositions, and phantasies, to name only a few—and we experience them, as well as objects, by way of intentional horizons. And it would be misleading also to think that phenomena always give themselves in the same way. Numbers give themselves in cognition, and in doing so exhaust their phenomenality; my fountain pen reveals itself to me in profiles; and my seminar next semester gives itself to me now by way of anticipation, but it will manifest itself in several other ways when it occurs and in memory when it has passed. Often we look *through* things. I might regard a tree at my window, for example, as an object and my view of it as subjective, and in doing so I would fail to see the structure of its appearing: its aspects, profiles, and its unity in a manifold of different perspectives. Yet if I suspend my habitual reliance on thinking of the tree as objectively real and my consciousness as an inner theater, I can begin to look directly *at* it. I can bring forward, as it were, its structure of appearing and investigate it, passing from one side of it to another. There is no question of saying that the tree relies for its existence on my consciousness, only that the meaning of the tree appears in a particular way, which in turn modifies my own being. I need not be limited to perception; I can anticipate the tree, fantasize about it, remember it, and so on; and in each situation the tree's mode of being will have given itself to me differently.

A poet like Robert Gray must not only attend to phenomena but also present them to us in memorable language. In a poem a particular tree that has been seen or imagined by a poet gives itself to me as absent: perceptions, desires, affects, memories, must be evoked in the language itself. No phenomenon is fully received by a pure consciousness for a poet; it always is caught in the sticky web of language, which is why Husserl thought that art is only akin to phenomenology. Yet poetry is not seeking to give us certain knowledge of the world; it is concerned with pathos and joy as well as cognition. There is much to be said for the impure phenomenology that much poetry is. Of course, a poem often hosts various phenomena that manifest themselves in distinct ways. The texture of a floor covering does not show itself in the same way as the anticipation of poverty or the recollection of a shared life. A farm does not become visible in exactly the same way to the farmer and the farmer's wife; and the farm's appearance is different again when it is perceived directly and when it is read about in a poem. All these things can appear in the same flow of experience.

I have just been evoking, from several angles, Robert Gray's poem "The Farm Woman Speaks." It is an early piece from *Creekwater Journal* (1973), though in that collection Gray is already in his first maturity as a writer, and the poem can now be read as foreshadowing aspects of his later work. A farmer's wife speaks, very simply, about the ruin of a crop, her family, and her everyday fears. Let us listen to her:

We can't take a bad year,
but the lino looks like an over-ripe banana:
there's no help pacing the floors.
Leaves panic with claws on the verandah.[4]

The woman sees the yellow linoleum, now blackened with wear, as "an over-ripe banana." The simile tells us exactly *how* the linoleum is seen, in the context of worried pacing to and fro because the season is the worst for years. She does not just see; she *feels* the seeing, and she does so by way of concern as well as perception. We surmise that other years have been lean through frost or flood or birds wrecking havoc with crops, and made her wear down the linoleum: the word "but" tells us all that. We gather from the simile that she most likely lives on the north coast of New South Wales, and has seen bananas grow old and rotten all the time, though probably not in her own house, there being little money and three children. Certainly there are no bananas to be had now; it is winter, and they would be far too expensive to buy when they have been shipped from north Queensland.

A phenomenon always gives itself in two ways at once: in the genitive (an appearing *of* something) and in the dative (an appearing *to* someone in a particular situation).[5] So we see not just leaves on the verandah, and hear the exact sound they make in the wind (little animals running on wood with claws), but in addition we apprehend how the anxious woman receives that sound. "We can't take a bad year," she says, because she knows what a bad year can do and how precarious the family situation is. The children are already having only broth for lunch, and when she shows them "trees rocked by a cruel cough" she does not need to tell them or us what it is like to be sick. To *take* a bad year: the verb is passive, used in the sense that one takes a punch in a fight. Pacing does not help anything, will not deflect the hit, but she cannot stop doing it. As we read the poem we anticipate more of this anxiety, this sense of "there's no help," and imagine a disaster coming or perhaps a final stoicism on her part. Yet we cannot tell for sure. If the loose lines and imperfect rhymes suggest the speaker's naiveté, the imagery she uses underlines her intelligence. We must remember that she is telling us a story, and we also wonder what will win out: her naiveté or her intelligence. For her, the results of crop failure is partly given now in her pacing and partly in the as yet unrealized act of being struck, perhaps repeatedly and from different points, in the months to come. Along with her, though, we also experience something else, the tenderness between herself and her husband:

There are still the times when he will turn to me.
At night, I drowse by the persimmons in the log,

And, first, he puts an arm around me—.
Only, those flames then feel like a striding flag. (4)[6]

We did not anticipate a turn like this in the poem: her life of "care // about three children," of strain and work, is fortified by a simple embrace. This is the one moment when the poem that has lived in the density of sight and sound involves actual touch.

Of particular interest is the way in which the final line begins—"Only, those flames …"—that is, with a conjunctive adverb meaning "except that" or "were it not that." The thought of the consequences of a bad year can be managed, barely, because of the couple's shared intimacy: the husband is active in turning to his wife, in embracing her, even in the face of having to "take" a bad year. Being touched by misfortune is overcome in part by touching one another. We are not told that the flames *look* like a striding flag but that they *feel* like one to her, which is not the same thing. We have passed from burning being coded as negative ("crops burnt by frost") to flames as a sign of affirmation: a flag in high wind that rallies those who see it. There may be none of the urgency or the metaphysical depth that one feels when Valéry cries, "Le vent se lève! … il faut tenter de vivre!"[7] Yet the woman's renewed affirmation of the future is spoken with a dignity that is as impressive in its way as the voice that once more grips life in "Le Cimetière Marin."

*

"I saw, at the same time, the transcendence of the real-life things: how much they exceeded any renderings of them, and so appeared more deeply themselves."[8] Gray has just been telling us in his memoir *The Land I Came Through Last* (2008) of his introduction to comic books as a child, and his encounter with cartoons is framed by an uncertain sense that he will die young because of a lesion in his heart. It is through the drawings, and the brooding of mortality in the background of his country-town life, that he comes to attest the irreducible reality of the world about him, including his own body. A little later in his narrative, recalling the convulsions of his grandmother as she was dying, Gray also remembers his mother, a Jehovah's Witness, trying to find out about demons, doubtless thinking that her mother was possessed. Years later, the son gives a counter-*credo*: "I could not believe in such things in that lazy small town, at the edge of the blue steppe of the ocean. From that time, I gave up all those indulgent fantasies of mine, and the world became for me completely physical. There was only this. Things were as they showed themselves to be" (152).

Reflection on popular art gives the young Gray a sense of the transcendence of the physical world, and then a rejection of the beliefs of an isolationist religious sect leads him to affirm the power of things to display themselves. In each case, avowal of the natural world goes through criticism of something caricaturing nature or claiming to belong to another order; and this will become a general principle for him: "Experience is corrected by experience" (349). Illusions are amended by a second look or by bringing another sense to bear on the situation, and in poetry one image will correct another in the attempt to define ever more precisely how something appears and how one feels about it. When he reaches this insight into experience Gray has been reminiscing about his travels in Scotland, and telling us of his admiration for David Hume. "The world is reliably as it appears" (349): such is what Hume's empiricism comes to mean for Gray. It is the Scotsman's theory of knowledge that strikes and consoles him, not his ethics, and the epistemology in question is a starting point and not a finishing point. Hume's skepticism is allowed to go out of focus while his emphasis on sturdy common sense is retained. No mention is made of Hume's aesthetics, his great *History of England*, his occasional forays into literary criticism, or his Tory politics. "It is permissible to stand on the shoulders of giants" (349), Gray reminds us, and it is equally true that when we stand there we tend to put both feet on only one shoulder.

It is noticeable that when Gray settles on philosophical formulations for his mature beliefs his phrasings are more often in tune with Husserl than with Hume. "*Only in seeing can I bring out what is truly present in a seeing*": so says Husserl, though one might think it was Gray speaking.[9] And when Gray uses the word "transcendence" it is roughly in the main sense that Husserl gives to it: that which exceeds purified perceptual acts. When I turn to look at the tree in my garden, what appears is the tree itself, not a representation of it; but of course only one aspect of the tree is actually appearing to me at any one time. I would have to walk around the tree and gaze at its topmost branches from my rooftop in order to take in the whole organism, and even then it would give itself to me only in terms of where I stand at any one moment. The tree transcends my acts of perceiving it. Also, the rejection of the two-world theory is exactly what Husserl proposes. The idea of another world hovering behind or beyond the one in which we live, a world in which there are immutable forms or noumena, is purely speculative, he thinks.[10] "There was only this," Gray says firmly, "Things were as they showed themselves to be."

The vocabulary of "only this" and self-showing is that of phenomenology, not empiricism. An empiricist thinks of investigating nature, of the mind taking in the data gathered by the senses, while a phenomenologist looks at the issue the other way round: phenomena manifest themselves to us, and we work out their meaning by recognizing how they are embedded concretely in our intentional horizons. We do not start with the ὕλη of a tree—the greenness of its leaves, the stickiness of its sap, the roughness of its bark—but with the phenomenon. We may seek the ὕλη, although only in terms of the intentional object that already interests us. When William Carlos Williams writes about "the reddish / purplish, forked, upstanding, twiggy / stuff of bushes" he gets about as close to non-intentional ὕλη as a poet can while still keeping our attention, but in general "Spring and All" responds to the phenomenon of Spring's arrival.[11] Recall the lines that follow those I have just quoted: "Lifeless in appearance, sluggish / dazed Spring approaches—." Spring manifests itself here only in the aspect of its slow approach.

A phenomenologist will convict an empiricist of abstraction; things may be independent of my consciousness in terms of their being but they have meaning only by virtue of the "constitutive duet" of intuition and intentionality.[12] "The world is reliably as it appears," and it is this staunch commitment to the self-showing of nature that dominates Gray's poetry. All of his books could have as an epigraph what Husserl imagines each and every object to call out to us: "There is still more to see here, turn me so you can see all my sides, let your gaze run through me, draw closer to me, open me up, divide me up; keep on looking at me over and over again, turning me to see all sides. You will get to know me like this, all that I am, all my surface qualities, all my inner sensible qualities."[13] Husserl does not stop at the level of objects, however; he seeks to describe intentional states, doxic modifications, psychic phenomena, moral and aesthetic values, and even the possibility of God as the absolute monad.[14] Unlike Husserl, Gray denies the possibility of God being present in human consciousness or in the world. And yet this poetry is not devoid of reverence; on the contrary, it is itself a series of spiritual exercises, meditations on matter, its ceaseless trans-formations, and the ways in which we can become entangled in it.

*

Writing to Hugo von Hofmannsthal in 1907, Husserl said that in "pure art" the aesthetic gaze is kin to the phenomenological gaze.[15] What the philosopher has in mind here is that the artist, merely in the making of art, passes from the natural attitude toward the phenomenological attitude. As soon as one writes the first word of a poem, or perhaps even before one picks up a pen, one is no longer following routine habits of perception. One is already departing from the uncritical realism—reductive physicalism, really—that is tacitly assumed when we make everyday judgments about our experience, and that bifurcates reality into an "outer world" and an "inner world."[16] Irrespective of his or her notional or real commitments and ideologies, the true artist passes, without thinking explicitly about it, from seeing the world in terms of *that* or *why* to seeing it in terms of *how*. One poet might not stay there for long; another might make an oeuvre out of playing on and around the borderline of the natural attitude (Cesare Pavese's *Lavorare Stanca*, say) or by letting it fade almost entirely from view (Paul Éluard's *La vie immédiate*, for example); and yet another might make a poem out of the conversion of the gaze (Olav Hauge, for instance).[17] But everyone slips away from it at least a little so that there is a poem to write and not a diary entry or a memo.

In 1907, Husserl discovered what he then called the epistemological reduction, and he was to spend the rest of his life determining distinct species of reduction, right up to his separation of ἐποχή and transcendental reduction, but nowhere does he try to persuade Hofmannsthal or any artist to adopt his vocabulary.[18] The artist is already to some extent a phenom-enologist, someone wakeful, a person who has cultivated "eidetic seeing" [*Wesenserschauung*] and is able to see the structure of a phenomenon.[19] More, the artist is someone who, when producing art, has performed the transcendental reduction and become an onlooker on his or her own life, able to fathom that things and events have concrete meaning because they appear in horizons that he or she projects but that are usually hidden by the natural attitude. Art is not attention; it is a change in the quality of attention so that we can see that we have already been in contact with what we see. We see that this being in contact, this intentional rapport with the things of the world, has always and already edged us away from being a self-contained subject. Of course, it is the poet's business to present that meaning, not to explicate it or get caught up in explaining how it comes to be. When Gray writes,

> The torch beam
> I feel with, through the pouring night,
> is smoke (70),

he gives what he *sees* after having suspended the natural attitude, not what has been decoded and then encoded in another way. What is contemplated in that fresh perception is also given indirectly, though at the same time, in other intentional horizons that the very perception may block from view. The striking visual image is not the entire import of the poem; rather, the poem involves horizons of imagination, desire, and memory that come to light only upon reflection. The poem niggles the reader until one realizes that it isolates a moment, first of frustration (one cannot see what one is looking for because of the rain), and then wonder (what one *can* see is beautiful), and more broadly evokes the pathos of human limits of time and achievement. We are invited to consider the horizons we neglect in life but that give it meaning.

*

We need to distinguish what, from a phenomenological point of view, a poet does and what a reader does when reflecting on a poem. The poet suspends the natural attitude and sees an event, a configuration, or whatever. This seeing is one with the act of writing; only seldom is it a question of representation. Ink has eyes of its own. Doubtless too the poet performs reduction, passing from *what?* or *why?* to *how?* When Merleau-Ponty evokes the reduction, he also gives us an image of poetic seeing. In reflection consciousness "steps back to watch the forms of transcendence fly up like sparks from a fire; it slackens the intentional threads which attach us to the world and thus brings them to our notice; it alone is consciousness of the world because it reveals that world as strange and paradoxical."[20] No reduction is ever complete, Merleau-Ponty adds; there is no total withdrawal to the immanence of consciousness, for consciousness is always sending out its feelers, even to its own productions. Besides, the act of writing frustrates any triumph of a presumed inner life: there is always a gap between writing and full presence.[21] All the same, one may ask how radical a reduction an artist is prepared to make. Considerable self-discipline is involved in stepping back from one's empirical self, lingering on the border of psychic life, and observing the infinite field of meaning being made and remade. Assuredly some poets experience the "awful tremor" involved in doing just that, some so successfully that they not do even notice it after a while.[22] And assuredly too they experience it in distinctive ways. What John Ashbery finds in "Self-Portrait in a Convex Mirror" (1975) is not the same as what Francis Ponge encounters in *Le parti pris des choses* (1942) or what Paul Celan discovers in *Die Niemandsrose* (1963). Reduction does not always have the same angle, go to the same depth, last for the same amount of time, and the person performing it does not always have the same inkling of where it will arrive.

One might say that the limits of reduction are the limits of individual poets, for reduction is at heart a measure of the strength of creativity. Yet this formulation is inadequate. It is not enough to view the field of meaning; one must make new meaning, and that requires looking *at*, to see the phenomenon in relation with other things or even to discern the internal relations that make up its εἶδος. The good poet performs reduction, not only phenomenological or transcendental, but also eidetic. Think of Vasko Popa's "The Little Box": imaginative variation leads us in the end to catch the structure of the little box, or at least to think we do.[23] For the poet is as free to explore multi-stable, Meinongian and topological objects as well as ordinary ones. The reader of poetry performs the same reductions, though not always in the same way or to the same extent. One must seek to find the εἶδος of what is read (and so to resist seeking its negative, seductive counterpart, the *Wesen*). Yet the reader is more likely to explicate the intentional meanings of the poem, to identify and contemplate the hidden horizons, including those that have him or her reading this particular work and not another one. In a sense, the reader is more likely to analyze his or her lived experience of the poem: its textual strata, its social conventions. Regardless of how effectively this is done, however, a strong poem will always transcend the reader's analysis. It keeps something of itself in reserve for the next reading, for one always comes to the poem as a new dative. That the poet is a reader too goes without saying; but the critical edge of a poem tends to be an assertion of the value of a gap in another poem, a missed opportunity, a connection not drawn by another poet because it was overlooked or simply did not appeal to the one writing.

Needless to say, it would be possible to read Gray's poems as partial readings of the writers from whom he has learned. To read him as a reader of Robert Louis Stevenson, Thomas Hardy or Raymond Chandler, D. H. Lawrence, Kenneth Slessor, Gary Snyder or late T'ang poets or Japanese Zen poets is only part of the story, however: the discovery of empirical influence or a deep structure of influence.[24] The other part, more pressing and certainly more difficult, would be to find the gaps and missed connections in Lawrence or Slessor or anyone else, the paths they did not take for whatever reason, and that can be discerned by a vigilant consciousness in the activity of forging a unique idiom and keeping it alive, giving it space to explore its possibilities, a space that, from one view, is merely the gap between one line and the next in an admired poem, and from another view is the opening of an entire field in which how things are may be seen and poems may be written.[25] We could read Gray and Tranströmer as close readers of Slessor's "Five Bells," but we would read them well only by recognizing that they found different gaps in that poem and filled them in their own ways that sent them on paths we now recognize to be unique. They adopted singular strategies of using imagery, and found other ends to which imagery can be put that were never entirely legible in "Five Bells" until they read the poem. And we could do that well only if we are aware of how they have read other authors, other vanishing points of their poetic worlds.

*

"A good simile refreshes the intellect," Wittgenstein once wrote in his notebook.[26] One might also say that it refreshes how we see the world or see ourselves within the world. When Tranströmer writes, "I am carried in my shadow / like a violin / in its black case," the simile points us inward; it involves us in a mystery, and is wholly contained in a discrete imaginative field.[27] Compare this with an equally short poem by Gray: "Figures racing to the surf / strike the silver water, crooked / as roots of ginger" (69).[28] Where Tranströmer's perception turns on the "I," Gray's elides all subjectivity. The simile points us outward, into the world, and also out of the plane in which the rest of the poem has been contained. In the same way that Caravaggio allowed dirty feet, horse's rumps, and other unpleasant reminders of the "real world" to jut toward us out of the picture plane in order to enhance his realism, so Gray sometimes places images so that they come out of the plane in which the rest of the poem takes place. The figures running into the surf are "crooked / as roots of ginger," and of course the allusion to ginger simply doesn't fit into the economy of the poem. In a small way the poem questions the presumed triumph in art of form and order over brute reality. Only for a moment, however: for we then see people running into the surf, their arms and legs going in many directions, like the branches of the ginger rhizome. We are invited to see the swimmers gasping as they strike the cold water in terms of the pungency of the ginger. Art opens toward the world, but it must always close and leave the world behind. Gray allows it to close askew in order to remind us of the angularity of the physical world and of the sharpness of its claim upon us. That is the sort of phenomenon that interests him.

Philosophers often talk of the need for evidence to justify claims, and we might wonder what the equivalent would be in poetry. There would be various sorts of evidence that we look for, depending on the "claim" (an insight, a judgment, a feeling, a mood): a distinctive idiom may be the sort of evidence we need to keep going when reading long verse paragraphs when more is spoken than is shown, while imagery, of one species or another, might supply evidence of a vital engagement with the world. I am thinking with Husserl of *Evidenz*, the making evident of something. Gray is unusually good at supplying striking visual images, and a simile by him usually does two things: it captures how something manifests itself to someone, and makes strongly evident a perception or feeling. So when he writes of "our mind, that is too often like / a knocked-over / hive" (38) we do not respond first and foremost to the intelligence that makes the simile but to a fulfillment of an intention, in this case, the intention to give body to the feeling of a social slight. The feeling of having been snubbed or looked down on, and the hurt and angry thoughts it releases, has become present to the reader in exactly the way it feels. Or consider another image: "The night as filled with rain as a plank with splinters" (116). The image fulfills the intention of suggesting a stormy downpour, yet it does more; it also fulfills an intention of the feeling of being tightly enclosed by the rain: a feeling that is at first disturbing and then comforting.

*

Most poets express their pedagogy in their writing—sometimes a way to read their work, sometimes a way to live, and sometimes both—and it shows up in various ways. On occasion with Gray it is lightly marked in his imagery. He describes hearing frogs on a hot night as follows:

> The frogs' hollow, ringing, regular
> 'clonk, clonk', from the scrub—
> exactly the sound of a distant hammer
> on framework. Going after some labouring job. (91)

The slight over emphasis, the snap of pleasure that "exactly" brings to the line, indicates that Gray wishes us to recognize his poetics of precision and teach us its value.[29] Elsewhere, he is more blunt, telling us that Christianity has the "hollowest metaphysics" (6), that in good Stoic fashion "one must adapt to nature" (72), that Wittgenstein is right to say in the *Tractatus*, "Things as they are are what is mystical" (221), that "Our only paradise is the ordinary" (222), and a whole lot more in "Illusions" (245–7) where he can appear somewhat dogmatic.[30] To read the poems from beginning to end is to see how Gray engages in a long debate with Buddhism, resisting those early elements in it that disparage the physical world as illusory and embracing those teachings that regard it as reliable in its self-manifestations to us and equally to be trusted as self-transforming in ways that will surprise us. In the end, perhaps, he comes to embrace a Taoist criticism of the Buddhist prizing of indifference, for fear that indifference and cruelty live in each other's pockets.

When Gray avows the transcendence of things he does so with two senses of immanence in play. The first is cosmic: there is only this world, and all that happens within it is the consequence of internal causes and their effects. And the second, not asserted but presumed, is phenomenological. When I become aware of hearing something—the sound of a distant hammer, for example—that act of becoming aware is immanent. Whether the sound is of a hammer on framework or frogs going "clonk, clonk" is not of primary importance. That the frogs' sound is like someone hammering nails into wood depends partly on the speaker's disposition, his resolution to go "after some labouring job." One cannot doubt that the speaker has become aware of a sound, though Gray takes care to supply *Evidenz* that we know how he is hearing it. He also refers us immediately—and this is characteristic of him—to a transcendent act. We are pointed to the world outside the self in which frogs croak and laborers hammer while building a house. Reality is given, and given as experience: there is a realism that Gray and Husserl share.

*

There is a sense in which we can say that Gray is a philosophical poet, perhaps even a religious poet, if we thoroughly rinse both adjectives and use them with care. There is a philosophy that runs through the poetry, and sometimes the poetry itself becomes a history of philosophy, or addresses, in its own way, philosophical topics. Because the philosophy that interests him converges with some schools of Buddhism—Abhidharma Buddhism, or the Sōtō school, for example—we can allow "philosophy" and "religion" to cohabit for a while. As soon as "religion" appears outside Buddhism, however, an edge become palpable in Gray's voice. "Telling the Beads" has nothing to do with the holy mysteries on which one meditates when praying the rosary. If anything, it is a poem that expresses relief when "all the Christians [are] out of the house, and gone to church" (88). Then Gray can at last be alone with nature, here represented by beads of water on a nasturtium leaf and blades of long flat grass. "This is authentic manna," he says, "it contains / no message and no promise" (88). There is a hidden path that runs from those Christians being out of the house to manna falling sweetly on the ground for the children of Israel to another image of water drops: "one thinks of lenses, floating upon each other, / dreamed by Spinoza" (87). We recall that because the young Spinoza could no longer accept orthodox interpretations of Scripture he was excommunicated from the Synagogue in Amsterdam in 1656, and that he later subjected the Hebrew Bible to uncompromising criticism in his *Tractatus Theologico-Politicus* (1670). And we also recall that it was Spinoza who in the *Ethics* (completed in 1675) proclaimed substance to be *deus sive natura*, God or nature. Undoubtedly the philosopher who confessed, "I do not know why matter should be unworthy of the divine nature," would greatly appeal to the Gray who claims "*Materia* is *mater*" (187).[31]

Gray is a hardened and shameless reviser of his poems, and in an earlier version of this lyric, he ventured, tongue in cheek, to canonize one of his philosophical heroes, calling him "St Benedict de Spinoza."[32] Not all saints are canonized; and it is possible to have a saintly aura without being Christian: think of Simone Weil or the Delai Lama, for example. Yet the honorific was dropped, doubtless because it introduced a distraction into the poem. Spinoza was saintly, and we may be attracted to saintly persons; but often we find the saints themselves far too difficult to deal with. Besides, what centrally interests Gray in "Telling the Beads" is the claim that the beads of water are "the most fragile particulars." The lyric becomes philosophical with that slightly chilly noun only to be warmed a little by Gray passing from the third to the second person ("You are the mushrooms // conceived on the pure walls of the air") before returning to the impersonal first person ("one thinks"). Of course, it is the adjective "fragile" that weighs more than the noun in "fragile particulars," and this pressure gently sets the poem moving toward closure:

Run the drops from a stalk across your lip

they're lost
in the known juice of yourself, after the ungraspable

instant. Long-reputed but unresponsive
elixir. (88)

Along with the "fragile particulars" it is the "ungraspable / instant" that
endlessly attracts Gray, not because it is "the ambassador who declares the
order of God" (as de Caussade has it in a fine phrase) but because he wishes
simply both to release and preserve it.[33]

A formulation like "release and preserve" recalls Hegel, and few poets are
more finely aware than Gray of the sharpness of this philosopher's remarks
on sense certainty. Thinking of those who base certainty on a "Here" or
a "This," Hegel observes, "the This of sense, which is 'meant', cannot be
reached by language, which belongs to consciousness, i.e. to what is inher-
ently universal. In the very attempt to say it, it would, therefore, crumble ...."[34]
Chances are that a reader of Gray's poetry will have a divided response to this
argument. On the one hand, it will be objected that "Telling the Beads" is not
concerned to establish certainty but to present experience. The concluding
couplet sums up the poet's response to these fragile particulars and this
fleeting instant: "Experiencing you, I see before me all the most refined /
consolations of belief and thought" (88). It is in our everyday encounters with
nature, a part of which is learning to adapt to it, that we are consoled; we
find peace not in longing for self-transcendence but in transcendence of self.
On the other hand, it will be admitted that "Telling the Beads" traces the
withdrawal of the singular event before comprehension's inexorable demand
for the universal. The poem organizes itself around an empty place where
it seemed, once again, that the absolutely singular was to present itself.
Absence has its own modes of phenomenality.

*

"Telling the Beads" has a speaker who talks to the "this" and the "now."
It is not one of Gray's more common gestures. "Dharma Vehicle," his most
substantial philosophical-religious poem, meditates on the status of particulars
as much as it sensuously evokes them. The poem is a vehicle of *dharma*, the
means of showing us the virtuous way of living in the world, which for Gray
involves tracing the history of Buddhism and showing its decisive turn toward
nature, and also showing how it converges with certain movements in the
West, principally materialism. We live virtuously when we live as seekers of
the truth, putting away our illusions about the world. (And we write morally,
he implies, when we seek the truth in our poems: true literature is a criticism
of mere literature.[35]) So we are told that the religion originated in India where
its dominant message was "insensibility / to the world" (72). When the
religion spread to China, however, there occurred a "complete reversal of such

dharma" (73). It is this reversal, this firm endorsement of the sensibility of the world, which wins the poet's approval: "There is the Other shore, / it is here" (73). Gray says this while camping in a fibro shack on a beach on the north coast of New South Wales. He is sleeping on a bed of cut fern, reading classical Chinese philosophy. I interrupt him a minute or two after he has started:

> I turn out the lamp.
> Leaves, twigs, berries falling
> on the tin like rain
> in the night
> —It was the monk
> Fa Ch'an-ang, in China,
> dying
> heard a squirrel screech
> out on the moon-wet tiles, and who told them
> "It's only this."

*

> Only this.
> A wide flat banana leaf,
> wet green,
> unbroken, leaning on
> the grass.
> The mother-of-pearl of a cloudy dawn. (73)

In the moment from "It's only this" to "Only this" almost everything that Gray wants to tell us is said.

Fa Ch'an-ang confides to the monks gathered around his deathbed that there is "only this," what is here and now: a squirrel's screech on the tiles that is already passing. There is no after life, no transcendence *of* the world only transcendence of things *in* the world. Reality is no more than (and no less than) sensuous particulars perpetually coming into existence, manifesting themselves to us, and then passing out of existence. Yet when Gray takes up the monk's insight in his own voice, he adjusts it very slightly. "Only" passes from being an adverb to being an adjective, and the emphasis now falls on the uniqueness of phenomena and on the way in which they present themselves. Only things here and now exist—this banana leaf, this grass, this dawn—and their preciousness abides in their ordinariness as well as their beauty, for both are here and now only fleetingly. We might be tempted to say that the first "only" indicates a philosophical response to experience while the second bespeaks a poetic response; but the very poem we are reading gives us reasons to doubt that the distinction can be drawn so neatly. Indeed, a little later Gray entwines the two senses of "only" when looking around the room in which he is writing:

So that these transient things, themselves, are what is Absolute;
these things
beneath the hand, and before the eye—
the wattle
lying on the wooden trestle,
pencils, some crockery,
books and papers, a river stone,
the dead flies and cobwebs
in the rusty gauze. (77)

The Absolute, that which for Hegel absolves itself of all conditions, is not something that has abstracted itself from particulars (and hence from the senses) but precisely the "fragile particulars" themselves. Nothing conditions them, no *Geist* that becomes ever more concrete, and no metaphysical ground on which we might stand and gaze at them.[36]

*

To perform the reduction, Fink tells us, is to allow transcendental subjectivity to awaken and become self-conscious; it is not the human being who finally sees the world when it is viewed properly, with an eye to finding its meaning, but something behind or beside the human. In that moment, Fink assures us, "the one who philosophizes" becomes "the player of the world [*Weltspieler*]," like one of the gods, as Heraclitus imagined them.[37] Phrased differently, this idea is the basis of thinking of the poet as a "little God," little because no poet creates *ex nihilo* and no poet can stop the flux that Heraclitus saw when he looked at the world.[38] In his memoir Gray writes, like many a poet before him, "I wanted with my imagination, to pluck the things I valued off the river of time, as it went careering by; to save them, or at least the feeling of them" (202). When those things are pulled from time each becomes a world in one of Gray's poems. Especially in the longer, later poems—"*Curriculum Vitæ*," "Mr Nelson," "The Hawksbury River," among others—one enters a richly imagined place with its major and minor characters, its changing backgrounds, and ordinary people living out lives that are by turns banal and, by dint of an act of kindness or empathy, extraordinary. It is at times like being in a Chekhov story or a Chandler novel ("Emptying the Desk" is as good an example as any), while at other times it is like being in a landscape painting, in the midst of a canvas by Tom Roberts or Max Meldrum.

Always, though, the artist in Gray, the one who spins those worlds, is doing more than practicing and advocating realism as an aesthetic; he is also affirming an ethics, as we have seen. Also, he is avowing a metaphysics that he takes to be co-ordinate with both. He is forever whispering to us beneath each poem, "Becoming *is* being." That said, one of the distinguishing features of Gray's poetry on its surface is the dynamic between noetic and hylētic phenomenology: phenomena manifest themselves, and then we are brought up face to face with ὕλη.[39] In "Smoke," for example, Gray comes up almost unbearably close to the sunlight playing on a Moreton Bay fig—

it comes sliding between that Gaudi-like, visceral architecture;
a slow
egg-thickened, steamy
mixture, precisely-sliced, and
in rows. Gently conveyor-belted down (108)

—and then suddenly pulls back: "I watch across a road of / cattle-race traffic, and above the wall."[40] We move backward from ὕλη to the world in which it is a part, one which "a gardener is at work: / his leaf-smoke / only visible within the slatted sun" (108). This shuttling from phenomenon to ὕλη and back again is one of the main lessons that Gray wishes to teach us—that everything that shows itself to us is at heart matter. Note also how Gray introduces Gaudi into the scene he describes. The allusion to a painter momentarily breaks the minute attention to nature, reminding us that this too is art and not a rival of nature.

Everything that shows itself to us is at heart matter: this lesson in metaphysics is unlikely to be philosophically persuasive, in large part because it overly restricts the scope of transcendence. We can distinguish several senses of the word "transcendence," each of which is necessary if we are to treat the world justly. There is the transcendence of physical objects with respect to consciousness, as we have seen, but there is also the transcendence of meaning over experience; it is rare for the full meaning of an event to coincide with its occurrence. There is also the transcendence of another's consciousness over my own: I may try to make out your thoughts and feelings from how you look and act, but the chances are that I will not wholly succeed and may miserably fail. And finally, there is the transcendence of those things that exceed any number of our experiential acts. A materialist may not believe in the God of the Abrahamic faiths but must be able to give an account of mathematical objects, transcendentals, even (in advanced physics) of matter itself with its "matter waves" and "quantum excitations," not to mention "strange matter" and "dark energy." It is difficult also for a reductive materialist to offer a decent explanation of qualia (or, for that, phenomenality) and intentionality.⁴¹ The more reductive and consequent the materialist, the less likely it is that a convincing account can be given. And it must be said that Gray is a highly consequent materialist, at least when he theorizes about matter.

For Gray, the enlightened mind is capable of "reflecting / things as they are—" (152), and so it is in Chinese and Japanese Buddhism, though as soon as we place that judgment in context a modification is called for. Gray is evoking a return to his childhood home on the north coast of New South Wales:

Into my mind there has always come, when travelling,
images of the twisted Hawksbury bush
crackling in the heat, and scattering its bark and twigs about,
white sunlight flicked
thickly on the frothy surges
and troughs of its greenery; and within those forests,
great pools of deep fern, afloat
beneath a sandstone rock-lip; and of the Platonic blueness
of the sky; and recollections of Coleday and Thirroul
on their clifftops, where sea-spray
blows among the pines and eucalypts; and, most of all, of those forests,
cool-light flouncing, with white female limbs,
and the yeasted green pastures,
where my mind first opened, like a bubble from a glass-blower's tube,
and shone, reflecting
things as they are—
there, where I have felt, anxiously, I would find them
a while longer,
after passing Kempsey, once more, on the mail train of an early morning.
(152)⁴²

This beautifully paced polysyndetic sentence twists and turns, looking up and down, from side to side, inside and outside. We pass "into" his mind and go "out of" his mind (the spatial metaphors being delusive), into his past and back into his present. The sentence does many things; one thing it does *not* do is passively reflect "things as they are." There are no adjectives in nature, and no images, either.⁴³ Instead, this sentence ascribes meaning to things from the doubled perspective of someone who has grown up among them and is returning to them, anxious that they still be there and not turned into parking lots, with the horizons of perception, imagination and memory intensely at work. "Things as they are" display themselves to Gray here, but note that they manifest themselves *to him* and that the meaning that they bear that is necessary for the poem to be a duet between intuition of what is there and the overt and covert intentionalities that pick it up.

To register the particulars of nature is, for Gray, a spiritual exercise: not an appeal to another world behind or above this one but a meditative discipline to see this world as it is. Matter is not regarded as base but as something to be praised. "True Mind" (16) is attained when one sees nature for what it is, not for what one might hope it is: a hard lesson to learn, though one that was admirably taught by the Japanese monk Dōgen (1200–53), who studied with Ju-ching in China, established Ch'an (Zen) in Japan, and founded the Sōtō school of Zen. In "To the Master, Dōgen Zenji" Gray takes over the monk's views, bypassing the cultic elements of Dōgen's practice, and speaking them in his own voice and on his own account.[44] What we find is a characteristic modern Western understanding of Zen as a philosophy without religious ritual:

The world's an incessant transformation, and to meditate
is awareness, with no

clinging to,
no working on, the mind.
It is a floating; ever-moving; "marvellous emptiness."

Only absorption in such a practice will release us
from the accidents, and appetites,
of life.

And upon this leaf one shall cross over
the stormy sea,
among the dragon-like waves. (33)[45]

The impulse to explain or preach in poetry should almost always be resisted. Yet Gray's voice carries the teaching; and who would give up the first eight lines if one also had to give up the final three? The waves resemble dragons, to be sure, yet we know too that for Dōgen the dragon is the figure for the truly enlightened, water is the palace of the dragon, and life is a boat.[46] To meditate on the world in the present moment without being attached to it is the way to become a dragon. Gray's teaching is austere, yet he finds ways of sweetening it. So when he tells us in another poem that "it feels now as though something that's in me / will have to keep onward in this way, going barefooted through the stars" (106) he is not affirming personal immortality of a Platonic kind but rather saying that the stardust from which he has been made will be transformed once again. He will "live forever, like the dust," as Robert Bly says in "Poem in Three Parts."[47]

*

I started by listening to a farm woman speak about an impending disaster, and I end by listening to the daughter of a farmer who has already been taken by misfortune. "In Departing Light," one of Gray's later poems, brings us deeply into the phenomenon of extreme old age. No longer is there anything of a sharp realism to hear in a female voice. Gray's mother, "all of ninety has to be tied up / to her wheelchair":

> Her mouth is full of chaos.
> My mother revolves her loose dentures like marbles ground upon each
>   other,
> or idly clatters them,
> broken and chipped. Since they won't stay on the gums
> she spits them free
> with a sudden blurting cough, which seems to have stamped out of her
> an ultimate breath.
> Her teeth fly into her lap or onto the grass,
> breaking the hawsers of spittle.
> What we see in such age is for us the premature dissolution of a body
> as it slips off the bones
> and back to protoplasm
> before it can be decently hidden away.
> And it's as though the synapses were almost all of them broken
> between her brain cells
> and now they waver about feebly on the draught of my voice
> and connect
> at random and wrongly
> and she has become a surrealist poet.
> "How is the sun
> on your back?" I ask. "The sun
> is mechanical," she tells me, matter of fact. Wait,
> a moment, I think, is she
> becoming profound? From nowhere she says, "The lake gets dusty." There
>   is no lake
> here, or in her past. "You'll have to dust the lake."[48]

Just as the surreal is in excess of the real (and therefore to be distrusted by Gray), so, too, this mother has survived too long in life, which paradoxically means, as the poem makes painfully clear, has not truly survived at all. If she clings to her beliefs as a Jehovah's Witness that she will survive death, they are, for her son, no more than superstitions. The poem moves in this grid of the surreal, survival, and superstition; it looks on different modes of excess, and seeks the cure of realism for each. Surrealism is countered by the naturalism of the poem; survival by a cool, hard look at how extreme old age manifests itself to the individual and those about her; and superstition by a final deflation of immortality.

The poem's final verse paragraph is worth quoting in full. It continues in the broken, looping lines that have marked it from the very beginning, itself an extreme of what can be risked in *vers libéré*:

My mother will get lost on the roads after death.
Too lonely a figure
to bear thinking of. As she did once,
one time at least, in the new department store
in our town; discovered
hesitant among the aisles; turning around and around, becoming
a still place.
Looking too kind
to reject even a wrong direction,
outrightly. And she caught my eye, watching her,
and knew I'd laugh
and grinned. Or else, since many another spirit will be arriving over there,
    whatever
those are—and all of them clamorous
as seabirds, along the wall of death—she will be pushed aside
easily, again. There are hierarchies in Heaven, we remember; and we
    know
of its bungled schemes.
Even if "the last shall be first," as we have been told, she
could not be first. It would not be her.
But why become so fearful?
This is all
of your mother, in your arms. She who now, a moment after your game,
    has gone;
who is confused
and would like to ask
why she is hanging here. No—she will be safe. She will be safe
in the dry mouth
of this red earth, in the place
she has always been. She

who hasn't survived living, how can we dream that she will survive her death? (23–4)[49]

"It's only this" Fa Ch'an-ang said on his deathbed. To which Gray responds, as an echo, centuries later, with "Only this." The counterpart to that observation in this poem is the tender statement, "*This is all /* of your mother, in your arms [my emphasis]," meaning this is her, all of her, and also this is all that is left of her. Note that Gray has to change from the first to the second person before he can say these words. He must put aside two things: his own austere teaching about human survival after death as learned from Dōgen, and the fantasy, supposedly Christian, of the souls pushing his mother aside in their rush to reach Heaven and its rewards. He has to step aside from himself for a moment before regaining enough poise to be reassured about her ("She will be safe"). Yet his own teaching cannot be put aside completely or convincingly: even this reassurance, far more minimal than immortality, is itself a dream. At death, for Gray, there can be no "she" who is there to be safe. No matter how often he says "will" in these lines, there is no future for his mother. Nevertheless the "will" is essential for the pathos of the poem. "Shall," said without any sense of volition, would drain the poem of its power.

   Superstition, one of Gray's constant targets, is a word that most likely derives (the *OED* tells us) from an attempt to say "standing over a thing in amazement or awe." For Gray, though, awe is to be disconnected from the transcendent deity of the Abrahamic faiths, which he assimilates too readily to superstition, and from the aesthetics of the sublime. It is to be completely rethought by way of the ordinary, not the sacred or a figure for the sacred. "We are given the surface again, but renewed with awe," he says in "A Testimony" (221). How those surfaces are given to us is his great theme, one to which he has remained faithful and, what is more impressive, to which he has remained creative in his fidelity. The awe he feels when accepting what the surfaces give to him is endlessly refreshed in his poetry, coming in ever-new ways from the deep conviction that matter is our true mother, and that our mother can be transformed endlessly and will never leave us. The mother appears in endlessly new forms, and performs an infinite number of arabesques on sheer nothingness. He understands "that even in life there is nothingness, an unfathomable emptiness against which we must defend ourselves even while being aware of its approach; we have to learn to live with this emptiness. We shall maintain our fullness, even in nothingness."[50] Those are words about Robert Antelme, not Robert Gray; but even as we acknowledge the differences between these two great writers—their utterly dissimilar circumstances, and the uniqueness of each man's writing—we can still hear the rightness of the remark for the poet as well as the prose writer. For in poem after poem Gray views the mother's movements and the void beneath them and running through them with a mixture of unflinching honesty and pathos that is entirely his own.

PART FOUR

Religio Poetæ

11

A voice answering a voice

Philippe Jaccottet and the "Dream of God"

Toward the end of *Orlando* (1928), Virginia Woolf's main character muses on a poem she wrote long ago:

> Was not writing poetry a secret transaction, a voice answering a voice? ... What could have been more secret, she thought, more slow, and like the intercourse of lovers, than the stammering answer she had made all these years to the old crooning song of the woods, and the farms and the brown horses standing at the gate, neck to neck, and the smithy and the kitchen and the fields, so laboriously bearing wheat, turnips, grass, and the garden blowing irises and fritillaries?[1]

The passage is important to Philippe Jaccottet. He quotes it (in French translation) without comment in his notebook for July 1981, now gathered in *La Seconde semaison* (1996), and takes from it the title of his second volume of articles, homages, prefaces and reviews, *Une Transaction secrète* (1987).[2] It is an apt title for a collection of criticism, although the image of a voice answering a voice is perhaps more telling for how he sees the writing of poetry in the first place. Call and response, the innocence of response, the non-response of the dead, signs from another world, communication across borders, the figures of welcome and the gaze, even prayer (but not addressed to a divinity), organize much of Jaccottet's writing, while the question of how to respond properly to lived experience and the natural world generates his ethics of writing.[3]

The opening poem of Jaccottet's first collection, *L'Effraie* (1953), turns on hearing a cry, even, in a way, "the old crooning song of the woods," and the poem itself is a complex response to it, one that is addressed to his partner who sleeps beside him, to himself, and of course to us. At first only a wind that has come a long way to the poet's bed in a sleeping city one June night is heard. Drifting off to sleep, the poet thinks that the wind breathes, and that a hazel tree rustles in response. Yet this breath merely presages a cry that at the threshold of sleep is heard as a call, "cet appel / qui se rapproche et se retire" [this call / that approaches and recedes].[4] And then, in an aside, we overhear the poet say to his partner, who is perhaps still sleeping, "Cet appel dans la nuit d'été, combien de choses / j'en pourrais dire, et de tes yeux" [This call in the summer night, how much / I could say about it and about your eyes]. It is a bird, "l'effraie," a barn owl (or screech owl or ghost owl) that calls.[5] Hearing the owl's hoot, the poet does not take it to be a natural sound unconcerned with him—a declaration of the borders of its territory or part of a courtship duet—but, in a gesture at once astonishing and ordinary, responds to it and in doing so makes him and his partner the ones called.

What could he say about the call? That he hears there a summons of mortality, to be sure, since the owl, a nocturnal creature and a predator, is a figure of death. Apuleius tells us in his *Metamorphoses* that owls were nailed to people's doors in order "to expiate with their own sufferings the disaster threatened against the family by their ill-omened flight."[6] The poet himself talks almost classically of "les ombres qui tournoient, dit-on, dans les enfers" [the shades turning about, as people say, in the underworld], the plural—"les enfers"—serving to distance him from any confessional belief in hell. Yet in parts of France people say that an owl that is seen on the way to the harvest can foretell a good crop, and that a pregnant woman who hears an owl may be sure she will give birth to a girl. Folklore about owls is extensive and contradictory. What can be said about the call when heard alone and what can be said about the call when thinking of his partner's eyes are perhaps two quite different things. Yet, with the approach of dawn, when dreaming is over, and when the owl has finished hunting or mating, the poet is left in no doubt of what he has heard. He does not reply to the call itself (one does not talk with the agents of death) but one can respond without replying; and in identifying the owl's cry as a call he has already responded to it, acknowledging his mortality. Death is a predator or is seducing him; either way he now has a felt relation with it. His response is deflected by way of his partner and the reader, "Et déjà notre odeur / est celle de la pourriture au petit jour, / déjà sous notre peau si chaude perce l'os" ["And already our smell / is that of the decay of morning, / already under our warm skin the bone pierces"]. If we think of Baudelaire in general when reading these lines, we also think of his sonnet "Les Hiboux" and of "L'Effraie" as a response to it. Yet *Les Fleurs du mal* marks out its urban territory very firmly, and after *L'Effraie* Jaccottet leaves its mating calls unanswered.

"En moi, par ma bouche, n'a jamais parlé que la mort" ["Nothing but death has ever spoken through my mouth"], Jaccottet writes in *La Semaison* (1984) for November 1959. "Toute poésie est la voix donnée à la mort" ["All poetry is the voice given to death"], he adds.[7] The position is also common to Yves Bonnefoy and Maurice Blanchot who reached it by way of Alexandre Kojève's reading of Hegel.[8] Jaccottet, though, is not to be too quickly identified with either of his contemporaries on this point. First, he inherits his view of death more surely from Rilke than from Hegel, as is clear from the explanation he gives of the association of poetry and death, "Que notre ruine loue, célèbre" ["So that our downfall may praise, celebrate"] (29). We think of lyrics such as "O sage, Dichter" and "Rühmen, das ists!" And second, in tension with the first view, he distrusts words because of their inability to stop death and because of the facility with which they can be used to speak of it. It should also be noted, with appropriate shading, that for Jaccottet the response to death occurs mostly in verse, extensively in works such as *Leçons* (1969) and "Plaintes sur un compagnon mort" (1983) yet, sometimes in a more muted way, throughout the lyrics. Prose, especially highly lyrical pieces such as *Paysages avec figures absentes* (1970; augmented 1976), *Beauregard* (1981) and *Le Cerisier* (1986), is his preferred place to evoke moments of earthly happiness. *L'Obscurité* (1961), an early *récit* about the death of a mentor who yields to despair and the gradual separation of the disciple from the master's dark vision, is an exception to the general rule. So, too, is *À Travers un verger* (1975), at least in part. "Je sais bien que je vais seulement tomber en poussière comme un objet fragile projeté contre un mur" ["I am well aware that I am going to fall to dust like a fragile object thrown against a wall"], he says there, and we hear how the demise of his friends and family, along with his own death, cuts across his desire to write.[9] "Qu'ils disent légèreté ou qu'ils disent douleur, les mots ne sont jamais que des mots," he confesses ["Whether they speak with frivolousness or in sorrow, words are only ever words"] (559). "À de certains moments, devant certaines réalités, ils m'irritent, ou ils me font horreur" ["At certain times, facing certain realities, they irritate me, or they horrify me"] (559).

Jaccottet's lyrical prose pieces are difficult to characterize; they participate freely in the prose poem as well as in the *récit* and the reverie, without belonging exclusively to any of them. If at times we are reminded of the Rousseau of the *Rêveries du promeneur solitaire* (1782), at other times it is the Francis Ponge of "Le Pré" who comes to mind. The Romantic impulse to ascribe meaning and value to natural things is tempered by a phenomenological insistence that things be allowed to reveal themselves in their own ways. "Au col de Larche," from *Après beaucoup d'années* (1994), is exemplary: "je ne l'oublie pas: ce n'est pas une voix, malgré les appearances; ce n'est pas une parole; ce n'est 'de la poésie' ... C'est de l'eau qui bouscule les pierres, et j'y aurai trempé mes mains" ["I don't forget: it's not a voice, despite appearances; it's not words; it's not 'poetry' … It's water that hurries over the stones and I will have dipped my hands there"].[10] One could be forgiven for thinking also of Thoreau, although Jaccottet read *Walden* only just before writing *Nuages* (2002). Of particular interest is the way in which these prose works respond to an encounter with something in the landscape around Grignan, south of Grenoble. Take *Le Cerisier* for example:

> Cette fois, il s'agissait d'un cerisier; non pas d'un cerisier en fleurs, qui nous parle un langage limpide; mais d'un cerisier chargé de fruits, aperçu un soir de juin, de l'autre côté d'un grand champ de blé. C'était une fois de plus comme si quelqu'un était apparu là-bas et vous parlait, mais sans vous parler, sans vous faire aucun signe; quelqu'un, ou plutôt quelque chose, et une « chose belle » certes; mais, alors que, s'il s'était agi d'une figure humaine, d'une promeneuse, à ma joie se fussent mêlés du trouble et le besoin, bientôt, de courir à elle, de la rejoindre, d'abord incapable de parler, et pas seulement pour avoir trop couru, puis de l'écouter, de répondre, de la prendre au filet de mes paroles ou de me prendre à celui des siennes— et eût commencé, avec un peu de chance, une tout autre histoire, dans un mélange, plus ou moins stable, de lumière et d'ombre, alors qu'une nouvelle histoire d'amour eût commencé là comme un nouveau ruisseau né d'une source neuve, au printemps, pour ce cerisier, je n'éprouvais nul désir de le rejoindre, de le conquérir, de le posséder; ou plutôt : c'était fait, j'avais été rejoint, conquis, je n'avais absolument rien à attendre, à demander de plus; il s'agissait d'une autre espèce d'histoire, de rencontre, de parole. Plus difficile encore à saisir.[11]

> [This time it was a cherry tree; not a cherry tree in bloom, which speaks to us in a clear language; but one full of fruit, seen one June evening on the other side of a large wheat field. Once again it was as if someone had appeared and would talk with you without talking with you, without making a sign; someone, or rather something, and a "thing of beauty" to be sure; but if it had been a human figure, a woman out walking, my joy would have been mixed with embarrassment and the need to run right to her, to be with her, unable to speak at first, not only because of having run so fast, then listening to her, answering her [*répondre*], catching her in the net of my words or being caught in hers—and might have started, with a little luck, a completely different story, in a more or less stable mix of light and shadow, then a new story of love would begin just there like a new brook from a new source, in the Spring, but with the cherry tree, I had no desire to reach it, to conquer it and possess it; or rather, it had all happened, I had been met and conquered, I had nothing at all to expect, nothing more

to ask for; it was another sort of story, of encounter, of words. Even more difficult to grasp.]

The ordinary event of encountering a cherry tree in summer is charged with extraordinary significance. The tree speaks without speaking: the very syntax of "*X* without *X*" ("vous parlait, mais sans vous parler") bespeaks the ineffable and goes back side street by side street over the centuries to St. Augustine's *Literal Commentary on Genesis* where God is figured as "Measure without measure," "Number without number" and "Weight without weight."[12] For Jaccottet, though, it is the natural phenomenon that is ineffable.

Yet if we evoke the category of the sacred here, or anywhere in Jaccottet, we must do so with care.[13] Following Jacques Derrida, we may say that the two sources of religion are the sacred and faith, but only the former applies to Jaccottet; and the sacred for him is not an epiphany of something beyond the world but of what is immediate, innocent and ineffable within it.[14] "Il y a assurément un autre monde, mais il est dans celui-ci" ["There is surely another world, but it is within this one"], says Ignaz-Vitalis Troxler in an expression now usually (and mistakenly) ascribed to Paul Éluard.[15] To which Jaccottet responds, as it were, in "Les Pivoines" by observing of the flowers, "Elles habitant un autre monde en même temps que celui d'ici; c'est pourquoi justement elles vous échappent, vous obsèdent" ["They abide in another world at the same time as in this one; that's exactly why they slip away from you, obsess you"].[16] In *À Travers un verger* he tells us "mes yeux ont vu quelque chose qui, un instant, les a niés" ["my eyes have seen something that, in an instant, has blinded them"], but he will not translate that "something" into a theme.[17] "Dieu est un souffle" [God is a breath] he observes in his notebook for March 1960, a breath that carries and nourishes poetry.[18] It is the most that he will say of God.[19]

A brief comparison with René Char's prose poem "Congé au vent" will help bring one aspect of *Le Cerisier* into focus. Here is Char's poem, followed by my translation:

À flancs de coteau du village bivouaquent des champs fournis de mimosas. À l'époque de la cueillette, il arrive que, loin de leur endroit, on fasse la recontre extrêmement odorante d'une fille dont les bras se sont occupés durant la journée aux fragiles branches. Pareille à une lampe dont l'auréole de clarté serait de parfum, elle s'en va, le dos tourné au soleil couchant.

Il serait sacrilège de lui adresser la parole.

L'espadrille foulant l'herbe, cédez-lui le pas du chemin. Peut-être aurez-vous la chance de distinguer sur ses lèvres la chimère de l'humidité de la Nuit?[20]

[Camping on the hillsides beside the village are fields of mimosa. At
harvest time it may happen that, far from there, you come across the
special fragrance of a girl whose arms have been busy all day in the light
branches. Like a lamp with an aura of perfume, she goes her way, her back
to the setting sun.

To speak to her would be sacrilege.

Rough shoes crush the grass—let her go by. Perhaps you can make out
on her lips the image of humid Night … .]

For Jaccottet, the event falls slightly more on the side of the natural than the
human, while for Char it is the other way around. One might think that the
event is more freighted with erotic possibilities for Char, and that Jaccottet
is pleased to accept his passivity and is challenged by the new space that
opens before him. Yet this would be to pass over Char's directive "cédez-lui
le pas du chemin" [let her go by]. Awed by the sacred moment, Char can only
stand back and let it revolve in its own space and in its own time. One finds
in Char a delicate folding of Eckhart's and Heidegger's motif of *Gelassenheit*,
releasement, and neither that motif nor anything like it is to be found in
Jaccottet.[21] If Jaccottet's poems have any particular philosophical resonance
it is projected before them, not drawn forth from behind them.

"Once again": the event has happened before, having been remarked in
Paysage avec figures absentes and *Beauregard*. In the former we are told,
close to the start, "Je crois que c'était le meilleur de moi qui entendait
cet appel, et j'ai fini par ne plus me fier qu'à lui, négligeant l'une après
l'autre toutes les voix qui auraient pu m'en détourner et sur lesquelles je
ne m'attarde pas ici, leurs objections me paraissant vaines, en dépit, de ce
qu'elles peuvent avoir de persuasif ou d'autoritaire, contre l'immédiateté et
la persistance de cette parole lointaine" ["I believe that it was the best of
me that heard this call, and in the end I trusted it alone, overlooking one by
one all the voices that could have distracted me from it and which I won't
consider here, their objections, however persuasive or authoritative, seeming
vain when set against the immediacy and persistence of this distant voice"].[22]
Another of these events is the occasion of *À Travers un verger*, and it is worth
seeing what happens there before going on.

Walking past an orchard of almond trees, Jaccottet says, "je me suis dit
qu'il fallait en retenir la leçon" [I have told myself that I should hold fast to the
lesson].[23] It is a pedagogical scene, but of what? We are told that the trees
stop you "mais sans vous héler" ["but without hailing you"] (554). There is
no call but something else, "Signes d'un autre monde, trouées" [Signs of
another world, openings] (554), that—so we hear later—"m'avait fait signe"
["had beckoned me"]. Something that abides in the orchard has signaled to
the poet, "Elle a ouvert, elle a fermé les yeux" ["It (She) has opened, then

closed its (her) eyes"] (556). ("Orchard," remember, is *un verger*, masculine.) Far from being joyful, Jaccottet responds with shame, "mais je me suis arrêté, inquiet, honteux, moi plein de rêveries sur les fleurs, faux sage, douteux juge, piètre vivant" [but I stopped, uneasy, ashamed, a man full of daydreams about flowers, a false sage, an uncertain judge, inadequate] (563). The orchard teaches the poet something. The lesson is less about whether to respond to natural beauty when there is so much suffering in the world. (That is something that Jaccottet tries to teach himself, as is made plain at the start of *Paysage*.) Rather, the poet is prompted to consider the ethics of responding to the simple and the natural. To respond well—richly, accurately, honestly—to the real, so that its phenomenality is respected as well as the aspects and profiles of the phenomena that manifest themselves, is what Jaccottet learns from the orchard. He wants what he calls in his acceptance speech for the Montaigne prize, "À la source, une incertitude. . ." (gathered in *Une Transaction secrète*), "le visage insoutenable du réel" ["the unbearable face of the real"].[24] Yet Jaccottet's shame remains, since poetry does not always respect the hard, innocent reality of the natural world but masks it, distracts us from it; and this shame is articulated in an iconoclasm that he folds into his verse and prose.

I say iconoclasm and not negative theology. Jaccottet is right to note in *Paysage* that the expression "negative theology" is misused when applied to his writing.[25] There is no affirmation of divine transcendence in his work. Some negative theologies are thoroughgoing iconoclasms; others work in concert with a devotion to icons. Jaccottet's iconoclasm is more attuned to ethics and poetics than to religion and epistemology. To see it clearly would require a close reading of several passages in his writings, "Oiseaux invisibles" in *Paysage*, among them, and the tone and intent of his iconoclasm would need to be distinguished from that which animates Bonnefoy's poetics and some of his poetry. A number of Jaccottet's poems include a critique of poetry—a gesture that goes back in modern times to Jena Romanticism—but none of them would declare in a programmatic way "L'Imperfection est la cime," as Bonnefoy does in the poem of that title, although À Travers un verger, with its sequence of prose poem and critical meditation, almost seems in its own way to fulfill the program of Lévinas's philosophical iconoclasm as set out in "La réalité et son ombre" (1948).[26] Almost: for while Jaccottet keeps in full view the fact that his meditation is a made object, once half-done and then returned to, he has no interest in advancing a philosophical critique of the image, of urging us to replace the image with the concept, but only of not being misled by images. In general, Jaccottet affirms poetry as experience, as Blanchot does with respect to Lautréamont and Rimbaud, but not in the sense of the poet suffering exposure to the perilous approach of the Outside. Only a few groups of lyrics—"On Voit," for instance—give any sense of the fragmentary. In general, his verse aspires to wholeness, and if he walks in fear of images in poetry it is not because of a prior commitment to the imaginary as the space where being ceaselessly perpetuates itself as nothingness, such as we find in *L'Espace littéraire*.[27]

Foregoing a long detour on the poetics and theology of the image, let us stay with one or two passages from the poet. We read in *La Semaison* for September 1965: "Aucun mot d'assez de poids ni assez simple pour tenir, semble-t-il, à côté de l'innommable; c'est lui qu'on voudrait trouver" ["No word is weighty or simple enough, it seems to me, to hold its own beside the unnameable; and that's what one wants to find"].[28] The words he finds, especially images, deflect the response that seems to be fitting. To return to *À Travers un verger*:

> Une fois encore: comme on est vite entraîné, en écrivant, en rêvant, en «pensant», loin des choses, loin du réel! Comme se dissout vite une saveur qui est la seule chose essentielle! Toutes ces pages ont été écrites à partir d'une très fraîche et très tremblante, merveille aperçue en passant sous un certain ciel, un certain jour; et d'une autre chose infiniment malmenée et douloureuse vue au travers; et en peu d'instants, on se retrouve très loin de l'une et de l'autre, ou pire que cela, car il ne peut plus être question de distances: dans un autre univers, dans une poussière ou une suie de mots.[29]

> [Once again: how quickly you are carried away writing, dreaming, "thinking," far from things, far from the real! How quickly a taste dissolves when it's the sole essential thing! All these pages have their beginning in something very fresh and trembling, a wonder seen in passing under a certain sky on a certain day; and something infinitely afflicted and sorrowful seen across it; and in a few moments, you are far from both, or worse than that, since it's not a matter of distances, in another universe, in a dust or soot of words.]

Jaccottet may well want to remove himself from the indulgence granted to the image by surrealist poets—René Daumal, Robert Desnos and Paul Éluard, for example—but there can be no question of doing without images altogether—or not all the time, at any rate.

As early as May 1958, Jaccottet writes, while on the island of Majorca, "Image possible à un moment donné, mais qui doit être franchie, effacée" ["An image is possible at any given moment, but it should be surpassed, effaced"].[30] Here, the thought seems to be a project of poetics, one that strikes an English reader as more than a little willful. Gerard Manley Hopkins comes to mind as a counter example and as a counter weight. Here, surely, is someone who speaks freshly and memorably of the natural world without denying himself images. Jaccottet admires Hopkins whose work he read in the late 1950s and continues to read—see his essay, "G. M. Hopkins ou le bon usage de la parole" in *Une Transaction secrète* and "Comme le Martin-Pêcheur prend feu" in *Et, néanmoins* (2001)—although Hopkins in French translation is a very pale thing. The Ignatian thinks in images; the Protestant tries to think himself out of them. At other times, Jaccottet's view of images can be presented with the air of a spiritual exercise as recorded in a journal. "Méfie-toi des images" [Distrust images], he says to himself and anyone close to him, in *À Travers un verger*.[31] "Peut-on jamais savoir si elles mentent, égarent, ou si elles guident?" ["Can you ever know if they deceive, distract, or guide?"] (23). One almost could be reading Evagrius—or, closer to home, Calvin—on prayer rather than Jaccottet on poetry. At other times, as in part six of "Parler," collected in *Chants d'en bas*, he says plainly, "J'aurais voulu parler sans images, simplement / pousser la porte" ["I would have wished to speak without images, simply / to open the door"].[32] And here one could be reading Eckhart on spiritual birth rather than Jaccottet on poetry.

Part of what disturbs Jaccottet is that whenever he tries to talk about being it vanishes.[33] It is an old story: we try to speak of existence in all its concreteness and end up talking about essence. More particularly, he is concerned that the singular escapes language. Of course, for scholasticism this is true of God who exists *a se*. Yet it is also true, as Hegel knew, of all immediate singularity, which can express itself only by negating itself and thereby abolishing itself as such.[34] For Hegel, the annihilation that comes with comprehension is required for the dialectic, while for Jaccottet it is the image that is at issue, not the concept. The image is to be distrusted not because it raises us to a more highly determined level of experience but because it masks experience, and does so by dint of its precision and its allure: "l'objet évoqué efface l'objet à saisir" [the object evoked effaces the object to be grasped"], he writes in Éléments d'un songe (1961).[35] And in *Paysages avec figures absentes* we read: "*L'immédiat*: c'est à cela décidément que je m'en tiens, comme à la seule leçon qui ait réussi, dans ma vie, à résister au doute, car ce qui me fut ainsi donné tout de suite n'a pas cessé de me revenir plus tard, non pas comme une répétition superflue, mais comme une insistance toujours aussi vive et décisive, comme une découverte chaque fois surprenante" ["*The immediate*: this is decidedly what I hold to, as the only lesson that been able to resist doubt in my life, for what was also given to me at once has never ceased to return to me later, not as a superfluous repetition, but as an insistence that is always live and decisive, like a discovery that surprises each time"].[36] The immediate is the poet's chosen teacher, not the master of *L'Obscurité*. And not only the immediate: *Leçons* begins with the poet telling us, when faced with death of his father in law, of "me couvrant d'images les yeux" ["covering my eyes with images"].[37] To which it will be objected that the line is a memorable image itself. Yet iconoclasm helps to shape Jaccottet's poetry in more than one way. On the one hand, it leads him to the "poème-discours" of *L'Effraie*, *L'Ignorant* and *À la lumière d'hiver* (1977); while on the other hand, it points to the stripped down lyricism of *Airs* (1967).

À la lumière d'hiver provides us with many examples of the "poème-discours" at its best. Take this untitled poem for example, followed by a bare transliteration in English:

> Une étrangère s'est glissée dans mes paroles,
> beau masque de dentelle avec, entre les mailles,
> deux perles, plusieurs perles, larmes ou regards.
> De la maison des rêves sans doute sortie,
> elle m'a effleuré de sa robe en passant
> —ou si cette soie noire était déjà sa peau, sa chevelure?—
> et déjà je la suis, parce que faible
> et presque vieux, comme on poursuit un souvenir;
> mais je ne la rejoindrai pas plus que les autres
> qu'on attend à la porte de la cour ou de la loge
> dont le jour trop tôt revenu tourne la clef …
>
> Je pense que je n'aurais pas dû la laisser
> apparaître dans mon cœur; mais n'est-il pas permis
> de lui faire un peu de place, qu'elle approche
> —on ne sait pas son nom, mais on boit son parfum,
> son haleine et, si elle parle, son murmure—
> et qu'à jamais inapprochée, elle s'éloigne
> et passe, tant qu'éclairent encore les lanternes de papier
> de l'acacia?
>
> Laissez-moi la laisser passer, l'avoir vue encore une fois,
> puis-je la quitterai sans qu'elle m'ait même aperçu,
> je monterai les quelques marches fatiguées
> et, rallumant la lampe, reprendrai la page
> avec des mots plus pauvres et plus justes, si je puis.[38]

[A stranger has crept into my words, / beautiful cloak of lace with, between stitches, / two pearls, several pearls, tears or glances. / No doubt come from the house of dreams, / she has lightly touched me with her dress when passing by— / or is this black silk already her skin, her hair?— / and already I follow her, because [I'm] weak / and getting old, as one seeks a memory; / but I will not join her any more than the others who one waits for at the door of the courtyard or the cabin / where the key is turned by day that has returned too early. . .

I think that I should not have let her / appear in my heart; but isn't it allowed / to make a little place for her, when she approaches /—her name isn't known, but one drinks her perfume, her breath, and if she speaks, her murmur— / and that forever unapproached, she withdraws / and fades, as long as the paper lanterns on the acacia are still giving light?

Let me let her fade, having seen her one more time, / can I leave her without her having even seen me, / I will climb with tired steps and, relighting the lamp, take up the page again / with words more poor and more just, if I can.]

Who is this stranger? A muse, certainly, though the word *masque*—"mask," "cloak," "disguise," "pretence"—should warn us and the poet to act with care when dealing with her. She has come from the house of dreams, though whether through the door of ivory or the door of horn we are not told. The allure of poetry, understood as a beauty that has detached itself from the world and that competes with it for our attention, is strong, even in age. Yet Jaccottet mimes a prayer, presumably to his higher self, to renew his vocation as a poet in a less intoxicated and more truthful way. He will forego rhetoric and imagery in order to remain true to the natural world as it manifests itself to him. Never quite becoming a lyric, the poem is deflected to be a "poème-discours," a "bref récit légèrement solennel, psalmodié à deux doigts au-dessus de la terre," as he says in *La Semaison* for March 1960 [a loosely formal short *récit*, chanted a little above the earth].[39] Put in more familiar terms, "Une étrangère" is a matrix of Romantic gestures that have become largely constitutive of post-Romantic poetry: accommodation to loss of vision, followed by vision regarded as ambivalent in any case (there is an ethical struggle of poetry with poetry itself). One might speak here of religion within the limits of poetry alone.

Which can also be expressed like this: "Une étrangère" looks to a model of poem as icon and as iconoclasm; it entertains the muse who makes it possible in the first place and then criticizes her (and the devotion she inspires) for blocking the self-manifestation of the world. That the "poème-discours" is Jaccottet's main mode as a writer of verse is scarcely to be doubted. Yet it is not the only mode he practices, and not the most severe or the most moving. For *Airs* shows Jaccottet at his most rigorous as an iconoclast, and at his most accomplished as an artist. Jaccottet seems to have been alerted to the possibilities of a new mode of writing by reading R. H. Blythe's four-volume *Haiku* (1950–2), following Jacques Masui's hint in a review of *La Promenade sous les arbres* (1957) that it might be congenial reading.[40] In August 1960 Jaccottet records his encounter with *Haiku* and says simply, "capital."[41] Then a little later in the month, "Il m'est arrivé de penser plus d'une fois, en lisant ces quatre volumes, qu'ils contenaient, de tous les mots que j'ai jamais pu déchiffrer, les plus proches de la vérité" ["It has occurred to me more than once when reading these four volumes that of all the words I could make out they contained those that are the closest to the truth"] (55). Since he is reading Japanese poetry translated into English, a language he does not know well, it is difficult to know what he receives from the poems. Yet creativity is not bound to turn on accurate reading.

In his essay on Blythe's translations, "L'Orient limpide," now gathered in *Une Transaction secrète*, Jaccottet affirms the haiku as "une poésie sans images" ["a poetry without images"].[42] Yet one could just as well say that haiku consist of nothing but images. In a sense it is the speed of the haiku, its perception of the world that is direct but does not reduce the mystery of being, that Jaccottet finds compelling. Without a doubt, his encounter with the haiku was well prepared for. In March 1960 he writes in his journal, "Toute l'activité poétique se voue à concilier, ou du moins à rapprocher, la limite et l'illumité, le clair et l'obscur, le souffle et la forme" ["All poetic activity devotes itself to reconcile, at least to bring in touch, the limit and the unlimited, the clear and the obscure, breath and form"].[43] And he adds, "Il se peut que la beauté naisse quand la limite et l'illimité deviennant visible en même temps, c'est-à-dire quand on voit des formes tout en devinant qu'elles ne disent pas tout, qu'elles ne sont pas réduites à elles-mêmes, qu'elles laissent à l'insaissable sa part" ["It may be that beauty is born when the limit and the unlimited become visible at the same time, that's to say when one sees forms while guessing that they don't say everything, that they are not reduced to themselves, that they leave the unknowable its share"] (354). Not giving the unlimited or the mysterious its part to play in poetry is, he says, "le malheur d'aujourd'hui" [the current sickness] (356). If haiku offers Jaccottet a model of the "poème-instant," another pole than the "poème-discours," it is not something that he has found simply by reading Blythe. The Giuseppe Ungaretti of *Allegria* (1919) and beyond had already shown him a way, and the Hölderlin of "Halfte des Lebens" (1805) had already taught him something about the innocence of response to the natural world.[44] Perhaps too he had heard something in the Jules Supervielle of a lyric such as "Dans la forêt sans heures" or—more likely, if my ear is accurate—the Salvatore Quasimodo of "Antico inverno."[45]

The lyrics of *Airs* are neither haiku nor do they eschew images altogether. His dream of poetry without images was never held for very long, as he admits in *De la poésie* (2005). Yet the poems are tightly constructed and keep a tight rein on images. The following untitled lyric is characteristic:

Là où la terre s'achève
levée au plus près de l'air
(dans la lumière où le rêve
invisible de Dieu erre)

entre pierre et songerie

cette neige: hermine enfuie[46]

[There where the earth [the world, dominions] ends [completes itself] /
raised very close to air [sky, heavens] / (in the light where the invisible /
dream of God wanders [goes astray]) // between stone and reverie // this
snow: ermine fleeing]

Looking at mountains in winter, the world seems to end. More than that, it
appears to complete itself: there is a sense of wholeness in the silence, as
though history were finally over. Earth has been lifted close to the heavens;
the border between this world and the other world seems close. It is up
there, in that cold light, that the invisible dream of God wanders. This is not a
poem of belief, though, for all we have is a *dream* of God, one that wanders
aimlessly, and has no visible images to give us. The rhyming of "rêve" with
"s'achève" delicately undercuts any decisive eschatological sense that might
linger from the first two lines, while "erre" leans on its Latin base of going
astray, being uncertain or mistaken. Reading this lyric, I am reminded of what
Jaccottet says, with admiration, of Giorgio Morandi, "this toned-down art, this
art of almost nothing."[47]

Does the dream of God wander between the stone and the reverie? To
be sure it does; and perhaps, "pierre" goes back along a familiar path to
"Peter," and thus the Church, though I think it unlikely. If "pierre" goes in that
direction, the dream of God roams between ecclesial structures—dogma,
ritual, prayer—and the imagination. Or are we being told that between the
stone and the reverie snow can be seen? To be sure we are; and the white
spaces around the line "entre pierre et songerie" play a part in suggesting
snow. We are told that the snow is like an ermine, a short-tailed weasel that
is fleeing, perhaps because it has been frightened or because it is hunting
for rodents. We see only white, and perhaps the black of its eyes, nose, and
the tip of its tail (like rocks sticking up through snow). Ermine conventionally
suggests honor and purity; in France, the robes of judges are edged with
their fur. Divine justice, a final reckoning in the heavens at the end of time,
is doubtless only a dream; and human justice too is hard to capture in this
world, as is the justice that poetry owes to the world in its dealings with it.
The closest we have to honor and purity, Jaccottet suggests, is the snow

of the natural world about us. Held together by the rhyme of "songerie" and "enfuie," the final two lines also keep in tension the two slightly phased readings of the poem, each of which has an iconoclastic spirit. Here, as elsewhere in *Airs*, Jaccottet responds in an exemplary manner to nature's voices. He is "celle qui chante / avec la voix la plus pure / les distances de la terre" ["the one who sings / with voice most pure / the distances of earth"].[48]

12

Eugenio Montale and "the *other* truth"

At a celebration of Eugenio Montale's eightieth birthday in 1976, Italo Calvino spoke beautifully about a short lyric that *il maestro* had written in 1923, when he was twenty-seven years old.[1] Like most Italian schoolboys of his day, Calvino had learned poems by heart, and sometime after he completed the *liceo*, he continued the admirable practice, adding "Forse un mattino ...," among others from Montale's first two volumes of poetry to his personal mental collection. The lyric comes from the title sequence of Montale's first book, *Ossi di seppia* (1925), a group of poems that the poet once called "my 'rondels.'"[2] As these scare quotes warn us, these poems are not rondels in the strict sense, nor, for that matter, are they rondeaux. There is no *rentrement*, or partial repetition of the first line, and "Forse un mattino ..." has two, rather than three stanzas. This interruption and partial redirection of poetic form is characteristic of Montale:

> Forse un mattino andando in un'aria di vetro,
> arida, rivolgendomi, vedrò compirsi il miracolo:
> il nulla alle mie spalle, il vuoto dietri
> di me, con un terrore di ubriaco.
>
> Poi come s'uno schermo, s'accamperanno di gitto
> alberi case colli per l'inganno consueto.
> Ma sarà troppo tardi; ed io me n'andrò zitto
> tra gli uomini che non si voltano, col mio segreto.[3]
>
> [Perhaps one morning, walking in glassy air,
> I'll turn, and see the miracle take place:
> pure nothing at my back, just emptiness;
> such horrors as if I had the bottle ache.

And then, as on a screen, trees houses hills
will all rush in, the old illusion back,
but too late now; and I'll return, quiet,
with what I know, to men who don't turn round.]

By turning around so quickly, the poet perceives "the *other* truth," the one that almost all Western philosophers and theologians refuse to countenance, that the world is nothing more than an illusion generated by human subjectivity.[4]

Edoardo Sanguineti and Gilberto Lonardi agree that this lyric derives its central idea from Leo Tolstoy's memoir "Boyhood."[5] The Russian novelist tells how he was enticed by skepticism. "I fancied that besides myself nobody and nothing existed in the universe," he writes, "that objects were not real at all but images which appeared when I directed my attention to them, and that so soon as I stopped thinking of them these images immediately vanished."[6] And he adds: "In short, I came to the same conclusion as Schelling, that objects do not exist but only my relation to them exists. There were moments when I became so deranged by this *idée fixe* that I would glance sharply round in some opposite direction, hoping to catch unawares the void (the *néant*), where I was not" (159). Tolstoy's allusion is to the young Schelling who in his *Ideas for a Philosophy of Nature* (1797) argued that the subject creates the succession of representations of the world, a position he repudiated when older.[7] The novelist might just as well have cited Fichte, from whom the young Schelling learned a great deal. For Fichte, consciousness generates the distinction between subject and object by positing both the "I" and the not "I"; in the *Wissenshaftslehre* (1794), there is no objective world that precedes the subject.[8] Yet is the best explanation of Montale's view solely philosophical? Angiola Ferraris makes an acute observation in his *Se il vento* (1995) that in "Forse un mattino ..." Montale reworks the story of Orpheus. "It is the look of him who turns, like Orpheus, to bring Eurydice near that causes her to be irrevocably lost: this is the paradox of poetic language, which only *touches* things in order to evoke the silence that envelops their essence, rendering them ungraspable. Thus the 'usual deceit' [*l'inganno consueto*] of the world as representation is revealed."[9]

Ferraris plainly reads Montale's poem by way of Maurice Blanchot's "The Gaze of Orpheus," a haunting meditation on the loss of origin in literary composition.[10] Eurydice is the inspiration of the poem, yet when Orpheus the poet turns to face her directly, she is annihilated, and he is left with words that pass endlessly into one another, and keep him, as author, suspended between life and death. Yet I doubt that Montale is speaking of what the Frenchman calls "the original experience," the moment when an author encounters the origin of the work as an endless murmur, an empty repetition of something fearfully old, rather than as a clean start.[11] Calvino gets closer to "Forse un mattino ..." when he observes that, "The 'miracle' is the prime, never contradicted Montalean theme of the 'break in the meshes of the net,' 'the link that doesn't hold'; but our poem is one of the few occasions when the *other* truth presented by the poet beyond the continuing wall of the world is revealed in a definable experience."[12] Needless to say, Calvino knows that Montale writes as an atheist but, as he notes elsewhere, he is also well aware that Montale's atheism is "more problematical than Leopardi's, shot through with continual leanings toward something supernatural that is at once corroded by his basic skepticism."[13]

At least two things need to be considered here: the claim that Montale is committed to the general theme of the inadequacy of representation, and the suggestion that only rarely does he approach this theme from the perspective of experience. In his "Intentions (Imaginary Interview)" of 1946 Montale himself underlines the question of representation in *Ossi di seppia*:

> I wanted my words to come closer than those of the other poets I'd read. Closer to what? I seemed to be living under a bell jar, and yet I felt I was close to something essential. A subtle veil, a thread, barely separated me from the definitive *quid*. Absolute expression would have meant breaking that veil, that thread: an explosion, the end of the illusion of the world as representation. But this remained an unreachable goal.[14]

So the risk of writing *Ossi di seppia* was the possibility of truly showing that "the world as representation" is illusory. This is not to be understood as an application of Schopenhauer's philosophy.[15] Montale is concerned with piercing the veil of Maya by poetry, even if it be a poetry that offends against the norms of literature. The dream of "Absolute expression" is a species of what Jean Paulhan had diagnosed, only a few years before "Intentions," as literary terrorism: the desire to do away with rhetoric in order to have immediate contact with reality.[16] Dada and Surrealism are two of the boldest terrorist groups in modern art.

In his imaginary interview, Montale accepts the role of terrorist while recognizing, unlike many of his fellow assailants, that there is no escape from rhetoric as such. "I wanted to wring the neck of the eloquence of our old aulic language," he says, "even at the risk of a counter-eloquence."[17] Achieving a speech other than that of Gabriele d'Annunzio or Guido Gozzano, a language as stripped and sharp as cuttlefish bones, though doubtless with its own conventions and seductions, would be just one of the challenges that Montale had to face. To call representation into question is to court full presence or the void, two equally frightening companions, for each speaks the words of death in its own way. Full presence is perpetual stasis, and the void is emptiness.

The opening poem of *Ossi di seppia*, "I limoni" ("The Lemons"), suggest the attraction of probing nature's "final secret." In the silence of lemon trees:

talora ci si aspetta
di scoprire uno sbaglio di Natura,
il punto morto del mondo, l'anello che non tiene,
il filo da disbrogliare che finalmente ci metta
nel mezzo di una verità. (11–12)

[sometimes we expect
to find a gap in Nature,
the still point of the world, the link that will not hold,
the thread that, disentangled, will lead at last
to the center of a truth.]

This is as close as the young Montale comes to the *crepuscolari* poets, and one can hardly expect to find much danger in their world of serenity and solitude. The most we see among the lemon trees is "in every human shadow that retreats / some disturbed Divinity" ["in ogni ombra umana che si allontana / qualche disturbata Divinità" (12)]. It is in "Arsenio," the last poem that Montale composed for the revised edition of *Ossi di seppia* (1928), that we begin to learn what is involved in encountering "the center of a truth." Set in a seaside town on the Ligurian coast where Montale grew up, "Arsenio" performs and analyses a failed attempt at self-transcendence. The "tightly woven / hour" ["ore / uguali, strette in trama" (83)] experienced by Arsenio, a dramatized version of the poet, is suddenly contradicted by "a refrain / of castanets" ["un ritornello / di castagnette" (83)]. This is a "Sign of another orbit" ["segno d'un'altra orbita" (83)], which the poet tells Arsenio to follow. The poem has considerable semantic and tonal weight yet it moves with its namesake quickly from stanza to stanza by way of imperatives: "Descend to the horizon," "Hear among the palms the spluttering / spray of violins," "Go down into the falling dark" ["Discendi all'orizzonte," "Ascolta tra i palmizi il getto tremulo / dei violini," "Discendi in mezzo al buio che precipita" (83)].

Following these directives does not revitalize Arsenio, however. He finds himself standing out on the street when a tempest hits the town:

Così sperso tra i vimini e le stuoie
grondanti, giunco tu che le radici
con sé trascina, viscide, non mai
svelte, tremi di vita e ti protendi
a un vuoto risonante di lamenti
soffocati, la tesa ti ringhiotte

dell'onda antica che ti volge; e ancora
tutto che ti riprende, strada portico
mura specchi ti figge in una sola
ghiacciata moltitudine di morti,
e se un gesto ti sfiora, una parola
ti cade accanto, quello è forse, Arsenio,
nell'ora che si scioglie, il cenno d'una
vita strozzata per te sorta, e il vento
la porta con la cenere degli astri. (82)

[So, lost among wet wicker chairs
and matting, a reed that drags its roots,
you, muddy, no longer quick,
tremble with life, and reach out
to an emptiness thick with muffled cries, the crest
of an ancient wave
that swallows you again; and everything
that holds you fast—street portico
wall mirror—fixes you
in an icy mass of the dead,
and if a gesture touches you, if a word
falls near you, Arsenio,
perhaps it's the sign, in the dissolving hour,
of a strangled life risen in you, and the wind
carries it away with the ashes of the stars.]

The catalogue in the middle of this concluding stanza ("strada portico / mura specchi" ["street portico / wall mirror"]) recalls a similar gesture in "Forse un mattino ...," the usual illusion of "trees houses hills." Yet "Arsenio" is more dynamic than "Forse un mattino ...," it responds to a more vivid and forceful vision, and it does so publicly, not in the privacy of a secret. And unlike the earlier poem it concludes with apocalyptic fanfare. Strictly speaking, "apoca-lypse" [ἀποκάλυψις] means revelation or uncovering rather than the end of the world, and what is made manifest in the closing lines of the poem is that the miracle entertained by Arsenio, and evoked so poignantly years earlier in "Forse un mattino ..." will not take place. A world has ended, one in which Arsenio still had hopes of self-transcendence. An attentive reader of *Ossi di seppia* will recall a couple of lines from the book's *envoi*, "In limine": "Se procedi t'imbatti / tu forse nel fantasma che ti salva" (7) ["If you go forward you may chance upon / the phantom who will save you"]. Is this existential counseling or advice on what the reader may expect? Either way, "Arsenio" finishes with a phantom that is unable to redeem a "strangled life" suspended between life and death; the final allusion to the *Commedia*, each of whose three parts ends with *stelle*, is sharply ironic. Less calmly than in "Forse un mattino ...," the speaker glimpses the dark truth that existence cannot wrest itself from nothingness.

Yet this is not quite "the *other* truth" of representations being entirely subjective; it is the truth of a "strangled life" that subsists between life and death. The narrator has tersely instructed Arsenio to do this and that, led him to the very brink of transcendence, and then witnessed his final immobility. Arsenio will not part the "subtle veil." Yet the possibility remains that the narrator will be able to do so one day. His imperatives have authority, perhaps an overly confident authority in this context, and one can perhaps sense an anxiety behind his proud display. I will come back to the possibility of parting the "subtle veil," for Montale never abandons it, but now I would like to return to the general issue of composition insofar as it relates to the question of representation, and I will go there by way of Calvino. I have spoken of a dialectical relation, of being both inside and outside the poem, in the narrator's voice and in the character of the poem, and this is a familiar strategy of Montale's. He even touches on it in the *envoi* of *Satura* (1971).[18] Largely because of this, I think Calvino is mistaken to distinguish so sharply between "theme" and "definable experience" in Montale. Poetry is not a reliable means of reporting experience, for it invariably overlays the very experience it makes possible on what has already happened to the writer (in life or in imagination) and, in doing so, resets and redirects it.

I am not thinking of poetry as *Erlebnis*, lived experience, but as *Erfahrung*. A poem opens a space that, as Blanchot says, is "above or below existence."[19] This disjunction marks many difficulties that I cannot explore here, for the relation between being and the murmur is far from simple in Blanchot, while the link between being and existence itself calls for close and narrow discussion.[20] So I will say, all too quickly, that for Blanchot this space is below existence, in the sense that it is the non-originary origin of the murmur, and for Montale the space of literary experience is above existence. I do not mean to suggest an ethereal or Platonic realm. "Above," here, merely means not restricted to what has been attained in existence. Once the first words of a poem have been written, an immense number of possibilities for its continuation are foreclosed while with each successive line vast ranges of further possibilities are opened to view only to be dismissed by a stroke of a pen. This process occurs in the interval between the author's consciousness and language; it is framed on the one hand by the author's familiarity with the history of poetry and poetics and, on the other hand, by what can actually be done in the language of composition: English, French, Italian, or whatever. It is an activity that modifies this consciousness and is even capable, in the extreme instances, of modifying the language as well.

The incalculable excess of possibilities at any moment of writing a poem should make us speak of literary composition in terms of impossibility rather than possibility. ("My genre is wholly a waiting for the miracle," Montale wrote to Giacinto Spagnoletti in 1960.[21]) Any poem of value is a record of someone having allowed the impossible to engage the possible. In their very different ways Roberto Juarroz and Jacques Derrida have told us this and shown how it can occur.[22] The greatest poetry gives a sense of that engagement having been perpetual. We think: it is inconceivable that this poem could have been written. It is not the new (let alone the "avant-garde" or "experimental") that impinges, for even poems that have become very familiar insist that they cannot be domesticated by our intelligence or our culture. To have memorized poems by George Herbert, Charles Baudelaire, or R. M. Rilke is the equivalent of having too many cats prowling around deep inside our minds: they are never truly under our rule. At some level, strong poems remain inconceivable to their readers (even if we puzzle over drafts of what is before them) and sometimes also to their writers. I have a disbelieving response of pure admiration for many of Montale's poems, including "Portami il girasole," "Arsenio," several of the "Mottetti" and the "Silvae" section of *La bufera e altro* (1957), and were I to include poems that are only slightly less astonishing, the list would go on and on. Montale remains a poet of the impossible, even when I feel the distinct weight of *Tutte le poesie* in my hands.

I have given the titles in Italian, not because my command of that language is in any way adequate to the poems, but rather because it is hard to appreciate the magnitude of Montale's achievement when he is read in English. Jonathan Galassi's renderings of Montale's first three books (the most important in his *oeuvre*—although I would add "Xenia" as a magnificent supplement) point faithfully to the originals but from a polite distance. On occasion, William Arrowsmith gets a step or two closer.[23] Yet neither translator can suggest in English the vigor and harsh music of the poems in Italian, the "counter eloquence" that Montale risked. This is not to say that poets have succeeded in their stead—Robert Lowell's imitation, "The Eel," for example, is a prolix failure—only that we await someone who will perform the impossible.[24] What makes Montale all the more beguiling, all the more fitting to have in English (and hence my sympathy with all his translators), is that some of his greatest poems like "L'anguilla" ("The Eel") and "Xenia" give the impression that they fill gaps in our literary tradition.[25] But how could we think of such gaps before we had read those poems in Italian?

*

In all strong poetry the event of presentation is bound up with representation; the impossible is associated with the possible. "Transcendence in immanence" would be one clue for thinking about Montale's strongest poetry. Whether in its form, rhythm or tone, the poem brings into words something that refuses to settle into a definite meaning. There is nothing mystical here: the new significances we discover as we reread the poem fall against, between or beside our hardened and habitual feelings or thoughts, extending both in unforeseen ways. The poem stays in this world, challenging us to live here more deeply, if not more securely. Yet, as we have seen, there is a craving for transcendence in Montale that complicates the formal schema of "transcendence in immanence" by mimicking it on another level.

Talking to himself about contemporary philosophy in "Intentions," Montale says:

> For me, the miracle was evident, like necessity. Immanence and transcendence aren't separable, and to make a state of mind out of the perennial mediation of the two terms, as modern historicism proposes, doesn't resolve the problem, or resolves it with showy optimism. One needs to live his own contradiction without loopholes, but also without enjoying it too much.[26]

The most evident way in which our poet lived "his own contradiction" was by being powerfully drawn to two muses, two very different kinds of women, whom, by the time he was writing *La bufera e altro*, he called Clizia and Volpe. This is how Galassi distinguishes them: "if Clizia represented the goal of transcendence through sublimation, Volpe is the avatar of transcendence through immanence."[27] That last expression is not quite precise, for immanence cannot be used as a means of transcendence. I take it that Galassi is thinking of transcendence as a passage from one immanence to another, of Montale passing from his own, constricted world to Volpe, and finding himself happy there because she is herself and not a sign of something beyond.

"Clizia" is the Italian for "Clytie" who, as Ovid tells us in *Metamorphoses* 4 (234–70), is a nymph who falls in love with Apollo and is changed into a sunflower. For Montale, Clizia is always the imperious and luminous female who turns from earth to heaven. Who is she? Critics usually point to Irma Brandeis (1905–90) whom Montale met in Florence in 1933, though in truth Clizia is a complex figure, answering as much to Dante's Beatrice and Petrarch's Laura as to any living woman. That Brandeis is Jewish is important in *La bufera e altro*, the book in which Clizia appears so strongly, even in her many absences.[28] The great storm against which the poet's relationship with Clizia is played out is partly a whirlwind of passion and partly the tempest of war: both the Second World War, in which the Jews were persecuted, and the cosmic wars of light and darkness, life and death, spirit and matter. "La bufera," then, is a far more complex phenomenon than "la tempest" that strikes the coastal resort in "Arsenio." It is "La bufera infernal" that whirls and batters the souls of those who are punished for carnal passion in Dante's *Inferno*, 5 (31–3). And for a belated Zoroastrian like Montale, it is also the ceaseless struggle of good and evil that the prophet evoked in his dualistic theology of Ahura-Mazda's relentless fight against the malicious Druj.[29]

Relations between the storms of war and passion are negotiated with supreme delicacy. Consider the final stanza of "Il tuo volo" ("Your Flight"), for example, where Clizia is asked:

> Se rompi il fuoco (biondo
> cinerei i capelli
> sulla ruga che tenera
> ha abbandonato il cielo)
> come potrà la mano delle sete
> e delle gemme ritrovar tra I morti
> il suo fedele? (210)

> [If you break through the fire (blond,
> ash-gray your hair
> across the wrinkle that the heavens
> left tender)
> how will the hand of silks
> and gems ever find its faithful one
> among the dead?]

Clizia's hair is described as "cinerei," ash-gray, which, as Arrowsmith asserts, aligns her with "those who have been physically incinerated by the war."[30] Yet, as one comes to expect with Montale, far more is also being said in these lines: "ash-gray" alerts us to Clizia's passage through the flames of purgatory, and indeed she truly belongs in the heaven she has deserted ("the wrinkle that the heavens / left tender" ["ruga che tenera" (210)] is her brow). Descending to earth in a time of war, Clizia risks not being able to save her votary, the poet who adores her and needs to be redeemed by her.

With hindsight one can detect facets of Clizia in earlier characters in Montale, in the Esterina of "Falsetto" (1924), for instance. "Hai ben ragione tu!" (15) ["You're quite right!"] the young woman is told as she lies on the beach sunning herself without a care in the world:

> Non turbare
> di ubbie il sorridente presente.
> La tua gaiezza impegna già il futuro

ed un crollar di spalle
dirocca i fortilizî
del tuo domani oscuro.
T'alzi e t'avanzi sul ponticello
esiguo, sopra il gorgo che stride:
il tuo profilo s'incide
contro uno sfondo di perla.
Esiti a sommo del tremulo asse,
poi ridi, e come spiccata da un vento
t'abbatti fra le braccia
del tuo divino amico che t'afferra.

Ti guardiamo noi, della razza
di chi rimane a terra. (15)

                    [Don't bother
the smiling present with whims.
Your gaiety already engages the future
and a shrug of the shoulders
demolishes the forts
of your dark tomorrow.
You rise and head for the bridge
over the whirlpool,
profile engraved
upon a background of pearl.
At the end of a trembling plank
you baulk, then laugh,
and, as if caught by a strong wind,
throw yourself into the arms
of your divine friend who seizes you.

We behold you, we
who stay here on the earth.]

The transcendence of Esterina in that final couplet anticipates how Montale will come to view Clizia in *La bufera e altro*. Yet by the sheer pleasure she takes in the present moment, Esterina also prefigures the more voluptuous and sensual Volpe. "I flee / the goddess who won't appear in flesh" ["fuggo / l'iddia che non s'incarna" (202)] announces the speaker of "Gli orecchini" ("The Earrings"), and Volpe is precisely the goddess who will gladly remain flesh, and who offers salvation in and through the body.

It would be a mistake to see Clizia and Volpe emerging distinctly from earlier female figures and never merging again. They are principles as much as persons, and both can be found in the one process. Thus Montale in a letter to Silvio Ramat: "She [Clizia] was the eel as well, but it could have been the other one [Volpe]."[31] The poem Montale refers to here, "L'anguilla" ("The Eel"), is to my mind one of the most striking lyrics of the twentieth century. In one sentence, rising and sinking over thirty lines, Montale shows a drive for self-transcendence that never for a moment betrays the blessedness of life. The eel begins in northern seas, swims closer to Italy, until one day "a light shot from the chestnut trees / catches its sparkle in pools of dead water, / in ditches streaming / down Appenine cliffs to the Romagna" ["una luce scoccata dai castagni / ne accende il guizzo in pozze d'acquamorta, / nei fossi che declinano / dei balzi d'Appennino alla Romagna" (262)]. Once in the Romagna, the eel becomes a spirit, "arrow of Love on earth," yet never forsakes the earth in the name of that Love. She is always:

l'anima verde che cerca
vita là dove solo
morde l'arsura e la desolazione,
la scintilla che dice
tutto comincia quando tutto pare
incarbonirsi, bronco seppellito;
l'iride breve, gemella
di quella che incastonano i tuoi cigli
e fai brillare intatta in mezzo ai figli
dell'uomo, immersi nel tuo fango, puoi tu
non crederla sorella? (254)

[the green soul seeking
life where only
drought and desolation feast,
the spark announcing
that all begins where all appears
burnt black, a buried stick;
quick rainbow, iris, twin
of her your eye sets on
shining, whole—here,
where men luxuriate in your mud, can you
not see her as your sister?]

Far more resonant in Italian, the concluding lines are animated by the wonderfully apt rhymes of "gemella" (twin), "quella" (fem., that [one]) and "sorella" (sister). The final question has a sense of both inevitability and surprise about it. Can one see her as a sister? Having read the poem all of us—Clizia, Volpe, Montale, you and I—have no choice but to say, "Yes, I can."

*

As the eel swims further south into sunny Italy, it sometimes appears to people gazing at a stream as a "brief rainbow" ["l'iride breve"]. "Iride" bears many meanings in Montale's poetry, one of the most prominent being the biblical image of God's covenant with men and women (Gen. 9:13). Yet when in "Iride" ("Rainbow") the Jewish Clizia is hailed as "Iri del Canaan" ("Iris of Canaan"), the word "Iris" also takes on the function of a proper name. "Iri" reaches toward the "Irma" of "Irma Brandeis" (and indeed contracts the entire name, "Ir-is") while more surely bringing to mind Iris, the Greek goddess of the rainbow, messenger of the gods and proclaimer of the dawn. Immediately, though, the Iris of Canaan becomes "that nimbus of mistletoe and holly / which carries your heart / into the night of the world" ["quel nimbo di vischi e pugnitopi / che il tuo cuore conduce / nella notte del mondo" (248)]. The Christmas imagery serves to transform the Greek messenger of the gods into the Christian angel of the Annunciation.

This short exegesis suggests something of the difficulty of following Montale at his most compressed, especially at the remove of reading him in English translation. In "Intentions" he confirms that this interpretive matrix is more or less what he had in mind. "Iride" shows us Clizia returning "to us as the continuation and symbol of the eternal Christian sacrifice. She pays for all, expiates all."[32] Because Clizia is made to assume the full weight of Christian symbolism, it does not follow that Montale himself speaks in the voice of orthodoxy. He figures himself in the poem as "the poor / bewildered Nestorian" ["povero /Nestoriano smarrito" (247)] and he underlines that this is a deliberate choice: "he who recognizes her is the Nestorian, the man who knows best the affinities that bind God to incarnate beings, not the silly spiritualist of the rigid and abstract monophysite."[33] This is not the only time that Nestorius's influence is felt in the poetry and the prose, and so it is worth taking a moment or two to grasp its significance. To do so requires, as Montale hints, some awareness of Monophysitism, the counterpart of Nestorianism, the view that Christ has only one nature. Montale's spiritual world is divided between these two religious ideas, both condemned as heresies, and it is worth noting before saying anything about either of them that he does not entertain the orthodox position about the nature of the Christ. That said, Monophysitism takes two main forms: Eutyches (c. 380–c. 456) held that the divine and the human natures of Jesus Christ were fused into a new nature, while Apollinarius of Laodicea (d. 390) maintained that Jesus had a human body and the usual passions yet his soul was divine.[34]

Monophysitism was condemned at the Council of Chalcedon (451), twenty years after its counterpart, Nestorianism, had been rejected at the Council of Ephesus (431).

Nestorius became Bishop of Constantinople in 428, and by loudly protesting against the practice of calling Mary Θεοτόκος, bearer of God, he quickly found himself embroiled in a fierce Christological feud. Vigorously combated by Cyril of Alexandria, a very formidable opponent, Nestorius was condemned in 430 by a synod at Rome. Despite protests, the political machine worked smoothly: at the Council of Ephesus in 431 Nestorius was deposed and excommunicated. In 436 he was banished to Arabia, although he was actually sent to Upper Egypt. Such is the main line of a complicated and bitter controversy.[35] Nestorius was declared a heretic for affirming that Christ is two persons, one divine and one human connected by the πρόσωπον, rather than one person with two natures. Were Nestorius's account of Christ true, it would follow that he was merely a human being though whom God worked in a singular way. Yet Nestorius did not think that he was guilty of the "Nestorian heresy." He roundly condemned Adoptionism, and asserted that Christ is the union of Jesus of Nazareth and the Logos. The nature of this union, he maintains, is that the πρόσωπον of Jesus is to be predicated of the Logos and vice versa. Whether this argument is sufficient to absolve Nestorius from the charge of Nestorianism depends partly on whether there is enough overlap between πρόσωπον and "person," and partly on which lead us into technical questions of theology that have little to do with Montale's interest in Nestorius.[36]

Montale's Nestorius is primarily a man who rejects the idea of God as pure spirit, an omnipotent deity existing eternally *a se*. The divinity needs us and our world in order truly to become himself, Montale thinks, and this commitment to the here and now modifies any tendency he may have to touch the "definitive *quid*" by way of limit experiences or acts of literary terrorism. In his short essay "A Wish" (1944) he observes that "in us and through us a divinity is brought into being, earthly at first, and perhaps celestial and incomprehensible to our senses, which without us could not develop or become cognizant of itself."[37] This is the faith that sets him at variance with orthodoxy, the faith that informs a poem like "A mia madre." When Montale addresses his dead mother, a devout Catholic, he tells her that "il coro delle coturnici ... vendemmiati del Mesco" (211) ["the choir of rock partridge" [heading for] "the harvested cliffs of Mesco"] are "non è un'ombra, / o gentile, non è ciò che tu credi" (211) ["not a shadow, / o gentle one, not what you believe"]. The son professes that this world is unconditionally real (a *volte face* from "Forse un mattino ..."); and the afterlife that was so certain, and so consoling, for his mother remains "la domanda che tu lasci" (211) ["the question that you leave"].

The same sentiments expressed in "A Wish" may also be found in a prose poem that recalls a visit to the poet Sergio Fadin before his death in 1942. Fadi "had always lived humanely, that is, simply and silently" and consequently had "no need to refer to ultimate, universal questions." Yet Montale cannot rest with such a minimal theology:

And now to say you're no longer here is simply to say you've entered another order [un ordine diverso], given that the one we move in, we stragglers, insane as it appears, appears to our reason the only place where divinity can reveal its attributes, be recognized and assayed as an enterprise whose significance we don't understand. (Might it, in turn, have need of us, then? If this is blasphemy, alas, it's by no means our worst.)

The "other order" is not completely isolated from this world: God needs us as much as we need him. So when Montale seeks "the other truth ... beyond the continuing wall of the world," as Calvino puts it, he believes that the wall has many cracks and breaks. The "other truth" needs to be expressed in the sensuous flow of contemporary Italian, in the light of Clizia and in the carnal enjoyments of Volpe. It is a truth that is at home in poetry and, even more, one that blossoms and grows in poetry. In "Siria" Montale had doubted that his poetry could be "scala a Dio" (240) ["a stairway to God"], but in its own Nestorian way it surely was and is.

Perhaps this goes some way toward explaining the affinity that Oreste Marcì finds between Montale's poetics and Coventry Patmore's essay "Religio Poetæ."[38] Patmore claims, "the Poet always treats spiritual realities as the concrete and very credible things they truly are ... [God] is excellently intelligible, though for ever unutterable, by those who love Him."[39] By the same token, for Montale, it is love that gives us the best image of God. And so we have a lyric like "Nella serra" ("In the Greenhouse"):

S'empì d'uno zampettìo
di talpe la limonaia,
brillò in un rosario di caute
gocce la falce fienaia.

S'accese sui pomi cotogni,
un punto, una cocciniglia,
si udì inalberarsi alla striglia
il poney—e poi vinse il sogno.

Rapito e leggero ero intriso
di te, la tua forma era il mio

respiro nascosto, il tuo viso
nel mio si fondeva, e l'oscuro

pensiero di Dio discendeva
sui pochi viventi, tra suoni
celesti e infantili tamburi
e globi sospesi di fulmini

su me, su te, sui limoni ... (249)

[Moles were scampering all over
the lemon house;
in a rosary of watchful water drops
the scythe was gleaming.

A spark among apples, quinces:
a cochineal bug!
We heard the pony rear
when groomed—and then the dream began.

Rapt, lightheaded, I was soaked
with you, your form
my hidden breath, your face
merging with mine, and the dark

thought of God descended
on the few still living, through sounds
from heaven and little drums
and globes of lightning hanging

over me, you, and the lemons ...]

"Nella serra" comes from *La bufera e altro*, although it has the lightness of some lyrics in *Ossi di seppia*, and a nuanced comparison with "I limoni" would doubtless tell us a good deal about Montale's trajectory, how he regards his beginnings, how he imagines his destinations, and of what sense it makes it speak of the unity of his achievement.

Attending to one thing only, the theologies at work in the two poems, I would simply like to mark the distance between glimpsing a divinity in a human shadow and "the dark / thought of God" (359) ["l'oscuro / pensiero di Dio" (249)]. If there could be no question of union with a divinity in "I limoni," it is perhaps the central issue of "Nella serra." The lovers achieve an ecstatic fusion, anticipated by the blaze of cochineal insect among the quinces, and immediately the "dark / thought of God" comes to the few who are sufficiently sensitive to receive and honor the thought. Undoubtedly this same élite will relish the ambiguity of whether it is the very idea of God that is dark or whether, as in negative theologies, it is the repudiation of any human idea of God that is at issue. What is common to both alternatives is that God abides in mystery. It is this mystery that descends upon the children's drums, the lighting, the lemons, the speaker, his lover, and us. This is the other "*other truth*" in Montale at its most profound, and it is ultimately about otherness being both unsayable in principle and yet sayable in poetry. The greatest poetry, like Montale's, contains the unsayable in what it says.

13

"La poesia è scala a dio"

On Charles Wright's
"belief beyond belief"

Long ago, Socrates told us that "a poet is a light and winged thing, and holy," and the metaphor has enjoyed good fortune in European poetry.[1] The prestige of this image has not been constant in literary history, no more than has the status of the image itself, but it has survived degeneration into a merely "literary" ornament. Romanticism is a sharp reaction against the literary, Jean Paulhan assured us sixty years ago; it is a terrorist movement that prizes the experiences of purity and rupture and that sets its jaw against all rhetoric.[2] Yet only a breath or two later, the same critic taught us to distrust that very distinction, and to recognize the difficulty of deciding whether we are dealing with an audacious experience or an exotic trope. At the very least, however, we can say that the Romantics revived and relaunched Socrates's image. We have only to recall Coleridge's vision of the poet with "His flashing eyes, his floating hair!," a figure whose sheer imaginative vitality requires his audience to close their eyes "with holy dread."[3]

After the high Romantics, Socrates's image became more and more literary for poets and their readers. In 1823 when Pushkin wrote of "freeing a bird" and not muttering "Against God's providence," he may not have been thinking of the poet as "God's bird" yet many of his readers assumed he was.[4] The image maintains its force by moving elsewhere, chiefly to critical and philosophical projects. In 1844, when Emerson ruminated on the grand triumphs of the imagination, he concluded that, "The poets are thus liberating gods."[5] Yet he would have been the first to admit that the final word is a trope. Later still, in 1916, a line like Vicente Huidobro's "The poet is a little God" cannot avoid appearing somewhat facile.[6] What has happened? A steady loss of belief in religious transcendence drained energy from one side of the metaphor, while the Arnoldian hope that poetry would replace religion was never able to sustain the other side. Yet the metaphor did not vanish altogether; it was recast this way and that and has enjoyed a remarkable new life in poetry and criticism.

Two of the most intense witnesses of modernity's advent, Nietzsche and Hölderlin, offer diverging testimonies of what occurred. God is dead, says the one in *The Gay Science*.[7] God has withdrawn, says the other when commenting on Sophocles's *Oedipus* cycle.[8] Nietzsche did not say what role the poet was to play after the divine internment, although I suspect that Rilke gives us a better sense of it than Mallarmé does. If we look at poets who respond pointedly to God's death—Philip Larkin and Wallace Stevens, say—the very idea of there being a single "role" seems implausible. Stevens said, "The death of one god is the death of all," then added, years later, "We say God and the imagination are one ..."[9] Quite different in stance and tone is Larkin's biting line that religion is a "vast moth-eaten musical brocade."[10] There is a similar lack of convergence with those poets who display an affinity with Hölderlin, writers as unmatchable as René Char, Robert Duncan, and Stefan George. Yet Hölderlin sketched out a role for the poet. In a world in which God has withdrawn from humans, and humans have turned away from God, the poet must maintain a space between the two infidelities, while awaiting another revelation. On this understanding, the poet would serve neither the old myths nor the new demythologizing; the one tempts us with nostalgia, the other with reductionism. Instead, poetry would maintain a space where a new revelation might one day be made welcome again.

Hölderlin called this space "the holy," although it has received other names, including "the impossible."[11] Of more interest than its various appropriations in modern thought is the central, if unremarked point that "the holy" is not aligned with revelation but with revealability. Poetry, then, is not of interest for any spiritual truths it may proclaim but is of value for its preparation of men and women for such truths when they are finally made manifest. Needless to say, this is not quite how Hölderlin's redirection of the Socratic metaphor has been received. "The holy" is cited by way of making sense of those writers whose verse is meditative or spiritual but who subscribe to no confession and hold no hope of' personal salvation. Religiosity is mistaken for religion, and the slip leads admirers of Geoffrey Hill or Charles Wright, for example, to make hasty inductions. In Britain and the United States, we have been hearing for some years of' "post-Christianity," and, more recently, of "religion without religion."[12] Sometimes one encounters talk of "limit experiences" or, in a Romantic register, the sublime. But none of these expressions will take us very far by itself. We can get further more quickly by pondering a central question that many of these people face. In a reality held to be finite what sense, if any, can be made of transcendence?

I put to one side for the moment a set of problems that are consequent on Edmund Husserl's insistence that all transcendence, whether natural or divine, external, or internal, be bracketed. Included in this sequestering is the important point that one cannot simply suspend reference to transcendence in the case of a text, whether literary or otherwise. One can at best fold that reference.[13] It is important to begin with an allusion to phenomenology in order to make it plain that there is no necessary convergence of a distinction between transcendence and immanence and a distinction between outer and inner. Perhaps it is never possible fully to exclude philosophical from religious senses of "transcendence," and in any case doing so is not my concern. All I wish to point out is that the question I have posed is differently inflected in different contexts. Harold Bloom, for one, asks the question from within a personal appropriation of Gnosticism, and does so with hermeneutical aims in mind.[14] Emmanuel Levinas, for another, poses the question from within phenomenology but seeks his answers in ethics.[15] That said, the question has opened new avenues for reading T. S. Eliot's *Four Quartets*, and has supplied a new angle from which to read Wallace Stevens.[16] We might come to read William Blake more seriously as a Valentinian Gnostic, and we might reassess the tradition, if it is one, that runs from Whitman and Dickinson to Crane and Frost in the light or questions that at first appear more properly theological than literary.[17] Yet the question is never quite brought to the surface of literary debate and examined closely in its own right. There was more than enough conceptual acuity for this to happen in the heyday of literary theory three decades ago, but most of the theorists then were a good deal more interested in transgression than transcendence. Or if "transcendence" was a word in their vocabulary, it was used in Martin Heidegger's preferred sense, fundamental-ontological transcendence, in which it was presumed that a case against religious transcendence had been made successfully.[18]

Today the question tends to be posed in a more careful manner by those critics who read theology seriously. Literary critics without theology or philosophy as living resources have tended to muddle different senses of "finite," "infinite," "immanence," and "transcendence," and I will have something to say about this a little later in the chapter. All that I wish to say now is that the question, as usually received, uncritically presumes a connection between modernity and the finite. In other words, modernity is taken to be chiefly characterized by attempts to define and explicate the finite structures of our understanding. People adopting this position might argue whether modernity begins with Locke or Descartes, although there could be little disagreement about the centrality of Kant. From this viewpoint, the overridingly important issue for modern literature is the sublime, and debate centers on whether it is approached by way of rhetoric or psychology, and whether it is at heart a matter of aesthetics or religion. If modernity is construed by way of structures—a history that reaches from the eighteenth to the twentieth centuries, from associationalism to structuralism—then critics of modernity will convict it of a tendency to dissociate itself from the past and the future. To be modern, to speak "for now," becomes for these critics a veiled way of speaking for all times. On hearing this one might well have two reactions. First, one might have cause to think that the version or modernity on offer is somewhat truncated: perhaps it would look different were we to begin with Giordano Bruno and Nicholas of Cusa in lieu of Locke and Descartes.[19] A modernity that begins by linking immanence and the infinite could easily differ from one that turns on the finite and the transcendent. Second, one might wonder if the questioning, doubting and debating that are part and parcel or modernity are duly honored here, and if its spatialization of time is quite so all pervasive. More particularly for my purposes in this chapter, if modernity is held to be co-ordinate with the finite, in one or more senses, then the question of transcendence in modern writing is likely to be skewed in advance.

An existential awareness of mortality, an assent to cosmic relativity: these only shade the background of what "finitude" signifies in contemporary criticism. Heidegger brings us closer when speaking of the "finitude of being," by which he means not the containment of being in space and time but the judgment that being conceals itself in the very process of unconcealing itself.[20] This judgment does not in itself preclude a religious vocabulary; far from it. In his meditations on Hölderlin, Heidegger resets the poet's sense of the holy. Indeed, he calls the poet (in general) a "demigod," and valiantly tries to retune the old metaphor.[21] Of course, there are accounts of finitude in which the spiritual is put out or play, out or focus, or out of shape, and some or these derive from Heidegger. Maurice Blanchot's elaboration of what I have elsewhere called "the counter-spiritual life" comes to mind.[22] At the same time, one can consider finitude positively, "as the place where there can truly be—though not transparently—a testimony to the infinite."[23] That place is created, Jean-Louis Chrétien thinks, in the gap between the excess of what is given and our response to it (which is comparatively weak). In that gap or wound "our existence is altered and opened, and becomes itself the site of the manifestation of what it responds to" (122). These are impressive words, and they will echo in what I have to say. All the same, in order to be faithful to the poetry that interests me here, I will more often be answerable to these words: "*Finitude* does not mean that we are non-infinite—small, ephemeral beings within a grand, universal and continuous being—but it means that we are *infinitely* finite, infinitely exposed to the otherness of our own 'being' (or: being is exposed in us to its own otherness)."[24]

I quote Jean-Luc Nancy partly because of his authority in Romantic studies (on the philosophical end of the continuum) and partly because he brings a conceptual precision, if not a sharp verbal clarity, to a contemporary apprehension of human finitude. The sentence I have cited makes two claims. First, we are existences without essences: human being is "being singular plural."[25] And second, our being cannot be rendered present to ourselves or to others. The otherness of being that is evoked here is not a soul or spirit; it arises from an awareness of being unable to possess the beginning or end of life.[26] Nancy is not only a thinker of Romanticism but also, as we can see from his conception of finitude, a late Romantic himself. Our sense of finitude, he thinks, comes from an encounter with the sublime: not an apprehension of nature or art but a recognition that our being is not uniquely possessed by consciousness; it is shared in community. Human existence is therefore an "absolute fragment," unconditioned and incomplete, and if we see here a bold conjunction of eminent Romantic themes we will also recognize a counter Romantic tendency when reading them in the context of Nancy's recoding of transcendence as "transimmanence."[27] Nancy is quick to deny religious transcendence, and he does so a little too quickly perhaps, for testimonies of religious experience do not always coincide with philosophical understandings of the word.

Nancy draws deeply from Heidegger's notion of fundamental-ontological transcendence in which being is cast as Dasein's horizon; and, on this understanding, transcendence is a structural feature of Dasein, one that is oriented to its being in the world and that does not involve a relation to God in faith. Can one argue that transcendence, in the religious senses of the word, is ontic rather than ontological? Yes indeed, Nathan Rotenstreich says, and adds that it is distinguished by having an intentional rapport with the object of faith.[28] Heidegger will maintain that the ontic is merely regional with respect to the ontological, however, and this is where Nancy gains his confidence in dismissing religious transcendence. Even so, one can object and point out that ontological transcendence bypasses or reduces something to which the mystics testify time and again: the desire for union with the deity. In scholastic terms, Heidegger would be guilty of collapsing *unio*, the union itself, with *unitio*, the movement of transcendence that leads to union. Sooner than join the debate, which would quickly involve larger questions about the "theological turn" in phenomenology, I would like to point out another sense of religious transcendence, one that coheres more readily with a sense of finitude. I approach it by drawing out one assumption at the heart of the question I have posed. It is this: we distance transcendence from experience at the cost of rendering transcendence unintelligible. More often than not, I suspect, the poets are concerned with a movement of unrest within experience, a sense of irruption within the immanent. A response to the spiritual can be figured in this way as well, and perhaps the names of Eberhard Jüngel and Emmanuel Levinas can stand as end points of the spectrum.[29] Nancy himself is unconcerned with this response, and yet his formulation of transcendence as a "resistance to immanence" is of considerable use to a religious poetics and a poetics of religion.[30]

I have been speaking quite generally because the question of transcendence is widespread in the criticism of modern poetry and because it is not posed with sufficient rigor. In turning to the poetry of Charles Wright I am aware that these reflections and precautions might appear overly weighty, on the one hand, and insufficiently nuanced, on the other. For instance, I have said nothing of the American sublime as a refiguring of the transcendent, although the Wallace Stevens whose apparently severe reduction, "the sublime comes down / To the spirit itself," will remain in the background of my remarks.[31] So too will Emerson's lines from the first part of "Merlin":

> "Pass in, pass in," the angels say,
> "In to the upper door,
> Nor count compartments of the floors,
> But mount to paradise
> By the stairway of surprise."[32]

Emerson's lines gain their power partly by the sheer confidence with which they appropriate and refigure the image of the "soul ladder" among the Orphics and the image of Jacob's ladder in Genesis 28:12 among Jews and Christians.[33] When the two traditions converged, it became an image that was heavily worked in the patristic age. One finds it in *The Passion of Saint Perpetua*, in St. John Chrysostom's homilies on John, and in Theodoret of Cyrrhus's *History of the Monks of Syria*, although it is St. John Climacus who gives the image its definitive shape in the seventh century.[34] I have already specified my theme by way of finitude and transcendence. More narrowly, it could also be stated in terms of the ways in which two related figures, the "ladder of divine ascent" and the "stairway of surprise," engage one another in Wright's poetry.

I should say that Wordsworth will also remain with us, or better the poetry he bequeathed to us that figures redemption through memory. Wright's is a poetry that, as he says, is centered on "language, landscape, and the idea of God."[35] And poetry, he thinks, has a "true purpose and result," namely "a contemplation of the divine and its attendant mysteries."[36] He goes so far as to observe that, "all my poems are prayers and songs. Hymns," while saying of God that "I don't think He exists other than in a harmony, the geometry and physics of whatever it is that holds the universe together."[37] Wright's prayers often take the form of petitions to the divine but with another addressee, and this shift marks the sense that we live in a "post-Passionate world," one where a passionate response to the Passion is incredible.[38] "Goddess of Bad

Roads and Inclement Weather, take down / Our names," he writes. He also addresses Christ, though as a "God-fearing agnostic": "Tell me again, Lord, how easy it all is— / renounce this, / Renounce that, and all is a shining—."[39] All of which is beautifully condensed in a later poem,

> Belief in transcendence,
>   belief in something beyond belief.[40]

Wright's poetry abides in the ambiguity of "beyond belief": it distrusts dogma while remaining open to the divine or, rather, open to the attractions of structure, the "last ache in the ache for God."[41] This is not the poetry of an angel or prophet but of a pilgrim. We might agree without too much debate that it is a religious poetry that answers to experience more readily than creed. It is less clear, though, whether we should speak with Matthew Arnold of "The God of Experience" or with Karl Rahner of "The Experience of God."[42]

*

I would like to approach Charles Wright's poetry by way of a lyric he translated from the Italian in the early 1960s. "Siria," or "Syria," is taken from Eugenio Montale's third and finest collection, *La bufera e altro* (1956). First, the poem in Italian:

> Dicevano gli antichi che la poésia
> è scala a Dio. Forse non è così
> se mi leggi. Ma il giorno io lo seppi
> che ritovai per te la voce, sciolto
> in un gregge di nuvoli e di capre
> dirompenti da un greppo a brucar bave
> di pruno e di falasco, e i voltri scarni
> della luna e del sole si fondevano,
> il motore era guasto ed una freccia
> di sangue su un macigno segnalava
> la via di Aleppo.

And then in Wright's English translation:

> The ancients said that poetry
> is a stairway to God. Maybe it isn't so
> if you read me. But I knew it the day
> that I found the voice for you again, loosed
> in a flock of clouds and goats

bursting out of a ravine to browse the slaver
of thorn and bulrush; the lean faces
of the moon and sun became one face,
the car was broken down, and an arrow
of blood on a boulder pointed
the way to Aleppo.[43]

This terse, dramatic poem comes from the fourth section of *La bufera e altro*, which Montale eventually entitled "'Flashes' e dediche" ("'Flashes' and Dedications"). The English word "flashes" is appropriate here, for if these lyrics illuminate the reader they are also likely to blind him or her; certainly they do not reveal simply or steadily. In glossing these poems scholars usually distinguish two female figures. There is Clizia—by turns angel and goddess, woman and light—who shimmers behind so many of Montale's major poems and subtly links them to Ovid (through Clytie) and Dante (through Beatrice). And there is la Volpe, the Vixen, whose carnality and spirituality play a more totemic role for the poet and whose presence informs "'Flashes' e dediche" and "Madrigali privati." In "Siria" the Vixen helps the poet regain his voice, overcome false divisions, and reclaim life at a higher level. The poet is stranded; only in the wilderness can one hear a prophetic voice. An arrow of blood points the way to Aleppo (said to derive from the Semitic word for milk); only through suffering is spiritual nourishment possible. Such are the interpretative gestures familiar to scholars of Montale.

Let us see how Wright improvises on the same poem. The point he wishes to make is "that Montale is a religious poet of a unique sort":

"The ancients said that poetry is a stairway to God." Some of us still say that. I do. (I think Montale does.) The poem is allusive and aphoristic. Allusive. The way we think of real things, the poet as pick-pocket and pilgrim ... When the voice is found, then the right words are in the right order, the ladder descends and the steps are there ... The voice here comes from the wilderness, the lights come together and are one light, they become one face, today is broken down and useless and the blood of history, the blood or the way things are, becomes directional and points to The City.[44]

Just before making these remarks Wright alludes to Clizia, yet makes no mention of the Vixen. What intrigues him is not so much the female presence in the poem, or even the predicament of' the speaker, as the spirituality the lyric elaborates. For Wright, the closing lines—"an arrow / of blood on a boulder pointed / the way to Aleppo"—become an image of being directed not simply to Aleppo but to a transfigured place, "The City," which because of the capital letters seems to be the City of God. Now at a stretch, and in the midst of reservations, this could happen in a poem informed by Clizia. But in a poem attuned to the Vixen the poet is more likely to be guided back to a world of sights and smells. I am not suggesting that Wright is imposing an Alexandrian theology, based on allegoresis, or a Gnosticism on Montale who, as we saw in the previous chapter, leans toward Nestorianism in preference to Monophysitism.[45] I am only indicating the kind of religious perception that comes almost instinctively to the American poet. In Wright's words: "What first drew me to these poems was their strong, and strange, religious overtones. This was rare in Montale's work and, even here, it is not 'religion' per se, but a peculiar sort of mysticism, little apocalypses, immense journeys in tight and loaded little packets ... there sometimes appear certain perceptions (*lampi*) that carry almost metaphysical overtones of faith."[46]

In later editions of *La bufera e altro,* Montale changed the title of this group of lyrics from "Lampi e dediche" to "'Flashes' e dediche" partly to set these poems apart from others devoted to Clizia and partly to evoke the flash of cameras: these lyrics are concerned with preserving intensely personal moments of journeys. It is telling that Wright recalls the earlier title, for his own poetic practice is more a matter of *lampi,* lightning flashes, than camera flashes. We should not let that distinction close too quickly or too tightly, though. There are poems by Wright about photographs: "Bar Giamaica, 1959–60," "Lines on Seeing a Photograph for the First Time in Thirty Years" and "Portrait of the Artist in a Prospect of Stone," for example. To be sure, we can read them and find more rumination or memory than registration of detail. Yet we should not let this distract us from how photography has affected the image in general and how it affects Wright's poetics in particular. That photography encouraged a convergence of "image" and "detail" in modernism is well-known, though we should not let this blind us to a more fundamental linkage or the image and chance detail, which informed symbolism in its final years of growth.[47] And since Wright's poetics reach back to symbolism, while Wright himself courts chance in the very act of composition, we should be wary of drawing too sharp a distinction between the unifying power of metaphor or symbol and the singular detail that resists incorporation. It is one reason why, in speaking of Wright, we are wise to talk of image rather than metaphor. That said, one can see Wright deepening and ramifying two aspects of Montale's lyrics: their literary status as both poems and journal entries, and their metaphysical status as images. I will take these one at a time.

It is important to notice that Montale carefully places each of the "'Flashes' e dediche" poems, sometimes in a title (Siena, the Greve, Finistère, the Llobregat, Syria), sometimes underneath a title (Reading, London, Ely,

Glasgow, Edinburgh, Damascus), and sometimes within a poem (Sesto Calende, Palmyra). These lyrics are journal entries as much as snapshots, each marking and commemorating a singular event.[48] A characteristic move is Montale's presentation of a quotidian detail that is transfigured and thereby registers transcendence as a possibility. (Wright follows him to some extent in his "metaphysics of the quotidian."[49]) Or since we are being guided by the figure of "la scala a Dio" perhaps we should speak with Wallace Stevens's acquaintance Jean Wahl of "trans-ascendance," a bursting out of immanence toward the heights although without reconstituting itself at another, higher level in which it would resettle as immanence.[50] Perhaps: yet we need to keep in mind that there is no such thing as a simple ascent in Montale. Where there is a "spark / which rose," there is also someone who finds new life at the price of being "burned to ashes."[51] And we should also recall that Wright reworks this double image himself when writing of "A soft, ashen transcendence / Buried and resurrected once, then time and again."[52]

Much of Wright's early work, now gathered together in *Country Music*, can be as dense and singular as Montale's verse. "Tattoos," for example, incorporates a line from the Italian poet, yet it maintains an independent stance with respect to journals and transcendence alike. Hauntings and commemorations rather than diary entries, "Tattoos" nonetheless insists on particular dates: a year follows each lyric—1973, 1972, 1951, 1968, 1946—though the sequence does not progress in either a backward or a forward linear manner. Consider the final stanza of this lyric that answers to 1946:

Now I am something else, smooth,
Unrooted, with no veins and no hair, washed
In the waters of nothingness;
Anticoronal, released ...
And then I am risen, the cup, new sun, at my lips.[53]

The stanza presents the thoughts and feelings of an acolyte who faints from hunger while serving at altar; the boy has a *faux*-experience of transcendence or, more accurately, of trans-ascendance. This yearning to rise above the world is put under increasing pressure as Wright enters more and more fully into his vision. There is a sense in which, as the years go by, Wright moves from serving at the altar to giving homilies at the lectern. He can be more of a kakangelist than an evangelist, preaching the bad news that there is no trans-ascendance. And his texts are more likely to be from artists and mystics than Scripture:

When you die, you fall down,
                    you don't rise up

Like a scrap of burnt paper into the everlasting.
Each morning we learn this painfully,
      pulling our bodies up by the roots from their deep sleep.[54]

Inevitably we remember the lines, "Mercy upon us, / we who have learned to preach but not to pray."[55] But even Wright's homilies include a good deal of prayer, and are closer to wisdom literature than to sermons.

By the time we get to *Chickamauga* (1995), the poetry gains its peculiar pathos by regarding transcendence as a resistance to immanence instead of an escape from it. If it is to occur, the epiphany must be here, in our rootedness on earth, not in a state of being uprooted. "What other ladder to Paradise," Wright asks, "but the smooth handholds of the rib cage?"[56] Elsewhere, the question is required to pass through a medium of greater complexity and greater pressure. Consider "East of the Blue Ridge, Our Tombs are in the Dove's Throat." Late on a Sunday in Charlottesville, "We cross our arms like effigies, look up at the sky / And wait for a sign of salvation"; but none is forthcoming. It is a poet and not a prophet who provides the appropriate teaching, and in Wright's world there can be little distinction between them: "as Lorca has taught us to say, / Two and two never make four down here, / They always make two and two." This is how the meditation concludes:

But the numbers don't add up.
Besides, a piece of jar glass
      burns like a star at the street's edge,
The elbows and knuckled limb joints of winter trees,
Shellacked by the sunset, flash and fuse,
Windows blaze
      and the earthly splendor roots our names to the ground.[57]

I would like to linger over these lines by making two comments about them.

The first confirms what we have already seen about Wright's spirituality as disclosed in his impromptu remarks on Montale's "Siria." Lorca's observation occurs in a short prose piece, "Historia de Este Gallo." In Granada, he writes, "the day has only one immense hour, and that hour is spent drinking water, revolving on the axis of one's cane, and looking at the landscape … Two and two are never four in Granada. They are always two and two."[58] When quoting from Lorca's prose, Wright could easily have made a link between the lassitude of Charlottesville and Granada in midsummer, or allowed his aesthetic of attending to little things to mingle with Lorca's "aesthetics of the diminutive." Instead, the pressure of his own concerns makes the Spanish poet appear to deliver a spiritual—Alexandrian, almost Gnostic—statement about things not adding up "down here" when Lorca is simply remarking the inability of people in Granada to make anything happen. I turn to the second observation.[59] It is no more than a gloss on the word, "Besides": the word acts as a hinge around which the poem turns. "There is *no* transcendence," it says (meaning that trans-ascendance is merely an illusion, like late sunlight burnishing a piece of glass so that it appears to be a star) while also suggesting "There is a *finite* transcendence, an awareness of the other in the same." There is splendor but solely on the earth. Either way, there is an epiphany, as in Montale, but a *lampo* and not a flaring of magnesium. And as in the "'Flashes' e dediche" group, there is transcendence as illumination of what is rather than an ascent to what might be. Wright may be drawn to a Clizia but, if he has a muse, it would be a figure closer to Volpe than Clizia.

So Wright must find his own way back to Dante and Ovid, and in an unusual move he does so through the writing of journals, notebooks and meditations. For these open-ended forms give him the opportunity to brood on metamorphoses of all kinds, and to transform Dante from the celestial poet of otherworldliness to the exemplary poet of everyday life. "Thinking of Dante is thinking about the other side," he writes, "And the other side of the other side. / It's thinking about the noon noise and the daily light."[60] If the expansive contemplation that characterizes *The World of the Ten Thousand Things* keeps faith with Montale's *lampi* by prizing radiant moments, it also works with, beside and around another modern Italian poet, the Dino Compana of "La Verna (diary)."[61] Like Campana's, Wright's journals are notations of a pilgrim, although the American exploits the ambiguity of the journal—as a way of gauging spiritual advancement and as a saving record of the quotidian—in a more thoroughgoing manner than the Italian does. Wright may be drawn to the *scala perfectionis* but he doubts that it leads out of the world. (As he writes in *Littlefoot*, with a backward glance to Yeats, "Outside of nature, no transformation, I say."[62]) In fact if one were to link him to one of the mystics one would be wise to choose Walter Hilton in preference to John Climacus, for Wright tends to circle around the same themes rather than climb a vertical ladder.[63] All the same, that sort of restricted choice strikes me as misleading, if only because Wright is more drawn as poet to the figure of the pilgrim than the mystic. Consider the pilgrim of his book-length poem *China Trace* (1977) who sets out in childhood only to remain sorrowful at the end of his journey, caught in the "flat black of the northern Pacific sky."[64] Is this because his reservations about the *scala* keep him at the threshold of transcendence? Or is it because this is all the transcendence that is available to a pilgrim?

Only poetry, whose each line, Wright says, "should be a station of the cross," offers a path he can trust.[65] And perhaps this is why, in the later volumes especially, we find Wright appealing to then gently undercutting spiritual authorities from East and West alike:

Everything comes from something,
> only something comes from nothing,
Lao Tzu says, more or less.
Eminently sensible, I say. [66]

True, Wright sets up Lao Tzu for a fall, but the poem makes a serious point: on the spiritual path experience is to be trusted above authority. If it seems that Wright is drawn more and more over time to Eastern spirituality, we must remember that he also recoils to his native Christianity, though as a literary resource. In another poem he makes T. S. Eliot play the straight man to his comic foil:

The definer of all things
> cannot be spoken of.
It is not knowledge or truth.
We get no closer than next-to-it.
Beyond wisdom, beyond denial,
> it asks us for nothing,
According to Pseudo-Dionysus, which sounds good to me.[67]

That last minute swerve from the manner and tone of *Four Quartets* is perhaps not quick or resonate enough to prevent us from making a passing comparison with Eliot, one that is to the advantage of the senior poet.

Ironizing a relationship with the masters, whether in literature or religion, is not the whole story, however. Wright may have written in homage to Rimbaud, and may honor the surrealist image, but he knows full well that or themselves words offer no hope of transcendence, and may well detect one from the true path. Thus the closing lines of "Night Journal":

—Words, like all things, are caught in their finitude.
They start here, they finish there
No matter how high they rise—
> my judgment is that I know this
And never love anything hard enough
That would stamp me
> and sink me suddenly into bliss.[68]

I pause simply to admire the fine economy of "my judgment," its compression of the subjective and the objective. For it indicates *both* the speaker's darkest estimation of how he has lived *and* the sentence he has received: to know he has foregone bliss because he has believed poetry and not love to be a ladder to God. When Wright calls poetry "this business I waste my heart on," he acknowledges having followed a seductive and fatal path in life, Emerson's "stairway of surprise" rather than the *scala perfectionis*.[69] The important word is "waste." Writing poetry has desolated his heart and, worse, has not given him the opportunities he needs to fulfill his potential as a human being. Far from being an ascent to God, poetry is here a descent to the grave.

This ambivalent relation between life and art goes back to the very "scene of initiation" that Wright has evoked on several occasions. Wright recalls a day in 1959 when he was living in Verona. He was handed a copy of *The Selected Poems of Ezra Pound*, one he had earlier loaned to a friend, and told to visit Lake Garda where Catullus was believed to have had a villa and where Pound supposedly wrote "'Blandula, Tenulla, Vagula,'" his response to the Emperor Hadrian's address to a deceased lover or perhaps his own departing soul. Hadrian's lyric, "Animula vagula blandula," is a tantalizing poem, which I offer in my own translation:

> Poor little soul all lost: you were my guest,
> The fine friend of my flesh.
> Where since, so pale,
> So stiff, so naked? No fun now in the dark.[70]

Wright went to Lake Garda, read Pound's poem, and became a poet. Years later he included this scene of vocation in a poem called "A Journal of Southern Rivers," and cited the opening line of Pound's lyric:

> What lasts is what you start with.
> *What hast thou O my soul, with Paradise*, for instance,
> Is where I began, in March 1959—
> my question has never changed,
> Always the black angel asleep on my lips … [71]

Pound's question becomes Wright's, although the appropriation is far from simple. For the line forks through his life and work, being both a religious query about how to harmonize love for this world with a desire for transcendence, and an aesthetic question about the kind or poem that, if pursued and mastered, could lead to Wright being canonized as a poet. Throughout the work, one question shadows the other, and neither is fully answered: the poetry that deepens his soul perhaps puts that soul in danger. It is with this thought in mind that we notice that his relations with spiritual masters are not always ironized. He may not be a Christian but Wright can still pray, with feeling if not with faith, "St. John of the Cross, Julian of Norwich, lead me home."[72] It's a poetry that mimes *fides qua* and has no *fides quæ*.

To understand the line I have just quoted we need to know that both mystics believe God to abide within the soul: "for in vs is his haymelyeste hame," Julian writes, while John adds, "The soul's center is God."[73] Going home for Wright is venturing so deeply into his subjectivity that he passes beyond it. To go home, if it is a true home, is to transcend oneself. Yet it is a home never quite reached. Wright is always deflected from paradise and, in the last two books of his trilogy finds himself reading the Appalachian Book of the Dead, not the New Testament or the *Paradiso*.

I suggested earlier that Wright learned about the metaphysical status or images from Montale. What he gathered from *il maestro* was perhaps no more than a sense of the image as *lampo*, and which he was ready to learn because he had already read Ezra Pound. Wright is at least as interested in the image for its spiritual possibilities as for its cleansing or poetic technique. In a page written in 1994 for his graduate students at the University of Virginia, he tries to distinguish image from metaphor, and to do so in an even-handed fashion:

> If it is true (and I think it is) that an image is, as Pound put it, an intellectual and emotional complex in an instant of time, and if the "logic of metaphor" is, as Crane put it, constructed on a series of associational meanings and thought-extension, then the narrative of image and the narrative of metaphor are different...the narrative (or logic) of metaphor will be more of a time-release agent, giving the reader a slower, longer contemplation; more time to think about the associations. The poem is perhaps more susceptible to a flow-through story line *inside* the poem.
>
> The narrative (logic) of image, on the other hand, is more explosive, gives the reader less time to ruminate, opens itself to impressionistic perceptions. The flow, such as it is, is intermittent, interrupted, and tends to exist *outside* the poem, as though a series of things glimpsed quickly, but indelibly, from a fast train ... [74]

For those who know Wright's later work, it is evident that he is quietly electing image over metaphor, and is doing so as part of an oblique defense of his meditative style, *sottonarrativa* or undernarrative, in which the story runs under the surface of the poem, appearing only now and then, like a train disappearing into and emerging from many tunnels.[75]

"The Image is Zen, Metaphor is Christian."[76] So Wright tries to tell Charles Simic in a flyting which ensued after he sent his friend a copy of the page I have just quoted. Simic will have none of it, and if truth is told speculative philosophy is not Wright's strongest suit. Putting his metaphysics of the image to one side, it is worth recognizing that for Wright the image's power "is otherworldly and ultimately apophatic."[77] It is memorably put in "Chinese Journal":

> In 1935, the year I was born,
> > Giorgio Morandi
> Penciled these bottles in by leaving them out, letting
> The presence or what surrounds them increase the presence
> Of what is missing,
> > keeping its distance and measure.[78]

Just as the Pseudo-Dionysius insists that apophatic theology precedes positive theology, so Wright proposes the priority of a negative poetics. Both are concerned, in their different ways, about revealability and not revelation. In the end his theology and his poetics are yoked together. As he advises himself in a later poem, "Shorten your poems and listen to what the darkness says."[79]

*

We have already heard Jean-Luc Nancy telling us that finitude means being "infinitely exposed to the otherness of our own 'being.'" Understanding this thought concretely would involve establishing how I mark my plurality in a singular manner and how I form a singular contract with these pluralities. It is one of the critic's tasks to discern how Wright himself negotiates plurality and singularity, and it is a task that is best performed with a nuanced understanding of the distinction between life and work. Certainly one would be led astray by taking as one's guide W. B. Yeats's division between "Perfection of the life, or of the work."[80] I took as my point or entry the Charles Wright who translates Eugenio Montale, and in a longer essay I would extend that discussion in the direction of travel and cultural poetics; for a good deal of Wright's poetry is concerned to singularize plural experiences of Italy and the American South. It is not an act or cultural translation so much as a holding together of layers of experience, each with its own moment of unrest, and layers of imaginative sympathy, as in the appeals to China.

More generally, it is of course Wright's earlier selves who form the plurality that is singularized by his proper name. The past is not to be approached by way of the same, though, but by way of otherness:

> There is an otherness inside us
> We never touch,
> > no matter how far down our hands reach.

It is the past,

> with its good looks and *Anytime, Anywhere* ...

Our prayers go our to it, our arms go out to it

Year after year

But who can ever remember enough?[81]

Wright tells us that insofar as it genuinely touches the past, memory is an act of finite transcendence. Later, he will add in a complex phrase "memory signs transcendence," meaning that transcendence is in fact a possession of memory—it calls us inward, not outward—and this realization makes "scales fall from the heart."[82] Husserl would agree with at least a part of that. Wright can also say, in Wordsworthian (and Proustian) mode, "What I remember redeems me," for recollection is a species of resurrection, he thinks.[83] If it is, then the word "resurrection" is being used in a literary rather than a theological sense. Even so, such a redemption is at best partial not only because "I can't remember enough" but also because "Absorbed in remembering, we cannot remember."[84] One can recover "other time" in this way though not or course "time as other": states of insomnia, fascination or suffering when the present excuses itself from its duties of retention and protention and lets time wander in, around and behind consciousness. Yet the melancholy one comes to associate with Wright's rhythms, idiom, and tones has little to do with a dialogue with time as other, and much to do with finitude. It is because humans are mortal and things are transient that we keep them in memory, and a poetry like Charles Wright's that is informed by memory at every level is inevitably marked not only by mourning who or what has passed but also by a foretaste of mourning who or what is still here, including the poet himself. One of the vital tensions in Wright's work is between a longing for detachment, which he finds in Christian mystics and Eastern sages, and an intense attachment to who or what has passed and will pass.

Living in a world held to be radically finite, people seek transcendence while knowing that it is bound to be overtaken by immanence: an ascent above the world is momentary, at best, or it fails, as with the Hunter Gracchus, who keeps docking in Wright's later poems.[85] Like the ascetic, the poet subtracts from the visible in order to reveal the invisible (which is what Wright's poetry often says); but unlike the ascetic, the poet must continually be sidetracked from this *via negativa* (which is what Wright's poetry often does). Even "Via Negativa" talks more about southwest Virginia and California than "the narrowness / Between the thing itself and the naming of the thing."[86] This theme and practice occur time and again from *Hard Freight* to *Appalachia*, although seldom more strikingly than in "Apologia Pro Vita Sua":

Landscape's a lever of transcendence—
                              jack-wedge it here,
Or here, and step back,
Heave, and a light, a little light, will nimbus your going forth:

The dew bead, terminal bead, opens out
                              onto a great radiance,
Sun's square on magnolia leaf
Offers us entrance—
                    who among us will step forward,
Camellia brown boutonnieres
Under his feet, plum branches under his feet, white sky, white noon,
Church bells like monk's mouths tonguing the hymn?[87]

These lines are indeed an apologia, although they look back only in the barest way to Shelley and Sidney, let alone Newman. And yet there is a poetics here, for Wright is almost giving us a template for the composition of his poems, while also offering an insight into how he understands his spiritual pilgrimage. To say that Wright uses poetry to develop a natural theology would be only partly right because the poetry also speaks to us of the failure of poetry to approach the divine and because the poetry is also drawn in quite other religious directions, including that of negative theology."[88] If we re-read the whole of Wright's trilogy, from *Country Music* to *Negative Blue*, this hesitance with respect to a religious vision becomes more and more clear. The poetry of *Negative Blue* is marked by a tension between the poet who has long been on a pilgrimage, whose volumes are the record of his quest, and the man who is still searching for the right place at which to begin his pilgrimage. Wright's later poetry evokes the distinctive pathos of a man remaining at the threshold while becoming ever more experienced on the path. In the lines I have just quoted it is significant that he evokes an entrance and nothing more, and that the passage ends with a question—"who among us will step forward"?—, which includes himself. And I should add that it is unclear whether one steps forward in order to begin a spiritual pilgrimage or to begin climbing the ladder of divine ascent.

Notice too that Wright tells us little about where we might go if we do indeed enter. "A great radiance" is held out before us; we discern it through a lack of adequation between the landscape and our grasp of it, what he calls later in the poem "ripples of otherworldliness."[89] There is something in our engagement with the landscape that cannot be translated into knowledge by way of perception. This "something" is what he calls "transcendence"; and the way he presents it makes us think of a "finite transcendence," disturbance in immanence instead of a trans-ascendance. "O Something, be with me, time is short," he prays later, in "Night Rider," yet the very lyric that follows it, "Is," looks coolly at transcendence considered as trans-ascendance:

Transcendence is a young man's retreat,
                    and resides in a place
Beyond place, vasty, boundless.
It hums, unlike the beauty of the world,
                    without pause, without mercy.[90]

On my reading, Wright's aging pilgrim might be oriented to what Matthew Arnold and Harold Bloom, in a rare moment of consonance, could agree to name "the God of experience." Or, indeed, this same pilgrim might be oriented to what Karl Rahner calls "the experience of God": the unthematic fore-grasping of divinity through self-experience in concrete historical situations with others. Perhaps I should emphasize "with others" since, although Wright begins with landscape, he finishes out his apologia by way of anecdote about people he knows or has known.

Only a hasty reader would stop here and bypass the possibility that Wright evokes a transcendence of self rather than a self-transcendence. To be sure, this would be a dangerous experience because it would invite the pilgrim not to find transcendence in and through experience but to risk abandoning experience altogether. It is one thing to use poetry as a ladder to God, quite another to cast it aside when the summit has been reached. To do that is to risk not being remembered by "The landscape and wild chestnut," and "Apologia Pro Vita Sua" implies that this is a very bad thing indeed.[91] It is no surprise then that Wright's pilgrim is pictured walking over the boutonnieres and plum branches into a sky that is all white. We might think this is the blinding heat of noon, a heat that nourishes the beauty of the natural world, and that the pilgrim will continue to encounter this world. By the same token, we might think that the path ahead, if taken, will lead to the dissolution of the senses and language, and that such a course would be extremely dangerous for a poet. There is a sense in which mystics are terrorists, like the Romantics, because they prize experience over rhetoric; and the greatest among them are perhaps the greatest terrorists of all because they value non-experience over experience. Of course, there is poetry of non-experience—John of the Cross's "Una noche oscura" and Gerard Manley Hopkins's "No worst there is none," for instance—just as there is a poetry of renunciation, such as one finds in the later Goethe. But Wright's work is otherwise: it is poetry of experience that also questions if it is experience of the right path. On this reading, "Apologia Pro Vita Sua" is a defense of a life, and a life of writing, lived in the wake of answering the question "who among us will step forward [?]." The difficulties the poem poses, along with the work for which it stands, is that it sanctions many contrary and even contradictory answers: "Not I," "Not yet," "I will," "I have," and even "The question is badly put."

PART FIVE

Morning knowledge

14

Contemplation and concretion

Four Marian lyrics

The topic of contemplation gravitates toward the Virgin Mary from several directions. First of all, Mary is a biblical model of contemplation: she stands before God, listens to his word, and is ready to accept him in any way, at any time, and to any extent. She ponders what the shepherds tell her about her son (Lk. 2:19) and keeps in her heart what Jesus says about why he stayed behind in Jerusalem (Lk. 2:51). The participle "pondering," rare in English until William Tyndale chose it to render συμβάλλουσα, admirably captures one aspect of contemplation, "to weigh mentally" (*OED*), while we must also take into account a quite different aspect: a sense of lightness, even suspension, in mental flight.[1] Second, only when we are devoted to Mary, edified by the exemplary witness of her humility and her readiness to respond without reserve to God, are we in a position to receive the grace of infused contemplation.[2] And third, Mary is herself an object for active contemplation: she opens a spiritual path that we may follow and that, with divine grace, enables us to be brought to her Son and to his Father through the workings of the Holy Spirit. The woman who is *summa contemplatrix* is also *illuminatrix contemplatium*.[3]

Yet perhaps I am moving a little too quickly, and claiming for contemplation things that might be more appropriately assigned to meditation or even thought. One authority to whom we all must bow in this matter is the twelfth-century Augustinian canon regular Richard of St. Victor, *Magnus Contemplator* as he became known. In *The Mystical Ark* Richard distinguishes cognition, meditation, and contemplation:

> By means of inconstant and slow feet, thinking wanders here and there in all directions without any regard for arriving. Meditation presses forward with great activity of soul, often through arduous and rough places, to the

end of the way it is going. Contemplation, in free flight, circles around with marvelous quickness wherever impulse moves it. Thinking crawls; meditation marches and often runs; contemplation flies around everywhere and when it wishes suspends itself in the heights. Thinking is without labor and fruit; in meditation there is labor with fruit; contemplation continues without labor but with fruit. In thinking there is wandering; in meditation, investigation; in contemplation, wonder. Thinking is from imagination; meditation, from reason; contemplation, from understanding.[4]

Notice that, unlike many later thinkers of the spiritual life, those who lived in the fourteenth century and beyond, Richard does not divide meditation from contemplation by way of the use and abandonment of images. For him, meditation is rumination; contemplation is free suspension in mental flight.[5] Later, the meaning of "meditation" would shift to denote affective devotion stimulated by moments in the lives of Jesus and Mary in particular. No doubt we associate Mary with powerful mental pictures, from Annunciation to Coronation, and we pass steadily through all of them when saying the rosary, of which Richard could know nothing. Besides, he is concerned less with objects of the gaze than with modifications of it, as St. Thomas Aquinas is quick to pick up when responding to Richard in the *Summa theologiæ*. He quotes Richard as saying that "contemplation is the soul's penetrating and easy gaze on things perceived; meditation is the investigation of a mind occupied in the search for truth; cogitation is the concentration of a mind that is prone to wander."[6] One could add that this gaze is intellectual yet compassionate, and does not seek to objectify anyone as is often assumed today when speaking of the gaze.

Glance, survey, and gaze: with Mary it is mostly a matter of the gaze, as subject and also, for us, as object. That is because much that is to do with Mary concerns the fifth and sixth grades of contemplation in Richard's classification. The first grade, he tells us, is restricted to the use of images; the second considers the image-making faculty guided by reason; the third, reason based on this faculty; and the fourth, reason conducted within reason. Yet when we come to the fifth rank we are placed above reason though not contrary to it, and this for Thomas is the beginning of contemplation proper. We are at the sixth rank, the summit of the gaze, when we are above reason and contrary to it. The Marian doctrines of the Virginal Conception, the Virgin Birth, the Assumption and the Immaculate Conception are all situated at the sixth level and so call forth the very perfection of contemplation.[7] More generally, we may reverence Mary in various profiles: *Apostola apostolorum*, Assumption, Immaculate Conception, *Mater dolorosa*, *Mater misericordiæ*, Mediatrix of all Graces, Mother of the Church, Pietà, Queen of Heaven, Second Eve, *Stella maris*, Wisdom of God, and so on, right up to a title used by some today that points to a speculative theologoumenon, Mary as Co-Redemptrix. Mary is also honored by links with special places; she is Our Lady of Chartres, Guadaloupe, Lourdes, Fátima, and many other sites. Nonetheless, for all our devotion to Mary, we never rest our gaze finally on her; she prompts us to pass from her to the contemplation of God's grace and mercy in her.

Not everything to do with Mary takes place on the sixth level of contemplation, however; some things occur at the first and second levels. I am thinking of the visit to Elizabeth, the flight to Egypt, the presentation in the temple, the losing of the boy Jesus in Jerusalem at Passover, her presence at the crucifixion, among other stories related in the Gospels and Acts. To be sure, allegorical and other styles of theological exegesis are capable of imbuing these events with immense spiritual significance, yet these events are first of all moments in a human life. One of the most important tasks for a Catholic is to see how all the big occasions of Mary's life grow together with those of her Son's life, not just at the level of biblical narrative (where there are challenges, such as Jesus's apparently harsh words about Mary at Lk. 11:27-8 and to her at Jn 2:4), but also at the level of Mariology and Christology. This growing together is what Hegel calls "concretion"; and in his philosophy the aim is to register the particular ways in which the dialectic gathers all that there is and makes it into an ever more concrete reality.[8] Human beings and God both become more determinate for Hegel as the Idea unfolds in logic and over the course of history. It is a philosophy that has long been attractive to Protestant theology in the twentieth century, not in the whole but in some of its parts: Karl Barth Hegelianized in the *Church Dogmatics*, as he freely admitted, and Wolfhart Pannenberg exhibits a tendency to Neo-Hegelianism in his *Systematic Theology*.[9]

Modern Catholic theology is not oriented by Hegel's vision of the Idea alienated in Nature and, through its engagement with History, recuperated and affirmed as Spirit. Its roots are chiefly in Aristotle, the Fathers, and needless to say medieval philosophy and theology. Yet contemporary Catholic theology is committed to rendering the Gospel as concretely as possible. In doing so it is not content simply to recover an image of Joseph, Mary and Jesus as a family with its own troubles and satisfactions. To be sure, this everydayness is important to stress, especially in parish life, not least of all because it shows that for God the extraordinary takes place within the realm of the ordinary and, at the same time, the ordinary can be charged with the power of the extraordinary. Our daily lives press into the mystery of God, and God pulls us ever closer to him through our disappointments, grief and joys. Society today is fascinated by the spectacle of fame, and the Church needs to counter it with the contemplation of the extraordinary. To be famous is not within everyone's grasp, for which those of us who are not famous should be thankful. As Charles Wright says, "The ache for fame is a thick dust and weariness in the heart."[10] Yet to be extraordinary within the compass of the ordinary is something that we may attain with the grace of God. As a wife and mother, Mary shows us ways in which this is possible.

We are also invited to see how Christian existence deepens in and through spirituality when it is informed by attention to Joseph, Mary and Jesus. For it is Joseph and Mary who guarantee for us the particularity of Jesus as a human being: they save us, if you like, from the intellectual seduction of an abstract Christ whose purely supernatural existence would have distanced him from us while making him more acceptable to the educated human mind. Christianity turns on the Incarnation of God, which requires the *fiat* of Mary, and we must remember that the Incarnation is not just the moment of conception but more profoundly the entire orientation in life and death of Jesus, both before and after Easter. God elected Jewish flesh in history and for eternity. Finally, concretion is needed to establish the coherence of *sacra doctrina*. Our path to the Father is Jesus Christ, the Messiah who comes to us as a man of his times, and there is nothing in Jesus untouched by Mary. Likewise, there is nothing important in the study of Mary that is not marked in some way or to some extent by the study of Christ.

The central Marian doctrines are consequences of an orthodox understanding of the doctrines of the Christ, and this is a key truth for Catholic systematic theology. A theologian will speak, for example, of how the Immaculate Conception and the Virginal Conception protect the Savior from the primal dislocation from God that in the Latin West we call original sin. He or she will also distinguish from this doctrine those other Marian doctrines that revolve tightly around Mary rather than Christ: the Virgin Birth, Perpetual Virginity, and the Assumption.[11] That there are Marian doctrines that have no apparent Christological significance does not count against their importance. Yet they need to be just as rigorously proposed. Today we might ask if the doctrine of the Virgin Birth is truly held aloft from Docetism. It is no easy thing to say, despite the authority of the Lateran Council (649), Saints Irenaeus, Chrysostom, Jerome and others, right up to *Lumen Gentium*, the dogmatic constitution of the Church as proclaimed at Vatican II (1964).[12] The doctrine has been declared and esteemed more surely than it has been theologically established. It calls for close examination without the pressure of the cult of virginity that was so powerful in patristic times.[13] Here, as elsewhere, one cannot reach a settled theology without encountering unsettling theologoumena. There are moments in theology when one can say too much, or too much in one direction, and thereby detract from the truth that a doctrine seeks to promote.[14] Finally, it must be acknowledged that Marian doctrines are foundational for a normal Christian life. We shall not apprehend the mystery of the Christ if we do not approach it through the bond between

Jesus and his mother. What is most mysterious comes to us through what is most familiar.

With all that said, and with its various limits in mind, it must be conceded that biblical images of Mary are few and far between, and when they occur they may be memorable but they are also fleeting. We see Mary clearly in Mark 3:31–5, Luke 1–2, Matthew 1–2, John 2:1–2, 19:25–7, and Acts 1:14; and if we are wise we bypass false images of her, such as her time as a Temple Virgin (in the *Protevangelium of James*) and of fire coming from her mouth when she speaks of the Annunciation (in the *Gospel of Bartholomew*).[15] There is an impulse to turn the authentic images of Mary into narrative. Think of Epiphanius the Monk's *Life of the Virgin*, Pseudo-John the Theologian's *Transitus Mariæ* and Maximus the Confessor's *The Life of the Virgin*.[16] And think, too, of those who wish to tell a fuller story than those we have in Scripture, Apocryphra or the Fathers, such as the one supplied by Maria de Agrada in her life of the Virgin in her *City of God*.[17] And there is a counter-impulse to retain these images as images so that they may be contemplated. Biblical images are strong, and some doctrinal images (the Assumption, the Coronation) also lodge firmly in our minds. Whether they are low or high on Richard's hierarchy of contemplation, they call for the mind to turn and turn around them. The educated Catholic imagination responds vividly to this call, and is also nourished by concretion in a sense other than Hegel's. It was Edmund Husserl who proposed a new way of thinking specifically.[18] We approach the concrete, he thought, not dialectically, as with Hegel, or by placing a particular under a generality so that it comes into focus as an example of something, as with Aristotle. Not at all: it is a question of discerning how a phenomenon gives itself, its particular manner of self-manifestation and reception in a specific situation.

Important as they are, the questions "What?" and "Why?" yield in terms of concreteness to the question "How?" How does Mary's motherhood become meaningful for us? Not just by discussion of the "closed womb" or by discussion over whether she felt pain in the birth or was excused from this pain but by the faith that she showed in God's promise. Let us never let our cultural familiarity with the Christian faith allow us to forget that "God" is the most abstract of words, even for theologians, and that it assumes a local habitation and a name only as it shines through Jesus, in his earthly life, his passion, and his resurrected life. And never let us forget that this same light is refracted through Mary. We may not think at first that this concretion is called for more urgently by sacred doctrines than by biblical verses, and that it is harder to comprehend the determinate meaning of the Immaculate Conception (in essence, a teaching about Mary's need for sanctifying grace from the moment of conception) than the loss of Jesus in the streets of Jerusalem. When we hear of the Annunciation we believe that we can understand the anxiety and the joy of a young girl who is to become pregnant before she is married and whom God has assured that she has found favor with him. Perhaps we can apprehend these things, although visual artists from those in the catacombs to those in modern times have aided us a good deal.[19] Michelangelo, Botticelli, El Greco, along with many others, have tutored our imaginations.

Poets have also helped to present Mary to us in a concrete manner that offers her to our free and varied contemplation, that is, as Richard of St. Victor says, to our understanding. In approaching poems, reading them as I shall be doing here, we dip down from contemplation to meditation and cogitation—we have to work, to reason, to investigate before we can be sure of our reading— yet the finest poems always seek to convert our gaze, finally to launch us to a state of mental suspension over them and what they evoke. Contemplation is a reward of meditation. We engage in cognition and meditation, in what Nietzsche called "slow reading," in order to pass to contemplation.[20] If we press on this formulation and ask what specifically is the contemplation to be gained by reading poems about Mary, we shall find ourselves in the midst of an important and difficult problem. For Christian poetry inherits its contemplative dimension from different sources. Contemplation is, first, the mind dilating on the splendor of being (Aristotle), and it is also the setting of passions in a "cool place" (Wittgenstein).[21] Christianity, however, also figures contemplation as the counter-gaze that responds to a gaze that has first turned to us. We do not initiate a relationship with the divine; rather, we respond to a loving gaze, one that sometimes pierces us and humbles us before we can respond with the love that is called forth from us. A lyric poem is a kind of *templum* through which an aspect or profile of the divine is seen to pass: not as revelation but as relation. The relation another has with Mary or Jesus, one that is recorded in verse, becomes a way of seeing Mary or Jesus, one that we take to correct our own vision or to improve it.

I would like to ponder several Marian lyrics in order to indicate some ways in which Mary appears to us in poetry. Of course, in having Our Lady given to us in this way we are able to grow into the mystery of the coming of God and the reception of God. We shall find that poets, like painters (and also like theologians), can only give profiles of the Virgin. Yet a poem can lead us into the mystery of the Mother more economically than the tersest of theologians, and contemplation revolves around what beckons us but that ultimately escapes our conceptual grasp.

*

There would be reason to begin with Marian verse by Romanos (c. 490–c. 560) in the Greek-speaking Church or Venantius Fortunatus (c. 530–c. 600) in the

Latin speaking Church, but I shall focus only on vernacular lyrics, and only on those written in English. Many opportunities for discussion abound, including a range of anonymous medieval lyrics, Chaucer's *Invocatio ad Mariam*, poems by St. Robert Southwell, John Donne, G. M. Hopkins, and Geoffrey Hill.[22] I shall be highly selective, and shall comment on just four lyrics, on some more briefly than others.[23] I begin with a piercing Marian carol from the Sloane manuscript, which is also one of the consummate lyrics of the English language, one distilled from a thirteenth-century poem, "No this fules singet and maket hure blisse."[24] The carol I shall discuss is very well-known, although as always with the highest art it is also inexhaustible. It is known by its first line, "I syng of a myden":

> I syng of a myden
>> That is makeles:
> Kyng of alle kynges
>> To her sone che ches.
>
> He cam also stylle
>> Ther his moder was
> As dew in Aprylle
>> That fallyt on the gras.
>
> He cam also stylle
>> To his moderes bowr
> As dew in Aprille
>> That fallyt on the flour.
>
> He cam also stylle
>> Ther his moder lay
> As dew in Aprille
>> That fallyt on the spray.
>
> Moder and mayden
>> Was never non but che;
> Wel may swych a lady
>> Godes moder be.[25]

On a first reading one might think that here as elsewhere Mary is seen as passive and self-negating: she simply "is," we are told.[26] Later, she is in a "bower" and she "lays" there. A moment's reflection, though, will show us that the poet is responding to Luke's account of the Annunciation in which Mary is active: she accepts what the angel proposes, and does not ask permission of Joseph to respond to God's call. (For Matthew, on the other hand, the Annunciation revolves around Joseph.) Indeed, the anonymous poet goes further than Luke in stressing Mary's active role. Note that she *chooses* Jesus: "To her sone che *ches*" [my emphasis], the lyric quietly insists, and the rhyme word underscores the affirmative human response to the divine invitation.[27]

How does the Incarnation happen? That is the central question of the lyric, not "What is the Incarnation?" or "Why did the Incarnation have to happen?," which are questions for the theologian, and good ones to ask in the right places and at the proper times. Yet the lyric takes the question that leads to the most concrete meaning. The answer turns out to be a complex one with three stages, although it is given as simply as an answer can ever be given. Notice, first of all, that while the poet begins "*I* syng of a myden" [my emphasis] the lyric "I" withdraws after the very first word and never again appears in the poem; and notice also that his song of Mary takes as its focus the coming of Jesus: "*He* cam also stylle" [my emphasis] is repeated twice, each time with incremental development following it. The song is of Mary whose gaze is on her son. The Mary whose action is given in her choice properly becomes passive once her decision has been made; we move from "che ches" to "Ther his moder was." She has passed from willing to being. Not that the activity of God in Mary is marked dramatically; if anything, it is barely registered: Christ's coming is "stylle" and like a "falling." It is also quotidian in its manner, "As dew in Aprille," although in the service of the most extraordinary event in world history. For dew is also a metaphor for the Holy Spirit and divine grace. Let us look at this advent a little more closely.

First we are told that Christ comes to Mary, and that is all. "Ther his moder was": it is the barest predicate that is possible in English, indicating that she exists (and that she exists in a place). The whole cosmos has contracted for God to where one woman is. How does he come? Very simply: "As dew in Aprille / That fallyt on the gras." April is a month of the season of Spring, a time of rebirth, and perhaps we think too of the word's origin in the Latin verb *aperire*, "to open." The year opens once again, this time in a singular way. No sooner than Mary has chosen her son than Christ comes as dew, unseen yet needed for the grass to grow; and with great delicacy the poem suggests the maturing of the infant in Mary and the new morning of life on earth. He comes as dew on the grass, and then as dew on a flower, and finally as dew on a spray.[28] We think of manna coming to the Children of Israel (Exod. 16:13), of the dew on Gideon's fleece (Judg. 6:37–40), of the psalmist singing "God will help her, [and that] right early" (Ps. 46:5), and with respect to the triple repetition, we may well think of the triune action of the Incarnation.

The language of the carol is spare, entirely conventional, and apart from its particularity it owes little or nothing to the affective devotional style associated with the *Meditationes vitæ Christi* of Pseudo-Bonaventure that became so prominent in the fourteenth century and that encouraged meditation rather than contemplation.[29] The carol's language is restrained; it encourages wonder. This language is also thoroughly biblical: we are likely to recall Canticle 2:1-2, "I am the flower of the field, and the lily of the valleys," and Isaiah 11:1, "And there shall come forth a rod out of the stem of Jesse, and a Branch shall grow out of his roots." The complexity of human maturation in the womb is suggested in three uncluttered similes. Each time Christ approaches Mary as all so "stylle": a medieval theologian would speak of Christ coming *modus sine modo*, in a way without a way; and a medieval poet, with equal precision but more concretely, evokes the dew that falls on the earth without any sign of having come from anywhere.[30] Christ does not come just the once for Mary; he keeps coming, each time the more richly. He is "Kynge of alle kynges"—the title derives from the Hebrew Bible (Ps. 72:11)—not because he imposes his rule on the world but because he will save the world with the Kingdom.[31] Unlike worldly kings, but like his Father, Christ is a just ruler. He comes like dew not because the Incarnation is natural but because God's transcendence does not disable his immanence within Creation, and because his majesty not does overwhelm his condescension.[32]

The central stanzas of "I syng of a myden" respond to the "How"-question, and so give us a lyrical phenomenology of the Incarnation. Yet there can be no doubt that the carol also folds a complex sequence of theology into its short lines. This happens in the first and last stanzas, the *exordium* and *conclusio*. The poet sings of a maiden who is "makeless": matchless, first of all, yet also without a mate, and, finally, immaculate. The theologoumenon of the Immaculate Conception, as it once was, entered England sometime in the first half of the eleventh century, and gained theological support with Eadmer's *Tractatus de conceptione S. Mariæ* in the early twelfth century, as well as sharp opposition at the time and thereafter. The feast was added to the English liturgical calendar in 1139. By the fifteenth century, mostly due to Franciscan preaching, the teaching of the Immaculate Conception had taken root so firmly in the vernacular imagination that it could enter a lyric in just the one word and under the cover of a primary meaning. It is in the final stanza, however, that a major sequence of Marian theology becomes audible. Mary is "Moder and mayden": she has conceived as a virgin and given birth to a child, *utero clauso et obsignato*, and is singular among created beings, the only one worthy of *hyper dulia*. Yet the poem can end only with the confession of the oldest Marian doctrine, formulated at the Council of Ephesus in 431, that Mary is the Mother of God. No title has been given to the "maydn" until now, almost at the end of the lyric, when she is declared "swych a lady," worthy of all dignity as the mother of the greatest of all kings and, moreover, as the one who accepted the divine invitation to bear the Messiah. The theological doctrine is tacitly accepted by the modern reader of the poem, outside all liturgy and even belief, by dint of the middle stanzas of the poem that render the Incarnation determinate in the most delicate way. Poetically, the "How"-question has precedence over all others.

*

I turn from the late Middle Ages to the late seventeenth century, a period not noted for its devotion to Mary or for its Marian lyrics, and to a poem from Nahum Tate's *Miscellanea Sacra: Or, Poems on Divine and Moral Subjects* (1696). It is "The Blessed Virgin's Expostulation, When our Savior at Twelve Years of Age had Withdrawn Himself, Luke 2:42." Mary speaks the entire piece, presumably in Jerusalem after urgently returning from Lebonah or Akrabah, hamlets that were a day's journey from the holy city, where she and Joseph had discovered that Jesus was nowhere to be found in their company of travelers. It is an unusual moment of the episode on which to focus. We are used to reflecting on the end of the story where, as Dante indicates in the *Purgatorio*, we see Mary as a model of gentleness in distress.[33] Not so for Tate; his Mary is agitated as she walks the streets of Jerusalem:

> Tell me some pitying Angel, quickly say
> Where does my Soul's sweet Darling stray
> In Tygers, or more cruel *Herod's* Way?
> O! rather let his tender Foot-steps press
> Unguarded through the Wilderness,
> Where milder Salvages resort;
> The Desart's safer than a Tyrant's Court.
> Why, fairest Object of my Love,
> Why dost Thou from my longing Eyes remove?
> Was it a waking Dream that did foretel
> Thy wondeous Birth? No Vision from Above?
> Where's *Gabriel* now that visited my Cell?
> I call—He comes not—flatt'ring Hopes, Farewel.
> Me *Judah's* Daughters once Caress'd,
> Call'd me of Mother's the most Blest;
> Now (fatal Change!) of Mothers, most distress'd!
> How shall my Soul its Motions guide,
> How shall I stem the vatious Tide,
> Whilst Faith and Doubt my lab'ring Thoughts divide?

For whilst of thy Dear Sight I am beguil'd,
I Trust the God—But oh! I fear the *Child*.[34]

Strictly speaking, the poem is a Christian midrash on Luke 2:42; it seeks to give to contemplation what Scripture does not itself offer: Mary's distressed reaction to the loss of Jesus in the mode of an address first to an angel and then to her son.

In terms of Richard's classification, we are certainly well beneath the fifth and sixth levels of contemplation. We overhear Mary's fears and register a note of panic in her voice. Not knowing where her son actually is, and especially in a city so much vaster than the hamlet of Nazareth (and swollen to twice its usual size at Passover), her imagination runs free and, like all parents at such times, is drawn to the dark side of the spectrum of possibilities: Has he been taken by Herod Antipas whose father, Herod the Great, had sought to kill him as an infant? Herod Antipas would later have John the Baptist executed; the Court is indeed more dangerous than the desert. So we do not find ourselves raised to the heights above or beyond reason; no *sacra doctrina* is folded into the maternal psychology. If anything, there is a questioning of the basis of Marian doctrines. (After all, Tate came from Puritan stock in Ireland.) For whether the Annunciation actually happened is called into doubt, though not very forcefully. "Was it a waking Dream that did fortel / Thy wondeous Birth? No Vision from Above?" The questions open the possibility that the Annunciation was imagined, not real.

Yet it is the humanity of Jesus, not his divinity, which has caused his mother's acute anxiety. Ordinary boys get lost in crowds and wander down side streets, talk with strangers, and worry their parents. Mary apparently expects that her divine son will not act like a typical twelve-year old boy because he is divine. "Where's *Gabriel* now that visited my Cell?," she asks, less in disbelief in the angel than in dismay that no angel comes to help her search for the boy Jesus in the big city. We are invited to contemplate Mary as more like us than we usually think when reflecting on Marian dogma, to suspend ourselves in compassionate wonder before the humanity of the Mother of God. When things are going well, we live fluently within our world; yet when something goes awry the things of the world obtrude: we fumble, doubt and panic.[35] So now, when Jesus is lost and the reliability of her family life and her relationship with God are disrupted, Mary says, "Faith and Doubt my lab'ring Thoughts divide." Only for a moment, though, are we allowed to imagine that Mary doubts the Father's care for her family, and yet the poem leaves us with a strong sense of both the faith and the human fear that besets her: "I Trust the God—But oh! I fear the *Child*."

What Tate puts tangibly before our attention is the manner of doubt that perhaps troubled Mary. It is not that she is afraid, or what she is afraid of, that most moves us but rather the way in which her fear is given to us. To be sure, she questions the reality of the Annunciation yet only in the context of praying to an angel, and so her belief in the supernatural is not seriously eroded. As I have suggested, it is her sudden sense of the humanity of her son that seems to inspire doubt. Could God have given her a son who is so *fully* human that he can wander away from his parents and cause them anxiety? We are used to thinking of Jesus as fully God and fully Man but less familiar with the idea of Jesus as fully God and fully Child. Tate's lyric gives that image to our understanding and so brings Mary closer to all parents in a visceral manner. Mary emerges in the poem as a woman of faith, though one just as capable of being thrown by unexpected events as we are. Tate's poem is not a memorable lyric, not by any means, yet it is not without force. Part of its power is that it ends with Mary in distress, while we know, as readers of the infancy narrative of Luke, that Jesus will be found and say that he has been in the Temple going about his Father's business. Mary will ponder these things in her heart, and turn a distressing event into a topic of contemplation of the mystery of the Incarnation. The lyric points us to this mystery, but stops before reaching it, allowing the reader to see it in a parental perspective.

Quite different in its rhetorical tenor from Tate's poem and the anonymous carol with which we started is W. B. Yeats's fierce lyric "The Mother of God" from *The Winding Stair and Other Poems* (1933), also a dramatic monolog spoken by Mary, and like "I syng of a myden" intently focused on the Incarnation. In a way, "The Mother of God" is a Christian counterpart to the more famous (and far stronger) lyrics "The Second Coming" (1919) in which a rough beast slouches toward Bethlehem to be born, and "Leda and the Swan" (1923) in which Zeus in the form of a swan rapes a young woman. The poem about Leda takes its bearings in all likelihood from Ronsard's "La défloration de Lède"; the other ones, including the one about Mary, derive from Scripture and *sacra doctrina*, though only "The Mother of God" remains within the orbit of Christianity. "The Second Coming" exhibits a grim irony toward the faith.[36] What finally interests Yeats in the sonnet of 1919 is whether Leda was divinized as regards knowledge in the moment of the sexual act. "Did she put on his knowledge with his power / Before the indifferent beak could let her drop?" "The Mother of God" ends, though, with a more searing intimate question:

> The threefold terror of love; a fallen flare
> Through the hollow of an ear;
> Wings beating about the room;
> The terror of all terrors that I bore
> The Heavens in my womb.

Had I not found content among the shows
Every common woman knows,
Chimney corner, garden walk,
Or rocky cistern where we tread the clothes
And gather all the talk?

What is this flesh I purchased with my pains,
This fallen star my milk sustains,
This love that makes my heart's blood stop
Or strikes a sudden chill into my bones
And bids my hair stand up?[37]

The love of God experienced by Mary is terrifying: the angel's word is a flare
fallen into her ear; the sound of his wings in her room is frightening; and,
worst of all, she must bear "The Heavens" in her womb. Not "Heaven"
but "The Heavens": Yeats does not allow us to spiritualize the image in
any orthodox way, but instead makes us think of the heterodox theology
of the seven heavens and then has us imagine them shrinking to fit inside
a uterus.[38] Mary's confinement is not quiet or ecstatic, as popular piety
would sometimes have it, but rather marked by a *mysterium tremendum et
fascinans*.[39]

The second and third stanzas consist of two questions of different sorts.
The first is rhetorical, stating (in the mode of question) that she was content
in her everyday life in Nazareth.[40] The Mishna gives us a good idea of what
that daily life would have been like in a small farming community of twenty
to thirty families, and chances are that Mary would very likely have enjoyed
that life had another woman been chosen by God to bear his son. Yet *she*
was chosen, and so she asks another question, which is given in the third
stanza. Jesus is a "fallen star" to which she has given birth, with all the usual
pains of labor. (As a Protestant, Yeats does not subscribe to the doctrine of
the Immaculate Conception, which renders Mary immune from the pain of
giving birth.[41]) But what is the love that makes her blood stop, her bones go
cold, and her hair stand up? Is it her love for her divine child? Or is it God's
love for her? It is both, for both loves are sublime and accordingly touched
by terror as well as joy. The enormity of her situation as subject and object
presses hard on her. The ordinary contains the extraordinary in a spiritual
sense, yet psychologically the extraordinary bursts out of the ordinary. With
Yeats's poem, then, we have a late Romantic lyric account of the motherhood
of Mary, utterly distinct in manner and idiom from the medieval carol and the
late seventeenth-century monolog.

*

The final lyric I shall consider is "Pietà" from *Surprises of the Son* (1969) by James McAuley. It will be said that it is only indirectly a Marian lyric, since it concerns itself with a normal mother and her dead child. Yet the title lights the poem so as to associate the mother with Mary, Our Lady of Sorrows, and the lyric has a Christological dimension that cannot be put aside:

> A year ago you came
> Early into the light.
> You lived a day and night,
> Then died; no-one to blame.
>
> Once only, with one hand,
> Your mother in farewell
> Touched you. I cannot tell,
> I cannot understand
>
> A thing so dark and deep,
> So physical a loss:
> One touch, and that was all
>
> She had of you to keep.
> Clean wounds, but terrible,
> Are those made with the Cross.[42]

A baby is born prematurely, lives briefly, and then just before dying is given to the mother to be caressed. The child is not even held with both arms in a full embrace. One touch comprises all the love that the mother is permitted to express, and this single act is the focus of the poem. An entire life is contracted to a day and night, and all of motherhood is abridged to just one brush of a hand against the child's flesh. (The poem too is curtailed: it is a sonnet in iambic trimeter, not pentameter.)

In "Pietà," a father addresses his dead child on the first anniversary of his or her death. The lyric is conducted within the figure of prosopopeia, giving a face to the dead, although the address later turns to the speaker, outside the intimate relationship of mother and child. The father says, "I cannot tell, / I cannot understand / A thing so dark and deep." He cannot relate the grief of another; he cannot understand it from within the depths of his wife's grief: the poem marks a withdrawal of contemplation at the level of ordinary human discernment. Nor can the mother grasp what has happened; there is no theoretical knowledge that can be attained about the mystery of suffering. All that the mother has to keep through life is a touch, the exercise of a non-theoretical sense, offering no knowledge that could give intellectual comfort. Yet touch and taste are precisely how we communicate spiritually with God, as contemplatives from St. Augustine on through the centuries have indicated time and again.[43] If the sonnet concerns the pain of an ordinary mother and father through its octave and almost all the sestet, it becomes strongly Christological in its final two lines: "Clean wounds but terrible, / Are those made with the Cross." What are we to make of this authoritative final statement?

The lyric's title moves us to think of Mary holding her dead son, whose wounds were very far from clean, and we remember how the mother of "Pietà" is joined through grief to Our Lady of Sorrows with the loss of her child. At the Temple Simeon prophesied that a sword would pierce Mary's soul (Lk. 2:35), and it came to pass: the cross was that very sword. It was so in itself (for a cross looks like a giant sword thrust into the earth) and also metaphorically (for it was a sword of sorrow). This blade did not physically enter her body, and so it left clean wounds, but those psychological and spiritual wounds were indeed terrible. What could be worse than having one's innocent son tortured and then executed as a criminal in the vilest way imaginable? Only one thing: the thought that one's son was the Messiah. It is oneness or singularity that is marked heavily in the sonnet: "*A* year ago you came," "*a* day and night," "*Once* only, with *one* hand," "*A* thing," "*One* touch" [my emphases]. Yet all these singular events lead to many wounds ("Clean wound*s*" [my emphasis]) in the mother and the father. The mother of "Pietà" suffers intensely, as Mary does; it is not that her son has been crucified but that he has lived so very briefly, and that the maternal relationship can be no more than a touch. Each of us has a cross to bear, the poem suggests, and the mother's cross is the loss of her son. More: each and every Christian at baptism is marked with the sign of the Cross and consequently is wrapped both in the hope of rising with Christ and in the expectation of suffering with him. Perhaps the mother or father makes the sign of the Cross when the baby is taken away; perhaps the infant is baptized before death. But even if these things are beyond the scene the poem evokes, the poet speaks as a Christian and is contained in the sign of the Cross. Only by identifying with the suffering Christ, with the mystery of his atoning sacrifice, can one hope to find any healing at all. The sonnet withdraws contemplation at the level of human pain only to reinstate it at the level of the mystery of the atonement. McAuley's "Pietà" is a Marian lyric in the deepest way; it passes through the lens of Mary in order to see Jesus steadily.

*

Marian devotion can be difficult because of the paucity of biblical images of the Virgin, and by dint of the abstraction of some Marian doctrines, whether they revolve around Christ or Mary herself. Yet Mary is contemplated concretely in carols and other lyrics: her mysteries are offered to our wondering gaze, not just to meditative review. Art properly concerns itself with the question "How?," even if it also asks other questions or responds to them from time to time. It has always performed a conversion of the gaze, usually partial and usually temporary, and so offers itself as a phenomenology to some extent. And because it is concerned with the gaze above all, phenomenology is contemplative. When it addresses itself to the holy or to God poetry performs a phenomenology, once again usually partial, of religion. Samuel Johnson insisted in his "Life of Waller" in his *Lives of the Most Eminent Poets* (1779–81) that religious poetry is impossible, for the truths of religion will always put one in a higher state than will the elaborations of verse.[44] In a sense, he is right: religious poetry goes awry when it seeks primarily or exclusively to answer the question "What?" or "Why?"

Yet religious poetry is concerned less with elaborating doctrine than with the manner of the changing relationship of the believer and the object of his or her belief. In life we pass from intimacy with God to distance from him, from doubt to trust; from distance to intimacy, from trust to doubt; and we bring our sense of the deity into focus for the length of a prayer before we realize that in doing so we transform the Almighty into an idol. It is the same with Mary. Against Johnson, who is in general the wisest of literary critics, we may say that religious poetry is not illustrative but concretive: it shows us situations in which something abstract attains definite meaning, and in doing so it helps us to grow together with God, one part of which is attaining an ever more determinate understanding of the spiritual unity of Jesus and Mary.

15

Ambassadors and votaries
of silence

I begin with Aristotle in the *Metaphysics*: "The term 'being' is used in various senses."[1] And to this very familiar thesis, adopted as a foundational insight of phenomenology, I add another, this time from Samuel Beckett's novel *The Unnamable* (1958): "For it is all very fine to keep silence, but one has also to consider the kind of silence one keeps."[2] A phenomenology of silence must begin in the unlikely company of Aristotle and Beckett so that it may teach us how to identify the different ways in which silence presents itself as company. It must start by leading us back past the natural attitude that we routinely adopt, the default acceptance of modern science (and common sense) as accounting for the meaning of our encounters with people and things (and not just explaining them according to its lights). We must pass to our lived experience and remain stubbornly answerable to its structures.

That passage involves taking a step back from our everyday lives and becoming transcendental onlookers who no longer believe in the world in terms of specific theses about being such as the empirical and psychological "I" does. Our intentional relations with the world are relaxed a little. Then we can begin to recognize that phenomena are concretely embedded in horizons that we have tended to overlook. We can step aside from our rapports with the things of the world, investigate them, and see how we have charged them with meaning: purpose, use, value. When we do that we discover that "silence" is said in many ways: such is the method of phenomenology. And then we may discover that silence gives itself to us in many ways: such is the counter-method of phenomenology.[3] Whether we remain with method or pass to counter-method, we nonetheless find that there is no single phenomenon of silence, no irreducible being that we can isolate from a range of silences. We begin to understand that each phenomenon of silence has a genitive and a dative aspect: it is a silence *of* something or someone, and it is a silence made manifest *to* someone. That person is already concretely engaged with the silence insofar as it comes to light in an intentional relationship of believing, desiring, hoping, imagining, loving, perceiving, or whatever. Given to the person who, in a sense, renders the giving possible, the phenomenon is also given to interpretation—pre-reflectively, reflectively, and more fully in rigorous phenomenological reflection.

At first we may think that silence is restricted to just one of our five senses, and is only a privation of it. Yet this is not so. When I look admiringly at one of Fred Williams's paintings such as "Upwey Landscape II" (1965) or "Waterpond in a Landscape II" (1966), it presents itself to me in silence; I do not hear the rustling of the bush or the plashing of twigs falling into a pond, although, to be sure, it may prepare me better to do both when I next go to the outback. The world of the visual arts is mute; its silence is not a privation but a constitutive element of its characteristic way of being. Similarly, when I touch a sculpture, sniff the cork of a freshly opened bottle of Margaret River Sauvignon Blanc, or take the first sip of that same wine, these sensual experiences are themselves mute. This lack of the power of articulation in the worlds of the four senses other than hearing does not amount to a silence that is always the same, though. I remember the first time that I kissed a girl. The structure of the silence before the kiss differed from the silence afterward. The one was organized by anxiety and desire; the other, by satisfaction and renewed desire. We should not be slow to ascribe meaning—objective as well as subjective—to silences only because they are not linguistic utterances. Some silences have content or significance that is irreducible to the contents of our minds at any given moment; they serve a purpose, have a value, and are worthwhile. We speak, rightly, about coming upon a situation that has a tangible silence, and that tangibility can have distinct textures.

Silence is linked to all five senses, then, and its connection is especially important in hearing, one of the two "theoretical senses," according to Hegel.[4] Whether in music or speech, familiar or unusual noises, silence is an essential element of understanding what is heard. Consider the phenomenon of speech. There is a silence between words, as well as before and after them. We may not notice the quiet between words but without it we would not be able to talk to one another, no matter how quickly we speak. In a conversation I may be silent in order to allow someone else a turn, or because I cannot speak myself (I may be shy, have nothing to say, or be emotionally overwhelmed), or because I answer by raising an eyebrow, or because I want to cut the conversation short. Each of these silences is structured differently, and is registered by the person with whom I am talking even before thinking about it. The silence contributes to understanding or even wholly conveys what is to be understood. It may communicate something I did not want to be known, something far more significant than what is actually said.

Not all human silences have the same shading or the same weight. In his novel *A Beggar in Jerusalem* (1970) Elie Wiesel has one of his characters testify to the difficulty of telling one silence from another:

> "I love silence," Katriel continued, "But beware: not all silences are pure. Or creative. Some are sterile, malignant. My father can distinguish between them with ease; I only with difficulty. There is the silence which preceded creation, and the one which accompanied the revelation on Mount Sinai. The first contains chaos and solitude, the second suggests presence, fervor, plenitude. I like the second. I like silence to have a history and be transmitted by it."[5]

Surely Katriel overstates the case: no one would ever intuitively confuse an awkward and a dignified silence, an eloquent and a guilty silence, a comic and a tragic silence. Surely everyone would immediately accept the justice of George Herbert's rhetorical question, "What is so shrill as silent tears?"[6] It is the giving of a specific character to a silence (as Herbert does so well here) that requires genius and, as a part of that genius, moral insight. Difficulty in evaluating silence turns more surely on whether one is morally justifiable to keep silent in particular situations. Was Abraham right not to tell Sarah about his intention in taking Isaac with him to Mount Moriah? In asking this question Kierkegaard points us directly to the ethics of silence.[7] He is not the only one to do so. When Beckett's narrator says that we should consider "the kind of silence one keeps" he is not only indicating that we keep quiet in different ways—Eucharistic meditation, barely holding one's tongue in an argument, and everything in between—but also that if one routinely plays host to bitter, ignoble and tense silences, one would do well to think about the guests one entertains.

Let us return to sound and silence. It will be said that the distinction between words and silence presumes another, for there is a silence that enables words to be spoken in the first place. And this is true. So we may distinguish between silence as a *means* of manifesting something and as *what* is made manifest. Now one may well doubt if silence can ever appear as such. Think of John Cage's composition *4' 33"* (1952). This piece is scripted as nothing other than silence—the pianist plays no note in any of its three movements—and yet it is importantly a silence of what is present, not what is absent. The work becomes a means of disclosing many sounds to which one does not usually attend while at a concert or anywhere: a woman shifting on her seat, a page of a program being turned, the creak of a leather jacket, saliva being swallowed. It is as though a switch is pulled and background noise becomes foreground noise to the point of becoming the formerly unnoticed music of what is. Even the nameless islands that Jorge Carrera Andrade evokes—"islands where silence / is the highest offering" [*isles donde el silencio / es la más alta dédiva*]—are, we imagine, populated by birds and insects whose noises we hear from time to time and that help to make the background silence more manifest.[8] And even in anechoic chamber, sound proofed and designed so that sounds are absorbed rather than reflected as echoes, one hears a little noise, such as the blood coursing through one's body and the rumbling of one's stomach. The silence that one discerns in the world is relative, not absolute.

André Neher tells us that in the Bible "silence is the metaphysical form of the cosmos," that an eternal silence abides behind physical being.[9] True as that may be, the Bible is also the testimony of that silence being disturbed by the call to Abraham, the address of the burning bush, the parables of Christ, by the "thin voice of silence" that interrupts the silence of the cosmos. For generations the biblical witness to cosmic silence has gone hand in glove with what scientists have told us about the immense hush of space. Nowadays we are being told another story, one that is perhaps even more eerie: that the echo of the Big Bang may still be heard. The pitch of cosmic microwave background radiation is some fifty octaves beneath what human beings can make out, so it is not a part of our lived experience. And yet, since the sound has been raised all those octaves so that it can now be heard on a laptop, it has become one more possible item of experience in the twenty-first century.[10] Once there was indeed the sublime silence of space; it lasted a mere fraction of a second before the "organ pipes" of the universe were ready to sound. So now what overwhelmingly seems to be the silence of the universe is no longer an absolute silence for anyone who takes even a passing interest in cosmology. The eternal silence of space is slowly being replaced in human consciousness by a faint hiss, for the echo of the Big Bang is far from beautiful, and this noise may accord either with religious belief (Creation would be God prompting the Big Bang) or with atheism (the Big Bang would be unmotivated).

There is another distinction to be considered. We should draw a line between the silence *of* something and being silent *for* something. All the works of the visual arts abide in mute silence—granted; but only some of them require silence in order to communicate properly with us. You see a poster on a wall; it happens to be of the young Bob Dylan, and is a frame taken from the TV documentary *Don't Look Back* (1967). It does not ask to be regarded in silence; in fact it may become more dense and powerful if seen while the soundtrack of the documentary is being played or if glimpsed in passing across the room during a noisy party. Yet a Chinese vase or a Greek icon insists on our silence, not only so that we can concentrate on particular details but also so that we can receive it in general. In order to be precise, we need to go further and distinguish between the silence *of* the entity (the image of Dylan, the Chinese vase and the Greek icon are equally mute), the silence *in* it (not in the image of Dylan but in the vase and the icon), and the silence *behind* it (definitely so with the icon, which is not an artwork, almost certainly in the vase—I have in mind one of those beautiful decorated vases from the Zhou dynasty—and certainly in the image of Dylan, though at a depth to be determined by a theology of the *imago dei*).[11] There is a difference between what is left unsaid about the singer, the vase and the icon, and what confronts us as unable to be said in the silence behind all three.

Leaving aside for the moment the silence behind things, and the theological investigation proper to it, we can already see from the examples just considered that there are times when "silence of" and "being silent for" draw together. This may happen in quite different ways: entering a great Cathedral like Chartres or Cologne one hears its silence and feels called to be quiet to attend to it, yet this experience, whether of respect or awe, is completely different from the silence one keeps on parts of the New York subway. The silence there does not call one to be quiet (out of respect for the faith of others) or to respond to a silence behind the silence (awe) but merely to follow a social convention in order to avoid trouble. Certainly there are times when the convergence between the silence of something and being silent in order to attend to it is more complete. I wake around three in the morning, and listen for the silence of the night, a ground against which the rumble of trucks on the bypass cuts its figure. This silence may itself be variously freighted; its unearthly calm and vastness may reassure me so that I go back to sleep, they may frighten me, as they did Pascal, or I may recall the sound of the universe (like a burning fuse) that I have heard on my laptop and stay awake pondering it until morning.

Of course the gap between the silence of something and being silent in order to attend to it narrows almost to nothing when I hear my own silence, insofar as it is not prevented by the sound of my breathing or the steady thud of my heart. There are times when one catches, almost by accident, one's inner quiet: not, to be sure, a "solitary mental life," a silent monolog of pure expression without indication, but at least a sense of peace and contentment.[12] Yet in coming across it one disturbs it. Also, one can hear one's silence all too well when one has been silenced in a classroom or at a public meeting. Then the silence burns. And one can also hear one's own silence in a moment of self-criticism or self-condemnation. I say to myself that I should not have let X say that about Y, I should have objected to it in no uncertain terms. To hear one's silence may apply to a group of people, together or dispersed. In "Les Peuples meutris ...," the first of his darkly brilliant chronicles of the intellectual life written during the Occupation of France, Maurice Blanchot said of French writers that, "After many years of vain agitation, they have at last heard their own silence."[13] They have been silenced by the events of the war, but hearing their silence as a response to those events may well be the best thing that could have happened to them as writers. In his very next column, "Le Silence des écrivains," Blanchot pondered the gulf between those authors who continued to write and publish during the war and those who thought it immoral to speak "in the silence of a spiritual Pompeii."[14] There is a time to speak and a time to be silent, but, as Blanchot implies, no original writer should allow himself or herself to be silenced by silence.

For the most part, our experience of silence is merely relative; in listening for it we also hear breath, heartbeats, footfalls, snippets of conversations on cell phones, wind in the trees, the persistent whine of mosquitoes in the garden on a summer evening, regardless of whether it is a silence that is being made manifest (a gap in conversation, say) or a silence that allows a manifestation to take place (the conversation itself). Even the voice of conscience speaks to us amidst other voices that echo within us, and can sometimes be confused with it. ("Is that my conscience telling me what is right or my grandfather speaking to me from the dead about what *he* would have done?") Absolute silence belongs of course to the profoundly deaf, for whom the distinction between sound and silence is occluded. More generally, it belongs to the mute world, which includes transcendent and transcendental structures. Wittgenstein warned us in the *Tractatus* (1921), "What we cannot speak about we must pass over in silence."[15] Among other things, he had in mind philosophers who try to talk about the transcendent and the transcendental. There is Plato who teaches us about the Forms with which we were in contact before we had ears to hear, and he argues that we are metaphysically constrained to accept the reality of this anterior world.[16] There is also Descartes who argued that we have the idea of God because we have, before any experience of the world, the idea of the infinite in us.[17] And there is Schelling who evokes an "eternal past" before Creation, in which God posits Himself.[18] Doubtless there is a limit to what we can positively say about these mute anterior states. Neither Plato's nor Schelling's silent pasts impinge on most of us, but Descartes's may do so if one believes in God, and there are other silences that may do as well.

Consider Descartes again. He points us to an aspect of our *ego cogito* that immemorially precedes our relations with the world, a non-intentional consciousness that senses itself in unbroken darkness and silence.[19] Michel Henry fastens onto this enstatic consciousness, and argues that its auto-affection is original phenomenality, prior to any phenomenon. There are sufferings and joys that we silently experience without any representations of the outside world.[20] In another register entirely, Levinas proposes, by way of a transcendental argument, the reality of an immemorial past, a time that has never been present and never will, a time in which my obligation to help the other person was forged and which calls the integrity of my "I" into question even before it has been formed.[21] I may experience the *ego cogito* in dreams and daydreams, and I may experience the advent of another person (in the radical sense of being exposed to his or her irreducible otherness), without being able to encounter the absolute silence of the non-intentional consciousness or the immemorial past. These silences trouble Husserl's decision to make phenomenality coordinate with objects, and thereby to put out of play anything that cannot be represented or referred to a representation. Human being draws from non-intentional life as well as engaging in intentional life, and is drawn toward a silence after subjectivity (or the effects we call "subjectivity") has dissolved. We grasp what it is to be human when we are fully engaged in phenomenological life, or see ourselves under the sign of death, or find ourselves standing before God. There are silences, then, that change the starting points and destinations of phenomenology. Never present to intentional consciousness, they cannot be represented, and yet they impinge on us to the point of guiding our actions in life or even (as Henry would have it) being life itself.

A phenomenology of silence would be vigilantly aware of silences that cannot be represented but that nonetheless organize discourse and life. In some cases, language serves to defer silence; in other cases, it longs for silence. There is a broad day in the λόγος that wants to shed its light on everything, to cover the world with the splendor of a rich, varied voice that can bring the ten thousand things before us, and there is also a night in the λόγος that leads us to the silence behind things. I would like to consider each in turn.

*

Let us listen to St. John Climacus who in *The Ladder of Divine Ascent*, most likely written in the mid-seventh century, discusses talkativeness and silence in the eleventh of the thirty steps that lead from a sinful life to one pleasing to God. His words are exemplary of much monastic theology that came centuries later. "Talkativeness," he says, "is the throne of vainglory on which it loves to preen itself and show off. Talkativeness is a sign of ignorance, a doorway to slander, a leader of jesting, a servant of lies, the ruin of compunction, a summoner of despondency, a messenger of sleep, a dissipation of recollection, the end of vigilance, the cooling of zeal, the darkening of prayer."[22] Perhaps Climacus is drawing from Plutarch's well-known essay "Concerning Talkativeness," for there has long been a deep-seated fear that the garrulous threaten good society as well as an abiding sense that religion calls for silence: "in speaking," Plutarch says, "we have men as teachers, but in keeping silent we have gods."[23] Clement of Alexandria, for one, says that the Father is "not capable of expression by the voice, but [is] to be reverenced with reverence, and silence, and holy wonder, and supremely venerated."[24]

Climacus is directing his advice primarily to monks, and is concerned to help them struggle against passions that disturb the good order of monastic life, and only secondarily to those who need spiritual direction in general. To talk too much is merely *inanis gloria*, vainglory. Thomas Traherne (1637?–74) would echo Climacus's view. Before he learned to speak, he says in "Dumbness," he was shut in "A fort impregnable to any sin" but once he could speak "Whole legions enter'd, and the forts betray'd."[25] A century after Traherne's death some Romantics—Rousseau and Wordsworth, above all—continued to celebrate our infant state, although to quite other ends. They did not think of talk as vainglorious, and certainly not the talk of the poet who was, as Wordsworth said, "a man speaking to men."[26] Indeed, in its different styles modern poetry takes itself to have been granted the right to say everything, even when it may appear to be courting silence by speaking very briefly or with extreme restraint.

Modern poetry might be said to begin with the conviction that poetry should be able to ground itself by incorporating its theory into its practice. Such is the import of the idea of the "literary absolute" in Jena Romanticism, especially as proposed in *The Athenaeum* (1798–1800). It is the dream of "the union ... of poetry and philosophy," of poetry incorporating philosophy in order to ground itself and thereby free itself from all conditions.[27] Poetry begins to confuse the genres once carefully distinguished in Quintilian's *Institutio Oratoria* and Boileau's *L'art poétique* (1674), and fails to respect the differences between the classical and the modern, with the consequence that all manner of things may be said that could not before. Also, though, the idea that poetry should be able to say everything comes from a democratic resistance to censorship and from a modernist affirmation of formal and thematic liberation.[28] Nothing should be ruled inappropriate for a poet to take as a theme, and no language is to be deemed as "unpoetic." And so one finds all sorts of language in modern poetry, grimy details of the poet's personal life, and the mixing of genres that were previously thought inappropriate to poetry, including the detective story, Euclidean geometry, and the journal.[29] At one extreme, contemporary poetry feeds off language itself, prizing its music over form or meaning, and sometimes—as with Andrea Zanzotto's experiments in glossolalia—with spectacular results.[30] With most "sound poetry" close reading gives way to close listening, although the listening can seldom be referred to understanding. It is as though hearing's status as a theoretical sense is slighted, treated as though it were non-theoretical, like touch, taste or smell.

The Romantic desire to say everything is not opposed to silence, however. If anything, it seeks silence as its proper end, while forever finding itself having to say more about something—consciousness, liberty, love—from another direction, with deeper insights or better phrasing, and always finding the silences that it reaches to be inauthentic and themselves spurring the writer to say more and to say it better. Correctly understood, the antonym of "silence" is not "speech" but "chatter," which, as Kierkegaard rightly says, "is the annulment of the passionate disjunction between being silent and speaking."[31] Chatter, we might say, is the grayness of the λόγος: not the λόγος grown old but kept barely alive without the nourishment of either silence or speech. Heidegger and Blanchot will speak memorably of it, each in his own way.[32] This chatter can be challenged by literature, and nowhere has this been done better than by Louis-René des Forêts in *Le Bavard* (1946) where the narrator endlessly gabbles, emptying words of all meaning, and thereby exposing the nihilism inherent in talk just for the sake of talk. Yet even the chatterer eventually and reluctantly yearns to stop speaking. "Silence—that silence for which he feels that mingled terror and longing aroused by the mere imminence of something which is both desirable and dangerous, wonderful and dreadful, that silence to whose arid laws he had never consented to bow, which he has never ceased to hate, but to which nonetheless he remains bound by an aching nostalgia, he catches himself summoning it with secret wishes."[33] Here silence is seen from behind, as it were, as a "drab and sterile region" (102), a state to be endured only when worn out by excessive jabber. If for many of us silence is an index of freedom, an escape from the clamor of the outside world, for the chatterer it is a prison to which he must always return, convicted by himself as well as by others.

There is another literature that desires to say everything without falling into chatter, although, to be sure, language can sometimes idle in it. One example of a text, in which (thanks to Ezra Pound) not a word is wasted, is T. S. Eliot's *The Waste Land* (1922), a poem composed entirely of voices drawn (unequally) from East and West, from literature and pub conversation, Scripture and domestic scenes. To read Eliot's poem well would be to have mastered a certain view of world literature, one determined by a particular sense of "world" (a representation pictured from the heights of European high culture), and one whose many voices have been channeled into Eliot's own voice, which subtly orchestrates the whole. For all that, the poem indicates an escape from talk—"Looking into the heart of light, the silence" (64)—though one not actually taken until the *Four Quartets* (1942) when the "heart of light" (190) at Burnt Norton became the site for the lotos to rise "quietly, quietly" (190) and to set in motion a spiritual quest for the "still point of the turning world" (191). In its snatches of talk that bespeak anxiety, exile, and exhaustion, *The Waste Land* is a poem that answers to social and cultural breakdown as well as the poet's own psychological state. It is the kind of work valued highly by George Steiner in his signal essay, "Silence and the

Poet" (1966). He argues there that political violence in the twentieth century has debased and devalued language, requiring poets to choose between keeping silent or devising a poetics cognizant of the damage to communication that has been done. Too many people write poetry without a hard won poetics, and consequently make it difficult for us to hear "the valid and the genuinely new."[34] Steiner's criticism is partly a refusal of talent in the name of genius, partly a schoolmasterly silencing of chatterboxes, and partly a shying away from a new aesthetic that is at odds with that of the high European modernism that he reverences.

This new aesthetic was brazenly being practiced in America in the 1960s, at the time that Steiner was writing "Silence and the Poet," by poets who were less concerned than Steiner to say everything about high culture, or to think of high culture as saying everything, while nonetheless wishing to say everything. A. R. Ammons, for one, wanted to embrace the process of writing more fully than he did the final product. Saying everything becomes a way of avoiding the "self-conscious POEM."[35] In *Tape for the Turn of the Year* (1965), Ammons talks of his desire to find a level of language "that could take in all / kinds of matter/ & move easily with / light or heavy burden" (144). This long thin poem happily meanders for page after page, its narrator telling a few elephant jokes and even disarmingly confessing that "maybe I write / too much" (62), while also offering secular prayers, a credo, and an ode to love.[36] All the time Ammons abides by the external limit of the length and width of a roll of adding-machine tape on which he types the poem. There appears to be no internal limit to what can be said, and the reader suspects that, despite the occasional complaints about the length of the tape, had the roll been twice as long so would the poem.[37]

One of the most intriguing contemporary poets whose poetics are grounded in the quest to say everything is John Ashbery. The main poetic tradition we inherit from Wordsworth presents the poetic subject solely in the nominative, the first person singular, the "I." Ashbery takes the human subject in a far broader sense, and evokes its experience in a wider range of declension: the genitive, dative, and ablative. Experience is given to us as possession, reception, address, indirection, place, and so on, without clear lines being drawn between them. The first person singular nominative must take its chances with the rest of the declension of the self; it has no poetic right to prominence. Ashbery does not do away with "the subject," as some of his admirers say, but gives us a richer, stranger sense of human subjectivity than the one the Romantics bequeathed to us. A poem by Ashbery, especially one of his longer performances (*Flowchart*, for instance), at first gives the impression of being consumed by a singular consciousness freely ranging about in itself and the world, looking at anything and everything, moving quickly between things, letting things become visible and interesting by dint of the quirkiness of his vision, and calling that coming into visibility "meaning." And yet, at the same time, one might say that the poet is more passive than active, that Ashbery's poetry is taken up with freely receiving phenomena, things from outside or inside consciousness, without judging the nature of their reality or their value.

One of Ashbery's finest poems is entitled "Soonest Mended."[38] Less said, soonest mended, we sometimes say after a quarrel. Yet in the quarrel with himself, which Yeats said is the source of poetry, Ashbery refuses to say less, and attends instead to the incessant murmur of language, both in the street and in his consciousness.[39] Ashbery eschews the ladder of formal perfection for what Emerson called "the stairway of surprise."[40] In "Soonest Mended" we remain thickly inside a world of pure immanence but with a crack of transcendence available to us, in the ambition "To step free at last, miniscule on the gigantic plateau" which, if achieved, is grasped for only a moment. For the most part, when reading Ashbery we remain immured in long verse paragraphs, passages of which could be, for all one can tell, a translation of the silent joys and sufferings of the non-intentional ego. All in all, his poetry is a kind of literary cubism, in which the different facets of experience are given all at once, although Ashbery differs from language poets in being prepared to strike the *lachrimæ rerum* note at the right time. "We are all talkers," he says, though it is what is "underneath the talk" that motivates his long poems. Meaning, here, is not something winnowed out, the pure presence of expression, but rather the external indication; in any case, it ends up on the floor. Perhaps we may think of Eliot writing in the *Four Quartets*, "We had the experience but missed the meaning."[41] But there can be no question of assigning a meaning to experience when the experience is itself so fragmented and apparently so passively received.

Very distant from Ashbery in stance and style are those poets who wish to say everything in as few words as possible, and to do so by folding long sequences of philosophical or theological motifs into a phrase or a line, resetting them by way of ambiguity and paradox. The later poetry of Paul Celan, from *Lichtzwang* (1970) to *Zeitgehöft* (1976), works in this way, and when reading it one feels as though each word has been rinsed in silence before being spoken in the poetry. So too, though its pitch is quite different, would be the early poetry of Geoffrey Hill, which tries to say everything by remaining answerable to the bewildering complexity of our world in its moral, political and religious dimensions. In "Annunciations," as we have seen in Chapter 7, Hill writes, "Our God scatters corruption," which in context means both that God triumphantly overcomes corruption and that He sows corruption.[42] Both things are said at once, partly to indicate the truth of each and partly to suggest Hill's restraint in declining to support one side or the other precisely because God is powerful while the faithful all too often deviate from or even reverse the gospel in the very practice of religion. His is a "duck-rabbit" poetics that conserves words and intrudes on the empire of silence as little as possible.[43] At the same time, Hill keeps a wary eye on what he calls the "tongue's atrocities" (84), the habitual tendency of poets to write as though granted Pentecostal powers, to write as though they could truly raise the dead or even talk to them in the writing of elegies. The tongue acts badly too when its words are allowed to slide from moral concern to aesthetic gratification for author and reader alike. How is one to prevent that from happening? Only, for Hill, by an extreme exercise of self-consciousness, a weighing of silence against words. After elegizing a child, a victim of the Holocaust, in only thirteen spare, jagged lines, he concludes by saying, partly of his own lyric performance, "This is plenty. This is more than enough" (67).[44] This then is a poetry that keeps itself close to the edge of silence in order to sharpen its moral responsiveness.

Many poets could agree with Charles Simic when he evokes the rightness of "A voice that wanted / To equal the silence / That surrounds it."[45] But in agreeing with Simic they would not necessarily agree with one another. For some will take this as a challenge to produce a voice that will keep silence at bay, producing an immense oeuvre like Ashbery, Yannis Ritsos, or Pablo Neruda. And others will take it as an invitation to compare a poem with silence, as though the finest lyrics drew close to silence, caressed it, and drew from it. I think of poets such as Basho and Issa, Roberto Juarroz, and the Philippe Jaccottet of *Airs* (1967). The early poems of Giuseppe Ungaretti can be added to the list. Consider his tiny lyric "Mattina" (1917):

M'illumino
D'immenso.[46]

Is the poet saying in these few words that, in the morning, he illuminates himself with the immensity of the sunlight and, beyond that, the universe, or is the morning itself saying the same thing? The lyric was originally entitled "Cielo et mare," and so we may wonder if the sea is saying that it illuminates itself with the vastness of the heavens. Is this a poem about the external world or about inner radiance? Is it a poem in which the phonic play of *i*, *m*, and *n* promotes harmony, or does its slant rhyme (*-ino* / *-enso*) suggest a break in the circle, so that the poem's meanings would spiral ever outward? There are times when the closer a poet gets to saying nothing, to letting silence do the work, the more the poem can be heard to say.

Yet silence need not work only in the service of haiku and hermetic lyrics; it can be seen as the very condition of true poetry, of whatever kind. Francis Ponge tells us that "the function of poetry" is "to nourish the spirit of man by giving him the cosmos to suckle."[47] For that to happen, we must both "lower our standard of dominating nature" and "raise our standard of participating in it" (109). We will be saved—and Ponge, a devout materialist, does not hesitate to speak of salvation—by "a poetry through which the world so invades the spirit of man that he becomes almost speechless, and later reinvents a language" (109). Poets should not busy themselves talking about human relationships; they can leave that to novelists. For poets are "the ambassadors of the silent world" [*les ambassadeurs du monde muet*] (110), that is, of absolute silence. The poet represents his or her homeland, the mute world of the cosmos, in the foreign land of culture. To do that he or she must not simply learn the language of that culture but also, and far more importantly, reinvent a language. "As such, they stammer, they murmur, they sink into the darkness of logos [*la nuit du logos*]—until at last they reach the level of ROOTS, where things and formulas are one" (110). It is the darkness of the λόγος that will take us further, leading us into the company of the votaries of silence as well as its ambassadors.

*

Let us return to St. John Climacus. "Intelligent silence," he says in step eleven of *The Ladder of Divine Ascent*, "is the mother of prayer, freedom from bondage, custodian of zeal, a guard on our thoughts, a watch on our enemies, a prison of mourning, a friend of tears, a sure recollection of death, a painter of punishment, a concern with judgment, servant of anguish, foe of license, a companion of stillness, the opponent of dogmatism, a growth of knowledge, a hand to shape contemplation, hidden progress, the secret journey upward. For the man who recognizes his sins has taken control of his tongue, while the chatterer has yet to discover himself as he should."[48] I retain from this catalogue of commonplaces (as they became) about the uses of silence in monastic life the image of prayerful silence as "the secret journey upward," keeping in mind that "upward" is a metaphor ill at ease in a postmodern world that does not countenance a hierarchically arranged universe and perhaps no longer a universe at all but in what cosmologists call the multiverse.[49]

One could also think of silence as one of the journeys downward, as patristic and medieval mystical theology would have it, taken by God in his self-revelation. The Epistle to the Hebrews begins, "God, who at sundry times and in divers manners spake in time past unto the fathers by the prophets, hath in these last days spoken unto us by *his* Son" (Heb. 1:1-2). Now we might take "spake" here to mean that God performed illocutionary actions by means of his prophets.[50] Aquinas cannot do that, though, speech act theory not having been available to him. He notes instead that "divers manners" means corporeal, imaginary and intellectual visions, as well as plain and obscure speaking.[51] And he adds that God speaks to us through "the imparting of species in the minds of angels or men" and this is "ordained only to the knowledge of divine wisdom" (11). This is a silent speech: not the absence of speech but a speech that communicates in absolute silence.[52] Recall the story of Elijah. God did not speak to his prophet in the voice of a great wind, or in the voice of an earthquake, or in the voice of a fire, but as "a still small voice" (1 Kgs 19:12). Thus the King James edition of the Bible; the English Standard Edition renders the line more closely with "a thin silence." On hearing it Elijah "wrapped his face in his mantle" (1 Kgs 19:13). The silence is not a privation; rather, its holiness is affirmed. For Aquinas, it is pure subsistent *esse* that cannot be fitted to the categories; it impinges on us as an otherness that exceeds the distinction between same and other that operates in the cosmos, a presence that cannot be assimilated to ontic, ontological or epistemic presence.

In his epistle to the Ephesians, St. Ignatius of Antioch (50– c. 98–117) writes some striking words that resonate with those we have just heard in Kings and Hebrews. "He who has truly acquired the word of Jesus can also hear his silence, so that he may become perfect and act through what he says and be known through what he does not say."[53] We hear the Word of the Father and, in hearing it, we long to approach the Father, which we do by passing from Word to silence. Let us stay with Ignatius, this time listening to his epistle to the Megesians: "there is one God who manifested himself through Jesus Christ his Son, who is his Word which proceeded from silence and in every respect pleased him who sent him."[54] Christ, here, is not the indwelling reason that was to interest Clement of Alexandria among others but is rather the spoken word of the Father. The word comes from silence and returns to it. This silence of the Father, wholly shared by the Son and the Spirit, is an index of what we call mystery and that, stammering, we try to grasp by way of οὐσία and *esse*.[55] Here silence escapes the theoretical sense of hearing. To hear it well we must pass from knowing to unknowing, a pilgrimage made possible only by the grace of God and, even so, experienced as more than a hard road but as the experience of experience, an experience of exposure to absolute peril. "It is a fearful thing to fall into the hands of the living God" (Heb. 10:31).

It is important to stress that the apophatic movement from the light of Creation to the darkness of God is grounded in the self-revelation of the Father in the Son and through the Spirit. Other apophatic theologies abound in the West, especially in Neoplatonism and Gnosticism, and Christian theology has participated in them from time to time, not always to its benefit. In the more pure Neoplatonic systems, such as those of Plotinus and Proclus, one passes from the world of the many to the worldless One that abides beyond the multiplicity of being. The practice of φιλοσοφία may lead the sage to the

One, and in doing so the many words of philosophy will be quieted as the One, the "un-word" [*Unwort*], is approached by ascending the hierarchy of being.[56] The lines between the apophatic theologies of Middle Platonism and the apophatic theologies of the Cappodocians and Pseudo-Dionysius the Areopagite are divided and equivocal, but a distinction can still be drawn, one that is justified by the difference between their positive theologies as well as by the biblical witness to the incomprehensibility of God. As good a testimony as any here is Augustine's: he explicitly points out that what Christianity teaches—devotion, tears of confession, sacrifice, redemption, and so on—is not to be found in the *libri Platonicorum* that he once esteemed so highly.[57] Like St. Gregory of Nyssa, Augustine spoke of ἐπεκτεινόμενος or stretching forward, and Christian apophatic theology can be understood as the ἐποχή that ensures we stretch toward the God of Jesus Christ. It is the passage from the Word spoken, preached in the kerygma, to the Word contemplated. This is the "supra-word" [*Überwort*] that is worshipped in silent adoration.[58] In doing so the faithful become votaries of silence. They know, though in the mode of unknowing, that the universe is not mute, that the silence behind the silence is an affirmation, not a privation.

Equally important as the acknowledgement of the *Überwort* is the recognition that apophatic theologies can be detached from one form of transcendence and attached to another that mimics it and even at times parodies it. Neoplatonism and Christianity at least agree in construing transcendence by way of "transascendance" [my emphasis], as Jean Wahl calls it, an ascent to the otherness of the other, whether it is the One or God.[59] The "darkness of the logos" can also be found in "transdescendance," however: in theurgy, with Iamblichus as well as Bataille; in the roots of being and language that Ponge evokes; or, rather differently, in the appeal to the transcendental (Kant and the post-Kantians) as supplying the ground of our discourse, or to the quasi-transcendental (Derrida) as underwriting the meaning of our talk and our silences. The mirrored nature of the two forms of transcendence can be appreciated by comparing two well-known passages. First, Augustine in the *Confessions*:

> Therefore we said: If to anyone the tumult of the flesh has fallen silent, if the images of earth, water, and air are quiescent, if the heavens themselves are shut out and the very soul itself is making no sound and is surpassing itself by no longer thinking about itself, if all dreams and visions in the imagination are excluded, if all language and every sign and everything transitory is silent—for if anyone could hear them, this is what all of them would be saying, "We did not make ourselves, we were made by him who abides for eternity" (Ps. 79:3, 5)—if after this declaration they were to keep silence, having directed our ears to him that made them,

then he alone would speak not through them but through himself. We would hear his word, not through the tongue of the flesh, nor through the voice of an angel, nor through the sound of thunder, nor through the obscurity of a symbolic utterance. Him who in these things we love we would hear in person without their mediation [*sed ipsum quem in his amamus, ipsum sine his audiamus*].[60]

Next to this eloquent testimony of transascendance we may place a fine piece of philosophical gothic by Levinas in his evocation of transdescendance in *Existence and Existents* (1947):

Let us imagine all beings, things and persons, reverting to nothingness. One cannot put this return to nothingness outside of all events. But what of this nothingness itself? Something would happen, if only night and the silence of nothingness. The indeterminateness of this "something is happening" is not the indeterminateness of a subject and does not refer to a substantive. Like the third person pronoun in the impersonal form of a verb, it designates not the uncertainly known author of the action, but the characteristic of this action itself which somehow has no author. This impersonal, anonymous, yet inextinguishable "consummation" of being, which murmurs in the depths of nothingness itself we shall designate by the term *there is* [il y a]. The *there is*, inasmuch as it resists a personal form, is "being in general" ... The rustling of the *there is* ... is horror.[61]

Augustine and Levinas use roughly the same procedure to indicate how a radical alterity would manifest itself to us. The one finds the silence of God, immediately communicated in prayerful silence, while the other discloses the murmur of being from which we cannot escape and which we encounter in horror. Blanchot will speak in similar terms of the "narrative voice," the disquieting murmur of language being sifted by language that can be discerned beneath the author's voice.[62]

If the transdescendant discloses itself to Blanchot and Levinas in a murmur, for Derrida it is completely silent and has not the slightest trace of a phenomenon about it, even in his metaphors for it. He calls it *différance*, among other nicknames—*cindre, khôra, trace*, to give only three—and takes it as a structural precondition of linguistic meaning rather than an existential situation that is inherently meaningful. One thing we have learned from reading Derrida over the last few decades is that the quasi-transcendental is just as good as the transcendent in explaining the endlessness of signification. Appeals to the transcendent God as the author of Scripture can yield layers of meaning; while responses to the transcendental play of *la différance* can show the endlessness of signification in Scripture and secular writings alike. Seen from one viewpoint, Origen and Derrida stand back to back, the one looking up for levels of meaning and the other gazing directly ahead at the infinite play of text and context. Of course, deconstruction can only ever be a ghost of apophatic theology precisely because it answers to a structure of transdescendance and not a divine transascendance.[63] It can guide us only in the realm of the "bad infinity" of meaning, in which the perpetual deferment of the full presence of final understanding stands over and against finite human consciousness.[64] It teaches us to attend to delicate shades and tight knots of meaning in everything we read; but the silence behind the words that it discerns is neutral, strictly without meaning, even though it affirms signification without end.

The exemplary close reading of a Jacques Derrida can finally only hear the same silence behind everything, whether it is a poem by Hopkins or a *récit* by Blanchot. Not that this is a consequence of his singular practice as a reader, for his hermeneutic style is a culmination of the most sophisticated and subtle practices of reading since the Enlightenment. The issue is not one of preferring another way of reading or of refining the one so finely practiced by Derrida but rather of asking what the very success of this hermeneutic has made us overlook or leave unheard. Can we hear other silences behind poetry? Doubtless the question sounds strange, but its very strangeness prompts us to think otherwise about the reading of poetry, and perhaps our reading in general. Husserl taught us to perform the reduction in order to lead ourselves back to a state without presuppositions, for only then could we receive phenomena properly. In doing so, however, he made one undeclared presupposition: that phenomenality must be set at the level of the objectness of the object. Bracketing the natural attitude was to secure us against the risk of accepting the default explanations of science as "common sense" but only so that phenomenology, once fully elaborated, could ground the positive sciences adequately. The methodological priorities of *Ideas* I lead directly to the project of *Ideas* III, "the foundation of the sciences."[65] Husserl's decision in favor of limiting phenomenality was one with his insistence that the transcendence of God, considered as the ground of the world, must be excluded from phenomenology.[66] In uncovering this presupposition we may ask ourselves what happens if we do not limit phenomenality at all, restricting it neither to objects (Husserl) nor being (Heidegger), and instead granting everything the right and the power to manifest itself in whatever way is appropriate to it.

Certainly, this extension of phenomenality would open the possibility of a phenomenological theology and, with it, distinctive attunements to the God who declines the flattering role of grounding the world in favor of being love itself. Some adepts of phenomenological theology may wish to revive Schleiermacher's feeling of absolute dependence, for example, and rethink it not by way of natural feeling but by finding oneself *coram deo*, by way of ontological attunements such as awe, fear, joy, or wonder. Others may return to faith, taking care to bracket the supernatural attitude, the default acceptance of another, higher world, like ours but perfect, as explaining the life of the spirit. A word read or spoken, a silence, a gesture of a hand: all these things, if encountered at the right angle, as it were, can tear away the usual significance that something has, and can introduce eternity into time; our governance of life and the world is cancelled in a single stroke. Accordingly, theology would have its own reductions to perform, and would find inspiration for them in what Erich Pryzwara called the "*reductio in mysterium*" or in what Jean-Yves Lacoste calls the "liturgical reduction."[67] One would be led back to the mystery of God's silence, to silence as mystery, to the silence appropriate in being before God who is silence itself.

Every prayer is an ἐποχή that can make the writing of theology possible, and theology begins only when we are led back from the world we master and that tries to master us to a created world, one that is ontologically dependent on God. Then we can make the "secret journey upward." We can see the secular world still painting its gray on gray, not because philosophy always comes too late, as Hegel thought, but because the secular world is just so much "evening knowledge," as Augustine called it, a knowledge of things in their own natures.[68] Secular literary criticism is evening knowledge in that it reads poems in terms of one or another aesthetic, or, more recently, in attempts to depart from aesthetics in order to uncover social and political currents running in, through, or past a poem. We would perhaps see how this tradition, passing from before Johnson to after Eliot, tended to idealize poetry in terms of a self-contained meaning, present and unified, meeting our gaze and returning it enriched in terms that were already tacitly known.[69] If there were religious assumptions built into this criticism, usually by way of a Romantic theory of genius, there were also clear biases against religious poetry. For this school could only figure poetry as the consequence of experience understood empirically, not as the exposure to peril that is constitutive of being approached by the *il y a* or being in relation with God. Religious poetry, for secular criticism, has been invariably suspect, regarded as taking its cues only from what others have experienced, centuries ago in the time of Jesus or in the extraordinary graces of the mystics.

Yet if we were led back to the mystery, and the phenomenality appropriate to it, we would perhaps say that the best religious poetry—Herbert, Hopkins, Traherne, and Vaughan may stand as indices here—would be a prime example of "morning knowledge," as the way of knowing granted when things are seen as created, invisibly tied to God. Of course, morning knowledge was granted only to the angels, Augustine and Aquinas say, and since we do not have angelic cognition we can speak of ourselves only in terms of morning faith. To read a poem in that way would be to be attuned to the silence of God that abides behind it. The theological aesthetic at issue would be informed by an apophatic theology, one that questions the metaphysical structures of presence and unity, and one that, remaining answerable to the Bible, reprises all affirmative theology in its passage to praise. Read in this way, the poem would contain an iconic moment, a gaze as though coming from an icon, which crosses the reader's gaze, addressing or questioning him or her, consoling him or her, and always placing him or her in the mystery of incarnation, death and resurrection. To read within that gaze would be to fold "close reading" into *lectio divina*, while also gingerly extending the realm of *lectio divina* to include poetry.

In "Hurrahing in Harvest," Hopkins tells us that "I lift up heart, eyes, / Down all that glory in the heavens to glean our Saviour."[70] It is important to recognize that in these lines "heart" precedes "eyes," for only if the heart, as the biblical seat of affect, prepares the aiming of sight can there be a genuine theological perception of the harvest. In the very next line Hopkins reverses the order of heart and eyes. He asks, rhetorically, "éyes, heárt, what looks, what lips yet gave you a / Rapturous love's greeting of realer, of rounder replies?" The eyes have been prepared by prayer to see Christ in nature. A living relationship with God must precede the operation of the spiritual senses or, if you prefer, theological insight. In the octave of the sonnet we are told of the instress of the Welsh countryside, "These things, these things were here and but the beholder / Wanting." The beholder is of course Hopkins himself who, having prepared himself to encounter God, is ecstatic when the meeting takes place: "The heart réars wíngs bold and bolder / And hurls for him, O half hurls earth for him off under his feet." Having prepared the poet to see and hear Christ, the heart pushes off from the ground. Also, though, the beholder is you and I. For it is at this moment that the poem can flex inside out, and each of us is silently addressed, "The encounter with God is always to be had, but *you* are not there."

All Hopkins's great lyrics of 1877—"God's Grandeur," "Spring," "The Windhover," "Pied Beauty," "As kingfishers catch fire ..." and "Hurrahing in Harvest" chief among them—are morning poems, whether or not they are set in the morning or the afternoon. Sometimes the morning is powerfully present, as in the opening of "The Windhover," when Hopkins tells us, "I caught this morning morning's minion." Always, though, the lyrics are written in the eschatological hope of morning knowledge, and in the experience of inventing a language, unique in English poetry, to express wonder and praise. To regard them solely as works of evening knowledge would diminish them. They not only embody experience of inscape but also call forth the possibility, or even the desire, for that same experience in the reader. Later poems of Hopkins bear testimony to another silence of God, negative rather than affirmative. For there are times when God does not answer, when He seems completely absent. "And my lament," Hopkins says, piercingly, "Is cries countless, cries like dead letters sent / To dearest him that lives alas! away."[71]

It is one thing to hear the silence of God's absence, another to hear silence when it has become a test of faith in God. Melville wrote memorably of this situation in *Pierre, or, The Ambiguities* (1852) when his narrator evokes, "that profound Silence, that only Voice of our God" and asks, with derision, "how can a man get a Voice out of Silence?"[72] In the same spirit we recall Shusaku Endo's novel *Silence* (1969), especially the passage when Father Sebastian Rodrigues painfully reflects on the sound of someone snoring near his cell, which turns out to be the groans of peasants who are being tortured because he will not deny Christ:

> A great shadow passed over his soul like that of the wings of a bird flying over the mast of a ship. The wings of the bird now brought to his mind the memory of the various ways in which the Christians had died. At that time, too, God had been silent. When the misty rain floated over the sea, he was silent. When the one-eyed man had been killed beneath the blazing rays of the sun, he had said nothing. But at that time, the priest had been able to stand it; or, rather than stand it, he had been able to thrust the terrible doubt far from the threshold of his mind. But now it was different. Why is God continually silent while those groaning voices go on?[73]

That last question resonates with an earlier passage in the novel, directly after the martyrdoms of two Japanese peasants, Mokichi and Ichizo, who were crucified in the sea. "And like the sea God was silent," we are told. "His silence continued." Which leads the narrator to reflect, "From the deepest core of my being yet another voice made itself heard in a whisper. Supposing God does not exist" (117). Here silence is perhaps not God's absence but His nonexistence.[74] There are moments in theology and apophatic theology when one runs very close to the negation of the faith on which theology relies. Sometimes one cannot be either an ambassador or votary of silence, for silence can wound us more deeply than any word.

What of poems by nonbelievers? Let us return to Ammons, more of a devout naturalist with panentheist inclinations than a practicing Christian. Think of his lyric "The City Limits" in which he ponders air, the vacuum, snow, shale, squid, wolf, roses, lichen and sees that everything "is of a tune with May bushes."[75] When one recognizes that everything, no matter what, is in its right place in the cosmos, fulfilling its proper functions, and related to everything else in a grand ecology, then one passes from fear of the sheer immensity of the cosmos to praise for its order, variety and dynamism. This passage can attune one to a silence behind the poem: the awe of a harmonious cosmos, if not of a personal Creator. The poem is usually read, with reason, so that the "you" is a figure of the "I"; but it can also be taken as an address to the reader, one that he or she may take up, to consider the interrelatedness of things, the unacknowledged harmony of the universe or multiverse, and rather than being frightened by its silences or its faint hiss be moved to praise its on-going creativity.

"Cascadilla Falls," one of the poet's most beautiful lyrics, gives us a somewhat different instance of the same situation. There Ammons tells us that he goes down to the Falls and picks up a "handsized stone / kidney-shaped, testicular" and that he "thought all its motions into it," the spin of the earth, the displacement gained from the earth's circling around the sun, the movement of the galaxy. Doubtless the very shape of the stone—a fossilized testicle or kidney—suggests mortality. Yet the poem is not a mourning of the poet's finitude. Shaken by the recognition of the sublimity of the stone's (and his) situation in the world, he turns to the sky, stands still, and says,

oh
I do not know where I am going
that I can live my life
by this single creek. (62)

We can take these concluding lines as his testimony of being caught adrift in life, or we can let them attune us to another voice, speaking silently to us, and saying, "Do *you* know where *you* are going? Do *you* know how to live *your* life?"

It will be said, and rightly, that artworks considered exclusively as artworks can pose this same question just as sharply. Rilke made precisely that point in his "Archaïscher Torso Apollos" where, at the end of the poem, the torso says, "You must change your life' [*Du musst dein Leben ändern*].[76] The objection is well made because no distinction is to be drawn between poems that act as though they are icons and other poems that serve as idols.[77] The distinction between the idol and the quasi-icon is phenomenological: any poem, any work of art, can take on a quasi-iconic role, and the word "quasi" is to be retained because it relates here to a work of art and not a work of spiritual devotion. It will also be said that one simply cannot tell whether one is attuned to the silence of God, the silence in which being turns over and over—what Levinas calls the *il y a*—or the silence of a multiverse without a God. Arresting though the objection is, it is not well posed. There is no question of a neutral reception of either the one or the other. To some degree Hopkins the Jesuit might agree with Sartre the atheist. "If a voice speaks to me, it is always I who must decide whether or not this is the voice of an angel," says the existentialist.[78] But Hopkins would demur over the word "decide"; one must prepare to hear the voice of an angel, though after that preparation one may still have to decide if the voice is angelic or not. For faith, the encounter with God is always possible, and in the end the choice one makes is whether or not to be open to it and the risks it offers us.

Consider a lyric such as Wallace Stevens's "The Snow Man," as nihilistic a poem as has ever been written.[79] In the poem's well-known closing lines, in which the snow man "beholds / Nothing that is not there and the nothing that is," one hears the bleak silence of transdescendance, to be sure, but theological aesthetics allows one to catch something else. To write about irreducible nothingness, about beholding nothing, is already to have overcome the correlation of nothingness and meaninglessness; it is already to have taken the first step in finding meaning, not just signification. No one writes a poem without the possibility of it being read by another, without entering into human contact. Even a poem that is deeply committed to nihilism as a metaphysical doctrine, as this one surely is, is also open to the possibility of dialogue, of affirming the value of communication. A structure of transascendance is already in place, even if it remains solely at the level of the human and denies God's ever-attentive ear. If one discerns the *imago dei* in the very creativeness of the poem, one must also accept that not all readers will do so, and if one hails the *imago dei* in the possibility of sociality, in the poem bringing people together to ponder life at its most dark, one must accept that not everyone will do so. A theological aesthetics should know its limits.

A theological aesthetics should also know, as St. Bonaventure puts it in the title of a little work, *De reductione artium ad theologiam*, that the arts, including each and every poem, can be led back to theological categories.[80] They cannot always be led back to faith: some poets remain ambassadors of silence and have no desire to be its votaries. This, though, is not a reason to ascribe theological significance to the silence of the transdescendant, as well as the transascendant; indeed, in regarding theology as the proper lens for discussing the transdescendant, as well as the transascendant, one is simply following Bonaventure's lead, but along a new path, one marked out by phenomenological theology.

Notes

Introduction

1 See, for example, Kevin Hart, *Kingdoms of God* (Bloomington: Indiana University Press, 2014).

Chapter 1: Poetry and revelation: Hopkins, counter-experience and *reductio*

1 Thomas Sprat, "Upon the Poems of the English Ovid, Anacreon, Pindar, and Virgil, Abraham Cowley, In Imitation of his own Pindarick Odes," *The Works of the English Poets from Chaucer to Cowper,* ed. Alexander Chalmers, 21 vols (London: C. Wittingham, 1810), IX. Sprat's lines read, "You first the Muses to the Christians brought, / And you then first the holy language taught: / In you good poetry and divinity meet, / You are the first bird of Paradise with feet."

2 It has been argued that *Four Quartets* transcends Christianity. See the discussion of this case by Kristian Smidt, *Poetry and Belief in the Work of T. S. Eliot* (New York: The Humanities Press, 1961), 213–14.

3 T. S. Eliot, "Religion and Literature," *Selected Essays*, 3rd edn (London: Faber and Faber, 1951), 390.

4 See Eliot, "What is Minor Poetry?," *On Poetry and Poets* (London: Faber and Faber, 1957). Also see Christopher Ricks, "Notes away from the Definition of Minor Poetry," *Ploughshares* 4 (3) (1978): 115–21. The sense of "minor" proposed by Gilles Deleuze and Félix Guattari falls into another camp entirely, and might well be appropriate for the study of contemporary religious poetry. See their *Kafka: Toward a Minor Literature*, trans. Dana Polan, foreword Réda Bensmaïa (Minneapolis: University of Minnesota Press, 1986), Ch. 3. In general, it is hard to rehabilitate the judgment that literature is minor without making reference to the hierarchy of genres or another hierarchy that might be taken to have replaced it.

5 See Eliot, "Religion and Literature," 391, and "What is Minor Poetry?," 45–6. Is it that Eliot found that Herbert showed an awareness of more human passions than he first thought when reading *The Temple*? Or that he came to believe that Herbert was more sincere in his poetry than he surmised? Or is it that, over time, he found Herbert's poems to treat the whole of life from a religious angle, and to do so without prejudice? In any case, Eliot's claim—"Christian poetry ... has been limited in England almost exclusively to minor poetry" ("Religion and Literature," 391)—remains perplexing so long as we do not identify the modernity motivating the expression "Christian poetry." Are we to think that *Piers Plowman* is either unchristian or minor? Neither seems possible. Eliot maintained his view in *George Herbert* (London: Longman Green, 1962). He observed, the year before "Religion and Literature" appeared, "Why, I would ask, is most religious verse so bad; and why does so little religious verse reach the highest levels of poetry? Largely, I think, because of a pious insincerity ... People who write devotional verse are usually writing as they want to feel, rather than as they do feel," *After Strange Gods: A Primer of Modern Heresy* (London: Faber and Faber, 1934), 28–9. Note the slide from "religious verse" to "devotional verse."

6 See, for example, David Jones, "Art and Sacrament," in his *Epoch and Artist: Selected Writings*, ed. Harman Grisewood (New York: Chilmark Press, 1959).

7 See Erich Auerbach, *Mimesis: The Representation of Reality in Western Literature*, trans. Willard R. Trask (Princeton: Princeton University Press, 1953), Ch. 2.

8 See Søren Kierkegaard, *Attack Upon "Christendom,"* trans. Walter Lowrie (Boston: The Beacon Press, 1944).

9 Samuel Johnson, "Waller," *The Lives of the Most Eminent English Poets; With Critical Observations on their Works*, 4 vols, ed. Roger Lonsdale (Oxford: Clarendon Press, 2006), II, 53. Johnson excludes the tradition of didactic Christian verse that, we can see if we look past the *Lives of the Poets*, began with St. Gregory Nazianzus's *poemata dogmatica* and that found contemporary expression in Richard Blackmore's "Creation."

10 Johnson, *Lives of the Most Eminent English Poets*, II, 53.

11 Harold Bloom, *Ruin the Sacred Truths: Poetry and Belief from the Bible to the Present* (Cambridge, MA: Harvard University Press, 1989), 4.

12 Bloom, *Ruin the Sacred Truths*, 12.

13 See, for example, David R. Anderson, "Johnson and the Problem of Religious Verse," *The Age of Johnson* 4 (1991): 41–57.

14 See, for instance, John Tutchin's comment that "Part of the Sacred Writings were delivered in verse" in the preface to his *Poems on Several Occasions with a Pastoral* (London: Printed by J. L. for Jonathan Greenwood, 1685). Richard Blackmore made the same point in the introduction to his *A Paraphrase on the Book of Job* (1700) and Edward Young showed himself to be in agreement in his *Conjectures on Original Composition* (1759). How impressive the psalms are as poetry is made evident when comparing them with Ephrem the Syrian's hymns which, although often striking as religious writing, are less than convincing when considered narrowly as poems. See St. Ephrem the Syrian, *The Hymns on Faith*, trans. Jeffrey T. Wickes (Washington, DC: Catholic University of America Press, 2015).

15 Johnson's views on devotional poetry were criticized shortly after the appearance of the life of Waller. See Daniel Turner, *Devotional Poetry Vindicated, in Some Occasional Remarks on the Late Dr Samuel Johnson's Animadversions upon that Subject in his Life of Waller* (1785).

16 See Gregory of Nyssa, *The Lord's Prayer, The Beatitudes*, trans. Hilda C. Graef, Ancient Christian Writers (New York: Paulist Press, 1954), 36, John of Damascus, "An Exact Exposition of the Orthodox Faith," *Writings*, trans. Frederic H. Chase, Jr., Fathers of the Church, vol. 37 (New York: Fathers of the Church, 1958), Book 3, Ch. 24.

17 Johnson, *Lives of the Most Eminent English Poets*, II, 53. Also see Johnson's life of Yalden, *Lives of the Most Eminent English Poets*, III, 111.

18 For the notion of the "indefinite relation" or the "relation without relation," see Maurice Blanchot, "The Relation of the Third Kind (man without horizon)," *The Infinite Conversation*, trans. Susan Hanson (Minneapolis: University of Minnesota Press, 1993).

19 For the introduction of revelation, as distinct from illumination, see Thomas Aquinas, *Summa theologiæ*, 1a q. 1 *responsio*. I exclude, for the purposes of this essay, Blanchot's argument that the true revelation of Judaism is the possibility of dialogue with an infinite Other. I discuss this contention in *The Dark Gaze: Maurice Blanchot and the Sacred* (Chicago: University of Chicago Press, 2004) Chs 6, 7.

20 Johnson, *Lives of the Poets,* I, 291.

21 See my essay, "The Experience of Poetry," *Box-kite* 2 (1998): 285–304.

22 See Hans Urs von Balthasar, "Revelation and the Beautiful," *Explorations in Theology*, 4 vols, I: *The Word Made Flesh*, trans. A. V. Littledale with Alexander Dru (1964; rpt. San Francisco: Ignatius Press, 1989).

23 See Avery Dulles, *Models of Revelation* (New York: Doubleday and Co., 1983), Part I.

24 As indices of this "age," see William James, *The Varieties of Religious Experience* (1902) and Wilhelm Dilthey, *Das Erlebnis und die Dichtung* (1905).

25 See Max Charlesworth, *Religious Inventions: Four Essays* (Cambridge: Cambridge University Press, 1997), Ch. 1.

26 Christopher Wordsworth, *Memoirs of William Wordsworth,* ed. Henry Reed, 2 vols (Boston: Ticknar, Reed and Fields, 1851), II, 370, 359.

27 See Martin Heidegger, "What are Poets For?," *Poetry, Language, Thought*, trans. Albert Hofstadter (New York: Harper Colophon, 1975).

28 See Karl Rahner, "Poetry and the Christian," *Theological Investigations*, vol. IV, trans. Kevin Smyth (London: Darton, Longman and Todd, 1974), 357–67.

29 See Eliot, "The Social Function of Poetry," *On Poetry and Poets*, 24–5. Also see his reported remarks on the subject, made in 1948, in Smidt, *Poetry and Belief in the Work of T. S. Eliot*, 57.

30 W. H. Auden, "For the Time Being: A Christmas Oratorio," *Collected Poems*, ed. Edward Mendelson (New York: Random House, 1976), 307.

31 A. R. Ammons, "Hymn," *Collected Poems 1951–1971* (New York: W. W. Norton, 1972), 39.

32 See Chapter 14 in this volume.

33 See St. Maximus the Confessor, *On the Cosmic Mystery of Jesus Christ,* trans. Paul M. Blowers and Robert Louis Wilkin (Crestwood, NY: St. Vladimir's Seminar Press, 2003) 34, 104, 126.

34 See, for example, my *Kingdoms of God* (Bloomington: Indiana University Press, 2014).

35 See, for example, Helen Gardner, *Religion and Literature* (Oxford: Oxford University Press, 1971), 134.

36 A. S. P. Woodhouse counters Eliot by arguing that "The poem is not a mere record of an experience; it is the realization of the experience," *The Poet and his Faith: Religion and Poetry in England from Spenser to Eliot and Auden* (Chicago: The University of Chicago Press, 1965), 7. His point applies to theologians as much to critics, as can be seen when Ross A. Shecterle takes "Religious literature" to be "writings that are seen to be 'codifications' of 'divine revelation,'" *The Theology of Revelation of Avery Dulles 1980–1994* (Lewiston: Edwin Mellen Press, 1996), 54.

37 See Eliot, "Dante," *Selected Essays*, 258.

38 See, for example, William Empson's reading of George Herbert's "The Sacrifice" in *Seven Types of Ambiguity* (1930; rpt. Harmondsworth: Penguin, 1961), 262–70. Empson's reading of "The Sacrifice" was contested by Rosemond Tuve in the first part of her *A Reading of George Herbert* (London: Faber and Faber, 1952).

39 See Malcolm Mackenzie Ross, *Poetry and Dogma: The Transfiguration of Eucharistic Symbols in Seventeenth Century English Poetry* (New Brunswick, NJ: Rutgers University Press, 1954), viii.

40 See Kierkegaard, "The Difference between a Genius and an Apostle," *Without Authority,* ed. and trans. Howard V. Hong and Edna H. Hong, *Kierkegaard's Writings,* vol. XVIII (Princeton: Princeton University Press, 1997), 93–108.

41 Gerard Manley Hopkins, "God's Grandeur," *Poems of Gerard Manley Hopkins,* ed. Robert Bridges (London: Humphrey Milford, 1918), 26.

42 In one of his Bedford Leigh Sermons, Hopkins observes that faith is "to believe without doubting all that God reveals, hear him whenever he speaks to you. But is it not enough to be ready to believe anything God may reveal, who will not do that? We do not have faith unless we believe that he has spoken and can say what (in some however general way) and believe that," *The Sermons and Devotional Writings of Gerard Manley Hopkins,* ed. Christopher Devlin (London: Oxford University Press, 1959), 28.

43 Johnson, *Lives of the Most Eminent English Poets,* II, 53.

44 On this line see *The Sermons and Devotional Writings of Gerard Manley Hopkins,* 195.

45 In his letter to Robert Bridges of January 4, 1883 Hopkins notes, "I mean foil in its sense of leaf or tinsel, and no other word whatever will give the effect I want. Shaken goldfoil gives off broad glares like sheet lightning and also, and this is true of nothing else, owing to its zigzag dints and creasings

and network of small many cornered facets, a sort of fork lightning too,"
Claude Colleer Abbott, ed., *The Letters of Gerard Manley Hopkins to Robert Bridges,* 2nd edn (London: Oxford University Press, 1955), 169.

46 Torah gives us several examples of God as fire: Lev. 9:24, Num. 11:1, Deut. 4:23, Deut. 5:20, and Deut. 9:3.

47 See St. Bernard of Clairvaux, *On the Song of Songs,* trans. Kilian Walsh, intro. M. Corneille Halflants (Kalamazoo, MI: Cistercian Publications, Inc., 1971) 4 vols, I, sermon 15. St. Bernard returns to the theme in later sermons, especially sermon 16.

48 Quoted by Blanchot, *L'Écriture du désastre* (Paris: Gallimard, 1980), 16.

49 In later poems, such as "I wake and feel the fell of dark, not day" (1885?), experience refers to an exposure to God's distance, not his presence.

50 The Vatican dropped its opposition to the use of lightning rods in 1769. Before then it had been thought that such things impeded divine intervention in the world. The biblical ground for the Vatican's objection to lightning rods would most likely be Job 36:32.

51 On *intus legere* as the origin of *intellegere,* see St. Thomas Aquinas, *Summa Theologiæ,* II. ii. q. 8. Edith Stein proposes that Husserl's "intuition" and Aquinas's *"intus legere"* are the same. See her "Husserl and Aquinas: A Comparison," *Knowledge and Faith,* trans. Walter Redmond, *The Collected Works of Edith Stein,* VIII (Washington DC: ICS Publications, 2000), 45.

52 On the phenomenological sense of "experience," see Claude Romano, *L'Événement et le monde* (Paris: Presses Universitaires de France, 1998) III, A.

53 Eberhard Jüngel, *God as the Mystery of the World: On the Foundation of the Theology of the Crucified One in the Dispute between Theism and Atheism,* trans. Darrell L. Guder (Grand Rapids: William B. Eerdmans, 1983), 32.

54 See Jean-Luc Marion, *Being Given: Toward a Phenomenology of Givenness,* trans. Jeffrey L. Kosky (Stanford: Stanford University Press, 2002), books III and IV. Also see the general introduction in Kevin Hart, ed., *Jean-Luc Marion: The Essential Writings* (New York: Fordham University Press, 2013).

55 Marion, *Being Given,* 215–16.

56 See Marion, "The Banality of Saturation," trans. Jeffrey L. Kosky, *Counter-Experiences: Reading Jean-Luc Marion,* ed. Kevin Hart (Notre Dame: Notre Dame University Press, 2006), §6.

57 See Milton, *Paradise Lost,* I, 19–22.

58 Friedrich Hölderlin, *Poems and Fragments,* trans. Michael Hamburger, 3rd edn (London: Anvil Press, 1994), 395.

59 Robert Bridges objects that the final image is one of Hopkins's "efforts to force emotion into theological or sectarian channels," "Preface to Notes," *Gerard Manley Hopkins: The Critical Heritage,* ed. Gerald Roberts (London: Routledge and Kegan Paul, 1987), 78.

60 See Derek Attridge, "'This Strange Institution Called Literature': An

Interview with Jacques Derrida," in Derrida, *Acts of Literature* (London: Routledge, 1992), 44–5.

61 See Derrida, *Speech and Phenomena: And Other Essays on Husserl's Theory of Signs,* trans. David B. Allison (Evanston: Northwestern University Press, 1973), esp. Ch. 7.

62 See St. Bonaventure, *On the Reduction of the Arts to Theology,* trans. and intro. Zachary Hayes, Works of St. Bonaventure (St Bonaventure, NY: Franciscan Institute, 1996).

63 Erich Przywara, "Katholizismus", in *Ringen der Gegenwart,* 2 vols (Ausburgh: Filser, 1929), II, 667. Rahner folds the notion into his work when he says, "A theological statement is a statement which leads into the *mysterium,* "What is a Dogmatic Statement?," *Theological Investigations* V, trans. Karl-H. Kruger (London: Darton, Longman and Todd, 1966), 58. Of course, this living mystery is an aspect of the Kingdom, and to some extent the *reductio in mysterium* converges with what I call the basilaic reduction. See my *Kingdoms of God,* Ch. 6, and also Chapter 2 of this volume.

64 Jüngel, *God as the Mystery of the World,* 378. The notion also permeates von Balthasar's theology.

Chapter 2: "For the life was manifested": On "material spirit" in Hopkins

1 All quotations from the Bible will be from the King James translation.

2 See Paul L. Gavrilyuk and Sarah Coakley, eds, *The Spiritual Senses: Perceiving God in Western Christianity* (Cambridge: Cambridge University Press, 2012).

3 Augustine, "First Homily," *Homilies on the First Epistle of John,* intro., trans. and notes Boniface Ramsey, ed. Daniel E. Doyle and Thomas Martin (New York: New City Press, 2008), 22.

4 I leave aside, solely for reasons of economy, the question of the role of the sacraments. Hopkins's poetry is not a sacrament and does not deal with sacraments, although there is no reason not to think of it as a sacramental and dealing with sacramentals. See Chapter 1.

5 See Karl Rahner, "The Doctrine of the 'Spiritual Senses' in Origen," *Theological Investigations,* 16, trans. David Morland (New York: Crossroad, 1983), 81–103, and "The Doctrine of the 'Spiritual Senses' in the Middle Ages," *Theological Investigations* 16: 104–34, Hans Urs von Balthasar, *The Glory of the Lord,* I: *Seeing the Form,* trans. Erasmo Leiva-Merikakis, ed. Joseph Fessio and John Riches (San Francisco: Ignatius Press, 1982), 365–425, and "Bonaventure," *The Glory of the Lord,* II: *Studies in Theological Style: Clerical Styles,* trans. Andrew Louth et al. (San Francisco: Ignatius Press, 1984), esp. 317–26. Also see Stephen Fields, "Balthasar and Rahner on the Spiritual Senses," *Theological Studies* 57 (1996): 224–41.

6 Origen, *Contra Celsum,* trans., intro. and notes Henry Chadwick

(Cambridge: Cambridge University Press, 1965), 44, Gregory of Nyssa, *Commentary on the Song of Songs*, trans. and intro. Casimir McCambley, pref. Panagiotes Chrestou (Brookline, MA: Hellenic College Press, 1987), 195, St. John of the Cross, "The Ascent of Mount Carmel," *The Collected Works of St. John of the Cross*, trans. Kieran Kavanaugh and Otilio Rodriguez (Washington, DC: ICS Publications, 1979), Book II, Ch. 4, section 2. It should be recalled, though, that elsewhere in the commentary on the Canticle, Gregory holds that one encounters God only in the darkness of faith.

7   See Hugh of Balma, "The Roads to Zion," *Carthusian Spirituality*, trans. and intro. Dennis D. Martin, pref. John van Engen. Classics of Western Spirituality (New York: Paulist Press, 1997) and Jean Gerson, "Sermon on the Feast of Saint Bernard," *Early Works*, trans. and intro. Brian Patrick McGuire, preface Bernard McGinn, Classics of Western Spirituality (New York: Paulist Press, 1998), 128–48.

8   For Origen, the inner person and the outer person were created separately. See his *Homilies on Genesis and Exodus*, trans. Ronald E. Heine (Washington, DC: Catholic University of America Press, 1982), 1.13. It should also be remembered that Origen rejected Aristotle's notion of matter as the substrate of all properties, as stated in *Metaphysics* 1.iii.1, along with the teaching of the eternity of matter. See *On First Principles*, trans., intro. and notes G. W. Butterworth, intro. Henri de Lubac (Gloucester, MA: Peter Smith, 1973), 4.4.7.

9   See Tatian, *Oratio ad Graecos and Fragments*, ed. and trans. Molly Whittaker (Oxford: Clarendon Press, 1982), Chs 12, 13, 30.

10 For Origen, of course, the soul had cooled down from its original warmth when close to God, and so descended to the material world. See Origen, *On First Principles*, Book II, Ch. 8, section 3.

11 See, for example, Martin Heidegger, *Being and Time*, trans. John Macquarrie and Edward Robinson (Oxford: Basil Blackwell, 1973), 10.

12 On this theme see Ronald Bruzina, *Edmund Husserl and Eugen Fink: Beginnings and Ends in Phenomenology 1928–1938* (New Haven: Yale University Press, 2004), 6.3.1 and 6.3.2. I leave aside here a narrow discussion of the differences between Husserl and Fink on "spirit."

13 See Husserl's quotation from Augustine's *De vera religione* at the very end of his *Cartesian Meditations: An Introduction to Phenomenology*, trans. Dorian Cairns (The Hague: Martinus Nijhoff, 1977). For Husserl on the soul, and in particular his rejection of the soul as naturalistically conceived, see his *The Crisis of European Sciences and Transcendental Phenomenology: An Introduction to Phenomenological Philosophy*, trans. and intro. David Carr (Evanston: Northwestern University Press, 1970), 63, 116, 118, 170, 214.

14 One influential account of the spiritual senses identifies them strictly with the intellect and excludes the imagination and even the will. See A. Poulain, *The Graces of Interior Prayer: A Treatise on Mystical Theology*, trans. Leonora L. Yorke Smith, pref. D. Considine, 3rd impression (London: Kegan Paul, Trench, Trubner and Co., 1921), Ch. 6.

15 Edmund Husserl, *Ideas Pertaining to a Pure Phenomenology and to a*

Phenomenological Philosophy: Second Book, trans. Richard Rojecewicz and André Schuwer, Edmund Husserl Collected Works III (Boston: Kluwer Academic Publishers, 1989), 100, 259. "Spirituality," as *Geistigkeit* is translated, has a far wider semantic reach than "spirituality" usually has in English. Husserl uses the word to designate the world of culture, as distinct from nature, for example, and understands animals to have culture as well as human beings.

16 See Angela Ales Bello, *The Divine in Husserl and Other Explorations*, Analecta Husserliana XCVIII (Dordrecht: Springer, 2009), Part 1, Ch. 2.

17 See Husserl, *Ideas Pertaining to a Pure Phenomenology and to a Phenomenological Philosophy: First Book*, trans. F. Kersten, Edmund Husserl Collected Works II (Boston: Kluwer Academic Publishers, 1998), section 58.

18 I follow the later Husserl in distinguishing ἐποχή and reduction. See *The Crisis of European Sciences*, section 41.

19 Husserl, *Cartesian Meditations*, 46.

20 Husserl's expression for what phenomenology does is give "*Gegenstände im Wie.*" See his *On the Phenomenology of the Consciousness of Internal Time (1893–1917)*, trans. John Barnett Brough (Dordrecht: Kluwer Academic Publishers, 1991), 121.

21 Not only the Christian, of course, although I limit myself here to that religion. It should be noted that atheists also have the supernatural attitude, but only in negative: they deny that there truly *is* such an attitude to be taken seriously. On what I have called the "supernatural attitude" see Husserl's words as recorded by Dorian Cairns in his *Conversations with Husserl and Fink* (The Hague: Martinus Nijhoff, 1976), 47.

22 See Karl Jaspers, *Philosophical Faith and Revelation*, trans. E. B. Ashton (London: Coillins, 1967).

23 See on this topic Max Scheler, *On the Eternal in Man*, trans. Bernard Noble (Hamden, CT: Archon Books, 1972), 268–9.

24 Husserl, *Ideas* I, 117.

25 Husserl, A V 21, 128a. I quote James G. Hart's translation of the passage in his "A Précis of Husserlian Phenomenological Theology," *Essays in Phenomenological Theology*, ed. Steven W. Laycock and James G. Hart (Albany: State University of New York Press, 1986), 148.

26 It is tempting to examine the relations between Husserl's view of God and experience, as expressed here, and Karl Rahner's notion of "transcendental experience." I put this aside for another occasion. I also leave aside the interesting question of whether the divine mode of presence, as entertained by Husserl in this passage, bears any resemblance to St. Bernard of Clairvaux's understanding of the presence of God that cannot be traced in the mind. See his *On the Song of Songs*, IV, trans. Irene Edmonds, intro. Jan Leclercq (Kalamazoo, MI: Cistercian Publications, 1980), sermon 74.6.

27 Augustine, *The Literal Meaning of Genesis*, in *On Genesis*, intro., trans. and notes Edmund Hill, ed. John E. Rotelle, The Works of Saint Augustine (Hyde Park, NY: New City Press, 2002), XII. 6.15–7.16.

28 See Bello, *The Divine in Husserl*, Part 1 Ch. 2, section 2.

29 On this issue see Anthony J. Steinbock, *Phenomenology and Mysticism: The Verticality of Religious Experience* (Bloomington: Indiana University Press, 2008), esp. Chs 1 and 5.

30 Husserl looks at the matter from the other side: for him, the one who makes the ἐποχή is like a religious convert. See *The Crisis of European Sciences*, section 35.

31 See my *Kingdoms of God* (Bloomington University Press, 2014), esp. Ch. 6.

32 Maurice Blondel, "The Letter on Apologetics," *The Letter on Apologetics and History and Dogma*, trans. Alexander Dru and Illtyd Trethowan (1964; Grand Rapids, MI: William B. Eerdmans, 1994), 130.

33 For Christ as αὐτοβασιλεια, see Origen, *Commentarium in evangelium Matthaei*, 14.7.10.

34 See Eberhard Jüngel, *God as the Mystery of the World: On the Foundation of the Theology of the Crucified One in the Dispute between Theism and Atheism*, trans. Darrell L. Guder (Grand Rapids, MI: William B. Eerdmans Publishing Co., 1983), 32. Jüngel's sense of experiencing experience remains within the supernatural attitude, however.

35 Husserl, *Briefwechsel*, 10 vols, ed. Elizabeth and Karl Schuhmann (Dordrecht: Kluwer, 1994), III, 454.

36 Not only Bonaventure but also Karl Barth. See his *Church Dogmatics* I: *The Doctrine of the Word of God*, Part 2, ed. G. W. Bromiley and T. F. Torrance, trans. G. T. Thomson and Harold Knight (Edinburgh: T&T Clark, 1956), 470.

37 Husserl, *The Crisis of European Sciences*, 97.

38 See Ignatius of Loyola, "The Spiritual Exercises," trans. George E. Ganss, *Spiritual Exercises and Selected Works*, ed. George E. Ganss (Mahwah, NJ: Paulist Press, 1991), sections 121–5.

39 George Herbert, "Prayer" (I), *The Works of George Hebert*, ed. F. E. Hutchinson (Oxford: Clarendon Press, 1945), 51.

40 Claude Colleer Abbott, ed., *The Letters of Gerard Manley Hopkins to Robert Bridges* (Oxford: Oxford University Press, 1955), 56.

41 Gerard Manley Hopkins, *Poems of Gerard Manley Hopkins*, ed. Robert Bridges (London: Humphrey Milford, 1918), 30–1. I have added all Hopkins's accents.

42 See Hugh of St. Victor, "The Soul's Three Ways of Seeing," *Selected Spiritual Writings*, intro. Aelred Squire (New York: Harper and Row, 1962), 183. Also see his *Didascalicon*, trans. Jerome Taylor (New York: Columbia University Press, 1991), 99–100.

43 See Richard of St. Victor, *The Twelve Patriarchs, The Mystical Ark, Book Three of "The Trinity,"* trans. and intro. Grover A. Zinn, pref. Jean Châtillon (New York: Paulist Press, 1979), 71.

44 Ignatius, "The Spiritual Exercises," 148, 149, 150.

45 Christopher Devlin, ed., *The Sermons and Devotional Writings of Gerard Manley Hopkins* (Oxford: Oxford University Press, 1959), 175.

46 It should not be assumed that Hopkins's commentary on the *Spiritual Exercises* is undertaken exclusively in an Ignatian spirit. His interest in Scotus is clearly legible in his comments. However, I am more interested here in the habit of contemplation than the Scotist inflection that Hopkins gives to his Ignatian training. See Marucci, *The Fine Delight that Fathers Thought: Rhetoric and Medievalism in Gerard Manley Hopkins* (Washington, DC: The Catholic University of America Press, 1994), 188–98.

47 For St. Ignatius one contemplates the visible and meditates upon the invisible; in the monastic tradition it is usually the other way round. See David Anthony Downes, *The Ignatian Personality of Gerard Manley Hopkins* (New York: University Press of America, 1990), Ch. 6. For an account of contemplation as a gaze on the face of God, see St. Gregory the Great, *Morals on the Book of Job*, trans. by members of the English Church, A Library of Fathers of the Holy Catholic Church (Oxford: John Henry Parker, 1847), III:1, 56–7.

48 See Augustine, *De consensus evangelistarum*, I.5.8. The relevant passage reads, "*ista vero magis in fide et apud perpaucos per speculum in enigmate et ex parte in aliqua visione incommutabilis veritatis.*"

49 Richard of St. Victor, *The Mystical Ark*, Book 2, Ch.12.

50 Hopkins, *The Collected Works of Gerard Manley Hopkins*, IV: *Oxford Essays and Notes*, ed. Lesley Higgins (Oxford: Oxford University Press, 2006), 307.

51 See, for example, *Carmen* I. iv, II. xiv, and IV. vii.

52 Yet see *Sermons and Devotional Writings*, 136–8, where the "spiritual senses" are directed to consider the fires of hell.

53 On the traces of Ruskin in this poem, see Alison G. Sulloway, *Gerard Manley Hopkins and the Victorian Temper* (London: Routledge and Kegan Paul, 1972), 89.

54 Humphry House, ed., *The Journals and Papers of Gerard Manley Hopkins*, completed by Graham Storey (London: Oxford University Press, 1959), 289, and Claude Colleer Abbott, ed., *Further Letters of Gerard Manley Hopkins Including his Correspondence with Coventry Patmore*, 2nd edn (London: Oxford University Press, 1956), 373

55 John Milton, *Paradise Lost*, ed. Alastair Fowler (London: Longman, 1968), VIII:257–61.

56 Paul Mariani is right to point us also to the similar rhythm in the opening line of Swinburne's "Hermaphroditus": "Lift úp thy líps, turn róund, look báck for lóve." See Mariani, *A Commentary on the Complete Poems of Gerard Manley Hopkins* (Ithaca: Cornell University Press, 1970), 116 n.55.

57 House, *Journals and Papers*, 204.

58 For other "phenomenological I's," see Husserl, *The Basic Problems of Phenomenology: From the Lectures, Winter Semester, 1910–1911*, trans. Ingo Farin and James G. Hart, Edmund Husserl Collected Works (Dordrecht: Springer, 2006), section 39, and Husserl, *Analyses Concerning Passive* *and Active Synthesis: Lectures on Transcendental Logic*, trans. Anthony J. Steinbock, Edmund Husserl Collected Works IX (Dordrecht: Kluwer Academic Publishers, 2001), 52.

59   Husserl, *Phantasy, Image Consciousness, and Memory (1898–1925)*, trans. John B. Brough, Edmund Husserl Collected Works XI (Dordrecht: Springer, 2005), 606.

60   House, *Journals and Papers*, 230.

61   House, *Journals and Papers*, 205.

62   It should be noted, though, that Husserl allows imagination to fulfill empty intentions: the meaning, not the object, has intuition. See Husserl, "Psychological Studies in the Elements of Logic," *Early Writings in the Philosophy of Logic and Mathematics*, trans. Dallas Willard (Dordrecht: Kluwer Academic Publishers, 1994), 150–1, and *Logical Investigations*, 2 vols, trans. J. N. Findlay (London: Routledge and Kegan Paul, 1970), II, 725.

63   Hopkins, *Oxford Essays and Notes*, 313.

64   See Heidegger, *The Fundamental Concepts of Metaphysics: World, Finitude, Solitude*, trans. William McNeill and Nicholas Walker (Bloomington: Indiana University Press, 1995), Part I.

65   See Lynn Staley, trans. and ed., *The Book of Margery Kempe* (New York: W. W. Norton, 2001), 10.

66   Theodosa Gray, trans., *The Homilies of Saint Gregory the Great on the Book of the Prophet Ezekiel*, intro. Bishop Chrysostomos (Etna, CA: Center for Traditionalist Orthodox Studies, 1990), II. i.18. Also see Gregory's similar comment in his *Morals on the Book of Job*, III.1, 262. Gregory is not alone in this view. See, for example, St. Ambrose of Milan, *Exposition of the Holy Gospel According to Saint Luke*, trans. Theodosia Tomkinson (Etna, CA: Center for Traditionalist Orthodox Studies, 2003), 20, 30; and Grégoire Palamas, *Défense des saints hésychastes*, 2 vols, intro, texte critique, traduction et notes Jean Meyendorff, 2nd edn (Leuven: Spicilegium Sacrum Lovaniense, 1973), vol. 1, I, 3, 27.

67   In a different key, one that is almost Stevensian, J. Hillis Miller speaks of a "marriage of spirit and matter" in Hopkins. See his *The Disappearance of God: Five Nineteenth-Century Writers* (Cambridge: Harvard University Press, 1963), 290.

68   See Devlin, *The Sermons and Devotional Writings*, 151.

69   Henry D. Thoreau, *Journal*, vol. 3:1848–51, gen. ed., John C. Broderick, ed. Robert Sattelmeyer et al. (Princeton: Princeton University Press, 1990), 354–5. The entry was made on August 5, 1851.

70   House, *Journals and Papers*, 199.

71   Blondel, *Action: Essay on a Critique of Life and a Science of Practice (1893)*, trans. Oliva Blanchette (Notre Dame: Notre Dame University Press, 1984), 198.

72   See Richard of St. Victor, *The Mystical Ark*, Book V, Ch. 4.

73   Richard of St. Victor, *The Mystical Ark*, Book VI, Ch. 18. In Richard's schema

Hopkins the poet would be in the third stage of contemplation, with only three wings, whereas those who make spiritual leaps have six wings.

74 On anticipation, see Jean-Yves Lacoste, "La phénoménalité de l'anticipation," *La phénoménalité de Dieu: Neuf études* (Paris: Éditions du Cerf, 2008), esp. 150–7.

Chapter 3: Eliot's rose-garden: Some phenomenology and theology in "Burnt Norton"

1 "Burnt Norton" was first published in *Collected Poems, 1909–1935* (London: Faber and Faber, 1936), and was reproduced as a pamphlet in 1941 before appearing in *Four Quartets* (London: Faber and Faber, 1944). Also see, John Lehmann, "T. S. Eliot Talks about Himself and the Drive to Create," *The New York Times Book Review*, November 29, 1953, 5.

2 Eliot also alludes to Fragments 25 and 68 in the second movement of "Little Gidding."

3 John Burnett translates λόγος as "Word" in his *Early Greek Philosophy* (London: A. and C. Black, 1892). The French translation of Eliot's poem follows suit: "le Verbe." See Eliot, *Quatre Quatuors*, trans. Claude Vigée (London: Menard Press, 1992), 7.

4 See, for example, Peter Milward, *A Commentary on T. S. Eliot's "Four Quartets"* (Tokyo: The Hokuseido Press, 1968).

5 Quoted in John Sutherland, *Stephen Spender: A Literary Life* (Oxford: Oxford University Press, 2005), 125–6. According to M. J. C. Hodgart, Eliot was also listening to Bartok's Quartets. See Hugh Kenner, "Into our First World," in *T. S. Eliot, "Four Quartets": A Casebook*, ed. Bernard Bergonzi (London: Macmillan, 1969), 182.

6 On this issue, see Eliot, "The Music of Poetry," written in 1942, during the composition of *Four Quartets*, in *On Poetry and Poets* (London: Faber and Faber, 1957), 38.

7 See Edmund Husserl, *Logical Investigations*, 2 vols, trans. J. N. Findlay (London: Routledge and Kegan Paul, 1970), I, 408–10, 427, among other places. Also see Husserl, *Philosophy of Arithmetic: Psychological and Logical Investigations with Supplementary Texts from 1887–1901*, trans. Dallas Willard (Dordrecht: Kluwer Academic Publishers, 2003), 19–20. It is worth noting that Eliot had some acquaintance with Husserl's writings, though one should not presume any endorsement of phenomenology on his part. See Kristian Smidt, *Poetry and Belief in the Work of T. S. Eliot* (London: Routledge and Kegan Paul, 1949), 20.

8 Such is the view, for example, of Staffan Bergsten, *Time and Eternity: A Study of the Structure and Symbolism of T. S. Eliot's "Four Quartets"* (New York: Humanities Press, 1973), 75.

9   See Donald Hall, "The Art of Poetry 1: T. S. Eliot," *Paris Review* 21 (1959): 57. Also see E. Martin Browne, *The Making of T. S. Eliot's Plays*, 2nd edn (Cambridge: Cambridge University Press, 1970), 345–52, and Helen Gardner, *The Composition of "Four Quartets"* (New York: Oxford University Press, 1978), 16.

10 Kenneth Paul Kramer, *Redeeming Time: T. S. Eliot's "Four Quartets"* (Lanham, MD: Cowley Publications, 2007), 33.

11 Eliot, "Dante," *Selected Essays*, 3rd edn (London: Faber and Faber, 1951), 257.

12 Eliot, "Charybde et Scylla: Lourdeur et frivolité," *Annales du Centre Universitaire Meditérranéan* 5 (1951–52): 77. Eliot and F. R. Leavis agree here. See Leavis, *Education and the University: A Sketch for an "English School"* (New York: G. W. Stewart, 1948), 94. For Eliot's knowledge of the "middle way," see Cleo McNelly Kearns, *T. S. Eliot and Indic Traditions: A Study in Poetry and Belief* (Cambridge: Cambridge University Press, 1987), 76–84. Also see A. David Moody, *Tracing T. S. Eliot's Spirit: Essays on his Poetry and Thought* (Cambridge: Cambridge University Press, 1996), Ch. 2.

13 See for example, "If the present and the future / Depend on the past, / Then the present and the future / Would have existed in the past. // If the present and the future / Did not exist there, / How could the present and the future / Be dependent upon it?," Jay L. Garfield, trans., *The Fundamental Wisdom of the Middle Way: Nāgārjuna's " Mūlamadhyamakakārikā"* (Oxford: Oxford University Press, 1995), 50.

14 See J. M. E. McTaggart, "The Unreality of Time," *Mind* 17 (new series, 68) (1908): 458.

15 Kenner, "Into our First World," 171. At the antipodes of my reading there stands A. Kron's argument in "A Semantics for the First Quartet by T. S. Eliot," *Algebra and Logic* 38 (4) (1999), 209–22. Kron formalizes the opening five lines of "Burnt Norton" and establishes their truth in a rigorous fashion. However, he translates "perhaps" by $\exists$, the existential quantifier, which may be questioned. See page 219. Another favorable reading is offered by C. O. Gardner, "Some Reflections on the Opening of 'Burnt Norton'," *Critical Quarterly* 12 (4) (1970): 326–35.

16 See, for example, Martin Heidegger, *What Is Called Thinking?*, trans. J. Glenn Gray (New York: Harper and Row, 1968), 102–3, and *Logic: The Question of Truth*, trans. Thomas Sheehan (Bloomington: Indiana University Press, 2010), 173. Also see, for example, Jacques Derrida, *Of Grammatology*, corrected ed., trans. Gaytri Chakravorty Spivak (Baltimore: Johns Hopkins University Press, 1997), 112.

17 On indefinite intentions, see David Woodruff Smith and Ronald McIntyre, *Husserl and Intentionality* (Dordrecht: D. Reidel Publishing Co., 1982), 18.

18 Cf. Agatha's remark to Harry, "I only looked through the little door / When the sun was shining on the rose-garden: / And then a black raven flew over" in *The Family Reunion* (New York: Harcourt Brace, 1939), 104. Also see Harry to Mary in the same play: "You bring me news / Of a door that opens at the end of a corridor, / Sunlight and singing," 59. In addition, see the lines about the "Lady of silences" in part two of "Ash-Wednesday." The rose-garden as a theme in Eliot's poetry was discerned quite early.

See Leonard Unger, "T. S. Eliot's Rose Garden: A Persistent Theme," *The Southern Review* 7 (4) (1942): 677–81.

19   In his commentary on *Four Quartets* Peter Milward suggests that the thrush is a symbol of the Holy Spirit. Yet I cannot conceive of Eliot maintaining that the Holy Spirit is capable of deceit. See his *A Commentary on T. S. Eliot's "Four Quartets,"* 23. We also remember the "hermit thrush" singing in part five of *The Waste Land*.

20   See Helen Gardner, *The Composition of "Four Quartets,"* 39–40. Eliot himself mentions Kipling's story "They" in a letter of February 1, 1946 to a French translator of *Four Quartets*. See Eliot, *Quatre Quatuors*, 55. It is worth noting that Alice, on entering the garden down the rabbit hole, encounters a "large rose-tree near the entrance of the garden: the roses growing on it were white, but there were three gardeners at it, busily painting them red," *Alice's Adventures in Wonderland* (London: Folio Society, 1961), 68.

21   See James M. Barrie, *Dear Brutus,* ed. and inrtro. William-Alan Landes (Studio City: Players Press, Inc., 2007), 35.

22   See Guillaume de Lorris et Jean de Meun, *Le Roman de la Rose*, ed. Félix Lecoy, 3 vols, Les Classiques Français du Moyan Age (Paris: Libraire Honoré Champion, 1965), I, *ll*. 659–72, 1249–56. Also see *The Romance of the Rose*, trans. Charles Dahlberg, 3rd edn (Princeton: Princeton University Press, 1995), Part 1, Book 1.

23   On suspension of belief and non-belief, see Eliot, "Dante," 258.

24   See Husserl, *Ideas Pertaining to a Pure Phenomenology and to a Phenomenological Philosophy: First Book*, trans. F. Kersten (Dordrecht: Kluwer Academic Publishers, 1983), Section 32, and Heidegger, *The Basic Problems of Phenomenology*, rev. edn, trans., intro. and lexicon Albert Hofstadter (Bloomington: Indiana University Press, 1988), 21.

25   See Eugen Fink, *Sixth Cartesian Meditation: The Ida of a Transcendental Theory of Method* with textual notations by Edmund Husserl, trans. and intro. Ronald Bruzina (Bloomington: Indiana University Press, 1995), 42.

26   Barbara Everett is somewhat hasty, it seems to me, in figuring the presences as ghosts. See "A Visit to Burnt Norton," *Critical Quarterly* 16 (3) (1974): 199–224, esp. 207–8, 212.

27   See Husserl, "Psychological Studies in the Elements of Logic," *Early Writings in the Philosophy of Logic and Mathematics*, trans. Dallas Willard (Dordrecht: Kluwer Academic Publishers, 1994), 150–1, and *Logical Investigations*, II, 725.

28   See John Keats, "Ode on a Grecian Urn," *Poems*, ed. John Barnard (Harmondsworth: Penguin, 1988), and St. John of the Cross, "Cantico Espiritual," in Kieran Kavanagh and Otilo Rodriguez, ed., *The Collected Works of St. John of the Cross* (Washington, DC: ICS Publications, 1979), 44.

29   Christopher Marlowe and Thomas Nash, *The Tragedy of Dido Queen of Carthage*, III. i, Tudor Facsimile Texts (Oxford: Clarendon Press, 1914). See Donne, "The Ecstasie":

> Our hands were firmly cimented
>   With a fast balme, which thence did spring,
> Our eye-beames twisted, and did thred
>   Our eyes, upon one double string.

30 Steven Carroll proposes an entirely naturalistic interpretation of the event in a novel based on Eliot's visit to Burnt Norton with Emily Hale. See his *The Lost Life: A Novel* (London: Fourth Estate, 2009), 7, 22.

31 Marcel Proust, "La Coeur aux Lilas et L'Atelier des Roses: Le Salon de Mme. Madeleine Lemaire," *Essais et articles*, ed. Pierre-Clarac et Yves Sandre, presentation de Thierry Laget (Paris: Gallimard, 1994), 155.

32 Philip Wheelwright points us to the flowers in Botticelli's "Primavera" and da Brescia's "Madonna in the Rose Garden" to get a sense of flowers that seem to be looked at. See his "Eliot's Philosophical Themes," *T. S. Eliot: A Study of His Writings by Several Hands*, ed. B. Rajan (London: Dennis Dobson Ltd, 1947), 99. I must confess, however, that I am unable to discern any visual evidence in these two paintings for the sense that Eliot proposes in "Burnt Norton."

33 Joseph Aspdin invented "Portland Cement," which is still used today, in 1824. I am unsure as to the history of the renovations and improvements of the garden and house that Eliot visited.

34 See Robert W. Hill, Jr., ed., *Tennyson's Poetry: Authoritative Texts, Juvenilia and Early Responses, Criticism* (New York: W. W. Norton, 1971), 48.

35 Mashaharu Anesaki, who taught Eliot at Harvard, evidently observed (in Manju Jain's words) that the lotos "is perfect because it has many flowers and many fruits at once. The real entity is represented in the fruit, its manifestation in the flower, so that there is a mutual relation of the final reality and its manifestation," Manju Jain, *T. S. Eliot and American Philosophy: The Harvard Years* (Cambridge: Cambridge University Press, 1992), 199.

36 I expand on the significance of the lotos in "Fields of *Dharma*: On T. S. Eliot and Robert Gray," *Literature and Theology* 27 (3) (2013): 267–84.

37 De Lorris, *Le Roman de la Rose, l.* 1569.

38 See Dante, *Paradiso*, xxxii, 47.

39 Eliot expressed regret about not having children. See Ronald Bush, *T. S. Eliot: A Study in Character and Style* (New York: Oxford University Press, 1984), 192.

40 See Augustine, *Confessions*, trans. and intro. Henry Chadwick (Oxford: Oxford Univesity Press, 1991), XI, xx (26).

41 See Husserl, *Phenomenological Psychology: Lectures, Summer Semester; 1925*, trans. John Scanlon (The Hague: Martinus Nijhoff, 1977), 141.

42 See Eliot, "A Prediction in Regard to Three English Authors: Writers Who, though Masters of Thought, Are Likewise Masters of Art," *Vanity Fair*, 22 (6) (1924): 29. I am summarizing Jain's view in *T. S. Eliot and American Philosophy*, 227.

43 Kavanagh and Rodriguez, ed., *The Collected Works of St. John of the Cross*, 721. Eliot imitates the stanza pattern in part four of "East Coker."

44 See "The Dark Night," *The Collected Works of St. John of the Cross*, Chs 17–20.

45 See Augustine, *Confessions*, XI, xiii (15).

46 See the Sketch of Mount Carmel, *The Collected Works of St. John of the Cross*, 110–11.

47 Cf. Eliot, *The Rock: A Pageant Play* (London: Faber, 1934), 52. F. H. Bradley writes something that may have stimulated Eliot: "There will be many times, all of which are at one in the Eternal—the possessor of temporal events and yet timeless," *Appearance and Reality: A Metaphysical Essay*, 2nd edn (Oxford: Clarendon Press, 1930), 189.

48 Nicholas Watson and Jacqueline Jenkins, eds, *The Writings of Julian of Norwich* (University Park: The Pensylvania State University Press, 2006), 249.

49 See Jean-Luc Marion, *Being Given: Towards a Phenomenology of Givenness*, trans. Jeffrey L. Kosky (Stanford: Stanford University Press, 2002), sections 21–2.

50 Watson, *The Writings of Julian of Norwich*, long text, Ch. 51, 229.

Chapter 4: God's little mountains: Young Geoffrey Hill and the problem of religious poetry

1 Mary Webb, *Gone to Earth*, intro. John Buchan (1917; London: Jonathan Cape, 1952), 13.

2 Geoffrey Hill, *Broken Hierarchies: Poems 1952–2012,* ed. Kenneth Haynes (Oxford: Oxford University Press, 2013), 5.

3 In *For the Unfallen* (London: André Deutsch, 1959) and later editions of his poetry, Hill dropped the subtitle of "Genesis" and the reference to Blake in "Holy Thursday." Hill did not reprint "To William Dunbar" and "For Isaac Rosenberg."

4 See, for example, Hill, *Collected Critical Writings*, ed. Kenneth Haynes (Oxford: Oxford University Press, 2008), Chs 14, 25, 26.

5 Hill, "The Poetry of Allen Tate," *Geste* 3 (3) (1958): 11.

6 See Hill, "Richard Eberhart," *The Isis*, November 25, 1953, 31.

7 Allen Tate, "The Man of Letters in the Modern World," *The Man of Letters in the Modern World: Selected Essays: 1928–1955* (New York: Meridian Books, 1955), 20.

8 This train of questioning is continued in Chapter 6 of this volume.

9 See St. Basil of Caeserea, *Exegetic Homilies*, trans Agnes Clare Way, The Fathers of the Church, vol. 46 (Washington, DC: Catholic University of America Press, 1963); St. Ambrose, *Hexameron, Paradise, and Cain and Abel*, trans. John J. Savage, The Fathers of the Church, vol. 42 (New York:

Fathers of the Church, 1961); and St. Bonaventure, *Collations on the Six Days*, in *The Works of Bonaventure: Cardinal, Seraphic Doctor, and Saint* (Paterson, NJ: St. Anthony Guild, 1970), V.

10 In choosing, for convenience, to call the speaker "Hill" one should be aware that the "I" of the early poems is not encumbered with personal details. A remark from one of Hill's early pieces of criticism is worth quoting: "when a writer seeks to create a work of art he must, indeed, have modesty and 'keep himself in the background'. That is the true modesty of the artist ...," "A Writer's Craft," *The Isis*, February 17, 1954, 14.

11 Pascal, *Pensées*, ed. and trans. Roger Ariew (Indianapolis: Hackett Pub. Co., 2005), 32.

12 See Rudolf Bultmann, *The New Testament and Mythology and Other Basic Writings*, ed. and trans. Schubert M. Ogden (Philadephia: Fortress Press, 1984), 1–43.

13 The details of the new division between Course I, II, and III may be found in the *Handbook to the University of Oxford* (Oxford: Clarendon Press, 1932), 157.

14 See John Haffenden, *William Empson: Against the Christians* (Oxford: Oxford University Press, 2006), Ch. 14.

15 Haffenden, ed., "To Frank McMahon," *Selected Letters of William Empson* (Oxford: Oxford University Press, 2006), 571. Empson's letter is dated August 21, 1973. His fury with Neo-Christianity reached a height in his memorable *Milton's God* (London: Chatto and Windus, 1961). However, also see "Literary Criticism and the Christian Revival" (1966), *Argufying: Essays on Literature and Culture*, ed. John Haffenden (London: The Hogarth Press, 1988), 632–37.

16 See Empson, "The Satisfaction of the Father" (*c.* 1972), *Argufying*, 622. Tertullian uses the word *satisfacere* but not in the sense of "vicarious sacrifice." See Robert Roberts, *The Theology of Tertullian* (London: Epworth, 1924), 180. Tertullian evokes the fires of hell in his *Apology*, bound with *De Spectaculis*, trans. T. R. Glover, and Minucius Felix, *Octavius*, trans. W. C. A. Kerr, Loeb Classical Library (Cambridge, MA: Harvard University Press, 1966), XLVIII, 13–15.

17 See Martin Luther, "Lectures on Galatians," *Luther's Works*, ed., Jaroslav Pelikan and Walter A. Hansen, 55 vols, XXVI: *Lectures on Galatians*, 1535 (St Louis: Concordia, 1963), 280, and John Calvin, *Institutes of the Christian Religion*, 2 vols, ed. John T. McNeill, trans. Ford Lewis Battles (Philadelphia: Westminster Press, 1960), Vol. I, Book II, Ch. 16, section 1.

18 As Empson indicates, his main source for his understanding of the Atonement is part of an article in *The Catholic Encyclopedia*. He seems not to have read the Fathers on the topic of the Atonement, and bases much of his idea of the Atonement on Milton's sense of it.

19 I should add that Empson was not an unreserved admirer of Hill's poetry, which he felt, rightly, could be "artificial" and could "harden into mere mannerism." See "To Christopher Ricks," June 30, 1978, *Selected Letters of William Empson*, 645, 646. Similarly, Hill expresses reservations about

Empson's poetry in his review of the special number of *The Review* devoted to Empson. See Hill, "The Dream of Reason," *Essays in Criticism* 14 (1) (1964): 91–101.

20 See Empson, *The Structure of Complex Words* (London: Chatto and Windus, 1951).

21 See Hill, "The Art of Poetry," LXXX, interview with Carl Phillips, *The Paris Review* 154 (2000): 281.

22 See Hill's remarks on the "uneasy thunder" of the "Divine Voice" in his review of Blake's *Jerusalem*, *The Isis*, March 4, 1953, 22.

23 Hill changed the line in his *Collected Poems* (London: Pegnuin, 1985) to read "And yet the sky was riven" (17). Following this edition, William Logan bases his interpretation of "God's Little Kingdom" on "riven" rather than "cloven," and thereby misses part of its theological point of the poem. See Logan, "The Absolute Unreasonableness of Geoffrey Hill," *Conversant Essays: Contemporary Poets on Poetry*, ed., James McCorkle (Detroit: Wayne State University Press, 1990), 43–4. It should at least be mentioned that the goat can be valued affirmatively in the Christian tradition. St. Gregory of Nyssa observes, in his fifteenth homily on the Song of Songs, "A goat is honored because its thick coat provides an image of beauty for the bride. Another reason for praise is that a goat can pass over rocks with a sure foot, agilely turn on mountain peaks, courageously pass through difficult, rough places, and can go safely on the road to virtue," *Commentary on the Song of Songs*, trans. and intro. Casimir McCambley, pref. Panagiotes Chrestou (Brookline, MA: Hellenic College Press, 1987), 269. The image of the cloven hoof, however, surely overrides this positive image of the goat.

24 See Rabbi Isaac the Blind of Provence, "The Mystical Torah—Kabbalistic Creation," *The Early Kabbalah*, ed. and intro. Joseph Dan, trans. Ronald C. Kiener, pref. Moshe Idel (New York: The Paulist Press, 1986), 74.

25 See Harold Bloom, *The Anxiety of Influence: A Theory of Poetry* (Oxford: Oxford University Press, 1973).

26 Hill, "Letter from Oxford," *London Magazine*, 1:4 (1954), 72. Anthony Thwaite calls Hill a "runic visionary" in his essay "Geoffrey Hill," *The Isis*, November 18, 1953, 17.

27 Quoted from http://www.come-and-hear.com/sotah/sotah_5.html (accessed on September 8, 2008).

28 See *Midrash Tanhuma*, trans. John T. Townsend (Hoboken, NJ: KTAV Publishing House, 1997), II, 108. Also see "Tractate Bahodesh," *Mekilta de-Rabbi Ishmael*, trans. and ed., Jacob Z. Lauterbach, 3 vols (Philadelphia: The Jewish Publication Society of America, 1933), II, 224.

29 See Eugenio Montale, "Siria," *Tutte le poesie*, ed. Giorgio Zampa (Milano: Arnoldo Mondadori, 2005), 240. Also see my discussion of Charles Wright's translation of the lyric in Chapter 13 of this volume.

30 See John Climacus, *The Ladder of Divine Ascent*, trans. Coim Luibheid and Norman Russell, intro. Kallistos Ware, pref. Colm Luibheid (New York: Paulist Press, 1982), and Guigo II, *The Ladder of Monks: A Letter on the*

Contemplative Life and Twelve Manifestations, trans. and intro. Edmund Colledge and James Walsh (Kalamazoo, MI: Cistercian Publications, 1978). It should be noted that Hill is not a Zarathustra, either: this prophet descends the mountain with his hard words, and does not fall from it. See Nietzsche, *Thus Spake Zarathustra: A Book for Everyone and No One*, trans. and intro. R. J. Hollingdale (Harmondsworth: Penguin, 1969), 40.

31 Wallace Stevens, "Sad Strains of a Gay Waltz," *Collected Poetry and Prose*, ed. Frank Kermode and Joan Richardson (New York: Library of America, 1997), 100. "Tea at the Palaz of Hoon" appears on p. 51.

32 In "Tea at the Palaz of Hoon" Stevens is a visionary of a certain sort, although one would hesitate to generalize of all his poems, even those in *Harmonium*, that he is always a visionary. "The Snow Man," to name just one lyric, is as bleak a poem in terms of religious vision as one can imagine, and yet it is a visionary poem. Not all visions are comforting.

33 T. S. Eliot, "East Coker," *Collected Poems 1909–1962* (London: Faber and Faber, 1963), 201. Also see Hill, "Dividing Legacies," *Collected Critical Writings*, 377–8.

34 Hill, "The Bidden Guest," *For the Unfallen*, 22.

35 Hill, "Lachrimæ," *Tenebræ* (London: André Deutch, 1978), 16, 19. I discuss these matters in greater detail in Chapter 6.

Chapter 5: "it / is true"

1 See Italo Calvino, *Invisible Cities*, trans. William Weaver (New York: Harcourt Brace Jovanovich, 1974). For "free phantasy" see Edmund Husserl, Ideas *Pertaining to a Pure Phenomenology and to a Phenomenological Philosophy: First Book, Introduction to a Pure Phenomenology*, trans. F. Kersten (Boston: Kluwer Academic Publishers, 1983), section 70.

2 See Claude Romano, *Le chant de la vie: Phénoménologie de Faulkner* (Paris: Gallimard, 2005).

3 See "Husserl an von Hofmannsthal (12.1.1907)," *Briefwechsel*, 10 vols, VII: *Wissenschaftlerkorrespondenz*, ed. Elisabeth Schuhmann and Karl Schuhmann (Boston: Kluwer, 1994), 135. Also see Martin Heidegger, "The Origin of the Work of Art," *Poetry, Language, Thought*, trans. Albert Hofstadter (New York: Harper and Row, 1971); Roman Ingarden, *The Literary Work of Art: An Investigation of Ontology, Logic, and Theory of Literature*, trans. George G. Grabowicz (Evanston: Northwestern University Press, 1973); Maurice Merleau-Ponty, "Eye and Mind," *The Primacy of Perception and Other Essays on Phenomenological Psychology, the Philosophy of Art, History and Politics*, trans. James M. Edie (Evanston: Northwestern University Press, 1964); and Mikel Dufrenne, *Phenomenology of Aesthetic Experience*, trans. Edward Casey et al. (Evanston: Northwestern University Press, 1973).

4 "September Song" first appeared in *Stand* 8 (4) (1967): 41. The poem was revised a little for publication in *King Log*. In the magazine publication there is a semi-colon between "been" and "untouchable" in the first line, there are no commas around "sufficient," and "zyklon" is not given a capital "Z." Also, the lapidary inscription is divided by a semi-colon rather than a dash; in the later version it resembles more closely dates of birth and death.

5   See Wallace Stevens, "The Poems of Our Climate," *Collected Poems* (New York: Alfred A. Knopf, 1954), 193.

6   See Richard L. Rubenstein, *After Auschwitz: History, Theology, and Contemporary Judaism*, 2nd edn (Baltimore: The Johns Hopkins University Press, 1992). See in particular Rubenstein's reflection on the first edition of 1966 in his new preface.

7   Geoffrey Hill, *Broken Hierarchies: Poems 1952–2012*, ed. Kenneth Haynes (Oxford: Oxford University Press, 2013), 44. "September Song" was originally collected in Hill's second volume of verse, *King Log* (London: André Deutsch, 1968).

8   Merleau-Ponty, "Everywhere and Nowhere," in *Signs*, trans. Richard C. McCleary (Evanston: Northwestern University Press, 1964), 157.

9   Derek Attridge, "'This Strange Institution Called Literature': An Interview with Jacques Derrida," in Jacques Derrida, *Acts of Literature*, ed. Derek Attridge (New York: Routledge, 1992), 41.

10 See Jean-Luc Marion, *Being Given: Toward a Phenomenology of Givenness*, trans. Jeffrey L. Kosky (Stanford: Stanford University Press, 2002), 5. Marion's concern here is that what shows itself must first give itself; yet it is consistent with this claim to say that some phenomena give themselves but do not show themselves. Also see Michel Henry, *The Essence of Manifestation*, trans. Girard Etzkorn (The Hague: Martinus Nijhoff, 1973), section IV.

11 Derrida, *Speech and Phenomena and Other Essays on Husserl's Theory of Signs*, trans. and intro. David B. Allison, pref. Newton Garver (Evanston: Northwestern University Press, 1973), 46.

12 See Franz Brentano, *Psychology from an Empirical Standpoint*, trans. A. C. Rancurello, D. B. Terrell, and L. L. McAlister, 2nd edn, intro. Peter Simons (London: Routledge, 1995), 198.

13 David V. Erdman, ed., *The Complete Poetry and Prose of William Blake*, new and rev. edn, commentary by Harold Bloom (Berkeley: University of California Press, 1982), 409.

14 The theory of racial inequality was proposed by Arthur de Gobineau in his *The Inequality of Human Races*, trans. Adrian Collins, intro. Oscar Levy (London: William Heinemann, 1915). The book appeared in German translation in 1897. Affirmation of the Aryan "master race" became a key part of Nazi thought.

15 The point was first made by Jon Silkin in his "The Poetry of Geoffrey Hill," published in 1972 and reprinted in Harold Bloom's anthology, *Geoffrey Hill*, Modern Critical Views (New York: Chelsea House Publishers, 1986), 20. I am thankful to Silkin for introducing me to "September Song" in a lecture he gave at the Australian National University in 1974, and to Bloom for conversations about Hill.

16 The epigraph of "Ovid in the Third Reich" is taken from Ovid's *Amores*, III, xiv. It reads, "*non peccat, quaecumque potest peccasse negare, / solaque famosam culpa professa facit,*" which Guy Lee renders as follows, "Any woman who pleads Not Guilty is innocent; / only confession gives her a bad name," *Ovid's Amores* (London: John Murray, 1968), 175.

17 William Wordsworth, *The Prelude: A Parallel Text*, ed. J. C. Maxwell (Harmondsworth: Penguin, 1971), V, 389–90. In the 1805 version, the boy is not quite ten, while in the 1850 version, he is not quite twelve.

18 Gerard Manley Hopkins, *Poems of Gerard Manley Hopkins*, ed. Robert Bridges (London: Humphrey Milford, 1918), 51. Hill evokes the poem several times in his *The Orchards of Syon* now in *Broken Hierarchies*, 349–418.

19 See Merleau-Ponty, *Phenomenology of Perception*, trans. Colin Smith (London: Routledge and Kegan Paul, 1962), xiv.

20 For counter-experience, see Jean-Luc Marion, *Being Given: Towards a Phenomenology of Givenness*, trans. Jeffrey L. Kosky (Stanford: Stanford University Press, 2002), 215–16.

21 See Emmanuel Levinas, "The Ruin of Representation," *Discovering Existence with Husserl*, trans. Richard A. Cohen and Michael B. Smith (Evanston: Northwestern University Press, 1998), 121.

22 See Stevens, "Poetry is a Destructive Force," *Collected Poems*, 192–3.

23 Hill, "History as Poetry," *Broken Hierarchies*, 61. Also see "Tristia: 1891–1938" in which Hill declares of Mandelstam, "The dead keep their sealed lives," 58.

24 Eugen Fink as quoted by Ronald Bruzina in his *Edmund Husserl and Eugen Fink: Beginnings and Ends in Phenomenology, 1928–1938* (New Haven: Yale University Press, 2004), 354.

25 On Hill's use of brackets, see Christopher Ricks, "'The Tongue's Atrocities,'" *Geoffrey Hill*, ed. Bloom, 67–8.

26 See Dylan Thomas, "A Refusal to Mourn, the Death by Fire, of a Child in London,'" *Collected Poems* (London: J. M. Dent, 1952), 94. It would be possible to identify poems of the same period that evoke children in the camps. Randall Jarrell's "In the Camp there was One Alive" (1948) is an example. See his *The Complete Poems* (London: Faber and Faber, 1971), 405–6. Also see R. Clifton Spargo's "The Bad Conscience of American Holocaust Elegy: The Example of Randall Jarrell," *The Ethics of Mourning: Grief and Responsibility in Elegiac Literature* (Baltimore: The Johns Hopkins University Press, 2004), Ch. 6. On hearing a trace of Thomas's poem, see for example, Jahan Ramazani, *Poetry of Mourning: The Modern Elegy from Hardy to Heaney* (Chicago: The University of Chicago Press, 1994), 7.

27 The earliest reference to "A Refusal to Mourn" is in a letter Thomas wrote to Vernon Watkins on March 28, 1945. It is linked to "Ceremony after a Fire Raid," and it is worth citing Ralph Maud's note that "An alternate title for part II of 'Ceremony after a Fire Raid' is written on the Texas manuscript of that poem: 'Among Those Burned to Death Was a Child Aged a Few Hours,'" *Where Have the Old Words Got Me?: Explications of Dylan Thomas' Collected Poems* (Montreal: McGill-Queens University Press, 2003), 41. "A

Refusal to Mourn" appeared in Thomas's collection *Deaths and Entrances* (1946).

28 See Jean Wahl, *Existence humaine et transcendance* (Boudry-Neuchâtel: Éditions de la Baconnière, 1944), 37.

29 Theodore W. Adorno, "Cultural Criticism and Society," *Prisms*, trans. Samuel Weber and Shierry Weber (Cambridge, MA: MIT Press, 1981), 34.

30 Adorno, *Negative Dialectics*, trans. E. B. Ashton (London: Routledge and Kegan Paul, 1973), 362–3.

31 Levinas, "Reality and its Shadow," *Unforeseen History*, trans. Nidra Poller, foreword Don Ihde, intro. Richard A. Cohen (Urbana: University of Illinois Press, 2004), 90.

32 The invisible revelation of subjectivity is the burden of Michel Henry's *The Essence of Manifestation*.

33 See Paul Celan, "Die Fleissigen," *Threadsuns*, trans. and intro. Pierre Joris (Los Angeles: Sun and Moon Press, 2000), 112–15.

34 The German text and a translation may be found in Michael Hamburger, *Paul Celan: Poems, A Bilingual Edition* (New York: Persea Books, 1980), 50–3.

35 On this issue I refer to Jean-Luc Nancy's essay "Forbidden Representation," *The Ground of the Image*, trans. Jeff Fort (New York: Fordham University Press, 2005).

36 I quote from a poem by Hans Sahl, a ripose to Adorno, that Nancy discusses in "Forbidden Representation." The relevant lines read as follows: "*Wir glauben, dass Gedichte / überhaupt erst jetzt wieder möglich / geworden sind, insofern nämlich als / nur im Gedicht sich sagen lässt, / was sonst / jeder Beschreibung spottet.*" Fort's translation runs, "We actually believe that poems have only now become possible again, insofar as only the poem can say what otherwise mocks every description."

37 See, in particular, Derrida, *The Work of Mourning*, ed. Pascale-Anne Brault and Michael Naas (Chicago: University of Chicago Press, 2001).

38 See Maurice Blanchot, "Friendship," in *Friendship*, trans. Elizabeth Rottenberg (Stanford: Stanford University Press, 1997).

39 See Marcel Proust, *In Search of Lost Time*, 6 vols, 6: *Time Regained*, trans. Andreas Major and Terrence Kilmartin, rev. D. J. Enright (New York: The Modern Library, 1993), 309.

40 Levinas, *God, Death, and Time*, trans. Bettina Bergo (Stanford: Stanford University Press, 2000), 12.

41 See Levinas's reference to Henry in *God, Death, and Time*, 17.

42 See W. S. Merwin, *The Lice* (New York: Atheneum, 1977), 58.

43 See Levinas, *Totality and Infinity*, trans. Alphonso Lingis (The Hague: Martinus Nijhoff, 1979). Levinas might well remind us that Heidegger published his essay "Plato's Doctrine of Truth" in 1942, the year in which the child was deported.

44 See Levinas, *De l'oblitération: Entretien avec Françoise Armengaud à propos de l'œuvre de Sosno*, 2nd edn (Paris: Éditions de la Différence, 1990).

45 Consider Hill's interview with Carl Phillips: "Human beings are difficult. We're difficult to ourselves, we are mysteries to each other … Why is it believed that poetry, prose, painting, music should be less than we are? Why does music, why does poetry have to address us in simplified terms, when, if such simplification were applied to a description of our own inner selves, we would find it demeaning?," "Geoffrey Hill: The Art of Poetry, LXXX," *The Paris Review* 154 (2000): 276–7. For Empson's views on ambiguity and complexity, see his *Seven Types of Ambiguity* (1930; rpt. Harmondsworth: Penguin, 1972) and *The Structure of Complex Words* (London: The Hogarth Press, 1985). Also see Hill's essay on Empson, "The Dream of Reason," *Essays in Criticism* 14 (1) (1964): 91–101.

46 I take both expressions from Yves Bonnefoy. See his "Baudelaire contra Rubens," *Le Nuage rouge: Essais sur la poétique* (Paris: Mercure de France, 1992), 79, and "Lifting Our Eyes from the Page," trans. John Naughton, *Critical Inquiry* 16 (4) (1990): 198.

47 See, for example, Blanchot, *The Book to Come*, trans. Charlotte Mandell (Stanford: Stanford University Press, 2003), 45, 122; and Derrida, "'This Strange Institution Called Literature,'" 36–40.

48 It must be conceded that some of Hill's recent works are more garrulous. See, in particular, *Speech! Speech!* in *Broken Hierarchies*, 287–348.

49 See Ricks, "'The Tongue's Atrocities,'" 67.

50 See R. M. Rilke, *Selected Poems*, trans. C. F. MacIntyre (Berkeley: University of California Press, 1940), 39.

51 I am obliged to Michael L. Morgan for reminding me of the Da-Yaynu in this context.

52 Unlike Susan Gubar, I do not think the "This" includes the killing of the child. See her *Poetry after Auschwitz: Remembering What One Never Knew* (Bloomington: Indiana University Press, 2003), 212.

Chapter 6: Transcendence in tears

1 All quotations from Geoffrey Hill's poems are taken from his *Broken Hierarchies: Poems 1952–2012*, ed. Kenneth Haynes (Oxford: Oxford University Press, 2013). In an interview Hill remarks that "the grasp of true religious experience is a privilege reserved for very few" and observes that he "is trying to make lyrical poetry out of a much more common situation— the sense of *not* being able to grasp true religious experience," "Geoffrey Hill," *Viewpoints: Poets in Conversation with John Haffenden* (London: Faber and Faber, 1981), 89.

2 See Hill, "Poetry as 'Menace' and 'Atonement,'" *Collected Critical Writings*, ed. Kenneth Haynes (Oxford: Oxford University Press, 2008), 18–19.

3   See Hill, *Collected Critical Writings,* 264. Also see 365.

4   For a discussion of the music, see Diana Poulton, *John Dowland: His Life and Works* (Berkeley: University of California Press, 1972), Ch. 5.

5   Richard Barnsfield, "If Musique and sweet Poetrie agree," in George Klawitter, ed., *Richard Barnfield: The Complete Poems* (Selinsgrove: Susquehahanna University Press, 1990), 181. Thomas Campion also wrote a poem (in Latin) in praise of Dowland. See his "Ad. Io. Dolandum," *Poemata* (Londini, 1595). Barnsfield and Campion probably have in mind Dowland's settings to lute songs such as "Come away, come, sweet love" and "I saw my lady weep."

6   On tears and theology, see E. M. Cioran, *Tears and Saints,* trans. and introd. Ilinca Zarifopol-Johnston (Chicago: University of Chicago Press, 1995).

7   "Saint Peters Complaint," along with earlier versions of the poem, can be found in James H. McDonald and Nancy Pollard Brown, ed., *The Poems of Robert Southwell, S.J.* (Oxford: Clarendon Press, 1967). The translation of Tansillo, "[The] Peeter Playnt," is given in Appendix I. Louis L. Martz analyzed the poetry of tears in his *The Poetry of Meditation: A Study of English Religious Literature of the Seventeenth Century,* rev. edn (New Haven: Yale University Press, 1962), 199–203. It is important to note that he rightly pointed out that Protestant authors also wrote tears poetry: see his discussion of George Herbert's "Praise," 202. Richard Strier provides an important supplement to Martz in his "Herbert and Tears," *ELH* 46 (2) (1979): 221–47.

8   On the line of "tears poetry" that runs from Southwell to Crashaw, see the fine discussion by Alison Shell in her *Catholicism, Controversy and the English Literary Imagination, 1558–1660* (Cambridge: Cambridge University Press, 1999), Ch. 2.

9   Haffenden, "Geoffrey Hill," 80, 87. Hill alludes to Crashaw's poem "Wishes: To his (supposed) Mistresse" in the final poem of *For the Unfallen,* "To the (Supposed) Patron," *Collected Poems,* 57.

10   Richard Crashaw, "The Weeper," *The Poems: English, Latin and Greek,* ed. L. C. Martin (Oxford: Clarendon, 1927), 312. The poem is generally known as "Saint Mary Magdalene, or, The Weeper." Hill observes that he admires Crashaw's verse in his interview with John Haffenden, 80. Calvin Bedient's estimate of "Lachrimæ" as "mawkish" can only be regarded as a hasty judgment. See his essay "On Geoffrey Hill," *Geoffrey Hill,* ed. Harold Bloom, Modern Critical Views (New York: Chelsea House Publishers, 1986), 108.

11   René Char, *Les Matinaux suivi de La parole en archipel,* Collection Poésie (Paris: Gallimard, 1987), 105.

12   Dowland's sequence runs "Lachrimæ Antiquæ," "Lachrimæ Antiquæ Novæ," "Lachrimæ Gementes," "Lachrimæ Tristes," "Lachrimæ Coactæ," "Lachrimæ Amantis," and "Lachrimæ Veræ."

13   "The Masque of Blackness" adapts Francisco de Quevedo's sonnet "Retrato de Lisi que traia en una sortija," "Martyrium" is Hill's composition in its entirety, and "Pavana dolorosa" alludes to Peter Philips's composition for keyboard.

14 I discuss "Lachrimæ Veræ" in more detail in "Poetic Sequences: Ted Hughes and Geoffrey Hill," *The Cambridge Companion to Twentieth-Century English Poetry*, ed. Neil Corcaran (Cambridge: Cambridge University Press, 2008), 187–99.

15 Hill cites Joseph Carey's observation about Eugenio Montale's "Iride" with obvious sympathy: "a heretic's dream of salvation, expressed in the images of the orthodoxy from which he is excommunicate," *Three Modern Italian Poets: Saba, Ungaretti, Montale* (New York: New York University Press, 1969), 316. The dedication to Hill's *Without Title* (London: Penguin, 2006), reads, "in omaggio a Eugenio Montale."

16 Hill quotes Coleridge's note in "Poetry as 'Menace' and 'Atonement,'" 4.

17 Images of Christians carrying crosses are to be found in Luis de Granada's *Of Prayer and Meditation* (1582) and John Bucke's *Instructions for the Use of the Beads* (1589). See Brad S. Gregory, *Salvation at Stake: Christian Martyrdom in Early Modern Europe* (Cambridge, MA: Harvard University Press, 1999), 276.

18 J.-M. de Buck, S.J., ed., *Spiritual Exercises and Devotions of Blessed Robert Southwell, S.J.*, trans. P. E. Hallett (New York: Benziger Brothers, 1931), 59.

19 Henrik Ibsen, *Brand: A Version for the Stage*, 2nd edn, by Geoffrey Hill, introd. Inga-Stina Ewbank (Minneapolis: University of Minnesota Press, 1981), 69. Hill prepared his version of *Brand* in 1976–7, toward the end of the period he was composing *Tenebræ*. For the proximity of Brand and Kierkegaard, see George Brandes, *Henrik Ibsen, Björn-Stjerne Björnson: Critical Studies,* trans. Jessie Muir et al. (London: William Heinemann, 1899), 21.

20 The conjunction of Hill and Kierkegaard perhaps comes best into focus when we read Kierkegaard's remark, "A religious poet is therefore in a peculiar position. Such a poet will seek to establish a relation to the religious through the imagination; but for this very reason he succeeds only in establishing an aesthetic relationship to something aesthetic ... If the religious is in truth the religious, if it has submitted itself to the discipline of the ethical and preserves it within itself, it cannot forget that religious pathos does not consist in singing and hymning and composing verses, but in existing," *Concluding Unscientific Postscript*, trans. David F. Swenson and Walter Lowrie (Princeton: Princeton University Press, 1941), 347–8.

21 See W. S. Milne, *An Introduction to Geoffrey Hill* (London: Bellew Press, 1998), 133.

22 See Jean Wahl, *Existence humaine et transcendance* (Neuchâtel: Éditions de la Baconnière, 1944), 37. It should be stressed that "image," for Levinas, is far broader in scope than "image" as used by Ezra Pound, for example.

23 Emmanuel Levinas, "Reality and its Shadow," in *Unforeseen History*, trans. Nidra Poller, Foreword Don Ihde, intro. Richard A. Cohen (Urbana: University of Illinois Press, 2004), 78.

24 See J.-P. Sartre, *The Imaginary: A Phenomenological Psychology of the Imagination*, trans. Jonathan Weber (London: Routledge, 2004). Sartre argues that the imagination has an intentional structure, which is irreducible to perception. He also talks of the "original poverty" of the image on p. 16.

25 See Edmund Husserl, *Ideas Pertaining to a Pure Phenomenology and to a Phenomenological Philosophy, First Book: General Introduction to a Pure Phenomenology*, trans. F. Kersten (Dordrecht: Kluwer Academic Publishers, 1983), Section 43.

26 See Levinas, *De l'obliteration: Entretien avec Françoise Armengaud à propos de l'œuvre de Sosno*, 2nd edn (Paris: Éditions de la Difference, 1998).

27 See Philippe Lacoue-Labarthe and Jean-Luc Nancy, *The Literary Absolute: The Theory of Literature in German Romanticism*, trans. Philip Barnard and Cheryl Lester (Albany: State University of New York Press, 1988).

28 D. D. Page, ed., *The Letters of Ezra Pound* (London: Faber and Faber, 1951), 366. Hill quotes this sentence in his interview with Haffenden, 99; it is at the root of his equation of style and faith in Milton, Donne and Herbert.

29 On this issue, see Bloom, *Where Shall Wisdom Be Found?* (New York: Riverhead Books, 2004).

30 See Maurice Blanchot, "Two Versions of the Imaginary" in *The Space of Literature*, trans. Ann Smock (Lincoln: University of Nebraska Press, 1982), 254–63. Blanchot, of course, will not accept the mimetic account of art that Levinas assumes. See my exposition and analysis of Blanchot's position in my *The Dark Gaze: Maurice Blanchot and the Sacred* (Chicago: University of Chicago Press, 2004).

31 See Hill, "Poetry as 'Menace' and 'Atonement,'" 15.

32 See Ricks, "'The Tongue's Atrocities,'" *Geoffrey Hill*, ed. Bloom, 56.

33 Augustine, Letter 120 to Consentius (410), *Letters 100–155*, The Works of Saint Augustine, II:2, trans. Roland Teske, S. J., ed. Boniface Ramsey (Hyde Park, NY: New City Press, 2003), 130–40

34 Boris Pasternack, *Poems*, trans. Eugene M. Kayden (Ann Arbor: University of Michigan Press, 1959), 168.

35 Conversation with Richard Strier on the influence of Donne on Hill has been illuminating for me. Strier notes, in addition, that there are echoes of George Herbert in "Lachrimæ." The third stanza of Herbert's "Mattens" certainly resonates with the opening of "Lachrimæ Amantis": "My God, what is a heart, / That thou shouldst it so eye, and wooe, / Powering upon it all thy art, / As if that thou hadst nothing else to do?," *The Works of George Herbert*, ed. F. E. Hutchinson (Oxford: Clarendon Press, 1941), 62.

36 Haffenden, "Geoffrey Hill," 90.

37 See Husserl, *Ideas* I, xx. Also see Derrida's comments in his interview with Derek Attridge, "This Strange Institution Called Literature," *Acts of Literature* (London: Routledge, 1992), 44.

38 In his interview with Carl Philips, Hill uses the word "mystery," but almost as though it was synonymous with "difficulty": "Human beings are difficult. We're difficult to ourselves, we are mysteries to each other. . . Why is it believed that poetry, prose, painting, music should be less than we are? Why does music, why does poetry have to address us in simplified terms, when, if such simplification were applied to a description of our own inner selves, we would find it demeaning?," "Geoffrey Hill: The Art of Poetry, LXXX," *The Paris Review* 154 (2000): 276–7. That poetry should not simplify is surely right; that it should therefore be "difficult" does not follow. The difficulty of modern poetry is in part caused partly by internal procedures and literary inheritances and partly by its mimesis of situations in the world. On excess of intuition, see Jean-Luc Marion, *Being Given: Toward a Phenomenology of Givenness*, trans. Jeffrey L. Kosky (Stanford: Stanford University Press, 2002), Book IV.

39 See Samuel Johnson, "Waller," *The Lives of the Most Eminent English Poets*, II, 53; Donald Davie, ed., *The New Oxford Book of Christian Verse* (Oxford: Oxford University Press, 1981), xxviii–xxix. Needless to say, this tradition rejects the blend of prayer and rhetoric exemplified at a very high level by Augustine in his *Confessions*.

40 See Jules Supervielle, "Prière à l'inconnu," *La fable du monde* (Paris: Gallimard, 1950), 39; and Yves Bonnefoy, "La lumière, changée," *Poèmes* (Paris: Mercure de France, 1978), 211.

41 See, for example, Martial Lekeux, OFM, *The Art of Prayer*, trans. Paul Joseph Oligny, OFM (London: Sands and Co., 1962).

42 See Hill's stage version of Ibsen's *Brand*, 17. Also see the lines about martyrdom on 67 and the odious Dean's observation "Religion's like High Art," 148. Pierre Janelle, *Robert Southwell the Writer* (New York: Sheed and Ward, 1935), 286–7.

43 Hill, "The Absolute Reasonableness of Robert Southwell," *Collected Critical Writings*, 30. Also see 33.

44 See Hill's essay "Poetry as 'Menace' and 'Atonement,'" and Christopher Ricks, "*Tenebræ* and at-one-ment" in *Geoffrey Hill: Essays on his Work*, ed. Peter Robinson (Milton Keynes: Open University Press, 1985), 62–85.

45 "The Masque of Blackness" was originally the fifth of the sequence when "Lachrimæ" first appeared in *Agenda* (Winter–Spring 1975): 29–35.

46 See Francisco de Quevedo, *Obra Poética*, 3 vols, ed. José Manuel Blecua (Madrid: Editorial Castilia, 1969), III, 652–3.

47 See Ethel Carleton Williams, *Anne of Denmark: Wife of James VI of Scotland: James I of England* (London: Longman, 1970), 126.

48 Ben Jonson, *The Masque of Blackness*, ll. 146–8, in *Ben Jonson's Plays and Masques*, ed. Richard Harp (New York: W. W. Norton, 2001), ll. 146–8, 320.

49 See Williams, *Anne of Denmark*, Ch. 11.

50 Pico della Mirandola, as translated by Walter Pater, in his *The Renaissance: Studies in Art and Poetry* (New York: Macmillan, 1900), 42. Also see Giovanni Pico della Mirandola, "Oration on the Dignity of Man," in *The Renaissance Philosophy of Man*, ed. Ernst Cassirer et al. (Chicago: University of Chicago Press, 1948), 225.

51 Pico della Mirandola, "Oration on the Dignity of Man," 225.

52 Arthur Golding, trans., *Ovid's Metamorphoses*, ed., introd. and notes, Madeleine Forey (Baltimore: The Johns Hopkins University Press, 2002), XI, 139.

53 John Lyly, *Midas*, II: i, 46–8, in *The Complete Works of John Lyly*, 3 vols, ed. R. Warwick Bond (Oxford: Clarendon Press, 1902), III, 124.

54 See Shakespeare, *As You Like It*, II. i, 5. I should note that "not the penalty of Adam" is regarded as a textual crux by some editors who are inclined to render it as "but the penalty of Adam" or "yet the penalty of Adam." See Richard Knowles, ed., *A New Variorum Edition of Shakespeare, "As You Like It"* (New York: The Modern Language Association of America, 1977), 70. See also B. L. Joseph, *Shakespeare's Eden: The Commonwealth of England, 1588–1629* (London: Blandford Press, 1971).

55 See the interpretation developed by Cathrael Kazin, "'Across a Wilderness of Retrospection': A Reading of Geoffrey Hill's *Lachrimæ*," *Agenda* 17 (1) (1979): 43–57, esp. 46–8.

56 For Hill's meditations on the mask, see especially his *Scenes from Comus* (London: Penguin, 2005).

57 See Immanuel Kant, *The Critique of Judgment*, trans., James Creed Meredith (Oxford: Clarendon Press, 1952), Section 10.

58 See Kant, *Religion within the Limits of Reason Alone*, trans., intro. and notes, Theodore M. Greene and Hoyt H. Hudson (New York: Harper and Row, 1960), 182–3.

59 "About George Haydock and His Companions," *Publications of the Catholic Record Society*, 5: *Unpublished Documents Relating to the English Martyrs*, ed. J. H. Pollen (Leeds: Privately Printed by the Society by J. Whithead and Sons, 1908), 61.

60 Gregory discusses this incident in *Salvation at Stake*, 309.

61 See, for example, Henry Garnet's *Treatise of Christian Renunciation* (1593), the final chapter of which consists of quotations from the Fathers.

62 St. Ignatius of Antioch, "The Epistle of Ignatius to the Romans," Ch. 4, in *Ante-Nicene Fathers*, 10 vols, I: *The Apostolic Fathers with Justin Marytr and Irenæus* (1885; rpt. Peabody, MA: Hendrickson Publishers Inc., 1994), 75. St. Jerome perpetuated the image in his *On Illustrious Men*, trans. Thomas P. Halton (Washington, DC: The Catholic University of America Press, 1999), 33. Southwell quotes St. Ignatius in his *An Epistle of Comfort: To the Reverend Priests, and to the Honorable, Worshipful, and Other of the Lay Sort, Restrained in Durance for the Catholic Faith*, ed. Margaret Waugh, foreword Philip Caraman, S.J. (London: Burns and Oates, 1966), 229.

63 *The Martydom of Saint Polycarp*, 15. 2, in *The Didache, The Epistle of Barnabas, The Epistles and the Martyrdom of St. Polycarp, The Fragment of Papias, The Epistle to Diognetus*, trans. and annotated James A. Kleist, Ancient Christian Writers (Westminster, MD: The Newman Press, 1948).

64 Southwell, *An Epistle of Comfort*, 179.

65 Scott R. Pilarz, S.J. observes, "Southwell does more than merely 'allow passions'; he celebrates them when they are rightly ordered," *Robert Southwell and the Mission of Literature, 1561–1595: Writing Reconciliation* (Aldershot: Ashgate, 2004), 176.

66 Arthur Wills, trans., *The Notebooks of Simone Weil*, 2 vols (London: Routledge and Kegan Paul, 1956), I, 279.

67 See Hill, "Annunciations 2," *Broken Hierarchies*, 40.

68 See J. M. Cohen, ed., *The Penguin Book of Spanish Verse* (Harmondsworth: Penguin, 1956), 247. This is the text that Hill used when composing "Lachrimæ." The prose translation of the sestet reads as follows: "How many times did the angel say to me: 'Now, soul, look out of your window, and you will see how lovingly he persists in knocking!' And how many times, oh supreme beauty, did I reply: 'I will open to-morrow,' only to make the same reply upon the morrow!" The translation requires more commentary than I can offer here. For instance, Hill has Christ at his door in the first stanza and yet, in the third stanza, the angel tells him "your lord is coming." In what sense can Christ be present yet still to come? Colin Thompson begins work on a close reading of the translation in his fine essay, "'The Resonances of Words': Lope de Vega and Geoffrey Hill," *The Modern Language Review* 90 (1) (1995): 55–70. For a more literal translation of the original sonnet, see Henry Wadsworth Longfellow, "Tomorrow," *The Poets and Poetry of Europe: With Introductions and Biographical Notices* (Philadelphia: Carey and Hart, 1845), 701.

Chapter 7: Uncommon equivocation in Geoffrey Hill

1 Christopher Devlin, ed., *The Sermons and Devotional Writings of Gerard Manley Hopkins* (London: Oxford University Press, 1959), 123.

2 Geoffrey Hill, "Dividing Legacies," *Collected Critical Writings*, ed. Kenneth Haynes (Oxford: Oxford University Press, 2008), 377.

3 See Jacques Derrida, *The Ear of the Other: Otobiography, Transference, Translation*, ed. Christie V. McDonald, trans. Peggy Kamuf (New York: Schocken Books, 1985), 106–8.

4 Christopher Ricks, *T. S. Eliot and Prejudice* (London: Faber and Faber, 1988), 255.

5 Ricks, *True Friendship: Geoffrey Hill, Anthony Hecht, and Robert Lowell Under the Sign of Eliot and Pound* (New Haven: Yale University Press, 2010), 50.

6 Richard Hooker, *Of the Laws of Ecclesiastial Polity*, 5 vols, ed. George Edelen (Cambridge: Harvard University Press, 1977), I, vii. 7.

7 See Hill, *Collected Critical Writings*, 479.

8 For the reference to Freud, see Harold Bloom, "Introduction," *Geoffrey Hill* (New York: Chelsea House, 1986), 5.

9 Hill, *Broken Hierarchies: Poems 1952–2012*, ed. Kenneth Haynes (Oxford: Oxford University Press, 2013), 40.

10 See Bloom, "Introduction," 3.

11 See Kenneth Allott, ed., *The Penguin Book of Contemporary Verse 1918–60*, rev. edn (Harmondsworth: Penguin, 1962), 391–3.

12 See Stéphane Mallarmé, "Le Tombeau d'Edgar Poe," *Oeuvres complètes*, 2 vols, ed. Bertand Marchal, Bibliothèque de la Pléiade (Paris: Gallimard, 1998), I, 38, and T. S. Eliot, *Four Quartets* (New York: Harcourt, 1943), 54.

13 See Barth, *Die christliche Dogmatik im Entwurf* (Zürich: Theologischer Verlag, 1982), 149ff.

14 See Emmanuel Levinas, "Reality and its Shadow," *Collected Philosophical Papers*, trans. Alphonso Lingis (The Hague: Martinus Nijhoff, 1987), 1–13.

15 Hill, *Broken Hierarchies*, 44.

16 See G. W. F. Hegel, *The Phenomenology of Mind*, trans. and intro. J. B. Baillie (New York: Harper and Row, 1967), 667.

17 Edmund Husserl, *Analyses Concerning Passive and Active Synthesis: Lectures on Transcendental Logic*, trans. Anthony J. Steinbock (Dordrecht: Kluwer Academic Publishers, 2001), 98.

18 Hill, *Collected Critical Writings*, 3, 4.

Chapter 8: Susannah without the cherub

1 Karina Williamson, ed. and intro., *The Poetical Works of Christopher Smart*, 5 vols (Oxford: Clarendon Press, 1980), I: *Jubilate Agno*, 9.

2 See Henry Denzinger, *The Sources of Catholic Dogma*, trans. Roy J. Deferrari (London: B. Herder Book Co., 1957), 785–6. The history of Susannah is found only in the two Greek versions with no basis in any Hebrew scroll, and this is mainly why it was not accepted in some early canons.

3 The very fact that exegetes talk of adultery rather than attempted rape says much about how "a very fair woman" has been understood. See Jennifer A. Glancy, "The Accused: Susanna and her Readers," *Journal for the Study of the Old Testament* 58 (1993): 103–16.

4 For the association on the enclosed garden with the Virgin Mary, see Bernard of Clairvaux, *On the Song of Songs*, 4 vols (Kalamazoo: Cistercian Publications, 1979), III. 47. ii. 4.

5 For a discussion of cinquecento paintings, in which Susannah's naked body is illuminated, see Babette Bohn, "Rape and the Gendered Gaze: *Susanna and the Elders* in Early Modern Bologna," *Biblical Interpretation* 9 (3) (2001), 259–73. Margaret Miles argues, "In the paintings Susanna's innocence becomes guilt as her body communicates and explains the Elders' lust," *Carnal Knowing: Female Nakedness and Religious Meaning in the Christian West* (Boston: Beacon Press, 1989), 123. It should be noted that the illuminated flesh of Susannah is itself ambiguous. On the one hand, it marks a moral distinction (light and dark); on the other hand, it better shows Susannah's charms.

6 The association with baptism goes back to Hippolytus of Rome. See his "On Susannah," in *Fathers of the Third Century: Hippolytus, Cyprian, Caius, Novatian, Appendix*, Ante-Nicene Fathers, 5 (1886; rpt. Peabody, MA: Hendrickson, 1999), 192. Also see W. Brian Shelton, *Martyrdom from Exegesis in Hippolytus: An Early Church Presbyter's "Commentary on Daniel"* (Milton Keynes: Paternoster, 2008). It should be added that in the early Church Susannah was frequently cited as an example of chastity. Augustine tells his congregation in Sermon 196, "If you are looking for an example of married chastity, you have Susanna," III:6 (184–229Z), *Sermons on the Liturgical Seasons*, trans. Edmund Hill, ed. John E. Rotelle, The Works of Saint Augustine (New Rochelle, NY: New City Press, 1992), 61.

7 See Kathryn A. Smith, "Inventing Marital Chastity: The Iconography of Susanna and the Elders in Early Christian Art," *Oxford Art Journal* 16 (1) (1993): 3–24.

8 See, for example, Hans Ludwig Wagner, *Susanna: Eine Tragödie in 3 Aufzügen* (München: G. Müller, 1918).

9 See, for example, Carl Lampe, *Susanna und Daniel* (Berlin: Selbstverlag des verfassers, 1855).

10 See Steven C. Walker, *Seven Ways of Looking at Susanna* (Provo, UT: Center for the Study of Christian Values in Literature, 1984).

11 See, for example, Ralph Radcliffe's *The Delivery of Susannah, a Tragedy* (1540), Thomas Garter's *The Comedy of the Moste Vertuous and Godlye Susanna* (1578), and Robert Roche's "Eustathia, or the Constancie of Susanna Containing the Preservation of the Godly, Subversion of the Wicked, Precepts for the Aged, Instructions for Youth, Pleasure with profitte," *Eustathia* (1599). Later works on Susannah in England include Robert Aylett, "Susanna: Or the Araignment of The Two Unjust Elders" in his *Divine and Moral Speculations* (1654) and Elizabeth Tollet, "Susanna, Or Innocence Preserv'd," *Poems on Several Occasions* (1756?). The biblical story inspired equally many literary works on the Continent. See, for instance, Paul F. Casey, *The Susannah Theme in German Literature* (Bonn: Bouvier Verlag Herbert Grundmann, 1976).

12 All quotations from A. D. Hope's "The Double Looking Glass" are from *Collected Poems 1930–1970* (Sydney: Angus and Robertson, 1972). The period after "purposeful" in the nineteenth stanza, which is omitted in the *Collected Poems*, has been restored.

13 See Hope, "The Apocalypse of Christopher Smart," *The Pack of Autolycus* (Canberra: Australian National University Press, 1978), 104–21.

14 See Wallace Stevens, "Peter Quince at the Clavier," *The Collected Poems of Wallace Stevens* (New York: Knopf, 1954), 89–92. John Hollander contends, a little hastily I think, that the "meditative movement" of Hope's poem "turns in a direction almost opposite to that of Stevens' *Peter Quince at the Clavier*," "Introduction," *Poems of Our Moment: Contemporary Poets of the English Language* (New York: Pegasus, 1968), 19.

15 See Alice Bach, *Women, Seduction, and Betrayal in Biblical Narrative* (Cambridge: Cambridge University Press, 1997), 71.

16 See Hope, "Introduction," *Selected Poems* (Sydney: Angus and Robertson, 1963), viii. "Susanna al Bagno" is held at the Accademia Nazionale di San Luca in Rome; "Susanna e i Vecchioni" is held in the Kunsthistorisches Museum in Vienna. Note that in "Susanna al Bagno" Veronese has Susannah hiding her breasts when one of the elders seeks to touch them.

17 Although the poem is mentioned by several commentators on Hope, the only full essay on it is by R. F. Brissenden, "The Double Looking Glass," in *The Double Looking Glass: New and Classic Essays on the Poetry of A. D. Hope*, ed. David Brooks (St Lucia: University of Queensland Press, 2000), 94–108.

18 Pseudo-Dionysius maintains that "cherubim" means "fullness of knowledge." See his *The Celestial Hierarchy* 205b in *The Complete Works*, trans. Colm Luibheid, foreword, notes, and translation collaboration by Paul Rorem, pref. Rene Roques, intro. Jaroslav Pelikan, Jean Leclercq, and Karlfried Froehlich (Mahwah, NJ: Paulist Press, 1987).

19 See, for example, Gregory of Nyssa, *Commentary on the Song of Songs*, trans. and intro. Casimir McCambley, pref. Panagiotes Chrestou (Brookline, MA: Hellenic College Press, 1987), 96.

20 Origen, like various exegetes after him, took the lines to be spoken by the Bridegroom who is a figure of Christ. See Origen, *The Song of Songs: Commentary and Homilies*, trans. and annotated R. P. Lawson, Ancient Christian Writers (New York: The Newman Press, 1956), 176. Philo of Carpasius seems to have been the first to assign the lines to the Bride. See *The Song of Songs*, trans. and ed. Richard A. Norris Jr., The Church's Bible, gen. ed., Robert Wilken (Grand Rapids, MI: William B. Eerdmans, 2003), 92.

21 See *Midrash Rabbah: Song of Songs*, trans. M. Simon, in *The Midrash*, IX (London: Soncino Press, 1939), 94–9. Also see Harold Fisch, "Susanna as Parable: A Response to Piero Boitani," *The Judgment of Susanna: Authority and Witness*, ed. Ellen Spoksky (Atlanta: Scholars Press, 1996), 37–8.

22 For the association of the phoenix and the resurrection of Christ see, for example, Origen, *Contra Celsum*, trans., intro. and notes Henry Chadwick (Cambridge: Cambridge University Press, 1965), 4:98, and Cyril of Jerusalem, *Catechetical Lectures*, 18.8, in *Cyril of Jerusalem and Gregory Nazianzen*, Nicene and Post-Nicene Fathers, Second Series, ed. Philip Schaff and Henry Wace (1894; Peabody, MA: Hendrickson Publishers, 1999), vol. 7, 135–6.

23 Hope, "Introduction," viii. Hollander evokes the "Mallarméan completeness" of the poem, "Introduction," 19.

24 Stéphane Mallarmé, "L'Après-midi d'un faune," *Oeuvres complètes*, 2 vols, ed. Bertrand Marchal, Bibliothèque de la Pléiade (Paris: Gallimard, 1998), I, 163.

25 Paul Valéry, "Poetry and Abstract Thought," *The Art of Poetry*, trans. Denise Folliot, intro. T. S. Eliot, *The Collected Works of Paul Valéry*, ed. Jackson Mathews, vol. 7 (Princeton: Princeton University Press, 1958), 72–3.

26 Stéphane Mallarmé, "Crise de vers," *Oeuvres complètes*, 2 vols, ed.

Bertrand Marchal, Bibliothéque de la Pléiade (Paris: Gallimard, 2003), II, 208. Also relevant here is Mallarmé's interest in the remnants of a pure language. See his "Avant-dire au *Traité du Verbe,*" *Oeuvres complètes*, II, 677–8.

27   Gérard Genette, "Valéry and the Poetics of Language," *Paul Valéry*, ed. and intro. Harold Bloom, Modern Critical Views (New York: Chelsea House, 1989), 108. Also see Hope, *The New Cratylus: Notes on the Craft of Poetry* (Melbourne: Oxford University Press, 1979), 13–14. It should be noted that later in the book Hope says, "Mallarmé will last forever," 127.

28   See Valéry, *Oeuvres*, ed. Jean Hytier, Bibliothèque de la Pléiade (Paris: Gallimard, 1957), I, 82, 122–30, 403–21.

29   Arthur Golding, trans., *Ovid's Metamorphoses*, ed., intro. and notes John Frederick Nims (New York: Macmillan, 1965), 77.

30   Gladys I. Wade, ed., *The Poetical Works of Thomas Traherne* (London: Dobell, 1932), 81.

31   Traherne, "The Odour," *The Poetical Works*, 150.

32   See Jean-Luc Marion, *God without Being: Hors-Texte*, trans. Thomas A. Carlson, foreword David Tracy (Chicago: The University of Chicago Press, 1991), I. 2, 3, and *Being Given: Toward a Phenomenology of Givenness*, trans. Jeffrey L. Kosky (Stanford: Stanford University Press, 2002), 215–16. Also see Marion, "The Banality of Saturation," *Counter-Experiences: Reading Jean-Luc Marion*, ed. Kevin Hart (Notre Dame: Notre Dame University Press, 2007), 401–4.

33   The motif of the dream within a dream is one that Hope explores in a later poem, "The Countess of Pembroke's Dream," *A Late Picking: Poems 1965–1974* (Sydney: Angus and Robertson, 1975), 36–40.

34   Hope, "The Wandering Islands," *Collected Poems*, 26.

35   Hope, "Imperial Adam," *Collected Poems*, 83.

36   Hippolytus, "On Susannah," 193.

37   Hope, "Chorale," *Collected Poems*, 73.

38   See Franz Delitzsch, *Biblical Commentary on the Book of Job*, 2 vols (1866; rpt. Grand Rapids, MI: W. B. Eerdmans, 1949), II, 128–9.

39   See Mary Cletus Fitzpatrick, ed., trans., and commentary, *Lactanti de Ave Phoenice* (Philadelphia: n.p., 1933), 41. It is likely that Hope read Lactantius's poem in its Anglo-Saxon version. See George Philip Krapp and Elliott van Kirk Dobbie, ed., *The Exeter Book*, The Anglo-Saxon Poetic Records 3 (New York: Columbia University Press, 1936), 94–113.

40   It is worth noting that in his anthology of modern midrashic verse, David Curzon includes two poems by Hope but not "The Double Looking Glass." See his *Modern Poems on the Bible: An Anthology*, ed. and intro. David Curzon (Philadelphia: The Jewish Publication Society, 1994).

41   See Meir Sternberg, *The Poetics of Biblical Narrative: Ideological Literature and the Drama of Reading* (Bloomington: Indiana University Press, 1985), 41.

42   See Albertus Magnus, *On Animals: A Medieval "Summa Zoologia,"* trans.

Kenneth F. Kitchell Jr and Irven Michael Resnick, 2 vols (Baltimore: The Johns Hopkins University Press, 1999), I, 1623. More generally, see, Jean Hubaux and Maxime Leroy, *Le mythe du phénix dans les littératures grecques et latine* (Paris: Droz, 1939).

Chapter 9: Darkness and lostness: How to read a poem by Judith Wright

1   I discuss this in detail in *How to Read a Page of Boswell* (Sydney: Vagabond Press, 2000). For more recent reflections on the "great books," see Alex Bearne, *A Great Idea at the Time: The Rise, Fall, and Curious Afterlife of the Great Books* (New York: PublicAffairs, 2008), and Tim Lacy, *The Dream of a Democratic Culture: Mortimer J. Adler and the Great Books Idea* (New York: Palgrave Macmillan, 2013).

2   "Ultimately we read—as Bacon, Johnson and Emerson agree—in order to strengthen the self, and to learn its authentic interests," Harold Bloom, *How to Read and Why* (New York: Scribner, 2000), 22.

3   I borrow the insight into Descartes and Leibniz from Jacques Maritain. See his *Art and Scholasticism* and *The Frontiers of Poetry*, trans. Joseph W. Evans (Notre Dame: University of Notre Dame Press, 1974), 40.

4   Edward Hirsch, *How to Read a Poem: And Fall in Love with Poetry* (New York: Harcourt Brace and Co., 1999), 1.

5   See Marianne Moore, *Nevertheless* (New York: Macmillan, 1944).

6   I take the expression from Paul Virilio, although without importing all that he intends by the expression. See James Der Derian, "Is the Author Dead? An Interview with Paul Virilio," *The Virilio Reader,* ed., James Der Derian (Oxford: Basil Blackwell, 1998), 21.

7   Thomas à Kempis, *The Imitation of Christ,* trans. Ronald Knox and Michael Oakley (New York: Sheed and Ward, 1959), Book 1, Chapter 4.

8   Friedrich Nietzsche, *Daybreak: Thoughts on the Prejudice of Morality,* trans. R. J. Hollingdale, with an introduction Michael Tanner (Cambridge: Cambridge University Press, 1982), 5.

9   Judith Wright, *Collected Poems, 1942–1985* (Manchester: Carcanet, 1994), 112–13.

10 As an instance of the former, see Shirley Walker, *Flame and Shadow: A Study of Judith Wright's Poetry* (St Lucia: The University of Queensland Press, 1991), 76–7. And as an example of the latter, see Paul Kane, *Australian Poetry: Romanticism and Negativity* (Cambridge: Cambridge University Press, 1996), 162. Of the readings discussed in this chapter, Kane's is the most subtle and rewarding.

11 Bernard O'Reilly, *Green Mountains* (1941; rpt., Sydney: Environbook, 2000), 33.

12 "5 Die in Air Crash," *Sydney Mirror,* Wednesday, March 3, 1937. The story
was run on the front page of the paper.

13 O'Reilly, *Green Mountains,* 33.

14 The story of the Stinson crash was told in Queensland schools as recently
as the late-1960s when I was a schoolboy, and although the details of
the story were no longer sharply recalled, people who read Judith Wright
(and it must be said she held a very special place in the literary world of
Queensland) vaguely associated "The Lost Man" with a plane crash in the
Lamington Plateau. Meredith McKinney, Judith Wright's daughter, has kindly
confirmed after reading this chapter that, to the best of her recollection,
"The Lost Man" did spring from reflection on Bernard O'Reilly's *Green
Mountains.*

15 Kieran Kavanaugh, OCD and Otilo Rodriguez, OCD, *The Collected Works of
St. John of the Cross,* rev. edn (Washington, DC: ICS Publications, 1991),
111.

16 Walker, *Flame and Shadow,* 212.

17 T. S. Eliot, "East Coker," *Collected Poems, 1909–1962* (London: Faber and
Faber, 1963), 201. The poem first appeared in *New English Quarterly* (1940).
Wright's other main European influence, W. B. Yeats, can be detected in
the third stanza of the poem in the image of "the song of the gold bird
dancing."

18 See, for example, "Brihad-Aranyaka Upanishad" 4.4.10, *The Thirteen
Principal Upanishads,* trans. Robert Ernest Hume, 2nd rev. edn (London:
OxfordUniversity Press, 1931), 142. The image of "the thicket of delusion"
should be noted, however, in this context. See *The Bhagavad Gita,* trans.
W. J. Johnson (Oxford: Oxford University Press, 1994), 2:52.

19 See the letter from Judith Wright which Walker quotes in *Flame and
Shadow,* 212.

20 Kavanagh and Rodriguez, "The Dark Night," *The Collected Works of St. John
of the Cross,* 415.

21 Gerard Manley Hopkins, *The Poems of Gerard Manley Hopkins,* ed. Robert
Bridges (London: Humphrey Milford, 1918), 66.

22 See Hans Urs von Balthasar, *The Glory of the Lord: A Theological
Aesthetics,* 7 vols, I: *Seeing the Form,* trans. and eds, Erasmo Leiva-
Merikakis, Joseph Fessio, and John Riches (San Francisco: Ignatius Press,
1982), 411.

23 See Denys Turner, *The Darkness of God: Negativity in Christian Mysticism*
(Cambridge: Cambridge University Press, 1995), 251. My reservations about
Turner's reading of the medieval mystics are given in "The Experience of
Non-Experience," *Mystics: Aporias and Presence,* ed., Michael Kessler
and Christian Shepherd (Chicago: The University of Chicago Press, 2004),
188–206.

24 See Kane, *Australian Poetry,* 162. Quite correctly, Kane does not urge us to
use the Jungian association of Christ and water as a way of explaining "The
Lost Man." Wright mentions her reading of Jung in a letter to Shirley Walker.
See Walker's *Flame and Shadow,* 211.

25 See Walker, *Flame and Shadow*, 77.

26 See "The Spiritual Canticle," *The Collected Works of St. John of the Cross*, 49.

27 Brian Elliott, *The Landscape of Australian Poetry* (Melbourne: Cheshire, 1967), 320; Walker, *Flame and Shadow*, 77.

Chapter 10: "Only this": Some phenomenology and religion in Robert Gray

1 Edmund Husserl, *Logical Investigations*, 2 vols, trans. J. N. Findlay (London: Routledge and Kegan Paul, 1970), I, 252.

2 Husserl, *Psychological and Transcendental Phenomenology and the Confrontation with Heidegger (1927–1931)*, trans. and ed. Thomas Sheehan and Richard E. Palmer (Dordrecht: Kluwer Academic Publishers, 1997), 218.

3 See John Ashbery, "A Wave," in *A Wave* (Harmondsworth: Penguin, 1985), 68–89, and *Flowchart* (New York: Knopf, 1991).

4 Robert Gray, *New Selected Poems* (Sydney: Duffy and Snellgrove, 1998), 3. All quotations from Gray's poetry will be to this edition unless otherwise specified. *Cumulus* (Melbourne: John Leonard Press, 2012), a book of collected poems, omits some poems and revises others, as does the volume of selected poems *Coast Road* (Melbourne: Black Inc., 2014). I will include Gray's revisions of lines that I quote in endnotes. In *Cumulus*, the stanza quoted has a dash rather than a colon in the second line.

5 Such is Husserl's view. Not so for Martin Heidegger, however; see his *Four Seminars*, trans. Andrew Mitchell and François Raffoul (Bloomington: Indiana University Press, 2003), 36.

6 In *Cumulus* the lines read, "There are still the times when he will turn to me. / I drowse by the persimmons in the log, / and he draws an arm around me.— / Only, those flames then seem an undefeated flag," 3.

7 Paul Valéry, *Selected Writings*, trans. Denis Devlin et al. (San Francisco: New Directions, 1950), 48.

8 Gray, *The Land I Came Through Last* (Sydney: Giramondo, 2008), 121.

9 Husserl, *Formal and Transcendental Logic*, trans. Dorion Cairns (The Hague: Martinus Nijhoff, 1978), 159.

10 This does not lead Husserl to disbelieve in God, though: he thinks that divine transcendence is made known in consciousness in ways other than the constitution of physical things, but that it escapes phenomenological investigation. See Husserl, *Ideas Pertaining to a Pure Phenomenology and to a Phenomenological Philosophy*, I: *General Introduction to a Pure Phenomenology*, trans. F. Kersten (Boston: Kluwer Academic Publishers, 1983), section 51 note. Also see Dorion Cairns, *Conversations with Husserl and Fink*, foreword Richard M. Zaner (The Hague: Martinus Nijhoff, 1976), 47.

11 William Carlos Williams, "Spring and All," *The Collected Poems*, 2 vols,

ed. A. Walton Litz and Christopher MacGowan (New York: New Directions, 1986), I: *1909–1939*, 183.

12 Husserl, *Analyses Concerning Passive and Active Synthesis: Lectures on Transcendental Logic*, trans. Anthony J. Steinbock (Boston: Kluwer Academic Publishers, 2001), 52.

13 Husserl, *Analyses Concerning Passive and Active Synthesis*, 41.

14 See Husserl, *The Basic Problems of Phenomenology: From the Lectures, Winter Semester, 1910–1911*, trans. Ingo Farin and James G. Hart (Dordrecht: Springer, 2006), Appendix XIII. The word "monad" here is not used in the metaphysical sense associated with Leibniz. Also see Husserl's lectures on Fichte, especially the third one, in *Aufsätz und Vorträge (1911– 1921)*, ed. Thomas Nennon and H. R. Sepp (Dordrecht: Springer, 1987), 267–93.

15 See Husserl, "Husserl an von Hofmannsthal (12. 1. 1907)," *Briefwechsel*, 10 vols, VII: *Wissenschaftlerkorrespondenz*, ed. Elisabeth Schuhmann and Karl Schuhmann (Boston: Kluwer Academic Publishers, 1994), 135.

16 Husserl distinguishes the natural attitude from the naturalistic attitude. See, for example, Husserl, *Introduction to Logic and Theory of Knowledge. Lectures 1906 / 07*, trans. Claire Oritz Hill (Dordrecht: Springer, 2008), 401. Also see his *Thing and Space. Lectures of 1907*, trans. Richard Rojcewicz (Dordrecht: Kluwer Academic Publishers, 1997), 33, and "Philosophy as a Rigorous Science," *Phenomenology and the Crisis of Philosophy*, trans. and intro. Quentin Lauer (New York: Harper and Row, 1965), 79–122.

17 See, for example, Olav H. Hauge, "To a Mountain," *Don't Give Me the Whole Truth: Selected Poems*, trans. Robin Fulton et al. (London: Anvil Press, 1985), 28.

18 See Husserl, *The Idea of Phenomenology*, trans. William P. Alston and George Nakhnikian (Boston: Kluwer Academic Publishers, 1990), 4. For the difference between ἐποχή and transcendental reduction, see Husserl, *The Crisis of European Sciences and Transcendental Phenomenology: An Introduction to Phenomenological Philosophy*, trans. David Carr (Evanston: Northwestern University Press, 1970), section 41. For Husserl's extensive reflections on reduction, see his *Erste Philosophie (1923 / 24) Zweiter Teil Theorie der Phänomenologischen Reduktion*, ed. Rudolf Boehm (Dordrecht: Springer, 1996) and *Zur Phänomenologischen Reduktion*, ed. Sebastian Luft (Dordrecht: Springer, 2002).

19 On this theme, see Jacques Derrida, "'This Strange Institution Called Literature': An Interview with Jacques Derrida," *Acts of Literature*, ed. Derek Attridge (New York: Routledge, 1992), 45–8.

20 Maurice Merleau-Ponty, *The Phenomenology of Perception*, trans. Colin Smith (London: Routledge and Kegan Paul, 1962), xiii.

21 See Derrida, *Speech and Phenomena: And Other Essays on Husserl's Theory of Signs*, trans. and intro. David B. Allison, pref. Newton Garver (Evanston: Northwestern University Press, 1973), Ch. 7.

22 Eugen Fink, *Sixth Cartesian Meditation: The Idea of a Transcendental Theory* *of Method*, trans. and intro. Ronald Bruzina (Bloomington: Indiana University Press, 1995), 144.

23 See Vasko Popa, *Homage to the Lame Wolf: Selected Poems, 1956–1975*, trans. and intro. Charles Simic (Oberlin: Field Translations, 1979), 97–110.

24 For the deep structure of influence, see Harold Bloom, *The Anxiety of Influence: A Theory of Poetry*, 2nd edn (New York: Oxford University Press, 1997). The study of local influences in Gray is not of great interest. It would consist of finding borrowings or parallels of the following sort. Compare Gray: "I'll lose sight of the ferry soon— / I find it while it's on darkness / and savour it like honeycomb, / filled as it is with its yellow light" (45), and Reznikoff: "Feast, you who cross the bridge / this cold twilight / on these honeycombs of light, the buildings of Manhatten," Charles Reznikoff, *Poems 1918–1936*, ed. Seamus Cooney (Santa Barbara: Black Sparrow Press, 1976), 116. Gray has revised these lines: "I'll loose sight of the ferry soon— / I can find it while it's on darkness, / like tasting honeycomb, / filled as it is with its yellow light," *Cumulus*, 42, and *Coast Road*, 15.

25 I am indebted here to Derrida. See his *The Archeology of the Frivolous: Reading Condillac*, trans. John P. Leavey, Jr. (Pittsburgh: Duquesne University Press, 1980).

26 Ludwig Wittgenstein, *Culture and Value: A Selection from the Posthumous Remains*, ed. Georg Henrik von Wright in collaboration with Heikki Nyman, rev. ed. Alois Pichler, trans. Peter Winch (Oxford: Basil Blackwell, 1998), 3e.

27 Tomas Tranströmer, "April and Silence," *The Great Enigma: New Collected Poems*, trans. Robin Fulton (New York: New Directions, 2006), 199.

28 In *Cumulus* the lines read, "Racing to the surf, / they strike its silver crookedly / as roots of ginger," 53.

29 In *Cumulus* the lines read, "The frogs' hollow, ringing, regular / 'clonk, clonk', from the scrub— / the sound of a distant hammer / on scaffolding. Going after some labouring job," 73.

30 See Wittgenstein, *Tractatus Logico-Philosophicus*, trans. D. F. Pears and B. F. McGuiness, intro. Bertrand Russell (London: Routledge and Kegan Paul, 1961), 6.44.

31 Benedict de Spinoza, *Ethics Preceded by On the Improvement of the Understanding*, ed. and intro. James Gutmann (New York: Hafner, 1949), I. xv.

32 Gray, *Grass Script* (Sydney: Angus and Robertson, 1978), 49.

33 J. P. de Caussade, *Self-Abandonment to Divine Providence*, trans. Algar Thorold, newly edited by John Joyce, intro. David Knowles (Springfield: Templegate, 1959), 33.

34 G. W. F. Hegel, *The Phenomenology of Mind*, trans. and intro. J. B. Baillie (New York: Harper and Row, 1967), 159–60.

35 For literature as a criticism of literature (*bungei futei no bungei*), see Steven Heine, *The Zen Poetry of Dōgen: Verses from the Mountain of Eternal Peace* (Boston: Turtle, 1997), 19.

36 For more on "Dharma Vehicle," see my essay "Fields of *Dharma*: On T. S.

Eliot and Robert Gray," *Theology and Literature* 27 (3) (2013): 267–84. Gray
has added new lines to the poem. See *Cumulus*, 66–7.

37 See Ronald Bruzina, *Edmund Husserl and Eugen Fink: Beginning and Ends
in Phenomenology 1928–1938* (New Haven: Yale University Press, 2004),
354. Also see Fink, *Sixth Cartesian Meditation*, 121.

38 See Vicente Huidobro, "Ars Poetica," *Selected Poems*, ed. and intro. David
M. Guss, trans. David M. Guss et al. (New York: New Directions, 1981), 5.

39 See Husserl, *Ideas* I, §85.

40 In *Cumulus*, the final two lines quoted read as follows, "mixture, precisely-
sliced and, / in rows, gently conveyor-belted down," 84.

41 On qualia, see Edmund Wright, ed., *The Case for Qualia* (Cambridge, MA:
MIT Press, 2008). The word "qualia" is notoriously used in various senses.

42 In *Cumulus*, there have been several small changes: "cool, light flouncing,"
"like a bubble distended from a glass blower's tube," and the penultimate
line is folded into the line that precedes it, 112.

43 See Claude Roy, *Descriptions critiques* (Paris: Gallimard, 1949), 107.

44 To hear Dōgen's voice, which is quite different from Gray's in these lines,
see *Dōgen's Extensive Record: A Translation of the Eihei Kōroku*, trans.
Taigen Dan Leighton and Shohaku Okumura, ed. and intro. Taigan Dan
Leighton (Boston: Wisdom Publications, 2004).

45 In *Cumulus*, the lines read as follows: "And said, 'The world is in ceaseless
transformation, / and to meditate / is just awareness, with no // clinging
to, no working on, the mind. Letting thoughts go / as they arise, we are
borne on a "marvelous emptiness". // As there's no abiding self / there is no
delusion and no realization, / no Buddha and no troubled beings. // Things
tell us what we need to do. / Otherwise, we face the wall, cross-legged. / It
is nothing but sitting. Not a grain of merit is obtained," 27.

46 See Hee-Jin Kim, *Eihei Dōgen: Mystical Realist*, foreword Taigen Dan
Leighton (Boston: Wisdom Publications, 2004), 200, 172. It should also
be noted that for Gray, as for Dōgen, the word "like" does not denote
resemblance so much as thusness [*ze*]. See *Eihei Dōgen*, 85.

47 Robert Bly, *Silence in the Snowy Fields* (Middletown: Wesleyan University
Press, 1962), 21.

48 Gray, "In Departing Light," *Nameless Earth* (Manchester: Carcanet, 2006),
20–1.

49 In *Cumulus*, some of the lines now read, "Looking too kind / to reject
outright / even a wrong direction," 238.

50 Maurice Blanchot, "In the Night that is Watched Over," *On Robert Antelme's
"The Human Race": Essays and Commentaries*, ed. Daniel Dobbels, trans.
Jeffrey Haight (Evanston: Northwestern University Press, 2003), 56.

Chapter 11: A voice answering a voice: Philippe Jaccottet and the "Dream of God"

1   Virginia Woolf, *Orlando: A Biography* (New York: Harcourt, Brace and Co., 1928), 325.

2   Philippe Jaccottet, *La semaison: Carnets 1980-1994*, in *Oeuvres*, ed., José-Flore Tappy with Hervé Ferrage, Doris Jakubec, and Jean-Marc Sourdillon, Preface Fabio Pusterla (Paris: Gallimard, 2014), 876–7. All quotations from Jaccottet will be from this edition unless otherwise noted.

3   See "Jour de janvier," for a recent example of a poem that is a non-theistic prayer, Jaccottet, *Ce peu de bruits*, in *Oeuvres*, 1224.

4   Jaccottet, "L'Effraie," *Oeuvres*, 3.

5   Jaccottet returns to the owl's call in *La semaison*, *Oeuvres*, 617. Also see 618, 661.

6   See Apuleius, *Metamorphoses*, ed. and trans. J. Arthur Hanson, 2 vols (Cambridge, MA: Harvard University Press, 1989), I. iii. 23.

7   Jaccottet, *La Semaison: Carnets 1954–1979*, *Oeuvres*, 347.

8   See Alexandre Kojève, *Introduction to the Reading of Hegel: Lectures on the "Phenomenology of Spirit,"* assembled by Raymond Queneau, ed. Allan Bloom, and trans. James H. Nichols, Jr (New York: Basic Books, 1969), 141; Yves Bonnefoy, "Les Fleurs du mal," *L'Improbable, suivi de Un rêve fait à Mantoue* (Paris: Mercure de France, 1980), 34; and Maurice Blanchot, "Literature and the Right to Death," trans. Lydia Davis, *The Work of Fire*, trans. Charlotte Mandell (Stanford: Stanford University Press, 1995), esp. 323. For a discussion of Blanchot and Bonnefoy on this issue, see my *The Dark Gaze: Maurice Blanchot and the Sacred* (Chicago: University of Chicago Press, 2004), Ch. 3.

9   Jaccottet, *À Travers un verger*, *Oeuvres*, 561.

10 Jaccottet, *Après beaucoup d'années*, *Oeuvres*, 853.

11 Jaccottet, "Le Cerisier," *Oeuvres*, 745–6.

12 See Augustine, *The Literal Meaning of Genesis*, 2 vols, trans. John Hammond Taylor (New York: Paulist Press, 1982), I. 3. 8.

13 See, in this regard, Jaccottet, *La Semaison*, *Oeuvres*, 623.

14 See Jacques Derrida, "Faith and Knowledge: The Two Sources of 'Religion' at the Limits of Reason Alone," trans. Samuel Weber, *Religion*, ed. Jacques Derrida and Gianni Vattimo (Cambridge: Polity Press, 1998), 33.

15 Paul Éluard, *Oeuvres complètes*, préface et chronologie de Lucien Scheler, textes établis et annotés par Marcelle Dumas et Lucien Scheler, 2 vols. (Paris: Gallimard, 1968), I, 986.

16 Jaccottet, *Après beaucoup d'années*, *Oeuvres*, 821.

17 Jaccottet, *À Travers un verger*, *Oeuvres*, 567.

18 Jaccottet, *La Semaison*, *Oeuvres*, 354.

19 Yet see *Élements d'un songe*, *Oeuvres*, 322–7.

20 René Char, *Oeuvres complètes*, intro. Jean Roudaut (Paris: Gallimard, 1983), 130.

21 Jaccottet, however, cites Eckhart in *La semaison*, *Oeuvres*, 357.

22 Jaccottet, *Paysages avec figures absentes*, *Oeuvres*, 469.

23 Jaccottet, *À Travers un verger*, *Oeuvres*, 553.

24 Jaccottet, *Une Transaction secrète: Lectures de poésie* (Paris: Gallimard, 1987), 306.

25 See Jaccottet, *Paysages avec figures absentes*, *Oeuvres*, 529.

26 See Yves Bonnefoy, *Poèmes* (Paris: Mercure de France, 1986), 117; and Emmanuel Levinas, "Reality and its Shadow," *Collected Philosophical Writings*, trans. Alphonso Lingis (The Hague: Martinus Nijhoff, 1987), 1–13.

27 See Blanchot, *The Space of Literature*, trans. and intro. Ann Smock (Lincoln: University of Nebraska Press, 1982), 242–3.

28 Jaccottet, *La Semaison*, *Oeuvres*, 386.

29 Jaccottet, *À Travers un verger*, *Oeuvres*, 565.

30 Jaccottet, *La Semaison*, *Oeuvres*, 337.

31 Jaccottet, *À Travers un verger*, *Oevures*, 557.

32 Jaccottet, *Parler*, *Oeuvres*, 543.

33 Consider the following: "À tout instant les choses peuvent de nouveau se défaire, c'est à peine si je les tiens, si j'en tiens l'ombre. Je dévore comme nourriture souhaitable ce qui n'est peut-être qu'absence," *La Semaison*, *Oeuvres*, 371.

34 See G. W. F. Hegel, *Phenomenology of Spirit*, trans. A. V. Miller, Foreword J. N. Findlay (Oxford: Clarendon Press, 1977), 77–9.

35 Jaccottet, *Éléments d'un songe*, *Oeuvres*, 284–5.

36 Jaccottet, *Paysages avec figures absentes*, *Oeuvres*, 469.

37 Jaccottet, *Leçons*, *Oeuvres*, 451.

38 Jaccottet, *À la lumière d'hiver*, *Oeuvres*, 577.

39 Jaccottet, *La Semaison*, *Oeuvres*, 359.

40 See Jacques Masui, "L'Expérience poétique de Philippe Jaccottet," *Cahiers du Sud* 128 (1958): 138–43, esp. 143.

41 Jaccottet, *La Semaison*, *Oeuvres*, 363.

42 Jaccottet, *Une transaction secrète*, 128.

43 Jaccottet, *La Semaison*, *Oeuvres*, 354.

44 See José-Flore Tappy, éd., *Jaccottet traducteur d'Ungaretti: Correspondance 1946–1970* (Paris: Gallimard, 2008), 65.

45 See Jules Supervielle, "Le voyage difficile," *Oeuvres poétiques complètes*, éd. Michel Collot avec la collaboration de Françoise Brunot-Maussang et al. (Paris: Gallimard, 1996), 291; and Salvatore Quasimodo, "Antico inverno," *Ed è subito sera*, con una saggio di Sergio Solmi, Tutte le opera (Verona: Arnoldo Mondadori, 1965), 175. Jaccottet spent some time in Italy where he became friends with Giuseppe Ungaretti and became acquainted with

Quasimodo's poetry, some of which he translated into French. See Tappy, *Jaccottet traducteur d'Ungaretti*, 43.

46 Jaccottet, *Airs, Oeuvres*, 424. Cf *La semaison, Oeuvres*, 361.

47 Jaccottet, *The Pilgrim's Bowl (Giorgio Morandi)*, trans. John Taylor (London: Seagull Books, 2015), 51.

48 Jaccottet, *Airs, Oeuvres*, 421.

Chapter 12: Eugenio Montale and "the *other* truth"

1 Italo Calvino, "Eugenio Montale, 'Forse un mattino andando,'" *Why Read the Classics?*, trans. Martin McLaughlin (New York: Pantheon Books, 1999), 209.

2 Eugenio Montale to Angelo Barile (August 12, 1924), quoted by Jonathan Galassi in his translation of the poet's works, *Collected Poems 1920–1954* (New York: Farrar, Straus and Giroux, 1998), 453.

3 Montale, "Forse un mattino ...," *Tutte le poesie*, ed. Giogio Zampa (Milano: Arnoldo Mondadori, 2005), 42. All translations from the Italian are mine unless otherwise noted.

4 See Calvino, "Eugenio Montale, "Forse un mattino andando," 212.

5 See Eduardo Sanguinetti, "Forse un mattino andando," *Letture montaliane: in occasione dell'80° compleanno del poeta* (Genova: Bozzi, 1977), 50; and Gilberto Lonardi, *Il vecchio e il giovane e altri studi su Montale* (Bologna: Zanichelli, 1980), 45.

6 Leo Tolstoy, "Boyhood," *Childhood, Boyhood, Youth*, trans. Rosemary Edmonds (London: Penguin, 1964), 158–9.

7 See F. J. W. Schelling, *Ideas for a Philosophy of Nature as Introduction to the Study of this Science*, trans. Errol E. Harris and Peter Heath, intro. Robert Stern (Cambridge: Cambridge University Press, 1988), 23–9.

8 See, for example, Fichte's letter to Karl Reinhold on July 2, 1795, in J. G. Fichte, *Early Philosophical Writings*, ed. and trans. Daniel Breazeale (Ithaca: Cornell University Press, 1988), 398–9.

9 Angiola Ferraris, *Se il vento: Lettura degli "Ossi di seppia" di Eugenio Montale* (Rome: Donzelli, 1995).

10 Maurice Blanchot, *The Space of Literature*, trans. Ann Smock (Lincoln: University of Nebraska Press, 1982).

11 See on this topic my essay, "The Profound *Reserve*," *After Blanchot: Literature, Criticism, Philosophy*, ed. Leslie Hill, Brian Nelson and Dimitris Vardoulakis (Newark, DE: University of Delaware Press, 2005), 35–57.

12 Quoted by William Arrowsmith in his notes to his translation of *Cuttlefish Bones (1920–1927)* New York: W. W. Norton, 1992), 216. Also see Calvino, "Eugenio Montale, 'Forse un mattino andando,'" 212.

13 Calvino, "Montale's Rock," *The Uses of Literature*, trans. Patrick Creagh (New York: Harcourt Brace Jovanovich, 1986), 289.

14 Montale, *The Second Life of Art: Selected Essays*, ed. and trans. Jonathan Galassi (New York: Ecco Press, 1982), 300. Cf. 317.

15 Schopenhauer alludes to the "veil of deception" in both volumes of *The World as Will and Representation*, trans. E. F. J. Payne (New York: Dover, 1969).

16 Jean Paulhan, *Les Fleurs de Tarbes, ou la Terreur dans les letters* (Paris: Gallimard, 1941).

17 Montale, "Intentions (Imaginary Interview)," *The Second Life of Art*, 300.

18 Montale, ["*I critici ripetono ...*"], *Tutte le poesie*, 283.

19 Blanchot, "À Toute Extrémité", *La Nouvelle NRF* 26 (1955): 290.

20 See my book, *The Dark Gaze: Maurice Blanchot and the Sacred* (Chicago: Chicago University Press, 2004).

21 Quoted by Arrowsmith, *Cuttlefish Bones*, 173.

22 See Roberto Juarroz, *Vertical Poetry*, trans. W. S. Merwin (San Francisco: North Point Press, 1988), 136; and Jacques Derrida, *The Other Heading: Reflections on Today's Europe*, trans. Pascale-Anne Brault and Michael B. Naas (Bloomington: Indiana University Press, 1992), 41.

23 See Arrowsmith's translations of *Cuttlefish Bones, The Occasions* (New York: W. W. Norton, 1987); and *The Storm and Other Things* (New York: W. W. Norton, 1985).

24 See Robert Lowell, "The Eel," *Imitations* (New York: Farrar, Straus and Cudahy, 1961), 125–6. The whole of my version may be found in Harry Thomas, ed., *Montale in English* (New York: Handsel Books, 2004), 163–4.

25 F. R. Leavis made the point admirably when he observed of "Xenia," "I have said at various times ... that it was easy to think of 'Xenia,' though it was in Italian, as an English poem. But I must confess that ... we have nothing like it in English," "Xenia," in Montale, *New Poems*, ed. and trans. G. Singh (London: Chatto and Windus, 1976), xxxiii.

26 Montale, "Intentions," 299–300.

27 Montale, *Collected Poems 1920–1954*, 538.

28 I should add that Jewish women are important for Montale: Liuba and Dora Markus who also feature in Montale's poetry are both Jewish.

29 Arrowsmith quotes Montale, "I am perhaps a late follower of Zoroaster, and I believe that the struggle between the opposed powers of good and evil lies at the basis of life," *The Storm and Other Things*, 171. According to Arrowsmith, Montale said this in his address to the Swedish Academy in 1975 when accepting the Nobel Prize. If so, the passage has been erased in Galassi's translation of that speech in *The Second Life of Art*. However, Montale speaks of "the old battle of good and evil" in "A Wish," *The Second Life of Art*, 10.

30 Montale, *The Storm and Other Things*, 176.

31 Quoted by Galassi, *Collected Poems*, 594.

32 Montale, "Intentions," 304.

33 Montale, "Intentions", 304.

34 For a general introduction to Monophysitism, see W. H. C. Frend, *The Rise of the Monophysite Movement: Chapters in the History of the Church in the Fifth and Sixth Centuries* (Cambridge: Cambridge University Press, 1972).

35 The best-known brief history of the controversy is by Edward Gibbon in his *The Decline and Fall of the Roman Empire*, 6 vols (London: Dent, 1910), vol. 5, 16–26. A fuller history, without Gibbon's irony and with the benefit of modern scholarly findings, may be found in Nestorius, *The Bazaar of Heracleides*, trans. and ed. G. R. Driver and Leonard Hodgson (Oxford: Clarendon, 1925), xvii-xxix. Also see, especially for Cyril's part in the process, Susan Wessel, *Cyril of Alexandria and the Nestorian Controversy: The Making of a Saint and of a Heretic* (New York: Oxford University Press, 2004).

36 J. F. Bethune-Baker argues that Nestorius was not a Nestorian. See his *Nestorius and His Teaching: A Fresh Examination of the Evidence* (Cambridge: Cambridge University Press, 1908). Friedrich Loofs argues that Bethune-Baker overstates the case. See his *Nestorius and His Place in the History of Christian Doctrine* (Cambridge: Cambridge University Press, 1914), 76f.

37 Montale, *The Second Life of Art*, 10.

38 See Oreste Marcì, *Realtà del simbolo* (Florence: Vallechi, 1968), 80–1.

39 Coventry Patmore, "Religio Poetæ," in *Principle in Art, Religio Poetæ, and Other Essays* (London: Duckworth, 1913), 222.

Chapter 13: *"La poesia è scala a dio"*: On Charles Wright's "belief beyond belief"

1 Plato, *The Collected Dialogues,* ed. Edith Hamilton and Huntington Cairns (Princeton: Princeton University Press, 1961), *Ion,* 534b.

2 See Jean Paulhan, *Les Fleurs de Tarbes ou La terreur dans les letters* (1941; rpt. Paris: Gallimard, 1991).

3 S. T. Coleridge, "Kubla Khan," *Coleridge: Poetical Works,* ed. Ernest Hartley Coleridge (London: Oxford University Press, 1967), 295.

4 Walter Arndt, trans., *Pushkin Threefold: Narrative, Lyric, Polemic, and Ribald Verse* (New York: E. P. Dutton, 1972), 12. See Osip Mandelstam's remarks on the poet as "God's bird" in "On the Addressee" in his *The Collected Critical Prose and Letters*, ed. Jane Gary Harris, trans. Jane Gary Harris and Constance Link (London: Collins Harvill, 1991), 67.

5 Ralph Waldo Emerson, *Collected Works*, vol. 3: *Essays: Second Series*, intro. Joseph Slater, text established by Alfred R. Ferguson and Jean Ferguson Carr (Cambridge, MA: Belknap Press of Harvard University Press, 1983), 18.

6 Vicente Huidobro, *Selected Poetry,* ed. and intro. David M. Guss (New York: New Directions, 1981), 3.

7 Friedrich Nietzsche, *The Gay Science: With a Prelude in Rhymes and an*

Appendix of Songs, trans. and commentary Walter Kaufmann (New York: Vintage Books, 1974), section 125. Richard Poirier notes that Emerson and William James evoked the death of God before Nietzsche. See his *Poetry and Pragmatism* (Cambridge, MA: Harvard University Press, 1992), 155–7.

8   Friedrich Hölderlin, *Essays and Letters on Theory,* trans. and ed. Thomas Pfau (Albany: State University of New York Press, 1988), 101–8. In connection with these comments see Maurice Blanchot's remarks in "Hölderlin's Itinerary" in his *The Space of Literature,* trans. Ann Smock (Lincoln: University of Nebraska Press, 1982).

9   Wallace Stevens, "Notes Toward a Supreme Fiction," "Final Soliloquy of the Interior Paramour," *Collected Poetry and Prose,* ed. Frank Kermode and Joan Richardson (New York: The Library of America, 1997), 329, 444.

10 Philip Larkin, "Aubade," *Collected Poems,* ed. and intro. Anthony Thwaite (London: The Marvell Press, Faber and Faber, 1988), 208.

11 Blanchot comments on Hölderlin's space, "the holy" or "the sacred," in *The Space of Literature,* 273–6. Also see his essay "The Great Refusal" in his *The Infinite Conversation,* trans. Susan Hanson (Minneapolis: The University of Minnesota Press, 1993). I discuss the topic in the third chapter of *The Dark Gaze: Maurice Blanchot and the Sacred* (Chicago: The University of Chicago Press, 2004).

12 I take the expression "religion without religion" from Jacques Derrida. See his *The Gift of Death,* 2nd edn and *Literature in Secret* (Chicago: University of Chicago Press, 2008), 50. Also see his "Faith and Knowledge: The Two Sources of 'Religion' at the Limits of Reason Alone," trans. Samuel Weber, *Religion,* ed. Jacques Derrida and Gianni Vattimo (Cambridge: Polity Press, 1998). Also see John D. Caputo, *The Prayers and Tears of Jacques Derrida: Religion without Religion* (Bloomington: Indiana University Press, 1997).

13 On this issue see Jacques Derrida's pointed remarks in his interview with Derek Attridge, "'This Strange Institution Called Literature,'" *Acts of Literature,* ed. Derek Attridge (New York: Routledge, 1992), 44–5.

14 See, among other works of the same period, Harold Bloom, *The Breaking of the Vessels* (Chicago: The University of Chicago Press, 1982).

15 See, for example, Emmanuel Levinas, *Totality and Infinity,* trans. Alphonso Lingis (The Hague: Martinus Nijhoff, 1979).

16 See, for example, David Tracy, "Fragments: The Spiritual Situation of Our Times," *God, the Gift, and Postmodernism,* ed. John D. Caputo and Michael J. Scanlon (Bloomington: Indiana University Press, 1999), and David R. Jarroway, *Wallace Stevens and the Question of Belief: Metaphysician in the Dark* (Baton Rouge: Louisiana State University Press, 1993).

17 On Blake as a Gnostic, see Bloom, *The Visionary Company* (Ithaca: Cornell University Press, 1971). On the New England tradition, see Elisa New, *The Regenerate Lyric: Theology and Innovation in American Poetry* (Cambridge: Cambridge University Press, 1993).

18 See Martin Heidegger, *Being and Time,* trans. John Macquarrie and Edward Robinson (London: SCM Press, 1962), 415–17.

19 I refer again to David Tracy's essay "Fragments." Also see Hans

Blumenberg, *The Legitimacy of the Modern Age,* trans. Robert M. Wallace (Cambridge, MA: MIT Press, 1983).

20 The most probing account of this difficult issue is Joan Stambaugh's study, *The Finitude of Being* (Albany: State University of New York Press, 1992).

21 Heidegger, *Erläuterungen zu Hölderlins Dichtung* (Frankfort: Klostermann, 1951), 98.

22 See my essay "The Counter-Spiritual Life," *The Power of Contestation: Perspectives on Maurice Blanchot,* ed. Kevin Hart and Geoffrey Hartman (Baltimore: The Johns Hopkins University Press, 2004). Also see the conclusion to my longer study, *The Dark Gaze.*

23 Jean-Louis Chrétien, *The Unforgettable and the Unhoped For,* trans. Jeffrey Bloechl (New York: Fordham University Press, 2002), 122.

24 Jean-Luc Nancy, *La Communauté désoeuvrée,* nouvelle éd., revue et augmentée (Paris: Christian Bourgois, 1990), 259. All translations from the French are mine unless otherwise noted. Cf. Nancy, *Une Pensée finie* (Paris: Galilée, 1990), 9–53, esp. 48.

25 See Nancy, *Être singulier pluriel.* The title essay explores the ambiguity of the title.

26 The point was first made, and memorably so, by Maurice Merleau-Ponty. See his *Phenomenology of Perception,* trans. Colin Smith (London: Routledge and Kegan Paul, 1962), 215.

27 See Nancy, *The Sense of the World,* trans. Jeffrey S. Librett (Minneapolis: University of Minnesota Press, 1997), 152, 55.

28 See Nathan Rotenstreich, *On Faith,* ed. and Foreword Paul Mendes-Flohr (Chicago: The University of Chicago Press, 1998), 52–3.

29 See Eberhard Jüngel, *God as the Mystery of the World: On the Foundation of the Theology of the Crucified One in the Dispute between Theism and Atheism,* trans. Darrell L. Guder (Grand Rapids, MI: William B. Eerdmans, 1983), 32–3; Levinas, *Proper Names,* trans. Michael B. Smith (Stanford: Stanford University Press, 1996), 184–5, and *Outside the Subject,* trans. Michael B. Smith (London: Athlone, 1993), 149.

30 Nancy, *La Communanté désouvrée,* 88. Also see Nancy's *Résistance de la poésie* (Périgueux: La Pharmacie de Platon, 1997).

31 Stevens, "The American Sublime," *Collected Poetry and Prose,* 107.

32 Emerson, "Merlin," *Collected Poems and Translations,* ed. Harold Bloom and Paul Kane (New York: The Library of America, 1994), 92.

33 Pindar speaks of "the sacred stair of Olympus" in Fragment 20–30, *The Odes of Pindar, Including the Principal Fragments,* ed., trans. and intro. John Sandys (Cambridge, MA: Harvard University Press, 1968), 515.

34 See the vision recounted in *The Passion of Saint Perpetua,* ed. J. Armitage Robinson (Cambridge: Cambridge University Press, 1891), 19f. St. John Chrysostom says,

> "Thus, as it were, mounting step by step, let us reach heaven by Jacob's ladder. I say this for it seems to me that by the well-known vision Jacob's ladder was a figure of this, namely the ascent through

virtue, little by little, by which it is possible to ascend from earth to heaven, not by steps apparent to the senses, but by the emending and correcting of one's habits" (*Commentary* 41 (New York: Fathers of the Church Inc., 1960), homily 83, 416).

Theodoret of Cyrrus observes that "the nurslings of piety have devised many and different ladders for the ascent into heaven," *A History of the Monks of Syria,* trans. and introd. R. M. Price (Kalamazoo, MI: Cistercian Publications, 1985), Ch. 27, 177. Also see the whole of St. John Climacus, *The Ladder of Divine Ascent,* trans. Colm Luibheid and Norman Russell, intro. Kallistos Ware (New York: Paulist Press, 1982).

35 Charles Wright, *Quarter Notes: Improvisions and Interviews* (Ann Arbor: The University of Michigan Press, 1995), 123.

36 Wright, *Halflife: Improvisions and Interviews, 1977–87* (Ann Arbor: The University of Michigan Press, 1988), 5. In "Lost Language" Wright tells us, "I have a thirst for the divine," *A Short History of the Shadow* (New York: Farrar, Straus and Giroux, 2002), 20. Also see "'Metaphysics of the Quotidian': A Conversation with Stan Sanvel Rubin and William Heyen," *Charles Wright in Conversation: Interviews, 1979–2006,* ed. Robert D. Denham (Jefferson, NC: McFarland and Co., 2008), 41.

37 Wright, *Halflife,* 130, 109. In "Scar Tissue" Wright observes, "The urge toward form is the urge toward God," *Scar Tissue* (New York: Farrar, Straus and Giroux, 2006), 37.

38 Wright, *Sestets* (New York: Farrar, Straus and Giroux, 2009), 63.

39 Wright, *Scar Tissue,* 16, 3, *Sestets,* 24. Also see "Little Prayer," *Outakes: Sestets* (Louisville: Sarabande Books, 2010). Elsewhere, Wright addresses unnamed counterparts of Christ also given the title "Lord." See, for example, *Caribou,* 5, 14, 21, 24, 36, 63, 68.

40 Wright, *Negative Blue: Selected Later Poems* (New York: Farrar, Straus and Giroux, 2000), 113. As an index of Wright's inheritance from Stevens, compare Wright's line with Stevens's in "Flyer's Fall": "We believe without belief, beyond belief," *Collected Poetry and Prose,* 295.

41 Wright, *Negative Blue,* 45. A later variation on this theme occurs in "Why, It's as Pretty as a Picture": "It is a kind of believing without belief that we believe in," *A Short History of the Shadow,* 50. In "Polaroids" in the same collection Wright evokes "The lapis lazuli dragonflies / of postbelief," *A Short History of the Shadow,* 35.

42 See Arnold, "The God of Experience," *God and the Bible,* ed. R. H. Super, The Complete Prose Works of Matthew Arnold, vol. 7 (Ann Arbor: The University of Michigan Press, 1970); and Rahner, "The Experience of God Today," *Theological Investigations,* vol. 11, trans. David Bourke (London: Darton, Longman and Todd, 1974).

43 Eugenio Montale, "Siria," *Tutte le poesie,* ed. Giogio Zampa (Milano: Arnoldo Mondadori, 2005), 240; and *The Storm and Other Poems,* trans. Charles Wright (Oberlin: Field Translation Series, 1978), 84.

44 Wright, *Halflife,* 43–4.

45 See Chapter 13 of this volume.

46 Wright, *Quarter Notes*, 34.

47 See Yves Bonnefoy, "Igitur and the Photographer," trans. Mary Ann Caws, *PMLA* 114 (3) (1999), esp. 334, 338.

48 Montale returned to a highly literary inflection of diary writing later in life with *Diario del '71 et del '72* (Milano: A. Mondadori, 1973).

49 See "Metaphysics of the Quotidian," *Charles Wright in Conversation*, 39.

50 I take the expression "trans-ascendance" from Jean Wahl, *Existence humaine et transcendence* (Neuchâtel: Éditions de la Bacconière, 1944), 113. Wahl also speaks of "trans-descendance."

51 Montale, *The Storm and Other Poems*, 86.

52 Wright, *Negative Blue*, 197.

53 Wright, *Country Music: Selected Early Poems*, 2nd edn (Hanover: Wesleyan University Press, 1991), 60.

54 Wright, *The World of the Ten Thousand Things: Poems 1980–1990* (New York: Farrar, Straus and Giroux, 1990), 61.

55 Wright, *The World of the Ten Thousand Things*, 35. Also see *Scar Tissue*, 60.

56 Wright, *The World of the Ten Thousand Things*, 116.

57 Wright, *Negative Blue*, 43.

58 Wright takes the passage from Federico García Lorca, *Collected Poems*, ed. and intro. Christopher Maurer (New York: Farrar, Straus, and Giroux, 1991), xv. The passage in question may be found in Lorca's *Obras completas,* ed. Arturo de Hoyo, 3 vols (Madrid: Aguilar, 1986), III, 385–6.

59 Wright's interest in Gnosticism and its relations is most clearly seen in "Apologia Pro Vita Sua," which alludes to texts contained in the Nag Hammadi Library.

60 Wright, *The World of the Ten Thousand Things*, 45. Also see "L' Amor che Move il Sole e l'autre Stelle," *Caribou* (New York: Farrar, Straus and Giroux, 2014), 49–50.

61 Dino Compana, *Orphic Songs*, trans. Charles Wright (Oberlin: Field Translation Series, 1984), 51–62.

62 Wright, *Littlefoot* (New York: Farrar, Straus, Giroux, 2007), 9. Wright observes that his poems are "stairways to whatever god is for me," "An Interview by J. D. McClatchy," *Charles Wright in Conversation*, 64.

63 See Walter Hilton, *The Stairway of Perfection,* trans. and intro. M. L. Del Mastro (New York: Image Books, 1979). The title is unlikely to have been Hilton's. See pp. 15, 42.

64 Wright, *Country Music*, 156.

65 Wright, *Halflife*, 5.

66 Wright, *Negative Blue*, 3.

67 Wright, *Negative Blue*, 9. Deflation remains in Wright's repertoire. See, for example, "Ancient of Days," *Caribou*, 16–17.

68 Wright, *The World of the Ten Thousand Things*, 149.

69 Wright, *The World of the Ten Thousand Things*, 38. Yet also see "If this is where God's at, Why is that Fish Dead?," *A Short History of the Shadow*, 16.

70 See Kevin Hart, *Barefoot* (Notre Dame: Notre Dame University Press, 2017).

71 Wright, *The World of the Ten Thousand Things*, 224.

72 Wright, *Negative Blue*, 81. On the motif of prayer when one is not committed to belief in God, see Chrétien, "The Wounded Word: Phenomenology of Prayer," in *Phenomenology and the "Theological Turn*," trans. Jeffrey L. Kosky and Thomas A. Carlson (New York: Fordham University Press, 2000), 147–8.

73 Julian of Norwich, *A Book of Showings*, 2 vols., ed. Edmund College and James Walsh (Toronto: Pontifical Institute of Medieval Studies, 1978), I. 268. John of the Cross, *Collected Works*, trans. Kieran Kavanagh and Otilio Rodriguez (Washington, DC: Institute of Carmelite Studies, 1979), 583.

74 Wright, *Quarter Notes*, 57–8.

75 See *Quarter Notes*, 117–18, and also see Wright's amusing manifesto for "Titleism" in the same collection of prose.

76 Wright, *Quarter Notes*, 59.

77 Wright, *Quarter Notes*, 59.

78 Wright, *The World of the Ten Thousand Things*, 199.

79 Wright, *Negative Blue*, 22.

80 W. B. Yeats, "The Choice," *Collected Poems*, 2nd edn (London: Macmillan, 1950), 278.

81 Wright, *The World of the Ten Thousand Things*, 48.

82 Wright, *Negative Blue*, 163.

83 Wright, *Negative Blue*, 33.

84 Wright, *The World of the Ten Thousand Things*, 52, *Negative Blue*, 74.

85 See, for example, "'I'm Going to Take a Trip in that Old Gospel Ship," *Caribou*, 15. Also see, for a variation on the motif, "Toadstools," *Caribou*, 38.

86 Wright, *A Short History of the Shadow*, 63.

87 Wright, *Negative Blue*, 71–2.

88 However, we should keep in mind Philippe Jaccottet's wise words of warning about the inappropriateness of technical expressions such as "negative theology" when talking about lyric poems. See his *Paysages avec figures absentes* in *Oeuvres*, pref. Fabio Pusterla, ed. José-Flore Tappy et al. (Paris: Gallimard, 2014), 529.

89 Wright, *Negative Blue*, 81.

90 Wright, *A Short History of the Shadow*, 28, 32.

91 Wright, *Negative Blue*, 180.

Chapter 14: Contemplation and concretion: Four Marian lyrics

1 See William Tyndale, *Tyndale's New Testament*, ed. David Daniell (New Haven: Yale University Press, 1989). The editors of the King James Version of the Bible confirmed Tyndale's choice.

2 See Louis-Marie Grignion de Montfort, *Traité de la vraie devotion à Marie* (Luçon: S. Pacteau, 1909), 119.

3 See L. Reypens, "Rosa Mystica: Maria et la mystique," *Maria: Études du la Sainte Vierge*, ed. D'Hubert du Manoir (Paris: Beauchesne et ses fils, 1949), I, 747. Also see Aidan Nichols, *Chalice of God: A Systematic Theology in Outline* (Collegeville, MI: Liturgical Press, 2012), 81, and in the genre of spiritual writing Ignacio Larranaga, *The Silence of Mary*, trans. V. Gaudet (Boston: St. Paul Books and Media, 1991), esp. Chs 5 and 6, and Victorino Osende, *Fruits of Contemplation* (London: B. Herder Book Co., 1953), Ch. 10.

4 Richard of St. Victor, "The Mystical Ark," in *The Twelve Patriarchs; The Mystical Ark; Book Three of the Trinity*, trans. and intro. Grover A. Zinn, Preface Jean Châtillon (New York: Paulist Press, 1979), 155–6.

5 This understanding of meditation is common in the thirteenth and fourteenth centuries. See, for example, William of St. Thierry, *Meditations* 8 (5), in his *On Contemplating God, Prayer, Meditations*, trans. Sister Penelope, CSMV (Kalamazoo: Cistercian Publications, 1977).

6 Thomas Aquinas, *Summa theologiæ* II IIæ, Blackfriars edition, vol. 46, trans. Jordan Aumann (London: Eyre and Spottiswoode, 1966), q. 180 art. 3 ad 1. It is worth adding that Aquinas figures Mary as both active and contemplative. See his *Academic Sermons*, trans. Mark-Robin Hoogland (Washington, DC: The Catholic University of America Press, 2010), 246.

7 Aquinas, *Summa theologiæ* II IIæ q. 180 art. 3 ad 3.

8 See Ivan A. Ill'in, *The Philosophy of Hegel as a Doctrine of the Concreteness of God and Humanity*, 2 vols, ed. and trans. Philip T. Grier (Evanston: Northwestern University Press, 2010–11).

9 See Eberhard Busch, *Karl Barth: His Life from Letters and Autobiographical Texts* (Philadelphia: Fortress Press, 1976), 380. Also see Wolfhart Pannenberg, *Systematic Theology*, 3 vols, trans. Geoffrey W. Bromiley (Grand Rapids, MI: W. B. Eerdmans, 1991–8).

10 Charles Wright, "Three Poems for the New Year," *The World of the Ten Thousand Things: Poems 1980–1990* (New York: Farrar Straus Giroux, 1990), 95.

11 On this issue see Raymond E. Brown, *The Virginal Conception and Bodily Resurrection of Jesus* (New York: Paulist Press, 1973), 132.

12 See *Lumen Gentium*, §57.

13 Karl Rahner sensibly observes, "Her divine motherhood is effected by her faith (Lk. 1:43; 2:27ff.), and so it not a merely biological occurrence," and

"we must never view this motherhood as a merely physical one, but see it as a free, personal act of her faith," *Mary Mother of the Lord: Theological Meditations*, trans., W. J. O'Hara (New York: Herder and Herder, 1963), 13, 56.

14 Again, Rahner's view on the matter is prudent: "the motherhood of Mary, corresponding to her person and her sinlessness, must have been different in various respects. That may be sufficient to justify our speaking of her virginity in childbirth," *Mary Mother of the Lord*, 65.

15 See "Book of James or Protevangelium," 7–8, and "Gospel of Bartholomew," 22, *The Apocryphal New Testament: Being the Apocyphal Gospels, Acts, Epistles, and Apocalypses with Other Narratives and Fragments*, trans. Montague Rhodes James (Oxford: Clarendon Press, 1953).

16 See Epiphanius the Monk, *De vita b. Virginis*, *Patrologia Graeca*, 120:185–216, Pseudo-John the Theologian, *Transitus Mariæ*, in *Apocrypha Syriaca: The Protevangelium Jacobi and Transitus Mariæ*, ed. and trans. Agnes Smith Lewis (Cambridge: Cambridge University Press, 2012), and Maximus the Confessor, *The Life of the Virgin*, trans. Stephen J. Shoemaker (New Haven: Yale University Press, 2012). Also see Brian E. Daley, trans., *On the Dormition of Mary: Early Patristic Homilies* (Crestwood, NY: St. Vladimir's Seminary Press, 1998).

17 See Mary of Agrada, *City of God*, trans. Fiscar Marison, 4 vols (1902; rpt. Washington, NJ: Ave Maria Institute, 1971).

18 I distinguish concrete phenomenological analysis from Husserl's doctrine of *concreta*. For that doctrine, see Edmund Husserl, *Logical Investigations*, 2 vols, trans. J. N. Findlay (London: Routledge and Kegan Paul, 1970), II, Investigation 3: "On the Theory of Wholes and Parts." The account of *concreta* is more clearly given in the first edition of the work. See Husserl, *Logische Untersuchungen*, II Band 1 und 2 (Husserliana XIX/1), ed. Ursula Parker (The Hague: Martinus Nijhoff, 1984), III, section 12.

19 See Vincent Cronin, *Mary Portrayed* (London: Darton, Longman and Todd, 1968).

20 See Friedrich Nietzsche, *Daybreak: Thoughts on the Prejudices of Morality*, trans. R. J. Hollingdale, intro. Michael Tanner (Cambridge: Cambridge University Press, 1982), 5.

21 See Aristotle, *Nicomachean Ethics*, trans. H. Rackham, Loeb Classical Library (Cambridge, MA: Harvard University Press, 1934), X. vii. 5 and X. viii. 7, and Wittgenstein, *Culture and Value: A Selection from the Posthumous Remains*, 2nd edn, rev. edn G. H. von Wright in collaboration with Helkki Nyman, rev. ed. Alois Pichler, trans. Peter Winch (Oxford: Basil Blackwell, 1998), 4e.

22 See Geoffrey Chaucer, "Prologue to the Second Nun's Tale," *The Canterbury Tales*, intro. Jill Mann (London: Penguin, 2005), 622–6; Robert Southwell, "Our Lady's Salutation," *Collected Poems*, ed. Peter Davidson and Anne Sweeney (Manchester: Carcanet, 2007), 5; John Donne, "Upon the Annunciation, when Good Friday Fell Upon the Same Day," *The Complete Poems of John Donne: Epigrams, Verse Letters to Friends, Love-Lyrics,*

Love-Elegies, Satire, Religion Poems, Wedding Celebrations, Verse Epistles to Patronesses, Commemorations and Anniversaries, ed. Robin Robbins (New York: Longman, 2010), 490–4; Gerard Manley Hopkins, "The May Magnificat" and "The Blessed Virgin Compared to the Air we Breathe," *Poems and Prose*, ed. W. H. Gardner (Harmondsworth: Penguin, 1953), 37–9, 54–8; T. S. Eliot, "Ash-Wednesday" VI and "The Dry Salvages" IV, *Collected Poems, 1909–1962* (New York: Harcourt, Brace and World, 1970), 94–5, 197–8; W. H. Auden, "For the Time Being: A Christmas Oratorio," in *Collected Longer Poems* (New York: Vintage, 1975); Geoffrey Hill, "Hymns to Our Lady of Chartres," *Broken Hierarchies: Poems 1952–2012*, ed. Kenneth Haynes (Oxford: Oxford University Press, 2013), 155–68, and Henry Adams's "Prayer to the Virgin of Chartres," *Letters to a Niece and Prayer to the Virgin of Chartres* (Boston: Houghton Mifflin, 1920), 125–34. In addition, one might cite sonnets about Mary by Henry Constable, William Alabaster and William Wordsworth. See "To our blessed Lady," *The Poems of Henry Constable*, ed. Joan Grundy (Liverpool: Liverpool University Press, 1960), 189–91, "To the Blessed Virgin," *The Sonnets of William Alabaster*, ed. G. M. Story and Helen Gardner (Oxford: Oxford University Press, 1959), 20, "The Virgin," *The Ecclesiastical Sonnets of William Wordsworth: A Critical Edition*, ed. Abbie Findlay Potts (New Haven: Yale University Press, 1922), 151.

23 For further discussion of Marian lyrics, see Barry Spurr, *See the Virgin Blest: The Virgin Mary in English Poetry* (London: Palgrave Macmillan, 2007).

24 See W. W. Greg, "I Sing of a Maiden that is Makeless," *Modern Philology* 7 (2) (1909): 165–7. In particular, the later poem has incorporated versions of the lines "Of on ic wille singen that is makeles: / The king of halle kinges to moder he hire ches" and "Wel mitte he berigge of Godes Sune be."

25 Karen Saupe, ed., *Middle English Marian Lyrics* (Kalamazoo, MI: Medieval Institute Publications, 1998).

26 See Rosemary Radford Ruether, *Mary: The Feminine Face of the Church* (London: SCM Press, 1979), 3.

27 Bernard of Clairvaux draws attention to Mary's choice at the Annunciation. See Bernard of Clairvaux and Amadeus of Lausanne, *Magnificat: Homilies in Praise of the Blessed Virgin Mary*, trans. Marie-Bernard Saïd and Grace Perigo, intro. Chrysogonus Waddell (Kalamazoo: Cistercian Publishing Co., 1979), 4. 11. Thomas Jemielty underlines the importance of the courtly love motif in the lyric, maintaining that God acts as a knight and Mary as a medieval lady. See his "'I Sing of a Maiden': God's Courting of Mary," *Concerning Poetry* 2 (Bellingham: Western Washington State College, 1968), 53–71.

28 Bernard of Clairvaux notes that "Nazareth means flower," *Magnificat*, 1.3.

29 Pseudo-Bonaventure's work was variously adapted into Middle English dialects. See Denise N. Baker, trans., "The Privity of the Passion," *Cultures of Piety: Medieval Devotional Literature in Translation*, ed. Anne Clark Bartlett and Thomas H. Bestul (Ithaca: Cornell University Press, 1999), 85–106. On devotion to Mary in the Middle Ages, see Miri Rubin, *Mother of*

God: A History of the Virgin Mary (London: Allen Lane, 2009), Parts IV and V and, more generally for the earlier period, Rachel Fulton, *From Judgment to Passion: Devotion to Christ and the Virgin Mary, 800–1200* (New York: Columbia University Press, 2002).

30 On the relation of rain and Mary's womb, see Bernard of Clairvaux, *Magnificat*, 2.7.

31 For the title "King of all kings" as related to Christ, see 1 Tim. 6:15, Rev. 17:14, 19:16. Also see Matt. 28:18.

32 Accordingly, I disagree with Leo Spitzer's interpretation of the coming of Christ in the poem as a natural miracle, like the rising of the sun each day. See his "*Explication de Texte* Applied to Three Great Middle English Poems," *Archivum Linguisticum* 3 (1951): 155.

33 See Dante, *Purgatorio*, XV. 83–93.

34 Nahum Tate, *Miscellanea Sacra: Or, Poems on Divine and Moral Subjects*, 2nd ed. (London: Printed for Hen. Playford, 1698).

35 See Martin Heidegger, *Being and Time*, trans. John Macquarrie and Edward Robinson (London: SCM Press, 1962), section 16.

36 See Pierre de Ronsard, *Oeuvres complètes*, ed. Jean Céard, Daniel Ménager and Michel Simonin, 2 vols, Bibliothèque de la Pléiade (Paris: Gallimard, 1993), I, 774–80.

37 W. B. Yeats, *The Winding Stair and Other Poems* (London: Macmillan, 1933), 45–6.

38 The theology of the seven heavens is common in the Pseudoepigrapha. See, for example, Apocalypse of Abraham 15:4, Ascension of Isaiah 6:13, Slavonic Enoch 20:1. Yeats may or may not have been aware of these specific sources, though talk of the seven heavens is common enough in esoteric spiritual circles. Biblical warrant for the multitude of heavens is given in Job 38:37.

39 See Rudolph Otto, *The Idea of the Holy: An Inquiry into the Non-Rational Factor in the Idea of the Divine and its Relation to the Rational*, trans. John Wilfred Harvey (London: Oxford University Press, 1923).

40 See Henry Skrzynski, *The Jewess Mary, Mother of Jesus* (Kensington, NSW: Chevalier Press, 1994).

41 Pius IX declared the doctrine in 1854. Long before then, however, Christians did not believe that Mary suffered pain in birth. Maximus the Confessor, for instance, denies that Mary suffered any pain in giving birth to Jesus. Her *fiat* canceled "the debts of affliction." See his *The Life of the Virgin Mary*, 51, 65.

42 James McAuley, *Collected Poems, 1936–1970* (Sydney: Angus and Robertson, 1971), 179–80.

43 See Augustine, *Confessions*, trans. and intro. Henry Chadwick (Oxford: Oxford University Press, 1991), IX, 24–5.

44 See Samuel Johnson, *The Lives of the Most Eminent Poets; with Critical Observations on their Works*, ed. and intro. Roger Lonsdale, 4 vols (Oxford: Clarendon Press, 2006), II, 52–4.

Chapter 15: Ambassadors and votaries of silence

1 Aristotle, *Metaphysics I–IX*, trans. Hugh Tredennick, The Loeb Classical Library (Cambridge: Harvard University Press, 1933), 5, 1003a.

2 Samuel Beckett, *The Unnamable*, trans. Samuel Beckett (New York: Grove Press, Inc., 1958), 28.

3 See Jean-Luc Marion, *Being Given: Toward a Phenomenology of Givenness*, trans. Jeffrey L. Kosky (Stanford: Stanford University Press, 2002), 7–10.

4 See G. W. F. Hegel, *Aesthetics: Lectures on Fine Art*, trans. T. M. Knox, 2 vols (Oxford: Clarendon Press, 1975), I, 38. The other theoretical sense is of course sight.

5 Elie Wiesel, *A Beggar in Jerusalem*, trans. Lily Edelman and Elie Wiesel (New York: Random House, 1970), 108.

6 George Herbert, "The Familie," *The Works of George Herbert*, ed. F. E. Hutchinson, corr. edn. (Oxford: Clarendon Press, 1945), 137.

7 See Søren Kierkegaard, *The Sickness unto Death: A Christian Psychological Exposition for Upbuilding and Awakening*, trans. Howard V. Hong and Edna H. Hong, Kierkegaard's Writings, XIX (Princeton: Princeton University Press, 1980), Problem III.

8 Jorge Carrera Andrade, "Nameless Islands," *Secret Country*, trans. Muna Lee (New York: Macmillan, 1946), 5,

9 André Neher, *The Exile of the Word: From the Silence of the Bible to the Silence of Auschwitz*, trans. David Maisel (Philadelphia: The Jewish Publication Society of America, 1981), 9.

10 See Mark Whittle, http://astsun.astro.virginia.edu/~dmw8f/index.php. I am indebted to Professor Whittle for communications about the primordial sound of the Big Bang.

11 A full analysis would insist on a silencing in the artwork (and a silencing that comes from the icon). See Georges Bataille, *Manet*, trans. Austryn Wainhouse and James Emmons (New York: Skira, n.d.), 86. Also see Jean-Louis Chrétien on this topic in "Silence in Painting," *Hand to Hand: Listening to the Work of Art*, trans. Stephen E. Lewis (New York: Fordham University Press, 2003), 21.

12 See Jacques Derrida, *Speech and Phenomenon*, trans. and intro. David B. Allison, pref. Newton Garver (Evanston: Northwestern University Press, 1973), Ch. 6.

13 Blanchot, [sans titre], *Chroniques littéraires du Journal des débats avril 1941–Août 1944*, ed. Christophe Bident (Paris: Gallimard, 2007), 15.

14 Blanchot, "The Silence of Writers," trans. Michael Holland, *The Blanchot Reader*, ed. Michael Holland (Oxford: Basil Blackwell, 1995), 28.

15 See Ludwig Wittgenstein, *Tractactus Logico-Philosophicus*, trans. D. F. Pears and B. F. McGuinness, intro. Bertrand Russell (London: Routledge and Kegan Paul, 1961), 74.

16 See, for example, Plato, *Meno*, 86a. It should be added that for a later

Platonist such as Plotinus the Forms are a living world, involving, among other senses, "all that hearings hear, all tunes and every rhythm," *Enneads*, trans. A. H. Armstrong, Loeb Classical Library, 7 vols (Cambridge: Harvard University Press, 1988), 7, *Ennead* 6. 7. 12. 30.

17 Elizabeth S. Haldane and G. R. T. Ross, ed. and trans., *The Philosophical Works of Descartes*, 2 vols (Cambridge: Cambridge University Press, 1931), I, 166.

18 F. W. J. Schelling, *The Ages of the World*, trans. and intro. Jason M. Wirth (Albany: State University of New York Press, 2000), 39.

19 See, for example, *The Philosophical Works of Descartes*, I, 343.

20 For material relating specifically to Descartes, see Michel Henry, *The Genealogy of Psychoanalysis*, trans. Douglas Brick (Stanford: Stanford University Press, 1993), Ch. 1, esp. 27–8. Also see Marion, "Does the *Cogito* Affect Itself? Generosity and Phenomenology: Remarks on Michel Henry's Interpretation of the Cartesian *Cogito*," *Cartesian Questions: Method and Metaphysics*, trans. Jeffrey L. Kosky and others (Chicago: Chicago University Press, 1999), esp. 103–7. It should be noted that Edmund Husserl was not unaware of the non-intentional consciousness. See, for example, *The Basic Problems of Phenomenology*, trans. Ingo Farin and James G. Hart, Collected Works, vol. 12 (Dordrecht: Springer, 2006), Appendix 3.

21 See, for example, Levinas, "Diachrony and Representation," *Time and the Other*, trans. Richard A. Cohen (Pittsburgh: Dusquesne University Press, 1987), 111–14.

22 John Climacus, *The Ladder of Divine Ascent*, trans. Colm Luibheid and Norman Russell, notes, Norman Russell, intro. Kallistos Ware, Preface Colm Luibheid (New York: Paulist Press, 1982), 158.

23 See Plutarch, "Concerning Talkativeness," *Moralia*, 14 vols, trans. W. C. Helmbold (Cambridge, MA: Harvard University Press, 1939), 6, 417.

24 Clement of Alexandria, *Stromata, or Miscellanies*, VII. 1, *Ante-Nicene Fathers*, II: *Fathers of the Second Century*, ed. Alexander Roberts and James Donaldson (1885; rpt. Peabody, MA: Hendrickson, 1999), 523.

25 Thomas Traherne, *Selected Poems and Prose*, ed. Alan Bradford (London: Penguin, 1991), 22.

26 William Wordsworth, "Preface to Lyrical Ballads" (1850), *The Prose Works of William Wordsworth*, 3 vols, ed. W. J. B. Owen and Jane Worthington Smyser (Oxford: Clarendon Press, 1974), I, 138.

27 Philippe Lacoue-Labarthe and Jean-Luc Nancy, *The Literary Absolute: The Theory of Literature in German Romanticism*, trans. Philip Barnard and Cheryl Lester (Albany: State University of New York Press, 1988), 91. The idea of saying everything, *tout dire*, in literature is explored in different ways by Maurice Blanchot and Jacques Derrida. See, for example, Blanchot, *The Book to Come*, trans. Charlotte Mandell (Stanford: Stanford University Press, 2003), 45, 63, 122, 205, 219, and Derek Attridge, "'This Strange Institution Called Literature': An interview with Jacques Derrida," in Derrida, *Acts of Literature*, ed. Derek Attridge (New York: Routledge, 1992), 36–40.

28   See Derrida, "'This Strange Institution Called Literature,'" 37–8.

29   See, for example, James Cummins, *The Whole Truth* (San Francisco: North Point Press, 1986), Eugène Guillevic, *Euclideans*, trans. Teo Savory (Greensboro: Unicorn Press, 1975); and Charles Wright, *Zone Journals* (New York: Farrar, Straus and Giroux, 1988).

30   See Patrick Barron, ed. and trans., *The Selected Poetry and Prose of Andrea Zanzotto*, with additional translations by Ruth Fedlman and others (Chicago: The University of Chicago Press, 2006).

31   Søren Kierkegaard, *Two Ages: The Age of Revolution and the Present Age, A Literary Review*, ed. and trans. with intro. and notes Howard V. Hong and Edna H. Hong (Princeton: Princeton University Press, 1978), 97. For a full discussion of Kierkegaard on chatter, see Peter Fenves, *"Chatter": Language and History in Kierkegaard* (Stanford: Stanford University Press, 1993). And for a quite different account of the relations of silence and poetry, in which it is argued that "Poetry today has lost its relationship with silence," see Max Picard, *The World of Silence*, trans. Stanley Godman (Chicago: Henry Regnery, 1952), 141.

32   See Heidegger, *Being and Time*, trans. John Macquarrie and Edward Robinson (Oxford: Basil Blackwell, 1973), section 35 and the references to *schweigen* or keeping silent, and Blanchot, "Idle Speech," *Friendship*, trans. Elizabeth Rotenberg (Stanford: Stanford University Press, 1997), 124.

33   Louis-René de Forêts, "The Bavard," in *The Children's Room*, trans. Jean Stewart (London: John Calder, 1963), 102.

34   George Steiner, "Silence and the Poet," *Language and Silence: Essays 1958–1966* (Harmondsworth: Penguin, 1969), 75. The essay should be compared with Blanchot's essay on the silence of the writer, cited above.

35   A. R. Ammons, *Tape for the Turn of the Year* (New York: W. W. Norton, 1965), 144.

36   See, for example, *Tape*, 60–1, 98, 141–2, 192–4.

37   For the remarks on the length of the tape in the poem, see *Tape*, 3, 38, 59, 66, 75, 145, 164.

38   See John Ashbery, "Soonest Mended," *The Double Dream of Spring* (New York: The Ecco Press, 1976).

39   See W. B. Yeats, "Anima Hominis," *Essays* (London: Macmillan, 1924), 492.

40   Ralph Waldo Emerson, "Merlin" I, *Collected Poems and Translations*, ed. Harold Bloom and Paul Kane (New York: The Library of America, 1994), 92.

41   T. S. Eliot, "The Dry Salvages," *Collected Poems 1909–1962* (London: Faber and Faber, 1963), 208.

42   Geoffrey Hill, "Annunciations," *Collected Poems* (Harmondsworth: Penguin, 1985), 63.

43   In a recent collection of poetry, Hill identifies himself as one of those who crave "ambiguity in plain speaking" and in his earlier poetry he was, as he says in the same volume, one of those who wrote "the line … that quickens to delay," *A Treatise of Civil Power* (London: Penguin, 2007), 45, 51.

44   See Chapter 5 of this volume.

45 Charles Simic, *Dismantling the Silence*, intro. Richard Howard (New York: George Braziller, 1971), 41. Also see, for example, Eugénio de Andrade's "O Silêncio," *Forbidden Words: Selected Poems*, trans. Alexis Levitin (New York: New Directions, 2003), 98.

46 Giuseppe Ungaretti, *L'Allegria,* ed. Cristiana Maggi Romano (Milano: Fondazione Arnoldo et Alberto Mondadori, 1982), 66.

47 Francis Ponge, "The Silent World is our only Homeland," *The Voice of Things*, trans. and intro. Beth Archer (New York: McGraw-Hill, 1974), 109.

48 St. John Climacus, *The Ladder of Divine Ascent*, 158.

49 See Bernard Carr, ed., *Universe or Multiverse?* (Cambridge: Cambridge University Press, 2007).

50 On this topic see Nicholas Wolterstorff, *Divine Discourse: Philosophical Reflections on the Claim that God Speaks* (Cambridge: Cambridge University Press, 1995).

51 St. Thomas Aquinas, *Commentary on the Epistle to the Hebrews*, trans. Chrysostom Baer, Preface Ralph McInerny (South Bend: St. Augustine's Press, 2006), 9–10. Aquinas adds elsewhere that God spoke to Adam "through interior speaking." See *Truth*, 3 vols, trans. James V. McGlynn (Indianapolis: Hackett Pub. Co., 1995), II, q. 18 art 3 *responsio*. Also see *Summa Theologiæ*, 60 vols, vol. 45, trans. Roland Potter (London: Eyre and Spottiswoode, 1970), 2a2æ. q. 173 art. 2.

52 Also see Augustine, *Confessions*, trans. Henry Chadwick (Oxford: Oxford University Press, 1991), IX. x (25), and Kierkegaard's prayer "Thy Silence," in *The Prayers of Kierkegaard*, ed. Perry D. LeFevre (Chicago: The University of Chicago Press, 1956), 76.

53 Ignatius of Antioch, "Ephesians," *The Apostolic Fathers: A New Translation and Commentary*, vol. 4: *Ignatius of Antioch*, Robert M. Grant (London: Thomas Nelson and Sons, 1966), 15. 2.

54 Ignatius of Antioch, "Magesians," 8.2.

55 See Virginia Corwin, *St. Ignatius and Christianity in Antioch* (New Haven: Yale University Press, 1960), 123.

56 On negative theology and hierarchy, see Josef Hochstaffl, *Negative Theologie: Ein Versuch zur Vermittlung des patristischen Begriffs* (München: Kösel, 1976), 1. 3/2.

57 See Augustine, *Confessions*, VII. xxi (27).

58 Hans Urs von Balthasar, *Theo-Logic*, 2: *Truth of God*, trans. Adrian J. Walker (San Francisco: Ignatius Press, 2004), 107–22. I borrow Balthasar's distinction between "non-word" and "supra-word" but regard the tradition of mystical theology as more deeply Christian than he is disposed to do. Also see his essay "The Word and Silence," in *Explorations in Theology*, 4 vols, I: *The Word Made Flesh*, trans. A. V. Littledale with Alexander Dru (San Francisco: Ignatius Press, 1989), 127–46.

59 See Jean Wahl, *Existence humaine et transcendance* (Neuchatel: Éditions de la Baconnière, 1944), 37. Of course, at times the transascendant goes by way of the transdescendant. See Augustine, *Confessions*, X.

60 Augustine, *Confessions*, IX. x (25). In *City of God* Augustine observes, "The holy angels, be it noted, learn to know God, not by the sound of words, but by the actual presence of unchangeable truth, that is by his only begotten Word," *City of God*, 7 vols, trans. David S. Wisen, The Loeb Classical Library (Cambridge: Harvard University Press, 1968), XI, xxix

61 Levinas, *Existence and Existents*, trans. Alphonso Lingis (Boston: Kluwer, 1988), 57, 60.

62 See Blanchot, "The Narrative Voice (the 'he,' the neutral)," *The Infinite Conversation*, trans. Susan Hanson (Minneapolis: University of Minnesota Press, 1993), 385–7.

63 See Derrida, "Différance," *Margins of Philosophy*, trans. Alan Bass (Chicago: The University of Chicago Press, 1982), 6.

64 See Hegel, *Hegel's Science of Logic*, trans. A. W. Miller, Foreword J. N. Findlay (London: George Allen and Unwin, 1969), 139.

65 See Husserl, *Ideas* III: *Phenomenology and the Foundation of the Sciences*, trans. Ted E. Klein and William E. Pohl, Collected Works, I (The Hague: Martinus Nijhoff, 1980).

66 See Husserl, *Ideas Pertaining to a Pure Phenomenology and to a Phenomenological Philosophy. First Book: General Introduction to a Pure Phenomenology*, trans. F. Kersten (Boston: Kluwer Academic Publishers, 1983), section 58. Yet also see the earlier *The Basic Problems of Phenomenology*, Appendix 13, for speculation on God as the "all-consciousness."

67 See Erich Pryzwara, "Katholizimus," in *Ringen der Gegenwart*, 2 vols (Ausburgh: Filser, 1929), II, 667, and Jean-Yves Lacoste, *Experience and the Absolute: Disputed Questions on the Humanity of Man*, trans. Mark Raftery-Skehan (New York: Fordham University Press, 2004), 175. Also see my essay, "Poverty's Speech: On Liturgical Reduction," *Modern Theology* 31 (4) (2015): 641–7.

68 See Augustine, "The Literal Meaning of Genesis," *On Genesis*, trans., intro. and notes Edmund Hill, ed. John E. Rotelle, The Works of Saint Augustine, I/13 (Hyde Park, NY: New City Press, 2002), 268–71. Also see Aquinas, *Truth*, I, q. 8 art. 16, 17. For Hegel's remark on philosophy painting its gray on gray, see his *Philosophy of Right*, trans. T. M. Knox (Oxford: Oxford University Press, 1967), 13.

69 On the idealization of poetry and negative theology as a resource for literary criticism, see Harold Bloom, *Poetics of Influence: New and Selected Criticism*, ed. and intro. John Hollander (New Haven: Henry R. Schwab, 1988), 429. Also see his *Kabbalah and Criticism* (New York: Continuum, 1984), 122.

70 Gerard Manley Hopkins, *Poems and Prose*, ed. W. H. Gardner (Harmondsworth: Penguin, 1953), 31.

71 Hopkins, *Poems and Prose*, 62.

72 Herman Melville, *Pierre; or, The Ambiguities*, ed. Harrison Hayford, Hershel Parker, and G. Thomas Tanselle (Evanston: Northwestern University Press, 1971), 208.

73 Shusaku Endo, *Silence*, trans. William Johnston (Tokyo: Sophia University in cooperation with The Charles E. Tuttle Co., 1969), 266.

74 Perhaps. But note the ending of the novel when Father Rodrigues says, "Even now I am the last priest in this land. But Our Lord was not silent. Even if he had been silent, my life until this day would have spoken of him," 298.

75 Ammons, "The City Limits," *The Selected Poems 1951–1977* (New York: W. W. Norton, 1977), 89.

76 Robert Bly, trans., *Selected Poems of Rainer Maria Rilke* (New York: Harper and Row, 1981), 146–7.

77 Clearly, I am indebted here to Marion, *God without Being: Hors-Texte*, trans. Thomas A. Carlson, foreword David Tracy (Chicago: The University of Chicago Press, 1991), Ch. 1.

78 Jean-Paul Sartre, "Existentialism is a Humanism," *Existentialism is a Humanism*, trans. Carol Macomber, intro. Annie Cohen-Solal, notes and Preface Arlette Elkaïm-Sartre, ed. John Kula (New Haven: Yale University Press, 2007), 26.

79 Wallace Stevens, "The Snow Man," *Collected Poems* (New York: Alfred A. Knopf, 1954), 10.

80 St. Bonaventure, *On the Reduction of the Arts to Theology*, trans., intro. and commentary Zachary Hayes (St Bonaventure, NY: Franciscan Institute, 1996).

Index